**Historical Dictionaries of Ancient Civilizations
and Historical Eras**
Series editor: Jon Woronoff

1. *Ancient Egypt,* Morris L. Bierbrier, 1999.

Historical Dictionary of Ancient Egypt

Morris L. Bierbrier

Historical Dictionaries of Ancient Civilizations and Historical Eras, No. 1

The Scarecrow Press, Inc.
Lanham, Maryland, and London
1999

SCARECROW PRESS, INC.

Published in the United States of America
by Scarecrow Press, Inc.
4720 Boston Way
Lanham, Maryland 20706

4 Pledell Gardens, Folkestone
Kent CT20 2DN, England

British Library Cataloging in Publication Information Available

Library of Congress Cataloging-in-Publication Data

Bierbrier, M. L.
   Historical dictionary of ancient Egypt / Morris L. Bierbrier.
      p. cm. — (Historical dictionaries of ancient civilizations
and historical eras ; no. 1)
    ISBN 0-8108-3614-9 (alk. paper)
    1. Egypt—History—To 640 A.D.—Dictionaries. I. Title.
II. Series.
DT83.B56   1999
932—dc21
                                      98-50361
                                        CIP

TO MY WIFE

Lydia Collins

CONTENTS

EDITOR'S FOREWORD

This new series, Historical Dictionaries of Ancient Civilizations and Historical Eras, could hardly get off to a better start. The first volume is on ancient Egypt. If not quite the oldest civilization, it is certainly the grandest. It stands out for the vast area it covered, the amazing span of its history, and the exceptional works of art and architecture it left behind. Egypt is also the most "topical" of the ancient civilizations, its achievements studied in classrooms around the globe and its vestiges still visited by millions of people every year, whether in present-day Egypt or dozens of museums. There are few indeed who do not recognize the pyramids and the Sphinx, Luxor and the Valley of the Kings, Tutankhamun, and Cleopatra.

This series of historical dictionaries, like the others, provides information on significant persons, places, and events. In this case, two eras of achievements are presented, the old and the new. There are entries on ancient kings and queens, generals and workmen, and on the magnificent cities and tombs they created, as well as on the archaeologists who brought them to light and the sites which display them. Broader subjects, such as art, language, and religion, aspects of architecture and historical periods are also covered. The volume is supported by a chronology of the key events, an introduction placing them in context, a dynastic list and another of Egyptian collections; the extensive bibliography, carefully structured by subject, leads the reader to additional authoritative sources.

This *Historical Dictionary of Ancient Egypt* was written by Morris Leonard Bierbrier who, while providing the many fine points of Egyptology, has created a book that can be used by a broader public as well. The entries are informative, yet concise, covering an amazing share of a vast field within a reasonably short book. To do so, he drew on an impressive accumulation of knowledge and experience. Dr Bierbrier studied Egyptology at the Universities of Toronto and Liverpool and joined the Department of Egyptian Antiquities of the British Museum in 1976, where he has now spent more than two decades, currently in the position of assistant keeper. In addition, he is the author of numerous articles and several books, including *The Tomb-Builders of the Pharaohs* and *Who Was Who in Egyptology.* For such reasons this volume really is an excellent starting place for both the subject and the treatment.

Jon Woronoff
Series Editor

ACKNOWLEDGEMENTS

This dictionary could not have been written without the help and encouragement of my colleagues Mr W. V. Davies, Dr A. J. Spencer, Miss Carol Andrews, Dr John Taylor, Dr Stephen Quirke, and Dr Richard Parkinson, who has kindly read part of the text in manuscript and made valuable suggestions. No text of this nature is ever finite as new discoveries both archaeological and intellectual continue to advance and refine the history of ancient Egypt. The selection of topics and entries is my responsibility, but I have benefited from advice from my colleagues and from the editor, Mr Jon Woronoff.

This book could not have been completed without the assistance of my dear wife, Lydia Collins, who has not only advised and supported me throughout its production but herself entered most of the manuscript on computer. It is a pleasure to dedicate this volume to her.

M. L. Bierbrier

CONVENTIONS

The pronunciation of ancient Egyptian is uncertain as vowels were not written down. Thus the names of Egyptian people and places have been interpreted in different ways by Egyptologists over the years. Some have preferred to use Greek versions of royal names such as Amenophis or Sethos although Greek versions do not survive for all royal names and some are obviously garbled. In the following text, an Egyptian form is cited for most personal names although it is not always possible to be totally consistent with well-known names such as Ramesses. Place names are given the most commonly known form—Arabic, Greek, and rarely Egyptian.

The names, order, and dates of the rulers of ancient Egypt are not exactly fixed because of gaps in our knowledge. From the New Kingdom, there is a margin of error of about 25 years but it may be greater in earlier periods. Some dynasties are contemporaneous which adds to the confusion. New discoveries constantly refine our knowledge but many problems remain.

The use of bold-face type to highlight names in the dictionary indicates that these have a specific entry of their own elsewhere in the text.

CHRONOLOGY

200000–12000 BC	Palaeolithic Period.
12000–5000 BC	Epipalaeolithic Period.
5000 BC	Beginning of Neolithic Period.
5000–4000 BC	Badarian Culture.
4000–3500 BC	Naqada I Period.
3500–3100 BC	Naqada II Period.
3100 BC	Union of Egypt. Dynasty 1.
3100–2686 BC	Early Dynastic Period (Dynasties 1–2).
2686–2181 BC	Old Kingdom.
2686 BC	Beginning of Dynasty 3.
2660 BC	Construction of step-pyramid of Djoser. First stone building.
2613–2589 BC	Dynasty 4. Reign of Snefru. First true pyramids at Dahshur and Meidum.
2589–2566 BC	Reign of Khufu. First pyramid at Giza.
2558–2532 BC	Reign of Khafre. Second pyramid at Giza.
2532–2503 BC	Reign of Menkaure. Third pyramid at Giza.
2494–2345 BC	Dynasty 5. Cult of Re. Pyramids at Abusir.
2375–2345 BC	Reign of Unas. First inscribed pyramid at Saqqara.
2345–2181 BC	Dynasty 6.
2181–2040 BC	First Intermediate Period. Collapse of central authority and civil war. Dynasties 7–11.
2040 BC	Reunification of Egypt under Mentuhotep II of Thebes. Dynasty 11.
2040–1795 BC	Middle Kingdom.
1985–1955 BC	Reign of Amenemhat I, founder of Dynasty 12. Capital moved to Lisht in Middle Egypt.
1799–1795 BC	Reign of Queen Sobekneferu. End of Dynasty 12.
1795–1650 BC	Dynasties 13–14. Second Intermediate Period. Disintegration of central authority. Infiltration and conquest of the north by Hyksos.

1650–1550 BC	Rule of Hyksos. Dynasties 15–16 in the north. Dynasty 17 at Thebes.
1560 BC	Campaign of Thebes against the Hyksos begins.
1550–1069 BC	New Kingdom.
1550 BC	Sack of Avaris and expulsion of Hyksos. Reunification of Egypt under Ahmose I of Dynasty 18. Elevation of Amun as chief god. Expansion into Nubia.
1504–1492 BC	Reign of Thutmose I. Egyptian armies in the Levant. Founding of Deir el-Medina and Valley of the Kings.
1479–1425 BC	Reign of Thutmose III. Hatshepsut as regent.
1472–1458 BC	Reign of Hatshepsut. Expedition to Punt. Building at Deir el-Bahri.
1458 BC	Battle of Megiddo. Thutmose III consolidates Egypt's empire in Syria-Palestine and in Nubia.
1352–1336 BC	Reign of Akhenaten. Attempt at religious change to worship of Aten. Loss of northern part of Syrian province to Hittites.
1336–1327 BC	Reign of Tutankhamun. Return to former religious practices.
1295 BC	Dynasty 19.
1279 BC	Accession of Ramesses II.
1274 BC	Battle of Kadesh. Ramesses II fails to win back lost Syrian provinces from Hittites.
1258 BC	Egyptian-Hittite peace treaty.
1245 BC	Egyptian-Hittite marriage alliance.
1213 BC	Death of Ramesses II.
1186 BC	Inception of Dynasty 20 following civil unrest.
1184 BC	Accession of Ramesses III.
1179 BC	War against the Libyans.
1176 BC	War against the Sea Peoples.
1153 BC	Assassination of Ramesses III.
1153–1069 BC	Later Dynasty 20. Loss of Egyptian empire in Syria-Palestine and Nubia.
1069–945 BC	Dynasty 21. Division of Egypt between north and south. Third Intermediate Period.
945 BC	Accession of Sheshonq I. Dynasty 22.
925 BC	Campaign of Sheshonq I in Palestine.
850–715 BC	Gradual disintegration of Egypt into various principalities. Dynasties 22–24.

728 BC	Invasion of Egypt by the Kushite King Piye.
715 BC	Conquest of Egypt by Shabaqo. Dynasty 25.
690 BC	Accession of Taharqo. First definite date in Egyptian history.
671 BC	First Assyrian invasion of Egypt. Temporary flight of Taharqo to Nubia.
667/6 BC	Renewed Assyrian invasion. Retreat of Taharqo to Nubia.
664 BC	Reconquest of Egypt by Tantamani. Death of Nekau I. Flight of Psamtik I to Assyria.
663 BC	Assyrian invasion of Egypt. Sack of Thebes. Installation of Psamtik I of Dynasty 26 as vassal.
656 BC	Installation of Nitocris, daughter of Psamtik I, as God's Wife in Thebes.
525 BC	Persian conquest of Egypt. Dynasty 27.
404 BC	Expulsion of Persians.
404–343 BC	Dynasties 28–30.
343 BC	Second conquest of Egypt by Persia.
332 BC	Conquest of Egypt by Alexander the Great.
323 BC	Ptolemy becomes satrap of Egypt.
305 BC	Ptolemy I takes title of king.
51 BC	Accession of Cleopatra VII.
30 BC	Conquest of Egypt by Rome.
69 AD	Accession of the Emperor Vespasian.
130 AD	Visit of the Emperor Hadrian.
312 AD	Triumph of Constantine. Official recognition of Christianity.
391–92 AD	Edicts of the Emperor Theodosius against paganism.
394 AD	Last dated hieroglyphic inscription. Found at Philae.
395 AD	Division of Roman Empire. Egypt becomes part of Eastern (Byzantine) Empire.
452 AD	Last attested demotic inscription. Found at Philae.
617–629 AD	Persian (Sassanian) occupation of Egypt.
641 AD	Arab invasion. Surrender of Alexandria.
642 AD	Departure of Byzantine forces. Arab occupation of Egypt.

Map of Egypt

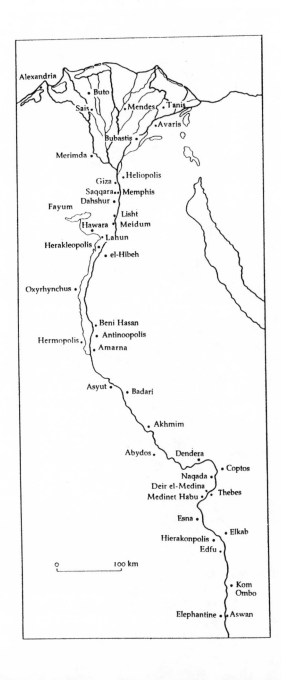

INTRODUCTION

Ancient Egypt owed its prosperity, wealth, and power to its geographic location alongside the banks and in the Delta formed by the river Nile. The annual floods of the Nile brought down rich silt from the interior which enriched the fertility of the soil and made food production dependable and plentiful. The agricultural area was protected in the east, west, and south by desert areas and in the north by the Mediterranean Sea, which tended to discourage, but not necessarily prevent, invasions. The desert areas were also rich in minerals and stone which could be exploited as tools and building materials.

The original inhabitants of Egypt appear to have belonged to the Hamito-Semitic group of peoples along with the ancient Libyans and Berbers. The Egyptian language had affinities with both the ancient Hamitic and Semitic languages but was an autonomous linguistic branch. The Egyptians clearly differentiated themselves from their Semitic neighbours to the north-east, the Libyans to the west, and the Nubians to the south. The Egyptians appear to have inhabited the Nile valley from the earliest times and remained essentially a homogenous group absorbing the intermittent flow of immigrants mainly from the north-east.

Inhabitants of the Nile valley can be identified from the Palaeolithic Period at various sites from 200,000 BC as hunter-gatherers living off the land and using flint tools. In the Neolithic Period farming communities developed, growing emmer wheat, barley, and flax. Domestic animals are attested as well as the use of pottery. Such sites have been found at Merimda Beni Salama in the Delta and in the Fayum, but the earliest phase of the Predynastic Period is known as Badarian from the site of el-Badari in Middle Egypt (5000–4000 BC). The subsequent phases of the Predynastic Period take their name from Naqada in Upper Egypt. Naqada 1 (4000–3500 BC) witnessed the growth of settlement sites in Upper Egypt noted for its black-topped red pottery. In the Naqada 2 Period (3500–3100 BC) the culture is attested as far north as the Delta at Minshat Abu Omar although an apparently separate culture is attested at Maadi near modern Cairo.

1

According to late Egyptian traditions, two kingdoms emerged in the late Predynastic Period—those of Upper and Lower Egypt which were merged to form the united kingdom of Egypt through the actions of the legendary king Menes. Modern historians have speculated that the historical king Narmer of Upper Egypt conquered Lower Egypt to unite Egypt, but the historical process was probably more complicated than this simple procedure. A strong kingdom under Dynasty 0 had emerged in the south possibly based at Hierakonpolis but those rulers were buried in mastaba tombs at Abydos. Little is known of developments in the north or even if the kingdom of Lower Egypt existed in fact, but certainly by about 3100 BC the country was unified under Dynasty 1.

The union of Egypt is also alleged to have led to the founding of a new capital at Memphis; certainly the tombs of officials such as Hemaka in the nearby cemetery at Saqqara testify to the early importance of Memphis, although the rulers continued to be buried at Abydos. The tombs became increasingly elaborate with niched facades and the royal tombs are surrounded by those of sacrificed retainers. Hieroglyphic writing had appeared in the late Predynastic Period as attested in the titulary of the rulers, who were identified with the sky-god Horus. The writing now became more complex, appearing on labels and surviving tomb inscriptions. During Dynasty 2 it appears that there were religious conflicts between the followers of the gods Seth and Horus which apparently were resolved by Khasekhemwy. During his reign the first bronze vessels and royal sculpture are attested. He was the last ruler to be buried at Abydos.

Dynasty 3 marked a shift in royal policy. The rulers were now buried at Saqqara. The mastaba tomb and royal sacrifices were abandoned in favour of the newly developed step-pyramid—a series of mastabas on top of one another using stone on a large scale. The step-pyramid was allegedly conceived by the vizier Imhotep, minister of King Djoser. The complex of Djoser also includes other buildings and reliefs of the king undertaking ritual activities. The names of the rulers of Dynasty 3 are attested at the mines of the Wadi Magara in the Sinai. Dynasty 3 marks the first appearance of the sun-god Re who was to become the main god, displacing the sky-god Horus. Some scholars include Dynasty 3 in the Old Kingdom; others begin the period with Dynasty 4.

Dynasty 4 marked the high point of royal power and control in the Old Kingdom. The forces of the first ruler Snefru campaigned in Nubia, and Egypt entered into commercial relations with Byblos and the Levant. Expeditions penetrated to Buhen in Nubia where a copper-smelting operation and supporting town site have been discovered and stone from quarries near Abu Simbel was used for royal statuary. The most visible sign of royal power were the royal tombs at Meidum, Dahshur, and later Giza where the true stone pyramid was now constructed to contain the royal burial. Each pyramid was in fact an architectural complex consisting of the royal pyramid to which was attached a mortuary temple linked by a causeway to a valley temple on the edge of the cultivation, where the royal body was received prior to its burial. Smaller pyramids of the queens would adjoin the main pyramid, which would be surrounded by the mastaba tombs of the princes and courtiers of the reign.

The royal court was unable to maintain the degree of economic control needed for the continual construction of stone pyramids in succeeding reigns. Three alone were built. Dynasty 4 ended in some chaos and future rulers were content to build pyramids with rubble case and only stone casing. The new rulers of Dynasty 5 enhanced the prestige of their patron deity the sun-god Re who was elevated to the top of the pantheon and in one form absorbed the sky-god Horus to appear as Re-Harakhty. New sun temples were built at Abusir where most of the rulers chose to be buried. The earliest known written documents on papyrus, temple accounts, date to this period. Dynasty 6 maintained control over the whole country but the minority and then long reign of Pepy II led to a loosening of central control. The dynasty apparently ended in confusion, and the central authority of the Old Kingdom collapsed, ushering in the First Intermediate Period.

The term Intermediate Period is used to designate phases when the central government was weak or non-existent and, partly as a consequence, written documentation is also less abundant. At the end of the Old Kingdom the country was divided into warring factions whose leaders adopted the titularies of rulers. Dynasties 7–8 briefly maintained themselves at Memphis but were superseded by two main contenders for power, the princes of Herakleopolis (Dynasties 9–10) and Thebes (Dynasty 11). Other provincial rulers or nomarchs increased their local power backing one side or the other. The surviving monuments of the period demonstrate the growth of different provincial schools of art as opposed to the previous uniform school emanating from the royal court of Memphis.

Around 2040 BC Nebhepetre Mentuhotep II of Dynasty 11 finally overcame the forces of Herakleopolis and reunited Egypt to establish the Middle Kingdom. A new capital was established at Thebes where the king built his funerary monument at Deir el-Bahri. Trade links were reopened with the south and the Levant. His dynasty did not long endure but was replaced by Dynasty 12 inaugurated by the southerner Amenemhat I, probably the vizier of the last ruler of Dynasty 11.

Amenemhat I proved a vigorous and inventive ruler. He strengthened Egypt's defenses on the Sinai by building fortifications to control the growing influx of Semitic peoples. He moved the capital to Itjtawy near the Fayum in the centre of the country and the region was further developed by his successors. Amenemhat I sought to ensure political stability by appointing his son Senusret I as his co-regent. During his reign the military occupation of Nubia was begun. His court also patronized writers who wrote favourably of the dynasty and the literature of the Middle Kingdom was to become the classic reading of the Egyptian literate classes long after with such stories as the tale of Sinuhe. This strong reign ended with the assassination of the ruler in obscure circumstances but his son was able to secure the throne and continue his father's policies.

Expansion continued south into Nubia as far as Semna under Senusret I and Senusret III and a series of fortifications were erected at strategic points to keep Nubia under control. The extent of Egyptian influence in the Levant is unclear. Trade links were maintained with the coastal cities such as Byblos. Egyptian couriers passed through Palestine and certainly the execration texts reveal an intimate knowledge of local rulers. Some texts reveal Egyptian military action in the Levant region. It is probable that Egypt maintained political influence here through diplomacy and the occasional military expedition. The period is distinguished by its fine and intricate craftsmanship, notably the production of jewellery, examples of which have been recovered from several royal tombs, such as those of the princesses Sithathoriunet and Nefruptah.

Dynasty 12 appears to have died out in the male line with Amenemhat IV who was succeeded briefly by his sister Sobeknefru, the first unequivocal female ruler. Her reign was brief and the succeeding Dynasty 13 is considered by most Egyptologists to have begun the Second Intermediate Period. At first the country remained stable and united although there was a continuous succession of rulers who mostly ruled for a very short period. However, the unity of Egypt began to dissolve with the creation of a contemporary Dynasty 14 at Xois. Egyptian forces withdrew from Nubia where a strong native kingdom emerged based at Kerma. The country also faced an increasing influx of Asiatic settlers from the east centering on the town of Avaris. Later Egyptian accounts infer a brutal invasion with much destruction. It is known that peaceful Asiatic settlement had gone on throughout Dynasties 12–13 but the final conquest of the north by the Asiatics or Hyksos may have been made under more violent circumstances. Certainly the Hyksos rulers of Dynasties 15 and 16 adopted Egyptian styles of titulary and so must have had some Egyptian advisers at court. The Hyksos appeared to have controlled Lower and Middle Egypt but Thebes remained independent under a series of rulers who also adopted royal titularies although they may at one point have been obliged to become vassals of the Hyksos rulers in the north.

It is clear that the Thebans and the Egyptians as a whole resented the rule of this foreign dynasty and as before the rulers of Thebes led the resistance to the Hyksos and sought to oust them from Egypt. The revolt against their rule appears to have been initiated by Tao of Dynasty 17 against the Hyksos ruler Apepi of Dynasty 15 according to a fragmentary literary tale. Tao may have died in battle but the struggle was carried on by his successor Kamose who besieged the Hyksos capital at Avaris and prevented a coalition between Hyksos and Nubian forces. He too appears to have failed and it was left to his successor Ahmose I to capture Avaris in about 1550 BC, expel the Hyksos forces from Egypt, and reunite Egypt under the control of his new Dynasty 18. The victorious Egyptians pursued their defeated foes into southern Palestine and under successive monarchs, notably Thutmose III, extended their domination of the Levant up to the Euphrates River, attempting to forestall any future Asiatic resurgence. At the same time Egyptian forces penetrated south of Elephantine (Aswan), destroying the Nubian kingdom based at Kerma and annexing much of Nubia as far south as Kurgus near the Fifth Cataract.

These further conquests brought wealth and prosperity back to Egypt. The rulers of Dynasty 18 embarked on important building projects, notably in the temple of Karnak at Thebes whose god Amun was elevated to chief god of Egypt and identified with the sun-god Re. The temples were also awarded large land-grants and portable wealth to confirm their support of the dynasty. The royal family altered its burial customs choosing the more secluded Valley of the Kings. The control of an empire and the southern gold mines made Egypt a superpower on the world stage. Direct contact was established with Greece, Asia Minor, and Babylon. Egyptian prestige reached its height in the reign of Amenhotep III whose harem was filled with many foreign princesses although his chief wife was an Egyptian commoner Tiy.

Religious discontent surfaced in the reign of his son Akhenaten who sought to suppress the cult of Amun in favour of his own patron deity Aton, a form of the sun-god Re. Although he tried to eliminate many of the old gods as well as Amun, he was not a monotheist, denying neither his own divinity nor that of his father. In his new capital at Amarna, a distinctive new art style developed. Akhenaten also faced the growth of a new superpower in the Hittite empire which annexed the Egyptian provinces of southern Syria. The failure of Akhenaten's program led to a return to the old gods and the old capital under his eventual successor Tutankhamun who was apparently the last of the royal line. The final rulers of Dynasty 18 sought to restore Egypt's position at home and abroad.

This new militaristic approach was favoured by the rulers of Dynasty 19 who came from a military background. The attempt to restore the former empire ended in failure about 1274 BC when Ramesses II was defeated by the Hittites. However, he held on to his inherited borders and eventually reached a peaceful accommodation with his enemy, relinquishing claims on lost territory and in due course marrying Hittite princesses. He was able to undertake major building projects at Abu Simbel and other temples and at his new capital of Pi-Ramesses. Egypt had become a cosmopolitan country no longer immune to outside influences in language and customs and even accepting foreign deities, but the era of Ramesses II marked the beginning of the end of Egypt as a prosperous and powerful superpower.

The successors of Ramesses II faced invasions from the west by the Libyans allied to the Sea Peoples as well as a civil war leading to the establishment of Dynasty 20. Ramesses III managed to fend off a further onslaught of the Sea Peoples who had apparently destroyed the Hittite empire, but his successors gradually became impoverished and withdrew from all Egyptian possessions in the east and Nubia. Another civil war led to the end of the New Kingdom and the beginning of the Third Intermediate Period.

The Third Intermediate Period is marked by the fragmentation of authority within the country, notably the division between north and south. During Dynasty 21 the authority of the pharaoh situated in the north was only nominally recognized in Thebes under the control of the high priest of Amun. Sheshonq I, of Libyan extraction, attempted to restore the unity of Egypt by establishing his son as high priest and he also sought to restore Egyptian prestige abroad by his invasion of Palestine. However, the tendency of Dynasty 22 to install princes in key areas of Egypt led to disunity and constant civil war with Dynasties 22 and 23 vying for nominal authority amid other local princes, notably of Sais (Dynasty 24). Unity was only restored with the invasion and conquest of Egypt by the Nubian kings Piye and Shabaqo who put an end to Dynasty 24 and reduced the local princes to vassals. The Nubian rule (Dynasty 25) in Egypt was brief as a weakened Egypt now faced new superpowers in the east who cast covetous eyes on the natural wealth and historic treasures of the country. A series of Assyrian invasions devastated the country culminating in the expulsion of Dynasty 25, the sack of Thebes, and the installation of a puppet ruler, Psamtik I of Sais, in 663 BC.

Psamtik I made use of his Assyrian master and later Greek mercenaries to eliminate all rival princes and he won control of the south through the adoption of his daughter as God's Wife of Amun at Thebes. His Saite dynasty (Dynasty 26) represented a brief revival of Egypt's prosperity and power. Artistic trends towards archaism and simplicity which began in the Third Intermediate Period continued. The hieratic written script gave way to the new more abbreviated demotic, which also indicated a shift in the spoken language. The weakening of Assyria allowed Egypt to become virtually independent and under Nekau II even to intervene in an attempt to support Assyria, which failed, and vainly to try to restore Egyptian influence in the Levant in the face of the new threat from Babylon. Closer relations were initiated with Cyrene in North Africa, sealed through a marriage alliance by Ahmose II, and with the Greek states leading to the designation of Naukratis as a Greek entrepôt in Egypt.

Egypt, however, remained too weak to resist the onslaught of the Persian king Cambyses who added it to his Persian empire as a province ruled by a satrap of royal birth. The Persian conquest (Dynasty 27) was deeply resented, especially as the Persian authorities appear to have limited the funds available to the temples, many of which had suffered during the invasion. There were a series of revolts, aided and abetted by the Greeks, which eventually succeeded in expelling the Persians about 404 BC. The new rulers of Egypt, Dynasties 28–30, were Delta dynasties recognized throughout Egypt, whose principal aim was to prevent any new Persian incursion. The most prominent were the rulers Nakhtnebef and Nakhthorheb who embarked on an ambitious building program on most of the temples of Egypt.

This last native dynasty was deposed by the reinvading Persians in 343 BC but their rule was brief as Egypt fell to Alexander the Great in 332 BC. Alexander was welcomed by the Egyptians as a liberator. His sojourn in Egypt was short but significant. He visited the Siwa Oasis where the oracle is alleged to have confirmed his divinity and made arrangements for the founding of Alexandria. On his death Egypt was secured by his general Ptolemy who founded a new dynasty and also secured Alexander's body for burial at Alexandria.

Unlike some of Alexander's successors, Ptolemy did not aspire to recreate his empire but was content to rule Egypt and its dependencies. This did not mean that he refrained from expanding Egypt's influence and control in Greece, Asia Minor, and especially Syria when possible, and the Ptolemaic dynasty became embroiled in frequent wars over Syrian territories with the Seleucid empire, which weakened both powers. Egypt was ruled from the court at Alexandria, which was almost exclusively Greek. Native Egyptians did not fill the top administrative positions and had to learn Greek for advancement. Greek settlers, mostly veteran soldiers, were given land, notably in the Fayum area where agricultural land was increased by better irrigation. Many settlers married local women so a bilingual class arose which acted as an intermediary between the Greek rulers and the bulk of the Egyptian population. Greek settlers also benefited from tax privileges denied to the locals. However, the court did patronize Egyptian temples and sponsored building works to win the loyalty of the priestly class. This did not prevent occasional rebellion on the part of the Egyptians, especially in the south where the rulers Harwennefer and Ankhwennefer maintained their independence for a time.

The Ptolemaic dynasty was severely weakened by civil war and the growth of Roman power in the Mediterranean. Ptolemy XII was forced to accede to Roman financial demands leading to his expulsion and reinstatement by Roman force of arms. Cleopatra VII was also put in power by Roman might but used her charms on Caesar and Marcus Antonius to expand Egyptian influence and restore its prestige in the Levant. Her partnership with Antonius was used by his enemies at Rome to blacken his reputation and led inexorably to a military clash with Roman forces under the future Augustus. His victory at Actium in 30 BC resulted in the conquest of Egypt and the suicides of Cleopatra and Antonius.

The Roman conquest resulted in a change of government in Egypt. Egypt was regarded as the private property of the Roman emperor, ruled in his name by the prefect, and the source of cheap grain to keep the Roman populace happy. Very few emperors visited Egypt after Augustus, most notably Hadrian. Roman senators were barred from entering the country without imperial permission. The Greek population in major cities—Alexandria, Naukratis, Ptolemais, and later Antinoopolis—were allowed to enjoy favoured tax status but the mixed Greek-Egyptian population of the provincial cities lost their special status, being regarded as equivalent to the native population, although prominent local citizens enjoyed some privileges. While the emperors occasionally endowed Egyptian temples, the Roman administration tended not to actively support ancient Egyptian institutions. The Egyptian language was no longer considered valid in the courts, where only Greek or Latin was recognized. As a result written Egyptian in the form of demotic and residual hieroglyphic writing gradually died out in ordinary usage although it was kept fitfully alive by the priesthood until the fifth century. The temples and the priests they supported grew steadily impoverished.

The weakened pagan culture was unable to resist the spread of Christianity, which gained official recognition under the Emperor Constantine. Egyptian Christianity was marked by a certain asceticism which led individual hermits such as Anthony to seek solace in isolated locations but soon under Pachomius gave rise to settled monastic communities, which helped to foster Christianity. Christians were intolerant of the pagan past, both Egyptian and Greek, and made destructive attacks on ancient temples and monuments, especially following the official suppression of paganism under the Emperor Theodosius I in 391–92 AD. Only the temple of Philae remained open because of its diplomatic importance in Egyptian-Nubian relations until the time of the Emperor Justinian when it was closed down in the 530s AD. Funeral customs also changed with the abandonment of mummification and substantial grave goods.

A new form of written Egyptian emerged known as Coptic. The ancient language was written in Greek letters with the addition of seven new letters to represent specific Egyptian sounds. The spoken language had already been altered through the influx of Greek words into the vocabulary. It is thought that the Coptic alphabet may have been devised by the early Christians to translate religious texts but it was also used for new religious compositions, biographical texts, letters, and administrative texts, notably in the new monastic communities. The development of Coptic was to prove of immense importance in the modern understanding of the ancient Egyptian language.

The adoption of Christianity and the suppression of the ancient cults did not lead to stability in Egypt. The division of the Roman Empire in 395 AD meant that Egypt was now ruled from Constantinople and became part of the Byzantine Empire. Attempts by the emperor to impose an agreed uniform Christian creed foundered on the doctrinal differences between orthodoxy as understood by Rome and the tendency towards monophysitism in the Coptic Church. Opposition to what the patriarchs at Alexandria such as Cyril and Dioscorus saw as unorthodox doctrines gradually estranged the Egyptian church from the imperial court, which vainly sought a compromise solution and then increasingly opted to impose orthodoxy by force, leading to the foundation of a Coptic Church separate from the Orthodox Church. Religious dissension weakened Byzantine rule and led sections of the population to welcome the Arab conquest of 641–42 AD.

The Arab conquest ultimately put an end to the last vestiges of the ancient Egyptian culture, in which the new rulers, like their Christian predecessors, had no interest. It was not their immediate intention to convert the entire population to Islam as this would have drastically affected their new revenues from the poll-tax on unbelievers. However, later bouts of fanaticism as well as social and economic pressure led to the conversion to Islam of the bulk of the population. Islamicization led to the adoption of Arabic as the common language of the new administration and its use also spread to the non-Muslim population so that Coptic had died out as a spoken language by the fifteenth century. It was preserved only in a few places in the Christian service although even the speakers no longer knew the meaning of the words. Ancient sites, when not despoiled or destroyed, were gradually buried and forgotten. Memories of ancient Egypt survived only in the neglected works of classical authors in European monastic libraries.

Very few Europeans visited Egypt in the medieval period apart from occasional pilgrims or merchants who brought back a few objects. The growth of learning in the Renaissance led to a rediscovery of classical antiquity and interest in Egypt. Coptic works including Biblical translations were acquired for Western libraries and the language was soon deciphered although it was not connected with ancient Egyptian. Haphazard excavations took place at Saqqara to supply *mumiya*—ground-up mummy dust, prized for its alleged medicinal properties—in the course of which minor Egyptian antiquities were uncovered. More substantial pieces were found in Rome where they had been imported during the period of Roman control. Minor pieces continued to arrive in Europe as a result of more intrepid travellers who penetrated further into Egypt in the course of the eighteenth century. The major impetus to the study of ancient Egypt came with the invasion of that country by Napoleon in 1798 as part of a plan to cut off the British from India. Napoleon took with him a team of scholars who went throughout the country recording and collecting monuments. The expedition ended in failure as the French were eventually forced to surrender to a combined Turkish-British force. The monuments which had been collected for shipment to Paris, including the Rosetta Stone, were awarded to the British by treaty and ended up in the British Museum. The French scholars returned with their papers and published the multi-volume *Description de l'Égypte* which made Egyptian sites and monuments available to a wider public.

Peace in Europe in 1815 and a stable government in Egypt under Mohammed Ali allowed scholars, artists, and collectors to visit Egypt, record its monuments, and collect antiquities with the permission of the Egyptian government. A major breakthrough was made by the decipherment of the hieroglyphic script by Jean-François Champollion using the Rosetta Stone and other bilingual monuments. His realization that the ancient Egyptian language was an earlier form of Coptic, which he already knew, greatly aided his work. His work was carried on by other scholars after his early death. The hieroglyphic, hieratic, and demotic scripts used by the ancient Egyptians can now be read although grammatical and lexical difficulties still remain.

The major European collections of Egyptian antiquities—the British Museum, the Louvre, the Turin Museum—were formed in the first part of the nineteenth century mainly by purchase from collectors, notably those of the British and French consuls in Egypt, Henry Salt and Bernardino Drovetti, who used agents such as Giovanni Battista Belzoni to acquire objects either directly from the locals or from excavations. The Egyptian government approved the export of most antiquities, in which it took no interest, until the efforts of Auguste Mariette persuaded the ruler to create in 1858 an Egyptian Antiquities Service to supervise and approve all excavations and exports of antiquities and a Cairo Egyptian Museum, opened in 1862, to display the best discoveries which were to remain in Egypt.

Serious excavation began towards the end of the century with the creation of the French Institute of Archaeology in 1880 and the Egypt Exploration Fund (now Society) in 1882. The method of excavation was revolutionized by the work of the British archaeologist Flinders Petrie whose attention to detail and small objects such as pottery enabled archaeological levels to be more clearly dated. Important contributions were made in the first half of the twentieth century by American institutions such as the Metropolitan Museum of Art of New York and the Boston Museum of Fine Arts under its excavator George Reisner. Under agreements at the time the chief finds remained in Egypt but a portion of the discoveries were awarded to institutions which financed excavations.

The discovery of the tomb of Tutankhamun led to increased public awareness of ancient Egyptian history and archaeology. Apart from interruptions due to wars, excavation and study of ancient Egypt have continued unabated. Following the revolution of 1952, the sale and export of antiquities from Egypt were banned apart from divisions of duplicate archaeological material with foreign archaeological missions. During the 1960s a major international rescue campaign was undertaken to excavate sites in Nubia which were in danger of flooding by the lake created by the Aswan High Dam. More recently excavation by the Egyptian Antiquities Service and foreign missions have shifted from desert sites to lesser known town sites especially in the Delta area. Continual discovery of new material necessitates constant revision of ancient Egyptian chronology and history, which still have many problems awaiting solutions. The more material that is recovered, the more we learn how little we know of ancient Egypt despite the riches of its archaeological heritage.

DICTIONARY

- A -

ABU ROASH. Modern name for the site of the funerary complex of **Djedefre** of **Dynasty 4** which includes the remains of his **pyramid** and associated **temples** as well as a major cemetery of the **Early Dynastic Period** and a pyramid of **Dynasty 3**. The site has been excavated by French expeditions from 1901, notably under Fernand Bisson de la Roque in 1922–24 and a Dutch expedition in 1957–59.

ABU SIMBEL. Modern name for the site in **Nubia** where **Ramesses II** erected two **temples**. The larger temple with four colossal statues of the king on the facade is dedicated to **Amun**-Re, **Re**-Harakhty, **Ptah**, and Ramesses II and aligned so the rays of the rising sun illuminate the cult statues in the interior sanctuary twice a year. The smaller temple with statues of the king and his queen **Nefertari** with their children on the facade is dedicated to the goddess **Hathor**. The site was rediscovered by the Swiss explorer Johann Ludwig Burckhardt in 1813 and the main temple was entered in 1817 by Giovanni Battista **Belzoni** who removed some of the statuary, now in the **British Museum**. The temples were cut up and moved to a higher site nearby from 1964–68 when the area was flooded in the wake of the construction of the new Aswan High Dam.

ABUSIR. Modern name for the area between **Giza** and **Saqqara** which served as the burial place for the kings and courtiers of **Dynasty 5** and also the location of **temples** dedicated to the sun-god **Re**. Four **pyramids** with their temples have been found here. The area was examined by a German expedition under Friedrich von Bissing and then under Ludwig Borchardt in 1898–1913, followed by a Swiss expedition in 1954–57, and has been excavated by a Czech expedition since the 1960s. See also **Neferirkare, Niuserre, Raneferef, Sahure**.

ABUSIR PAPYRI. The earliest written documents from Egypt consisting of **temple** accounts found in the temple of **Neferirkare** at **Abusir** dating to **Dynasties 5–6**. The texts are written in early **hieratic**. Similar texts have recently been found in the nearby temple of **Raneferef**. See also **Papyrus**.

ABYDOS. Greek name for the sacred city of *Abdju* in **Upper Egypt** and burial place of **Osiris**, god of the dead, located south of modern Sohag. The kings of **Dynasty 0** and **Dynasties 1–2** were buried there at the site now known as Umm el-Qaab. The local god Kentiamentiu became identified with the god Osiris who was believed to be buried there. In the **Middle Kingdom** with the growth in worship of Osiris, the site became a place of pilgrimage and a desirable location for burial. In the **New Kingdom, temples** were erected by **Sety I** and **Ramesses II** as well as a cenotaph for the god Osiris, the Osireion. The area was excavated by the French archaeologists Auguste **Mariette** from the 1850s and Émile Amélineau in 1894–98. The **Egypt Exploration Fund** worked here under Flinders **Petrie** and later other archaeologists in 1899–1904, 1909–14, and 1925–30 and also sponsored the copying of the temple of Sety I from 1928. Another British archaeologist, John Garstang, was active in 1907. Excavations have been carried out by an American expedition from 1967 and more recently by German archaeologists. See also **Aha, Anedjib, Djer, Djet, Den, Narmer, Qaa, Semerkhet.**

ACHAEMENES (fl. c.484–459 BC). Persian **satrap** of Egypt. Son of Darius I, king of **Persia**, and Atossa daughter of Cyrus the Great. He was appointed to office in 484 BC after a rebellion in Egypt and governed until he was killed in 459 BC during another rebellion against Persian rule led by **Inaros**.

AFTERLIFE. The ancient Egyptians firmly believed in an afterlife although conceptions of its nature varied. It was generally regarded as a continuation of the **agricultural** life along the **Nile** and hence servant figures or **shabtis** were required to avoid manual labour. It was also believed that the dead rested in suspended animation and only revived when the sun-god **Re** descended into the underworld during the hours of darkness on earth.

In order to enjoy an afterlife, the deceased would need to have led a virtuous life according to the precepts of *maat*. He would have to pass through the various gates of the underworld guarded by demons to reach the court of the god of the dead **Osiris** where he would be judged in the **weighing of the heart** ceremony. Various spells in the **Book of the Dead** were designed to ensure that this procedure was carried out successfully.

The Egyptians also believed that the body of the deceased had to be preserved as a home for the *ka* or life spirit and the *ba* or free spirit of the deceased in order that he or she might continue to live after death. The technique of mummification was developed to accomplish this. The **mummy** would be buried in the tomb after the opening of the mouth ceremony in which it was magically revived. Depending on the cost of burial, it could be buried in a series of wooden decorated coffins which might be placed in a large stone coffin or sarcophagus. The family or priests would then make periodic food offerings to the spirit of the deceased. Statues would also be provided in case the body decayed as a home for the spirits. The Egyptian expected to enjoy the same life after his decease as before and so was provided with appropriate grave goods. See also **Name**.

AGRICULTURE. Egypt was an agricultural country in which the bulk of the population were peasant farmers involved in work on the land. The fertility of the land caused by the **Nile** floods ensured that generally there were abundant crops; famines, while they did occur, were rare. The main crops were wheat and barley to make bread and beer, the staple diet of the people. Vegetable crops were also grown and vineyards are attested. Fodder was also grown for livestock.

The life of the countryside was dominated by the agricultural schedule as planting would follow the Nile flood in the early summer and the peasantry would be available for government forced labour towards the end of the season. Government inspectors would determine the amount of tax in kind due from the individual plots, and the collected grain could be stored and used to feed government employees as at **Deir el-Medina**. In Egypt's barter **economy**, a measure of wheat was used to value less expensive goods.

Most of the land was owned by the royal court, the **temples**, and the bureaucracy, but along with the large estates small private plots are also attested. Most of the population were presumably landless peasants who worked on the large estates as sharecroppers or labourers, but some peasants owned their own land by inheritance or gift of the crown. Enterprising farmers might own some land, rent out more from the estates, and hire labourers so the status of the agricultural population might be quite varied.

AHA (reigned c.3080 BC). Second king of **Dynasty 1**. Successor of **Narmer** as confirmed by the dynastic seal. He appears to have been buried at **Abydos**, and tombs of officials of his reign are known at **Saqqara**. Aha is probably not to be identified as **Menes**. He was succeeded by **Djet** who was probably his son.

AHHOTEP (fl. c. 1570–1540 BC). Sister and queen of probably Seqenenre **Tao** of **Dynasty 17** and thus daughter of Senakhtenre and **Tetisheri**. She was the mother of **Ahmose I** and his sister-wife **Ahmose-Nefertari**. Ahhotep apparently acted as regent of her son on his accession and exercised great influence throughout his reign. A second queen Ahhotep is known from a burial at **Thebes** and is probably to be identified as a queen of **Kamose.**

AHMOSE I (reigned c.1552–1527 BC). Throne name Nebpehtyre, founder of **Dynasty 18**. Probably son of Seqenenre **Tao** and Queen **Ahhotep**. He succeeded **Kamose**, who may have been his brother, apparently under the regency of his grandmother **Tetisheri** and his mother Ahhotep. Ahmose I continued the campaign of the rulers of **Thebes** against the **Hyksos** rulers in the north and his army successfully took the Hyksos capital **Avaris** and expelled them from Egypt, reuniting the country under his rule. His army penetrated at least into southern Palestine in pursuit of the enemy. He also began the Egyptian invasion of **Nubia**. His wife and probable sister **Ahmose-Nefertari** became regent for their son **Amenhotep I** on his death.

AHMOSE II (reigned 570–526 BC). Greek form Amasis. Throne name Khnumibre. A military commander of **Wahibre** (Apries) whom he overthrew following a brief civil war. He sought to ally Egypt with the Greeks to face the continuing threat of **Persia** including a marriage alliance with Laodike, a Greek lady from **Cyrene**. Ahmose II ruled effectively for 45 years and died conveniently just before the Persian invasion of 525 BC as a result of which his son **Psamtik III** was deposed and later executed. See also **Persia.**

AHMOSE (fl. c.1560–1500 BC). Military officer. Son of Baba, a soldier of King Seqenenre **Tao**, and his wife Ebana, from whose name her son is generally known as Ahmose son of Ebana. He was the owner of a tomb at **Elkab** which contains a major autobiographical inscription describing his exploits in the wars against the **Hyksos**. Ahmose was present at the siege of **Avaris** and later took part in campaigns in Palestine, Syria, and **Nubia** under **Ahmose I**, **Amenhotep I**, and **Thutmose I**.

AHMOSE. The name of several princes and princesses of **Dynasty 17** and early **Dynasty 18.** Their separate identities are confusing as Ahmose seems to have been used both as a distinct name and as part of a more complex name such as Ahmose-**Meritamun**, daughter of **Ahmose I** and wife of **Amenhotep I**. The most prominent prince seems to have been Ahmose Sipair, probably the eldest son of Ahmose I who predeceased his father. He was worshipped together with **Ahmose-Nefertari**, who may have been his mother, and Amenhotep I in the **Ramesside Period**.

AHMOSE (fl. c.1504–1470 BC). Sister-wife of **Thutmose I** and mother of **Hatshepsut**. Her parentage is not known, but she was not a royal princess as previously believed.

AHMOSE-NEFERTARI (fl. c.1550–1500 BC). Wife and probably sister of **Ahmose I** and thus daughter of Seqenenre **Tao** and **Ahhotep**. She appears to have been the first queen to use the title **God's Wife of Amun** and is portrayed with her husband on several monuments of the reign. Ahmose-Nefertari may have acted as regent for her son **Amenhotep I** and seems to have survived him. She was deified with him after his death and was worshipped with him especially at the village of **Deir el-Medina.**

AKHENATEN (reigned c.1352–1336 BC). Throne name Neferkheperure waenre. Original name Amenhotep IV. Son of **Amenhotep III** and **Tiy.** It is probable that he was not the eldest son as a Prince Thutmose is attested but presumably died young. It is also not clear if there was a **coregency** between his father and himself or whether he succeeded only on his father's death. Akhenaten sought to establish the primacy of the cult of **Re**-Harakhty in the form of **Aten**, the sun's disk. Following opposition in **Thebes** from the followers of **Amun**, he established a new capital at Akhetaten, now **Amarna.** His opposition to the older cults gradually grew more intense, and they were eventually proscribed. His religious beliefs have been wrongly described as monotheism as Akhenaten did not abandon those cults associated with the sun-god or with kingship, namely his deified father and himself.

His reign is also noted for a revolutionary new art style which is far freer than older Egyptian conventions and depicted the royal family and himself in a particular manner. Some have sought to identify a medical problem in this style, but it may simply have been a new artistic convention. His wife **Nefertiti** assumed a prominent role in royal scenes, and it has been suggested that she even succeeded him. The circumstances which ended the reign are unknown. Akhenaten's eventual successor **Tutankhamun**, who may have been his son, abandoned Amarna and reverted to the worship of Amun. Akhenaten's name and that of his immediate successors were later proscribed. See also **Amarna Period**, **Art**, **Ay**, **Horemheb**.

AKHETATEN see **AMARNA.**

AKHMIM. Modern name for the Egyptian *Khent-Min*, Greek Khemmis or Panopolis in the ninth Upper Egyptian **nome**. Little remains of the ancient city under the modern town. Home city of **Ay**. In 1981 colossal statues of **Ramesses II** and his daughter and queen **Meritamun** were discovered here. Unsupervised excavations at the end of the nineteenth century led to the discovery of many textiles and textile fragments from the **Coptic Period.** The nearby tombs of the **Old Kingdom** at el-Hawawish were copied and published by an Australian expedition from Macquarie University in 1979–92.

ALARA (reigned c.770 BC). Nubian ruler. The first known member of the later **Dynasty 25**. He is not known to have been active in Egypt, but his successor **Kashta** extended Nubian rule over the Theban area.

ALASIA. A foreign country which is named in Egyptian documents during **Dynasties 18–20**, notably in the **Amarna Letters**. The country could be reached by sea as described in the story of **Wenamun**. Alasia is generally identified with all or part of Cyprus although some authors would situate it on the Levant coast.

ALEXANDER THE GREAT (356–323 BC). King of Macedon and conqueror of the Persian empire including Egypt. Son of King Philip of Macedon and Olympias of Epirus. Alexander succeeded to the Macedonian throne on the assassination of his father in 336 BC and in 334 BC embarked on the conquest of **Persia**. In 332 BC his army entered Egypt whose **satrap** surrendered peacefully. Alexander assumed the status of an Egyptian ruler and visited the oasis at **Siwa** where he received an oracular pronouncement, later believed to indicate that he was the son of a god. He indicated the position of a new city to be built on the coast and named **Alexandria** after him. He left Egypt in 331 BC to continue his conquests elsewhere, arranging for the country to be divided under various officials the chief of whom was **Cleomenes**, the chief financial officer. Alexander died in Babylon in 323 BC on his return from India. See also **Ptolemy I**.

ALEXANDER II (IV of Macedon) (reigned 317–310 BC). Posthumous son of **Alexander the Great** and the Bactrian princess Roxana. He reigned jointly with his uncle **Philip Arrhidaeus** until the murder of the latter in 317 BC. Alexander II was imprisoned by Cassander and murdered in 310 BC, but he was still acknowledged as ruler until 305 BC when Cassander, **Ptolemy I,** and other Macedonian generals assumed independent kingships over parts of Alexander the Great's empire.

ALEXANDER HELIOS (b. 40 BC). Son of Marcus **Antonius** and **Cleopatra VII**. Twin of **Cleopatra Selene**. He was declared king of Armenia, Parthia, and Media in 34 BC and betrothed to Princess Iotape of Media. This prince was captured by **Augustus** in 30 BC and displayed in his triumph in Rome in 29 BC. His ultimate fate is unknown.

ALEXANDER, TIBERIUS JULIUS (fl. c.10–75 AD). Roman official. He was born in **Alexandria**, son of Alexander Lysimachus, head of the Jewish community. Alexander served as governor of Judaea (c.46–48) and as prefect of Egypt in which capacity he helped to engineer the accession of **Vespasian**. He served on the staff of **Titus** during the siege of Jerusalem.

ALEXANDRIA. City on the Mediterranean coast of the western Delta founded by **Alexander the Great** in 331 BC on the site of the Egyptian village of *Rakedet*, Greek Rakotis. It became the capital of Ptolemaic and Roman Egypt and included many fine buildings, notably the famed library and the *Pharos* or lighthouse regarded as one of the wonders of the ancient world. Alexander's body was preserved in a special mausoleum in the city. The city was also decorated with Egyptian monuments removed from earlier sites, notably **Heliopolis**. The large cosmopolitan population included Egyptians, Greeks, and Jews.

The city later suffered damage from earthquakes and invasion and declined following the move of the capital to Cairo after the Arab conquest in 642 AD. Many parts of the city appear to have sunk beneath the harbour. Little of the ancient city remains today apart from the area adjacent to the so-called Pompey's Pillar. Excavations by successive directors of the Graeco-Roman Museum have uncovered many local burial catacombs with reliefs in a mixed Egyptian-Roman style. From 1960 a Polish expedition has worked at the site of Kom el-Dikka uncovering a theatre and baths. Recent surveys by teams of French divers have begun to reveal the parts of the city now underwater and recovered Egyptian sculptures and reliefs.

AMADA. Modern name for a site in Lower **Nubia** of a **temple** built by **Thutmose III** and his son **Amenhotep II** in honor of **Amun**-Re and **Re**-Harakhty. The area has now been flooded by the lake formed by the Aswan High Dam, but the temple has been removed and re-erected on a higher level.

AMARA WEST. Modern name for a site in Upper **Nubia** where a major Ramesside settlement and **temple** have been discovered. The town appears to have been founded by **Sety I** with further construction by his son **Ramesses II**. It was probably the major administrative centre for Upper Nubia. It was excavated by the **Egypt Exploration Society** 1938–39 and 1947–50.

AMARNA. The modern Arabic name el-Amarna or Tell el-Amarna denotes the site of the capital city *Akhetaten* founded by **Akhenaten** in **Middle Egypt**. Akhenaten claimed to have chosen a virgin site to become the new capital away from the religious intolerance of **Thebes** and where he was free to pursue the worship of **Aten**. The site consists of the remains of royal palaces, villas, **temples**, private dwellings, and a workmen's village and the boundaries were marked by a series of **stelae**. The sculptor **Thutmose**'s workshop yielded the famous bust of **Nefertiti** now in the **Berlin Egyptian Museum**. Tombs were cut in the nearby cliffs for officials, and a royal tomb was built for the king in which he determined to be buried. The scenes on the walls are not fully preserved, but one depicts the death of the Princess **Meketaten** although the circumstances are unclear.

The city was abandoned by **Tutankhamun** and was used as building material by later rulers notably **Ramesses II**. The site was first excavated by Flinders **Petrie** in 1891–92 and then a German expedition in 1907, 1911–14. The tombs were copied by an expedition of the **Egypt Exploration Fund** in 1901–07. In 1921–36 further excavations were undertaken by the British organization, renamed the Egypt Exploration Society, and work was resumed under its auspices in 1977.

AMARNA LETTERS. A large number of clay tablets inscribed in cuneiform, the script used in Mesopotamia and western Asia, found at the site of el-**Amarna**. These consist of the diplomatic correspondence of the royal court at the end of **Dynasty 18** with the princes of Syria and Palestine under Egyptian control as well as other royal courts in Babylonia, **Assyria**, and Anatolia. Most of the documents date to the reign of **Akhenaten**, but some letters may belong to the time of his predecessor **Amenhotep III** or his successor **Tutankhamun.** The letters reflect a state of disarray in the Egyptian empire although the extent of its weakness may be exaggerated.

AMARNA PERIOD (c.1352–1327 BC). A term used by Egyptologists to denote the reigns of **Akhenaten** and his successors **Smenkhkare** and **Tutankhamun**. The period is notable for innovations in art and religious belief and ended with the abandonment of **Amarna** as Egypt's capital. The rulers of the Amarna period were later suppressed from Egypt's historical record by their successors. See also **Ay, Horemheb, Nefertiti**.

AMASIS see **AHMOSE II.**

AMENEMHAT I (reigned c.1985–1955 BC). Throne name Sehetepibre. Son of Senusret and Nefret. He is first attested as **vizier** of **Mentuhotep IV** of **Dynasty 11** and must be identical with the founder of **Dynasty 12** although it is not clear if he came to the throne peacefully or as a result of a coup d'état. Amenemhat I proved a strong and effective ruler, establishing a new capital at *Itjtawy*, now **Lisht** in the **Fayum**. He began the campaign of conquest of **Nubia** and also built a series of fortifications along Egypt's Sinai border known as the Walls of the Ruler. He apparently installed his son **Senusret I** as **co-regent** although this has been doubted by some Egyptologists. Amenemhat I was assassinated after 30 years of rule in an apparent palace conspiracy which was crushed by his son. He was buried in a **pyramid** complex at Lisht. A **wisdom** text in his name, *The Instruction of Amenemhat I*, was composed after his death, presumably in the reign of his son. See also **Intefyoker**, **Khety**, **Sinuhe**.

AMENEMHAT II (reigned c.1922–1878 BC). Throne name Nubkaure. Son of **Senusret I** of **Dynasty 12** and **Nefru**. He continued Egyptian expansion in **Nubia** and sent expeditions to the Red Sea and **Punt**. A recently discovered inscription gives details of campaigns in the Sinai and possibly further north. He maintained contacts with **Byblos**. He was buried in a **pyramid** complex at **Dahshur**. See also **Khenemet-nefer-hedjet**, **Senusret II**.

AMENEMHAT III (reigned c.1855–1808 BC). Throne name Nimaatre. Son of **Senusret III** of **Dynasty 12.** His principal monuments are located in the **Fayum** area which seems to have been extensively developed in his reign. He built two **pyramids**, one at **Dahshur** where he appears to have been buried and another at **Hawara** where his mortuary temple was later known to the Greeks as the Labyrinth. See also **Nefruptah**.

AMENEMHAT IV (reigned c.1808–1799 BC). Throne name Maatkherure. Son of **Amenemhat III** of **Dynasty 12**. He is principally known from several monuments in the **Fayum**. He appears to have died without issue and was succeeded by his sister **Sobeknefru**. His burial place has not been securely identified.

AMENEMHAT. The name of several Egyptian princes of **Dynasty 18**. One is known solely from an inscription on a coffin which had been made for his reburial towards the end of **Dynasty 20** or early **Dynasty 21** and was rediscovered in 1918–20 at **Deir el-Bahri**. He has been wrongly described as a son of **Amenhotep I**, but his actual parentage remains unknown. His very existence might be doubtful if the later embalmers were mistaken in their identification of the body which was that of a year-old child. The eldest son of **Thutmose III**, who died before his father, was named Amenemhat but cannot be identified with this child as his titles indicate an older individual.

AMENEMNISU (reigned c.1043–1039 BC). Throne name Neferkare. Second ruler of **Dynasty 21** of unknown origin. He was cited in **Manetho** by his throne name and this was generally considered to be an error until an inscription with his titulary was discovered in the tomb of **Pasebakhaenniut I** at **Tanis**. His reign appears to have been brief.

AMENEMOPE (reigned c.993–984 BC). Throne name Usermaatre sete-penamun with epithet meryamun. Fourth ruler of **Dynasty 21** and successor of **Pasebakhaenniut** I. Little is known of his reign. His burial was discovered at **Tanis** by the French excavator Pierre Montet.

AMENHERKHEPESHEF (fl. c.1285–1255 BC). Eldest son of **Ramesses II** by **Nefertari**. The prince appears to have been also known as Amenherwenemef and Setiherkhepeshef. He was named crown prince by his father and is attested until year 21 of the reign when he was involved in diplomatic correspondence with the **Hittites** along with his mother. He died before his father. He was presumably buried in the tomb of the sons of Ramesses II (no. 5) in the **Valley of the Kings.** A like-named son of **Ramesses III**, who died young, was buried in the **Valley of the Queens** (no. 55). See also **Dynasty 19.**

AMENHOTEP I (reigned c.1527–1506 BC). Throne name Djeserkare. The Greek form of his personal name is Amenophis. Son of **Ahmose I** of **Dynasty 18** and **Ahmose-Nefertari.** He seems to have succeeded as a child under the regency of his mother. In his reign the workmen's community at **Deir el-Medina** appears to have been founded and he was the first king to be buried in a cliff tomb in or near the **Valley of the Kings,** but this remains to be identified. He apparently died without issue by his sister and queen **Meritamun** and was succeeded by **Thutmose I.** He was later worshipped as a god, along with his mother, especially at Deir el-Medina. His body was recovered in the **royal cache** in 1881.

AMENHOTEP II (reigned c.1427–1401 BC). Throne name Akheperure. Son of **Thutmose III** of **Dynasty 18** and Merytre-Hatshepsut. On his accession he faced a revolt in his Asiatic domains which he ruthlessly crushed, exhibiting the remains of the rebels as far south as **Nubia.** His inscriptions boast of his athletic prowess. He appears to have largely maintained the northern conquests of his father. He was buried in tomb no. 35 in the **Valley of the Kings** and his body was recovered from his tomb in 1898 along with other rulers who had been buried there in a **royal cache.** He was succeeded by his son **Thutmose IV** by the lady Tiaa.

AMENHOTEP III (reigned c.1390–1352 BC). Throne name Nebmare. Son of **Thutmose IV** of **Dynasty 18** and **Mutemwia.** He may have succeeded as a child and reigned 32 years. His reign is known for its magnificence in construction and artworks. He maintained the Egyptian empire in Asia and was in communication with the many princes of the area as shown in the **Amarna letters**. His chief queen commoner **Tiy** was the mother of his eventual heir **Akhenaten** as it appears that his eldest son Thutmose predeceased him. He married several foreign princesses from **Mitanni** and Babylon. He also had several daughters, notably **Sitamun** whom he married. A proposed **co-regency** between father and son is debatable, and most Egyptologists reject it. He was buried in tomb no. 22 in the **Valley of the Kings**, and his body was recovered from the **royal cache** in tomb no. 35 of **Amenhotep II**. His mortuary temple featured the Colossi of **Memnon**. See also **Gilukhepa**, **Tadukhepa**.

AMENHOTEP IV see **AKHENATEN**.

AMENHOTEP SON OF HAPU (fl. c.1390–1360 BC). Overseer of works for **Amenhotep III**. He was born in **Athribis**. He probably was responsible for the construction of many of the king's monuments including his mortuary **temple** at **Thebes** and his **Nubian** temple at **Soleb** where he was commemorated. He was buried at Thebes. Amenhotep, son of Hapu, acquired a reputation for wisdom and was deified after his death, being worshipped in his own mortuary temple. See Colossi of **Memnon**.

AMENIRDIS. The name of two princesses of **Dynasty 25** who were adopted as **God's Wife of Amun**. Amenirdis I was the daughter of **Kashta** and Pebtama, and her adoption by **Shepenwepet** I was an indication of the control of **Thebes** now exercised by the ruler of **Nubia**. Amenirdis II, daughter of **Taharqo**, was adopted by Shepenwepet II as her heir, but it is not certain if she succeeded as Dynasty 25 was ousted from control of Thebes by **Psamtik I** of **Dynasty 26** who sent his daughter **Nitocris** to become God's Wife.

AMENMESSE (reigned c.1202–1199 BC). Throne name Menmire. Of unknown parentage, he contended with **Sety II** for the throne on the death of **Merenptah**. He was defeated and his memory largely obliterated. He had prepared tomb no. 10 in the **Valley of the Kings** for his burial. See also **Dynasty 19**.

AMENMOSE (fl. c.1504–1499 BC). Egyptian prince of **Dynasty 18**. He was the eldest son of **Thutmose I** possibly by the lady **Mutnefret**. He is attested in his father's reign with the title of general and in a tomb scene with his younger brother **Wadjmose**. Both predeceased their father and the throne eventually passed to their brother or half-brother **Thutmose II**.

AMENOPHIS see **AMENHOTEP**.

AMENY QEMAU (reigned c.1775 BC). An ephemeral king of **Dynasty 13**. His throne name is uncertain. His **pyramid** tomb was discovered at **Dahshur** in 1957 but has never been properly excavated or published. The name Qemau has been wrongly interpreted in the past with the meaning of "Asiatic". He may have been the father of **Harnedjitef** who also bore the epithet which might be read as son of Qemau. The name of Ameny Qemau might be interpreted to indicate that he was the son of a previous ruler named Ameny who in turn might be identified with one of the obscure rulers named Amenemhat of Dynasty 13.

AMUN. Chief god of the **New Kingdom** and later. Originally a minor god at **Thebes**, he rose to prominence in **Dynasty 12**, which came from the south, and was promoted to the head of the pantheon under the Theban **Dynasty 18** through a fusion with the sun-god **Re**, becoming Amen-Re, king of the gods. Amun is usually represented as a human figure with two plumed feathers but can have a hawk head. He is seen as one of the creator gods. His main **temple** was at **Karnak** in Thebes and he was later worshipped as one of the main gods in **Nubia** at Gebel Barkal and other temples. His sacred animals were the ram and the goose.

AMYRTAEOS (reigned 404–399 BC). Greek name for the Egyptian ruler of **Dynasty 28** Amenirdis of **Sais** who led a rebellion against the **Persian** occupation and succeeded in expelling them from the country. He apparently invaded Phoenicia to prevent a Persian counterattack. No inscriptions of his are known, but he is mentioned in a **demotic** papyrus. Amyrtaeos was in turn overthrown by **Nefaarud** I founder of **Dynasty 29**.

ANAT. Canaanite goddess of war. Her worship was adopted in Egypt in the **Ramesside Period** and **Ramesses II** gave his eldest daughter **Bintanat** her name. She was considered by the Egyptians as one of the wives of **Seth** along with **Astarte**.

ANCHMACHIS see **ANKHWENNEFER**.

ANEDJIB (reigned c.2935 BC). Sixth ruler of **Dynasty 1** and successor of **Den**. He was buried in a modest tomb at **Abydos** and his name has been erased in some instances so there may have been some unrest at the end of his reign. See also **Semerkhet**.

ANHUR. Egyptian god known to the Greeks as Onuris and considered a god of war. He is depicted as a bearded man wearing feathered plumes and carrying a spear. His principal place of worship was **Thinis** but he was also worshipped in combination with **Shu** at **Sebennytos**.

ANIBA. Site in Lower **Nubia** in the Second **Cataract** region. Egyptian *Miam*. A fortress was constructed here during **Dynasty 12** and was reoccupied in the **New Kingdom** when it became a major administrative centre for the area between the First and Second **Cataracts**. It was excavated by a German expedition in the 1930s and is now flooded by the lake of the Aswan High Dam. Some monuments from here were salvaged before the flooding.

ANKHESENAMUN (fl. c.1345–1327 BC). Formerly **Ankhesenpaaten**. Third daughter of **Akhenaten** and **Nefertiti** and wife of **Tutankhamun**. She joined her husband in the abandonment of her father's religious practices and capital at **Amarna** and changed her name to remove the reference to **Aten**. On the death of her husband, she wrote to the **Hittite** king to seek a Hittite prince as a new husband but he died mysteriously on the way to Egypt. Her subsequent fate is unknown although it has been conjectured that she married the next king **Ay**.

ANKHESENMERYRE (fl. c.2305–2270 BC). Otherwise Ankhesenpepy. The name of two sister queens of **Pepy I** and daughters of Huy. The elder became the mother of **Nemtyemsaf** I and the younger that of **Pepy II**. The pyramid of the younger Ankhesenmeryre/Ankhesenpepy was discovered at **Saqqara** in 1997.

ANKHESENPAATEN (fl. c.1345–1327 BC). Third daughter of **Akhenaten** and **Nefertiti** who later adopted the name **Ankhesenamun** as wife of **Tutankhamun**. A second princess Ankhesenpaaten-tasherit is attested on some monuments from **Amarna** and may be her daughter.

ANKHESENPEPY (fl. c.2220 BC). The name of a wife of **Pepy II**. Her **sarcophagus** was found in the tomb of **Iput**, another of his queens, at **Saqqara**. She was the mother of an ephemeral king of **Dynasty 7** or **8**

whose throne name was Neferkare. The queens **Ankhesenmeryre** are also sometimes called Ankhesenpepy.

ANKHNESNEFERIBRE (fl. c.590–525 BC). Daughter of **Psamtik II** and Takhut. She was adopted by her great-aunt **Nitocris** in 595 BC and succeeded her as **God's Wife of Amun** in 586 BC. She held the post until the **Persian** invasion of 525 BC after which there is no further record of her. She is the last attested God's Wife although a later classical source implies that the office continued. Her reused sarcophagus was discovered at **Deir el-Medina** and is now in the **British Museum**.

ANKHWENNEFER (reigned c.199–186 BC). Rebel ruler in the south during the reign of **Ptolemy V**. The Greek version of his name is Chaonnophris, previously wrongly read as Anchmachis. He succeeded **Harwennefer** and was able to regain **Thebes**, controlling as far north as **Asyut**. He was driven from Thebes in 191 BC and finally defeated and captured in battle in 186 BC. His ultimate fate is unknown.

ANTHONY (c.251–356 AD). Egyptian saint and hermit. He was the son of Christians from the village of Qiman, and on their death, gave away his worldly possessions and lived the life of an ascetic hermit near the village and later in the Eastern Desert. He inspired other hermits to live for a time near him, forming the first ascetic community although he himself moved to the desert to be on his own. Several of his letters survive, and his life, written by **Athanasius**, spread the idea of ascetic life in the Christian world. **Pachomius**, another ascetic, was to change the solitary existence of the hermit into that of a monastic community. See also **Coptic Church**.

ANTINOOPOLIS. Greek name of the city in **Middle Egypt** founded by **Hadrian** in 130 AD in honor of his favourite Antinous who had drowned in the **Nile**. Now modern Sheikh Ibada, it is located on the east bank of the Nile opposite **Hermopolis**. The inhabitants were drawn from the major Greek cities in Egypt. The site was originally an Egyptian city with a **temple** erected by **Ramesses II** and has remains dating from the **Predynastic Period**. It was excavated by the French archaeologist Albert Gayet 1896–1907.

ANTIOCHUS IV (reigned 175–164 BC). Ruler of the Seleucid empire encompassing Syria, Asia Minor, Mesopotamia, and parts of Iran. Son of Antiochus III and Laodice of Pontus and brother of **Cleopatra I**. He succeeded to the throne on the assassination of his brother Seleucus IV in association with his nephew Antiochus whom he adopted and later executed. Conflict with Egypt over Syria was renewed in 170–169 BC, but an invading Egyptian army was defeated. Antiochus in turn invaded Egypt, taking the border town of Pelusium and capturing **Ptolemy VI** and **Memphis**, but he failed to take **Alexandria** and withdrew in 169 BC. He invaded again in 168 BC and may have aimed to crown himself ruler of Egypt, but he was forced to withdraw under pressure from Rome. He then turned his attention eastwards to Iran and died at Tabae in 164 BC.

ANTONIUS, MARCUS (83–30 BC). Roman politician. Son of Marcus Antonius and Julia of the family of the Julii Caesares. He was an early supporter of his distant relation Caius Julius **Caesar** and sought to inherit his political power after the latter's assassination in 44 BC but was forced to ally himself with the future **Augustus** in order to crush their political opponents. He was given the eastern part of the empire in the division of the empire after their victory at Philippi in 42 BC and married Augustus's sister as part of their political alliance. He soon formed a political and personal connection with **Cleopatra VII** of Egypt which estranged him from Augustus, who used this oriental entanglement to vilify Antonius in Rome. Eventually war was declared against Egypt and Antonius was defeated at the battle of Actium in 31 BC and committed suicide in 30 BC as Augustus's forces entered **Alexandria**.

ANTYEMSAF see **NEMTYEMSAF**.

ANUBIS. Egyptian god of the necropolis and embalming represented as a jackal or a jackal-headed man. He was responsible for conducting the deceased to **Osiris**, god of the dead.

ANUKIS. Daughter of the god **Khnum** of **Elephantine** and **Satis**. She is depicted as a human female figure wearing a feathered headdress and was principally worshipped at Elephantine and in **Nubia**.

APEPI (reigned c.1585–1550 BC). Throne name Aawoserre. Greek version Apophis. Last or penultimate **Hyksos** ruler of **Dynasty 15**. He is attested as an opponent of the rulers of **Thebes**, **Tao**, and **Kamose**. He tried to fashion an alliance with the ruler of Kush against the Thebans, but this apparently failed. It is not clear if he was still reigning when his capital **Avaris** fell to the Theban forces under **Ahmose I**. Two other throne names, Aakenenre and Nebkhepeshre, are associated with Apepi and may refer to different monarchs or more likely the same man who changed his throne name. He may have been briefly succeeded by Khamudy, the last of the dynasty.

APEREL (fl. c.1370 BC). Northern **vizier** of **Amenhotep III**. His intact tomb was excavated at **Saqqara** from 1976 culminating in the opening of the burial chamber in 1987. His existence was hitherto unknown. Aperel's name is Semitic, but his burial was thoroughly Egyptian so it cannot be necessarily assumed that he was of foreign origin as Semitic names were sometimes used by Egyptians.

APION. Family of Egyptian landowners and officials in the **Byzantine Period**, known from documents from **Oxyrhynchus** where they had estates. The earliest known member appears to have been Flavius Strategius who is attested from 439 and died before 469. His descendant was Apion I who held an honorary consulship at the end of the fifth century AD and died between 524 and 532.

Other members of the family included Flavius Strategius Apion II, a patrician and vice-prefect of the East in 503–04 and later praetorian prefect in the East in 518–19; Flavius Strategius, honorary consul about 518 and prefect of Egypt from about 518–23; and Flavius Strategius Apion, consul in 539 who died about 577–79. The family appear to have supported the orthodox imperial view in the religious controversies. The last known member was Apion III who died in late 619 possibly a victim of the **Persian** invasion. The Apions represent one of the few Egyptian families to have exercised political influence at the imperial court.

APIS. Greek name for the sacred bull of **Memphis**, Egyptian *Hapi*. The bull was the living embodiment of the god **Ptah** and after death was identified with **Osiris**. He was recognized by distinct signs and housed in the **temple** complex. On his death a new bull would be sought born near the time of death of the old. The bulls were buried in the **Serapeum** at **Saqqara**. The mother of the bull was also accorded special honors and the burial catacombs for the cows were discovered by a British expedition in the 1970s. The cult is known from **Dynasty 1**, but became particularly important in the **Late Period**.

APRIES see **WAHIBRE.**

ARCHAIC PERIOD see **EARLY DYNASTIC PERIOD.**

ARIUS (c.270–336 AD). Egyptian Christian priest in **Alexandria**, of Libyan origin who enunciated the doctrine of Arianism, indicating that Christ had only one nature and it was human as against the orthodox view of two natures, human and divine intermingled. He was fiercely opposed by **Athanasius**, later patriarch of Alexandria, who forced him to leave the city. He died in Constantinople in 336. His doctrine found little support in Egypt although Athanasius was for a time deposed by an Arian, but it influenced several emperors and later spread to barbarian converts outside the empire.

ARMANT. Modern name for the Egyptian *Iuny*, Greek Hermonthis, capital of the fourth **nome** of **Upper Egypt** until superseded by **Thebes**. It was located on the west bank of the **Nile** opposite **Tod**. The principal deity of the site was the god **Montu** whose **temple** is now destroyed. Archaeological remains date from the **Predynastic** to the **Roman Periods** when it again became the nome capital. The burials of the sacred ram **Buchis** have also been located. The site was excavated on behalf of the **Egypt Exploration Society** in 1927–32.

ARSAMES (fl. c.423–404 BC). Persian **satrap** of Egypt during the reign of Darius II of **Persia** (423–04 BC). Member of the royal family. Part of his official correspondence written in Aramaic has been discovered. His governorship may have been ended by the revolt which brought **Amyrtaeos** to power.

ARSAPHES see **HERYSHEF.**

ARSINOE I (born c.300 BC). Daughter of Lysimachus, king of Thrace, and Nicaea. First wife of **Ptolemy II** and mother of **Ptolemy III.** She was exiled to **Coptos** in 279 BC on a charge of conspiracy after she was supplanted in the king's affections by **Arsinoe II.**

ARSINOE II (c.316–270 BC). Daughter of **Ptolemy I** and **Berenice I.** She married King Lysimachus of Thrace who killed his son by his first marriage possibly by her influence. This resulted in civil strife leading to the king's death in battle in 281 BC. She then married her half-brother

Ptolemy, king of Macedonia, who murdered two of her sons and died in battle with the Celts in 279 BC. She returned to Egypt and her third marriage about 276 BC to her full brother **Ptolemy II**. She was highly influential at court and was deified with her husband.

ARSINOE III (c.235–205 BC). Daughter of **Ptolemy III** and **Berenice II** and wife of her full brother **Ptolemy IV** whom she married in 217 BC. She was estranged from her husband and was apparently murdered by his courtiers shortly after his death to prevent her becoming regent.

ARSINOE (c.63–41 BC). Daughter of **Ptolemy XII** and possibly **Cleopatra VI Tryphaena.** She supported her brother **Ptolemy XIII** against **Cleopatra VII** and was taken to Rome by Julius **Caesar** to appear in his triumph in 46 BC. She later took refuge in Ephesus but was executed at the order of her sister Cleopatra VII in 41 BC.

ART. In ancient Egypt monumental and most private art was designed for religious not decorative purposes. The statue was originally developed as a substitute home for the spirit in the **afterlife**, and later statues were also placed in **temples** where the **name** of the deceased could be read, causing the deceased to live again. The block statue, which first appeared in the early **Middle Kingdom**, was particularly favoured because of the amount of space available for text. Incised reliefs and wall paintings in tombs depicted the goods and activities which the deceased wished to enjoy in the next life. Royal reliefs on temple walls showed the majesty and power of the king and the beneficence of the gods. Most statues and reliefs were in fact painted, but much of this paint has now worn away.

Egyptian artists worked to a canon of proportions for the human figure. A standard style was set by the royal court although regional variations appeared during the intermediate periods when central government and artistic patronage had broken down. Egyptian art was not static as the canon of proportions varied over time. The most obvious change occurred during the **Amarna Period** when the canon was changed and the human figure was depicted in an exaggerated style with a long narrow neck and full hips. In the **Late Period** the artists drew inspiration from the works of the **Old Kingdom** and **Middle Kingdom**.

Very little survives concerning the decoration in royal and private buildings. The surviving fragments of tiles and frescoes show that the decorative scheme of the royal palace sought to display the might of the sovereign as a conqueror although some more intimate scenes are known from the Amarna Period. Egyptian craftsmen were adept in the production of small functional objects such as cosmetic spoons and other toiletry objects in a highly decorative form. See also **Thutmose**.

ASKUT. Modern name for the site of a fortress in the Second **Cataract** region of **Nubia.** Egyptian *Djer Setiu.* It appears to have been constructed as part of a series of fortresses from **Buhen** to **Semna** by **Senusret III** to control the native Nubians. The fortress was abandoned in the **Second Intermediate Period**, but reused in the **New Kingdom**. It was excavated in 1962–64 by an expedition from the University of California at Los Angeles before the site was flooded by the lake created by the Aswan High Dam.

ASSYRIA. A kingdom situated in northern Iraq which was renowned for its war-like abilities. Assyria benefited from the destruction of **Mitanni** and the **Hittite** empire and expanded southwards to conquer Mesopotamia and westwards to Syria and Palestine whose states were annexed or reduced to vassal status. Assyria came into conflict with Egypt at the beginning of **Dynasty 25**, but its forces were kept at bay until the reign of Esarhaddon (681–69 BC) who invaded Egypt in 671 BC. The Nubian ruler **Taharqo** of Dynasty 25 was defeated and driven south and members of the royal family captured, but the Assyrian forces were eventually expelled.

The son and successor of Esarhaddon, Ashurbanipal (669–27 BC) renewed the campaign, took **Memphis**, and drove Taharqo south again. The local princes of the Delta submitted, notably **Nekau I** of **Sais** of **Dynasty 26** who became the chief Assyrian vassal after the other princes were executed for disloyalty. The new ruler of Dynasty 25 **Tantamani** invaded Egypt from **Nubia** in 664 BC after the departure of the main Assyrian forces and killed Nekau whose son **Psamtik I** fled to Assyria for protection. In 663 BC the Assyrians returned, defeated the Nubians, and sacked **Thebes**. During Psamtik I's long reign the control of Assyria gradually weakened due to internal difficulties and Egypt regained independence. When the Assyrian kingdom was destroyed in 612 BC, the remnants appealed to Egypt for help, and **Nekau II** invaded Palestine as an ally but was defeated by the Babylonians at the battle of Carchemish in 609 BC after which Assyria disappeared as a political entity.

ASTARTE. Canaanite goddess of love and fertility. Her worship spread to Egypt in the **New Kingdom**. She was considered one of the wives of the god **Seth** along with **Anat**.

ASWAN see **ELEPHANTINE.**

ASYUT. Arabic name for the Egyptian *Sauty,* Greek Lycopolis, capital of the 13th **nome** of **Upper Egypt.** The chief deity of the city was the god **Wepwawet.** Very little remains of the town, but the tombs of the **nomarchs** of the **First Intermediate Period** and the **Middle Kingdom** have been uncovered. Excavations took place by a French team in 1903, an Italian expedition in 1905–13, and British excavators in 1906–07 and 1922.

ATEN. The sun's disk and so a form of the sun-god **Re**-Harakhty. Aten was worshipped as a god in his own right towards the end of **Dynasty 18** and raised to position of supreme deity by **Akhenaten** in opposition to the cult of **Amun.** In his honour the king took a name compounded with that of the god and founded a new city at **Amarna.** The king sought to suppress the cults of other rival gods, but his new religion was not monotheistic since he did not proscribe cults connected with the sun-god such as the **Mnevis** bull or those deifying the kingship of his father or himself. Following Akhenaten's death, the cult of Aten was abandoned and proscribed although there are occasional references to the Aten in its old form as the sun's disk.

ATHANASIUS (c.296–373 AD). Egyptian Christian patriarch. He was born in **Alexandria** where he was educated and became the secretary of Patriarch Alexander whom he succeeded in 326. Prior to his accession he took part in the Council of Nicaea in 325 where the orthodox creed was laid down, and thereafter became a staunch opponent of the doctrine of **Arius.** He was exiled from 334–37 and deposed from 340–45 and 356–61, and briefly exiled in 363 and 365 by various emperors for his views. He set the example for opposition by the patriarchs of Alexandria to imperial policy when it conflicted with their religious beliefs. He died in May 373. His surviving writings include an influential life of St. **Anthony.**

ATHRIBIS. Greek name for the Egyptian *Hutheryib,* modern Tell Atrib, capital of the 10th **nome** of **Lower Egypt.** The town is attested from at least the **Old Kingdom** but was particularly prominent in the **Late** and **Graeco-Roman Periods.** Little remains on the site, but it was excavated by Flinders **Petrie** in 1907 and subsequently by Alan Rowe in 1939 and has been under excavation by a Polish expedition from 1957. The tomb of queen Takhut, wife of **Psamtik II** and mother of **Wahibre**, was discovered here in 1951.

ATUM. Primeval creator god who was believed to have arisen from chaos or **Nun** and then produced the deities **Shu** and **Tefnut** by spitting or masturbation. He can be depicted as a human figure or a serpent. He was worshipped at **Heliopolis** where he was soon identified with the sun-god **Re**. His sacred animal was the ichneumon or shrew.

AUGUSTUS (63 BC–14 AD). First Roman emperor. Original name Caius Octavius. Son of Caius Octavius and Atia and great-nephew of Caius Julius **Caesar** who adopted him in his will. He used his adoptive father's name and his own political skills following Caesar's assassination in 44 BC to become one of the rulers of the Roman world with Marcus Aemilius Lepidus and Marcus **Antonius**. He eventually forced Lepidus's resignation and clashed with Antonius and his ally **Cleopatra VII** whom he defeated and drove to suicide in 30 BC. He then annexed Egypt as the personal property of the emperor forbidding any senator to go there without imperial permission and putting Egypt under the control of a prefect. His rule restricted the rights of the native Egyptians and refused to recognize the use of Egyptian in official documentation. He was considered **pharaoh** by the Egyptians and his name appears in **cartouches** with the prenomen Autocrator, the Greek equivalent of Imperator, his official Roman designation.

AVARIS. Modern Tell el-Daba. Capital city of the **Hyksos Dynasty 15** situated in the Delta. Very little is known of its history. It was founded in **Dynasty 12** and settled by immigrants from Syria-Palestine and later served as the Hyksos stronghold. It was attacked by **Kamose** and later captured by **Ahmose I** of **Dynasty 18** after which it fell into ruins. Excavations on the site have been carried out by an Austrian expedition since 1966 and have revealed palace structures and wall frescoes in the Minoan style.

AY (reigned c.1327–1323 BC). Throne name Kheperkheprure. High official in the reign of **Akhenaten** and **Tutankhamun** with the title **God's Father** and **vizier**. It has been speculated that he was the brother of **Tiy** and the father of **Nefertiti**, but nothing definite is known about his family apart from the fact that his wife, also **Tiy**, was the nurse of Nefertiti. He succeeded Tutankhamun, probably against the wishes of Queen **An-**

khesenamun and conducted the burial rites for the late monarch as depicted in Tutankhamun's tomb. His reign was brief and he was buried in tomb no. 23 in the **Valley of the Kings**, discovered in 1816, but his **mummy** has not been preserved or identified. His memory was later suppressed in **Dynasty 19**.

- B -

BADARI, EL-. Modern name for a site in **Upper Egypt** dated to the **Predynastic Period**. The black-topped red pottery found here gave the name Badarian to a phase of predynastic culture.

BAHRIYA OASIS. An oasis in the Western Desert west of **Luxor**. Archaeological remains have been discovered from the **New Kingdom** to the **Byzantine Period** including tombs of local governors from **Dynasties 19** and **26**.

BAKENRENEF (reigned c.721–715 BC). Throne name Wahkare. The Greek form of his name was Bocchoris. Ruler of **Dynasty 24**. He succeeded his father **Tefnakhte** as prince of **Sais** and claimant to the throne of Egypt. The extent of his rule in Egypt is unclear, but he was opposed and finally defeated by **Shabaqo** of **Dynasty 25**. Later sources indicate that he was executed by the new ruler. See also **Third Intermediate Period**.

BAKETATEN (fl. c.1350 BC). Royal princess known only from a relief at **Amarna** where she is depicted with her mother Queen **Tiy**. It is presumed that she was an otherwise unattested daughter of **Amenhotep III**, but it is possible that she was in fact a granddaughter of Tiy and daughter of **Akhenaten**. See also **Amarna Period**.

BALAMUN, TELL EL-. Modern name for the site of the northernmost city of Egypt situated near the Mediterranean coast of the northeastern part of the Delta. Egyptian *Behdet*, later *Paiuenamun*. Greek Diospolis Parva. The city is attested from the **Old Kingdom** until the **Roman Period** and was the capital of the 17th **nome** of **Lower Egypt**, created in the **New Kingdom** although little now remains. The principal gods worshipped here were **Horus**, lord of Behdet, and later **Amun** to whom the main temple was dedicated in the New Kingdom. The site was briefly examined by Howard Carter in 1913 and an Egyptian expedition in 1977–78, but since 1991 has been excavated by an expedition from the **British Museum** which has traced the outlines of the main **temple** and subsidiary temples built from the **Saite Period** until **Dynasty 30.**

BALLANA. Modern name for a site in **Nubia** on the west bank of the **Nile** south of **Qasr Ibrim** where, together with the site of Qustul on the opposite east bank, many graves have been excavated from different phases of Nubian culture. Some 180 tombs, dating from the fourth through seventh centuries AD, were discovered of which 40 contained material of such richness that they might be called royal. The objects found included jewellery, notably crowns, weapons, horse fittings, and vessels. These are now in the **Cairo Egyptian Museum**. The site has given its name to the Ballana culture or X-group culture which can be identified from graves elsewhere in Nubia. The area was excavated by the Egyptian Antiquities Service in 1931–34 and more recently by an Egyptian expedition in 1958–59 and the University of Chicago in the 1960s in advance of flooding caused by the Aswan High Dam.

BASTET. Cat goddess of **Bubastis** represented as a cat-headed or lioness-headed human figure often with a sistrum rattle or kittens. The worship of her cult became popular in the **Late Period** from which time cemeteries of cats, killed as votive offerings to her, have been discovered. See also **Sakhmet**.

BAWIT. Modern name for a monastic site in **Upper Egypt** 28 kilometres south of **Hermopolis** which flourished from the late third century AD until at least the end of the twelfth century. It was apparently founded by the monk Apa Apollo. Excavations by French archaeologists in 1901–04 and 1913 uncovered part of the site and found architectural elements, stone and wooden sculpture as well as important paintings.

BAY (fl. c.1196 BC). The power behind the throne at the end of **Dynasty 19**. He claims to have arranged the succession of **Siptah**. It is not clear if he survived into the reign of **Tewosret**. Egyptian inscriptions give him the title of chancellor but a text from **Ugarit** calls him commander of the king's guard. He had a tomb (no. 13) in the **Valley of the Kings.** He has been identified as a Syrian by modern Egyptologists due to a later ambiguous reference, but there is in fact no firm evidence of his background. See also **Sethnakhte**.

BEIT EL-WALI. Modern name for the site of a **temple** of **Ramesses II** in **Nubia**, built early in his reign and depicting his wars. The area is now flooded by the lake of the Aswan High Dam, but the temple has been moved to a site near Aswan.

BELZONI, GIOVANNI BATTISTA (1778–1823). Italian adventurer and excavator. He was born in Padua on 5 November 1778 and later joined a circus troupe in London. He went to Egypt in 1815 to seek work as a technical adviser but was unsuccessful. He was employed by Henry Salt, the British consul-general, to move a head of **Ramesses II** from the **Ramesseum** for shipment to England to the **British Museum** and thereafter to acquire antiquities for Salt's collections which were later sold to the British Museum and the **Louvre**. Belzoni supervised excavations at **Giza**, **Thebes**, and **Abu Simbel** as well as acquiring material directly from locals. He quarrelled with Salt over the terms of his employment and in 1819 returned with some antiquities and watercolours of tomb scenes to London where he put on a successful exhibition and wrote his memoirs. Belzoni died at Gwato in Benin, West Africa, on 3 December 1823 during an expedition to seek the source of the Niger River.

BENI HASAN. Modern name for the site in **Middle Egypt** containing the rock tombs of the **nomarchs** of the 16th **nome** of **Upper Egypt** and other officials dating to **Dynasties 11** and **12**. One tomb is notable for the depiction of Asiatics who had travelled to Egypt. The site also contains a **New Kingdom** rock chapel dedicated by **Hatshepsut** and **Thutmose III**. The tombs were copied by an expedition from the **Egypt Exploration Fund** in 1890–91.

BENJAMIN (c.590–661 AD). Coptic patriarch of **Alexandria**. He was born at Barshut in the western Delta and in 620 joined a monastic community at Canopus. He later served the patriarch Andronicus of the **Coptic Church** as his assistant, succeeding him in 622. In 631 he opposed **Cyrus**, the newly appointed orthodox patriarch and prefect of Egypt who tried to end the religious divisions in Egypt by force. Benjamin fled into hiding, and the resultant instability undoubtedly aided the Arabic conquest of Egypt in 642. He was then restored to office, but the division of the Christians into Coptic and orthodox communities with separate patriarchs remained permanent. He remained on amicable terms with the new Islamic rulers. He died on 3 January 661.

BERENICE I (c.340–278/7 BC). Daughter of Magas and Antigone and wife of a Macedonian named Philip by whom she had several children. She came to Egypt with Eurydice, second wife of **Ptolemy I**, and soon became the mistress and then wife of the king. She was the mother of his successor **Ptolemy II** and his sister-wife **Arsinoe II.**

BERENICE II (c.273–221 BC). Daughter of King Magas of **Cyrene** and Apama. She was engaged to **Ptolemy III**, but her mother attempted to marry her to a Macedonian prince against whom she led a revolt ending in his execution. She married the Egyptian king in 246 BC. She was the mother of **Ptolemy IV** who apparently had her killed shortly after his accession.

BERENICE III see **CLEOPATRA BERENICE III.**

BERENICE IV (c.78–55 BC). Eldest daughter of **Ptolemy XII** and **Cleopatra VI Tryphaena.** When her father was expelled in 58 BC, she was named joint ruler apparently with her mother. She married firstly in 56 BC Seleucus, a Syrian prince whom she murdered shortly after the marriage, and secondly Archelaus of Cappadocia who was killed in 55 BC trying to defeat the Roman forces supporting his father-in-law. On his restoration, Ptolemy XII executed his daughter.

BERLIN EGYPTIAN MUSEUM. The museum was founded by the King of Prussia on 1 July 1828 following the acquisition of the collections of Heinrich von Minutoli and Giuseppe Passalacqua, who became the first director. The collection was increased during the expedition to Egypt in 1842–45 by Richard **Lepsius**, who became the second director in 1865. A new museum for Egyptain antiquities was opened in 1850. The collection was enriched by the gift of **Amarna** sculpture, notably the head of Queen **Nefertiti**, by a merchant who had financed the German excavations at Amarna. The museum was badly damaged during World War II and the collections later divided between East and West Berlin. The management of the Egyptian collection has now been unified, and plans are underway to rebuild the museum on its old site.

BINTANAT (fl. c.1280–1210 BC). Eldest daughter of **Ramesses II** and **Isitnofret**. She married her father and was influential during the latter part of his reign and into that of her full brother **Merenptah**. She had her own tomb (no. 71) in the **Valley of the Queens** where she is depicted with a daughter whose royal parentage is not explicitly stated.

BOOK OF THE DEAD. The name given to a type of **papyrus** which was often buried with the dead from the **New Kingdom** onwards. The papyrus contained a number of magical spells which would enable the deceased to successfully reach the next world. The most important concerned the ritual of the **weighing of the heart** against the feather of *maat* to determine the deceased's worthiness to enter the **afterlife**, and the spell was supposed to fix the balance in the deceased's favor. Some books of the dead were decorated with elaborate vignettes and scenes depicting the funeral and ritual scenes. Some were obviously produced as special commissions, but there were stock examples available for purchase in which the name of the deceased could merely be filled in in the blank spaces or in some cases not filled in at all.

BOSTON MUSEUM OF FINE ARTS. This museum was founded in 1872 and immediately acquired its first Egyptian objects from the collection of C. Granville Way who had purchased them from the estate of Robert Hay, an early traveller in Egypt. Further acquisitions were made from the collection of John Lowell of Boston, another early traveller and from donations from the **Egypt Exploration Fund**. In 1909 a new museum building was inaugurated. Following the appointment of George **Reisner** as curator of Egyptian Antiquities in 1910, the museum received substantial numbers of objects from his archaeological work at **Giza**, **Naga el-Deir**, **Deir el-Bersha**, and various **Nubian** sites.

BRITISH MUSEUM. The British Museum was founded in 1753 as a national museum of Great Britain to house collections which had then been bequeathed to the nation. It was funded by a lottery which allowed the purchase of a property in London, now on Great Russell Street. The original building was demolished and rebuilt in the first half of the nineteenth century. Small Egyptian items were present in the collection from the foundation, but major Egyptian antiquities were acquired in 1802 with the surrender of objects, including the **Rosetta Stone**, collected by the French invaders of Egypt who were defeated by a combined British and Turkish force. Egyptian holdings then expanded with the purchase of individual collections such as those of Henry Salt in 1823, Joseph Sams in 1834, and Giovanni Anastasi in 1839 as well as items acquired at auction sales or by donation. The collection was further enhanced by the efforts of the Keeper of Egyptian Antiquities E. A. Wallis Budge (1857–1934). From 1882 the Museum received a share of the objects excavated by the **Egypt Exploration Fund/Society**. From 1980 the British Museum has conducted its own excavations at **Hermopolis** and **Tell el-Balamun**. It has one of the finest collections of Egyptian antiquities outside the **Cairo Egyptian Museum**.

BUBASTIS. Greek name for the Egyptian city of *Per-Bastet,* capital of the 18th **nome** of **Lower Egypt**, now Tell Basta. The principal deity worshipped here was the cat- or lioness-headed goddess **Bastet**. Remains have been found from the **Old Kingdom**, but the town was most prominent in **Dynasty 22** which is said to have originated here. It was excavated by a British expedition from the **Egypt Exploration Fund**, 1887–89, and by Egyptian Egyptologists notably Labib Habachi in 1939 and 1943–44, Shafik Farid in 1961–67, Ahmad el-Sawi in 1967–71, and more recently Muhammad Bakr from 1978 and a joint expedition of the Universities of Zagazig and Potsdam from 1996.

BUCHIS. Sacred ram of the city of **Armant.** The Bucheum or catacombs of the rams were excavated from 1926–32 by a British expedition sponsored by the **Egypt Exploration Society** and date from **Dynasty 30** to the **Roman Period**.

BUHEN. Site in **Nubia** at the Second **Cataract**. The Egyptians had penetrated this far south during the **Old Kingdom** where remains of copper-smelting production have been found. A major fort was constructed in the **Middle Kingdom** as part of the Egyptian garrison. The site and its vicinity were excavated by a British expedition from the **Egypt Exploration Society** in 1960–65 before the area was flooded by the lake formed behind the Aswan High Dam.

BUTO. Greek name for the Egyptian twin cities of *Pe* and *Dep* also known as *Per-Wadjet*, modern Tell el-Farain. Ancient capital city of **Lower Egypt** whose principal deity was the cobra goddess **Wadjet**. Some remains can be traced from the **Predynastic Period** until Roman occupation. The site was briefly examined by Flinders **Petrie** in 1886 and excavated by Charles Currelly in 1904 and Veronica Seton-Williams for the **Egypt Exploration Society in** 1964–68 but has since been examined more extensively by an Egyptian and a German expedition from 1983.

BYBLOS. Major town and seaport on the eastern Mediterranean coast in modern Lebanon, ancient *Gubla*. It was the principal port through which timber and other goods were exported to Egypt from the **Early Dynastic Period** onwards. Relations are attested in the **Old**, **Middle**, and **New Kingdoms**. The city escaped destruction by the **Sea Peoples** and is mentioned in the Tale of **Wenamun** at the end of **Dynasty 20** when Egyptian influence there was negligible due to the weakness of the Egyptian state.

BYZANTINE PERIOD (395–642 AD). The period during which Egypt was ruled from Constantinople by the Eastern Roman emperor. This era is marked by increasing religious differences between the orthodox court and the monophysite church in Egypt which became increasingly nationalistic, eventually breaking away to form the separate **Coptic Church**. The period ended with the Arabic conquest of Egypt in 642 AD.

- C -

CAESAR, CAIUS JULIUS (100–44 BC). Roman dictator. Son of Caius Julius Caesar and Aurelia. He had a successful political career culminating in the consulship of 59 BC. Caesar obtained an appointment as governor of Roman Gaul (then only covering modern Provence) and exhibited exceptional military skill in conquering the whole of Gaul (modern France and part of Belgium). Attacked by political opponents at home, he invaded Italy in 49 BC and was proclaimed dictator. Caesar defeated his rival Gnaeus Pompeius at Pharsalus and followed the latter's flight to Egypt where he discovered that Pompeius had been murdered and Egypt was engulfed in civil war between **Ptolemy XIII** and his sister **Cleopatra VII**. He sided with Cleopatra, who became his mistress, and following the defeat and death of Ptolemy, installed her as ruler of Egypt with her younger brother **Ptolemy XIV**. She claimed that Caesar was the father of her son **Ptolemy XV**, known as Caesarion. Cleopatra was in Rome when Caesar was assassinated in 44 BC.

CAIRO EGYPTIAN MUSEUM. The largest and finest number of Egyptian antiquities are preserved in the **Cairo Egyptian Museum**. The Museum was established in 1862 by the Egyptian ruler Said at the request of Auguste **Mariette**, the head of the Antiquities Service, and opened at Bulaq in October 1863. The Museum was filled with objects from Mariette's excavations and subsequent work by Egyptian and foreign archaeologists. It supervised the division of antiquities agreed with foreign excavators and kept all important pieces in Egypt. In 1891 the Museum was moved to Giza and finally in 1902 to its present site in Cairo. A large selection of objects acquired last century and early this century were published in a series of catalogues by international scholars. Masterpieces in the collection include the **Narmer** palette, the statues of **Khafre** and **Menkaure** from **Giza**, royal jewellery from **Dahshur**, the **Tutankhamun** treasures, and the finds from the royal tombs at **Tanis**.

CAMBYSES (reigned 525–522 BC). Persian ruler, son of Cyrus, king of **Persia** and Mesopotamia. He carried out a successful invasion of Egypt in 525 BC overthrowing **Dynasty 26**. The invasion caused some damage although the extent of this cannot be determined. Cambyses adopted a few Egyptian royal customs including taking a throne name—Mesutire—chosen by **Udjahorresnet**. He cancelled many of the privileges of Egyptian **temples** and so became unpopular with the Egyptian priesthood. Later stories of his cruelty, including the murder of the **Apis** bull, cannot be substantiated and may be exaggerated.

CANOPIC JARS. Modern term for the four jars in which the soft internal tissues of the deceased were stored after the mummification of the body. Canopic chests in which packages of these organs (liver, lungs, stomach, and intestines) were placed are known from the early **Old Kingdom**, but actual jars with ovoid lids appear slightly later. By the **Middle Kingdom** the set of four jars dedicated to the four **sons of Horus** had evolved. The jars were all originally human-headed, but by the **New Kingdom** they bore separate heads—human, baboon, jackal, and hawk. From **Dynasty 21** the internal organs were wrapped in packages and placed in the body, but the funerary equipment continued to include dummy canopic jars. The use of actual jars was revived in **Dynasty 26**. The term canopic derives from confusion with Canopus—a deity depicted as a human-headed jar in the **Graeco-Roman Period**. See also **Mummy**.

CARACALLA (188–217 AD). Roman emperor. He was born on 4 April 188, eldest son of **Septimius Severus** and Julia Domna. His original name appears to have been Lucius Septimius Bassianus, but he was renamed Marcus Aurelius Antoninus after his father's accession. Caracalla was named co-emperor with his father on 28 January 198 and succeeded his father in 211 together with his younger brother Geta whose murder he ordered in late 211. In the same year he issued a proclamation granting Roman citizenship to all inhabitants of the empire in order to raise taxes. Caracalla conducted several military campaigns, notably an eastern war from 215. He visited Egypt that year and massacred part of the population of **Alexandria** whom he regarded as disrespectful. Caracalla was assassinated on the road between Edessa and Carrhae in Syria on 8 April 217.

CARTER, HOWARD (1874–1939). British excavator. He was born in London on 9 May 1874, the son of an artist who trained him in this calling. He was sent to Egypt in 1891 as an artist draughtsman at **Beni Hasan** by the **Egypt Exploration Fund** and later worked as an assistant to Flinders **Petrie** at **Amarna** and at **Deir el-Bahri**. Carter was appointed chief inspector for **Upper Egypt** in 1899 and transferred to **Lower Egypt** in 1904 but left the Antiquities Service in 1905 after a disagreement. He was employed by the Earl of Carnarvon from 1909 as his archaeologist in the Theban area, especially in the **Valley of the Kings** where he made significant discoveries before finding the intact tomb of **Tutankhamun** in 1922. Carter took 10 years to clear the tomb but he lacked the academic background to undertake a definitive archaeological report on his work. His detailed notes are preserved in the Griffith Institute, Oxford, and have been used to prepare a series of reports on groups of materials from the tomb.

CARTOUCHE. The modern French name used by Egyptologists to denote the ring which encircles the prenomen and nomen in the royal **titulary,** ancient Egyptian *shenu*. The identification of the cartouche as the marker of the royal name aided the decipherment of **hieroglyphic** writing.

CATARACT. The modern name for the rocky stone areas in the bed of the **Nile** which render navigation impossible. The First Cataract is situated just south of **Elephantine**, modern Aswan, and marked the original border between Egypt and **Nubia**. There are six numbered cataracts in the course of the Nile in the Sudan before it divides into the White and Blue Niles near Khartoum.

CHAMPOLLION, JEAN-FRANÇOIS (1790–1832). French scholar. He was born in Figeac on 23 December 1790. He very early conceived the desire to decipher the ancient Egyptian **hieroglyphic** script and prepared himself by studying oriental languages, including **Coptic**. He eventually obtained an academic post in Grenoble which gave him time to devote to his studies. Champollion first regarded the script as symbolic. However, the Englishman Thomas Young demonstrated that the names of the Ptolemaic rulers were written alphabetically. Champollion later disingenuously claimed that he was unaware of Young's research, but he adopted this approach and soon with the help of bilingual inscriptions such as the **Rosetta Stone** surpassed Young's work. Champollion established that the hieroglyphic script was both alphabetic and pictographic and was able to read ancient Egyptian for the first time and realize that it was an older form of Coptic.

He achieved wide recognition for his work and in 1826 was appointed first curator of Egyptian antiquities at the **Louvre Museum**. In 1828–29 he visited Egypt. Champollion was appointed professor of Egyptian history and archaeology at the Collège de France in Paris in 1831. He died in Paris on 4 March 1832. Although respected as a scholar, he was regarded as an arrogant and difficult man by his contemporaries.

CHEOPS see **KHUFU**.

CHEPHREN see **KHAFRE**.

CHRONOLOGY. The ancient Egyptian calendar consisted of a year of 360 days divided into three seasons of *akhet* (flood), *peret* (sowing), and *shemu* (harvest) plus five extra days at the end of the year. Each season comprised four months of 30 days and was in turn divided into three weeks of ten days of 24 hours split between night and day. Because the calendar did not include the extra one-quarter day of the earth's rotation, the civil calendar gradually diverged from the solar year so that the months moved and the two only harmonized briefly every 1,460 years. The solar year was measured from the annual rising of the star Sirius, which becomes visible around July of each year in the modern calendar.

A third calendar in use for administrative purposes was the regnal year based initially on the biennial cattle count in the **Old Kingdom** and from the **Middle Kingdom** on the king's actual years although his first year was foreshortened so the beginning of his second might coincide with the beginning of the civil year. This practice was abandoned in the **New Kingdom** when the full regnal year was dated from the king's accession, but calculation of the regnal year reverted to the old system in the **Late Period**. Thus three different dating systems—solar, civil, and regnal—were in use in the New Kingdom.

The conversion of Egyptian dates to the modern Julian calendar is not exact. Dating from the **Late Period** is fixed by synchronisms with Assyrian, Persian, Greek, and Roman dating systems. It is known that the solar and civil calendars coincided in 139 AD, and thus the previous coincidence would have occurred 1,460 years earlier—the period being known as a Sothic cycle, but the use of astronomical references to the rising of the star Sirius are too unclear to be of effective use. The most effective method for determining chronology is through use of the detailed king-lists known from documents such as the **Palermo Stone** or **Turin Royal Canon** or authors following **Manetho** supplemented by synchronisms with Mesopotamian or Hittite kings and astronomical dating when available. For earlier periods radio-carbon dating has proved most useful.

CLEOMENES (fl. c.350–322 BC). Born in **Naukratis**, Cleomenes was appointed the chief financial administrator of Egypt by **Alexander the Great** and soon became the leading power in the country. He undertook the building of **Alexandria**. He was executed by **Ptolemy I** following his appointment as **satrap** in 322 BC.

CLEOPATRA I (c.215–176 BC). Wife of **Ptolemy V** and daughter of Antiochus III, ruler of the Seleucid empire, and Laodice of Pontus. She was engaged to Ptolemy V in 196 BC and married him in 194–93 BC as part of a peace settlement between Egypt and the Seleucid empire. She had three children: **Cleopatra II**, **Ptolemy VI**, and **Ptolemy VIII**. On the death of her husband in 180 BC, she acted as regent until her own death between April and July 176 BC.

CLEOPATRA II (c.185–116 BC). Daughter of **Ptolemy V** and **Cleopatra I** and wife of **Ptolemy VI** and **Ptolemy VIII**. She was married to her brother Ptolemy VI in April 176 BC and declared joint ruler of Egypt in 170 BC in the face of the threat of invasion by the Seleucid king **Antiochus IV**. When her husband was captured by the enemy, she and her younger brother Ptolemy VIII held out in **Alexandria**. Antiochus IV was forced to abandon Egypt under Roman pressure, and the joint rule of the three siblings was restored. In 164 BC civil war broke out between the brothers and Ptolemy VIII was expelled to **Cyrene**. Cleopatra II bore four children to Ptolemy VI: **Ptolemy Eupator**, **Ptolemy VII**, **Cleopatra Thea**, and **Cleopatra III**. Her husband was killed in 145 BC, and she briefly acted as regent for her son Ptolemy VII until power was seized by her brother Ptolemy VIII who married her but murdered her son.

Cleopatra bore her new husband one son, **Ptolemy Memphites**, but he soon preferred her daughter Cleopatra III. Civil war broke out between the spouses in 132 BC during which Ptolemy VIII murdered his son Memphites before regaining control in 130 BC. Peace was eventually restored between the spouses in 124 BC when Cleopatra II was recognized as senior queen. She is last recorded in 116 BC having survived her second husband.

CLEOPATRA III (c.158–101 BC). Daughter of **Ptolemy VI** and **Cleopatra II**. She became the second consort of her uncle **Ptolemy VIII** about 141 BC which eventually led to a civil war between her mother Cleopatra II, who was the first consort, against her husband and herself. Peace was eventually restored in 124 BC. Cleopatra bore her husband five children: **Ptolemy IX**, **Ptolemy X**, **Cleopatra IV**, **Cleopatra Tryphaena**, and **Cleopatra V Selene**. On Ptolemy VIII's death in 116 BC, she was given the choice of which son would rule with her. She preferred her younger son Ptolemy X but was forced by public opinion to accept her elder son Ptolemy IX who was eventually ousted in favour of his younger brother in 107 BC. This led to civil war in Cyprus and Syria between the rival kings. Cleopatra III died in 101 BC allegedly murdered by her ungrateful son Ptolemy X.

CLEOPATRA IV (d. 113 BC). Daughter of **Ptolemy VIII** and **Cleopatra III**. Consort of her brother **Ptolemy IX** who was forced to divorce her by their mother about 116 BC. Cleopatra IV fled to Cyprus and then Syria where she married the Seleucid king Antiochus IX Cyzicenus. She was in Antioch when it fell in 113 BC to his rival Antiochus VIII Grypus whose wife, her sister **Cleopatra Tryphaena**, ordered her to be executed.

CLEOPATRA V SELENE (c.140/35–69 BC). Daughter of **Ptolemy VIII** and **Cleopatra III**. About 116 BC she married her brother **Ptolemy IX** after he was forced by his mother to divorce his first wife and their sister **Cleopatra IV**. She remained in Egypt when her husband was expelled in 107 BC and in 103 BC she married her cousin Antiochus VIII Grypus, ruler of Syria, son of her aunt **Cleopatra Thea**, and former husband of her sister **Cleopatra Tryphaena**. Antiochus VIII Grypus was killed in 96 BC. Cleopatra Selene then married two further rulers of Syria: Anti-

CLEOPATRA VII PHILOPATOR • 47

ochus IX Cyzicenus (died 95 BC), cousin of her husband but also his maternal half-brother through Cleopatra Thea and former husband of her other sister Cleopatra IV, and finally her step-son Antiochus X Eusebes (killed about 89 BC). She apparently had two sons by her first husband whose fate is uncertain and two sons by her last husband who aspired to rule in Syria. Cleopatra Selene was captured during an invasion of Syria by Tigranes, king of Armenia, and executed in Seleucia-on-the-Tigris in 69 BC. Because the former Cleopatra V Tryphaena and **Cleopatra VI Tryphaena** are now regarded as identical, Cleopatra Selene is cited in more recent scholarship as Cleopatra V Selene.

CLEOPATRA VI TRYPHAENA (d. 57 BC). Wife of **Ptolemy XII.** Her origin is unknown but she was presumably his sister or half-sister and so daughter of **Ptolemy IX.** She evidently remained in the country when her husband was expelled in 58 BC and ruled jointly with her daughter **Berenice IV.** Earlier scholars had supposed that the co-ruler was a sister of Berenice IV and counted Cleopatra V Tryphaena as the mother and Cleopatra VI Tryphaena as the daughter, but these are now regarded as one and the same; the designation Cleopatra V has now been assigned to **Cleopatra V Selene.**

CLEOPATRA VII PHILOPATOR (c. 69–30 BC). Egyptian queen. Daughter of **Ptolemy XII** and possibly **Cleopatra VI Tryphaena.** She succeeded her father together with her younger brother and consort **Ptolemy XIII** with whom she soon fell out. Their civil war was interrupted by the arrival in Egypt of Julius **Caesar** who soon sided with Cleopatra and defeated her brother's forces in 47 BC in which battle he was killed. Cleopatra VII was installed as ruler of Egypt with her still-younger brother **Ptolemy XIV** as consort, but she had become Caesar's mistress and claimed him as the father of her son Ptolemy Caesarion. She was in Rome in 44 BC when Caesar was assassinated and returned hurriedly to Egypt. Her brother soon died and was replaced as ruling pharaoh by her son as **Ptolemy XV.**

Cleopatra formed an alliance with Marcus **Antonius**, who was in charge of the eastern Roman Empire, and bore him three children. She used her intimacy with Antonius to aggrandize Egypt to the detriment of other eastern states. Their relationship gave Antonius's rival **Augustus** the opportunity to vilify him in Rome and to declare war on Egypt as a threat to Rome. The Egyptian forces were defeated at the battle of Actium in 31 BC and, after the fall of Alexandria in 30 BC, Cleopatra committed suicide rather than be taken captive to Rome. See also **Alexander Helios, Cleopatra Selene, Ptolemy Philadelphus**.

CLEOPATRA BERENICE III (d. 80 BC). Daughter of **Ptolemy IX** and **Cleopatra IV**. She became the official consort of her uncle **Ptolemy X** after he took over the throne from her father, and, following the former's deposition in 88 BC, of her father Ptolemy IX. She became sole ruler of Egypt on his death in 80 BC but was forced by the Romans to accept her first cousin and step-son Ptolemy XI Alexander II as her consort. He murdered her within days of the marriage in June 80 BC and was promptly killed himself.

CLEOPATRA SELENE (fl. c.40 BC–11/7 AD). Daughter of Marcus **Antonius** and **Cleopatra VII**. She was born in 40 BC with her twin brother **Alexander Helios**. She was captured by **Augustus** in 30 BC and displayed in his triumph in Rome in 29 BC. She was brought up by Octavia, the sister of Augustus and the Roman wife of Antonius and married to King Juba II of Mauretania (modern Morocco) about 20 BC. She may have acted as regent for her husband during his absences from the kingdom and appears on his coinage. She had at least one son, King Ptolemy of Mauretania who was executed by Caligula in 40 AD and is the last known descendant of the Ptolemaic dynasty.

CLEOPATRA THEA (c.165–121/0 BC). Daughter of **Ptolemy VI** and **Cleopatra II**. She was married in 150 BC to the Syrian pretender Alexander I Balas who was installed as Seleucid ruler with the aid of his father-in-law, but the allies soon fell out. Cleopatra Thea was given to his rival Demetrius II. Balas was defeated in battle by Ptolemy VI in 145 BC after which he was killed and Ptolemy died of wounds. Demetrius II was captured in battle with the Parthians in 139 BC and Cleopatra Thea married his brother Antiochus VII Sidetes who was himself killed in battle with the Parthians in 129 BC. Demetrius II was restored but proved unpopular and was killed at Tyre in 126/5 BC. His widow ruled alone or in association with her sons by Demetrius II, Seleucus V (allegedly killed by her), and Antiochus VIII Grypus. She was apparently poisoned by her son in 121/0 BC after her attempt to murder him had failed. Her other son Antiochus IX Cyzicenus by Antiochus VII became a rival to his half-brother Antiochus VIII Grypus. Both brothers married Ptolemaic princesses, the former **Cleopatra IV** and **Cleopatra Selene** and the latter **Cleopatra Tryphaena** and his brother's widow Cleopatra Selene.

CLEOPATRA TRYPHAENA (d. 112 BC). Daughter of **Ptolemy VIII** and **Cleopatra III**. She married her first cousin the Seleucid king Antiochus VIII Grypus, son of Demetrius II and **Cleopatra Thea**, but he faced a rival in his half-brother Antiochus IX Cyzicenus who was married to **Cleopatra IV**, sister of Cleopatra Tryphaena. When Cleopatra IV was captured in 113 BC, she was executed at her sister's behest. Cleopatra Tryphaena was then herself killed when she fell into the hands of Antiochus IX in 112 BC.

COPTIC. The final phase of the Egyptian language and writing in which Greek script, with the addition of six new letters, was used to write ancient Egyptian. It is believed that the script was developed by Christians to spread their faith to the Egyptian populace. The script was used to translate Christian religious works, including the Bible but also ordinary correspondence, business and legal texts, and funerary and other inscriptions in stone. Following the Arabic conquest in 642 AD, it was gradually superseded by Arabic and fell out of use by the sixteenth century except for certain religious phrases no longer understood by the priests or general populace. European scholars learnt the language from exported Biblical and other religious manuscripts but were unaware that the language was ancient Egyptian until the decipherment of the **hieroglyphic** script. Knowledge of Coptic greatly aided the decipherment and understanding of ancient Egyptian. See also **Champollion**.

COPTIC CHURCH. Egyptian Christianity developed from the first century AD under the patriarch of **Alexandria**. The **Coptic** script was used to translate the holy scriptures and religious works. Strains soon appeared between the orthodox formula for the nature of Christ—two natures, human and divine intermingled, as set down by the councils of Nicaea in 325 and Chalcedon in 451—and the belief in Egypt of one divine nature known as monophysitism.

After failing to find a compromise, the Byzantine emperors with the support of the Roman popes sought to impose orthodoxy in Egypt, leading to a schism when a Coptic patriarch of Alexandria was elected in opposition to the orthodox one. Most Egyptians supported the Coptic Church and their loyalty to the emperor was weakened, facilitating the Arab conquest. This in turn led to the eventual decline of the native church since large parts of the population eventually went over to Islam and the Coptic language was replaced by Arabic. The Coptic Church is more vigorous at present than for several centuries.

COPTIC MUSEUM (CAIRO). This museum was founded in 1902 through the efforts of Marcus Simaika Pasha and established in its current position in Old Cairo in 1908. It was taken over by the Egyptian Antiquities Service in 1931 and enlarged in 1947. The collection contains over 14,000 objects from the **Coptic** Period, including stone sculpture, frescoes, icons, textiles, objects in ivory, wood, metal, and ceramic, and important manuscripts such as the **Nag Hammadi Codices**.

COPTOS. Greek name for a site in northern **Upper Egypt**, modern Qift. Ancient Egytian *Gebtu*, capital of the fifth Upper Egyptian **nome**. The chief deity of the town was the fertility god **Min** who was also regarded as the god of the Eastern Desert. The importance of the town lay as a centre for expeditions into the desert to the stone quarries or to the Red Sea coast to connect to trade routes to **Punt** and other locations. The **temple** that survives dates to the **Ptolemaic Period** with Roman additions, but earlier remains have been found back to the **Early Dynastic Period**. The site has been partly excavated by Flinders **Petrie** in 1893–94 and a French expedition in 1910–11.

CO-REGENCY. A system of dual rule which was devised to ensure the automatic transfer of power to the junior ruler on the death of the elder. It seems first to have been employed by **Amenemhat I** who made his son **Senusret I** a joint ruler although in this case the succession was disputed. Two types of co-regency are known whereby the junior partner has a full royal **titulary** and regnal dates or simply the titulary and no separate year dates until his succession as sole ruler. Co-regencies have complicated the determination of the exact **chronology** of rulers as they are not always attested clearly or taken account of in the surviving **kinglists**. Some co-regencies proposed by some modern Egyptologists such as that between **Amenhotep III** and **Akhenaten** are disputed.

CRETE see **KEFTYU.**

CYPRUS see **ALASIA.**

CYRENE. An area of eastern Libya colonized by Greek settlers c. 630 BC. An independent dynasty emerged but later recognized the suzerainty of **Cambyses** and subsequently **Alexander the Great**. At first ruled by **Ptolemy I**, it became independent again but the country was annexed to Egypt through the marriage of **Berenice II** to **Ptolemy III**. It became independent again briefly under **Ptolemy VIII** before his accession and under Ptolemy Apion, the illegitimate son of Ptolemy VIII, who died childless in 96 BC and left his kingdom to Rome.

CYRIL (d. 444 AD). Patriarch of **Alexandria**. He was a nephew of the patriarch Theophilus and was educated at the monastery of Deir Anba Macarius in the Nitrian Valley. He became a priest in Alexandria and succeeded his uncle as patriarch in 412. He was a vigorous opponent of Neoplatonism and Nestorianism and took a leading part in the Council of Ephesus in 431 when the teachings of Nestorius were condemned as heresy. He died in Alexandria on 27 June 444 and was succeeded by **Dioscorus**. See also **Coptic Church**.

CYRUS (d. 642 AD). Byzantine official. Bishop of Phasis in the Caucasus until 631 when he was named by the Emperor **Heraclius** as prefect of Egypt and patriarch of **Alexandria** in opposition to the **Coptic Church** and its patriarch **Benjamin**. He was entrusted with putting an end to dissension by enforcing orthodoxy in Egypt and attempted to carry out this policy with ruthless persecution of the Copts. He was not successful. Cyrus faced the Arabic invasion in 641 and was forced to agree by a treaty of 8 November 641 to surrender Alexandria and Egypt to the invaders and withdraw imperial forces in the following year. He died in Alexandria on 21 March 642 before the end of Byzantine rule in the city. See also **Byzantine Period**.

- D -

DAHSHUR. Modern name for the area south of **Saqqara** where several royal tombs from **Dynasty 4**, **Dynasty 12**, and **Dynasty 13** are located. Two **pyramids**, the Bent and the Red, are assigned to **Snefru** and were the first built as true pyramids from the start. The pyramids of **Amenemhat II**, **Senusret III**, and **Amenemhat III** are also located here as well as the tombs of queens and princesses from which much fine jewellery has been excavated. The tomb of King **Hor** of Dynasty 13 has also been discovered. The area has been excavated by the French in 1894–95, the Egyptians under Ahmad Fakhry in 1951–55, and the German Archaeological Institute, later taken over by the New York **Metropolitan Museum of Art** from 1980.

DAKHLA OASIS. An oasis in the Western Desert west of **Luxor**. Excavations have uncovered remains possibly from the **Early Dynastic Period** and certainly from the **Old Kingdom** until the **Byzantine Period**. The site was visited by Herbert Winlock in 1908 and again examined by the Egyptian archaeologist Ahmed Fakhry in 1971–72. A settlement and tombs from **Dynasty 6** have been excavated at Balat by a French expedition from 1977, while a joint Canadian-Australian expedition has conducted a survey and excavations in the oasis from 1978 and found a Roman and Byzantine town site and associated **temples** at Ismant el-Kharb which has yielded documentary and literary texts on **papyrus** and wooden tablets.

DEIR EL-BAHRI. Modern name for a site on the cliffs of the western bank of the **Nile** opposite **Thebes**. It was apparently first used to construct the tomb and mortuary **temple** of **Mentuhotep II** of **Dynasty 11** and the tombs of his successors as well as the chief officials of the court. In **Dynasty 18** it was chosen as the site of the mortuary temple of Queen **Hatshepsut** the building of which was supervised by her official **Senenmut**. The temple is well preserved and is famous for its reliefs of the expedition to **Punt** and the transportation of an **obelisk**. Next to this a mortuary temple was constructed by **Thutmose III**, but this has been largely destroyed by a subsequent earthquake. The site became a **Coptic** monastery in the Christian period but was later abandoned.

Deir el-Bahri was first excavated by Auguste **Mariette** in 1850, 1862, and 1866. Major excavations were undertaken in the Hatshepsut temple in 1893–96 and the Mentuhotep II temple in 1903–07 by a British expedition of the **Egypt Exploration Fund**. Further work in the area was carried out by Herbert Winlock of the **Metropolitan Museum of Art** from 1911–31. The Mentuhotep II temple was re-examined by a German expedition from 1965–72 and the Hatshepsut temple has been the subject of excavation and restoration work by a Polish team from 1961 during which the Thutmose III temple was discovered.

DEIR EL-BALLAS. Modern name for a site in **Upper Egypt** north of **Thebes** where the remains of a major royal palace and town have been discovered. The area appears to have been occupied at the end of **Dynasty 17** and the beginning of **Dynasty 18**. It has been partially excavated by George **Reisner** from 1900–02 and more recently by an expedition from the **Boston Museum of Fine Arts** from 1980.

DEIR EL-BERSHA. Modern name for a site in **Middle Egypt** on the east bank of the **Nile** near **Hermopolis**. The most important features of the area are the rock-cut tombs of the governors of the 15th **nome** of **Upper Egypt** from **Dynasty 12**, notably the tomb of Djehutihotep which features a scene of the transport of a colossal seated statue from the quarry at **Hatnub**. The tombs were excavated and copied by expeditions of the **Egypt Exploration Fund** in 1891–92, the Egyptian Antiquities Service in 1897 and 1900–02, and the **Boston Museum of Fine Arts** in 1915 and 1990.

DEIR EL-GABRAWI. Modern name for a site in **Middle Egypt** on the east bank of the **Nile** north of **Asyut** where the governors of the 12th **nome** of **Upper Egypt** were buried in rock-cut tombs in **Dynasty 6**. Some of the scenes in one tomb served as a model for similar scenes in a tomb at **Thebes** dated to the **Saite Period.**

DEIR EL-MEDINA. Modern name for the site of the workmen's village on the west bank of **Thebes** near the **Valley of the Kings.** The village was founded either by **Amenhotep I**, who was worshipped there as a god, or his successor **Thutmose I** whose name appears on bricks on the site. The workmen were organized to construct the royal tombs in the Valley of the Kings, but little material has survived from **Dynasty 18** apart from several tombs of workmen such as the foreman **Kha**, whose tomb was found intact, and some **stelae.** The village may have been abandoned during the reign of **Akhenaten** but was certainly in operation under **Tutankhamun** and reorganized in the reign of **Horemheb.**

Much material survives from the **Ramesside Period** including stelae, **papyri, ostraca**, and tombs which give a detailed picture of life in the community. The village was under the direct control of the southern **vizier**, but was effectively governed by the two foremen of each side of the workforce, which was divided into two, and the scribe or scribes. Local disputes were settled in the village court made up of the chief men of the village, but criminal cases were sent to the vizier. The workmen were supplied with payments in kind of wheat and beer and other commodities, and surviving daybooks show that the work period was not overly onerous and there was generous time off. The workmen in their spare time prepared material for their own tombs and accepted commissions for tomb equipment from outside the community. The village possessed a series of small chapels in which gods and goddesses such as **Amun** and **Meretseger** were worshipped by the workmen themselves in the roles of priests. The village was abandoned at the end of **Dynasty 20** when royal burials ceased and conditions deteriorated due to Libyan raids. Some workmen remained at **Medinet Habu** and took part in the preparation of the **royal caches** in **Dynasty 21**.

The site was discovered in the early nineteenth century and objects were acquired by several museum collections, notably the **British Museum**, the **Louvre**, and the **Turin Egyptian Museum**. The site was excavated by an Italian expediton from Turin in 1905–06 and 1909, a German expedition in 1913, and has since 1917 been excavated and published by the French Archaeological Institute in Cairo. See also **Hesunebef**, **Kenherkhepeshef**, **Paneb**, **Ramose**, **Sennedjem**.

DELTA see **LOWER EGYPT**.

DEMOTIC. Term derived from the Greek for the cursive Egyptian script which was derived from and superseded **hieratic** from the **Saite Period**. It was used primarily on **papyri** and **ostraca** but occasionally on carved stone, notably the **Rosetta Stone**. Use of the script declined following the Roman conquest as it was no longer recognized in the courts and was then solely used by priests. The last known text has been found in the temple of **Philae** dated to 452 AD.

DEN (reigned c.2985 BC). Fifth king of **Dynasty 1**. Successor and probably son of **Djet** and Queen **Merneith** who may have acted as regent for her son. His tomb has been excavated at **Abydos** and among the finds were ivory labels which showed the king in various poses, including smiting Asiatics. See also **Anedjib**.

DENDERA. Modern name for the Egyptian city of *Iunet*, later known as Tentyris in Greek, capital of the sixth **nome** of **Upper Egypt**. The site is known from the **Early Dynastic Period** and there are tombs from the **First Intermediate Period** when the regional rulers were semi-independent. Its main feature is the magnificent Graeco-Roman **temple** dedicated to the goddess **Hathor**, from which came the famous Dendera zodiac now in the **Louvre**. The site was excavated by Flinders **Petrie** in 1897–98 and the University of Pennsylvania from 1915–18. The temple inscriptions are being published by a French expedition.

DENDUR. Site in Lower **Nubia** of a small **temple** built during the reign of **Augustus** to two deified brothers. The site has now been flooded by the lake behind the Aswan High Dam, but the temple was removed in 1963 and presented to the **Metropolitan Museum of Art** in New York.

DIOCLETIAN (reigned 284–305 AD). Roman emperor. Original name Diocles. Full name Gaius Aurelius Valerius Diocletianus. Born in Dalmatia on 22 December 243/5, he joined the army and rose to the rank of commander of the royal bodyguard. On the mysterious death of the Emperor Numerian, he was proclaimed emperor on 20 November 284. In a series of campaigns Diocletian reunited the empire under his rule. In 292 he crushed the revolt of the prefect of Egypt in **Alexandria**. Diocletian reorganized the empire and instituted the system of two emperors with a Caesar to assist each. He also undertook a systematic persecution of Christians in an attempt to restore old Roman values. Diocletian abdicated on 1 May 305 and retired to Salonae where he saw the empire relapse in civil war among his successors. He died in Salonae on 3 December 316 or possibly 311.

DIOSCORUS (d. 454 or 458 AD). Patriarch of **Alexandria.** He was possibly born in Alexandria and became archdeacon to the patriarch **Cyril** with whom he attended the council of Ephesus in 431 and whom he succeeded in 444. Dioscorus soon came into conflict with the pope in Rome when he headed the Second Council of Ephesus in 449 over the issue of monophysitism. Here his opponent the patriarch of Constantinople Flavian was deposed and died soon after as a result of ill-treatment by Egyptian monks in the entourage of Dioscorus. The orthodox view was reaffirmed at the Council of Chalcedon in 451 and Dioscorus was deposed and exiled to Gangra in Paphlagonia. The decisions of the Council of Chalcedon and the deposition of the Alexandrian patriarch increased the tension between the **Coptic** population of Egypt who supported their patriarch and the imperial power in Constantinople which was to lead to continued dissension in Egypt.

DIOSCORUS (c.520–585 AD). Egyptian landholder, lawyer, and poet. He was the son of Apollos, village headman of Aphrodito in **Middle Egypt**, modern Kom Ishgaw, and later founder and monk of the monastery of Apa Apollos. He received a good classical education, probably at **Alexandria**, and pursued a legal career during which he visited Constantinople. Many of his papers, which include both documentary and literary texts of his own composition, written in Greek and **Coptic**, were discovered in 1901–07 and are now divided among several museum collections.

DIVINE BIRTH. According to the official theology, each ruler of Egypt was a son of the chief god who impregnated the queen mother. This belief was reflected in the **Westcar Papyrus** where the first three rulers of **Dynasty 5** are described as the sons of **Re**. In the **New Kingdom** the mother of **Hatshepsut** is depicted embraced by the god **Amun** in reliefs at **Deir el-Bahri** and the mother of **Amenhotep III** is shown in a similar position in the **temple** of **Luxor.**

DJEDEFRE (reigned c.2566–2558 BC). Variant Redjedef. Eldest son and successor of **Khufu** of **Dynasty 4**. He is apparently mentioned in the destroyed section of the **Westcar Papyrus**. His reign is obscure, and he is mainly known from his funerary **pyramid** at **Abu Roash**. He was succeeded by his brother **Khafre**.

DJEDHOR (reigned 361–362 BC). Second ruler of **Dynasty 30**. The Greek version of his name is given as Tachos or Teos. Throne name Irmaatenre. Epithet setepenanhur. Son of **Nakhtnebef**. On his accession he embarked on a military campaign against **Persia** in Asia financed by a heavy levy on **temples** to pay his expenses, including Greek mercenaries. Djedhor left his brother Tjaihapimu as regent in Egypt, but the latter's son **Nakhthorheb** revolted against his uncle and won over the army whereupon Djedhor fled to Persia.

DJEDKARE (reigned c.2414–2375 BC). Personal name Isesi. Penultimate ruler of **Dynasty 5**. His **pyramid** complex was discovered at **Saqqara** by an Egyptian expedition but has not been fully published. See also **Menkauhor**, **Unas.**

DJER (reigned c.3050 BC). Third king of **Dynasty 1**. Successor of **Aha**. His tomb has been excavated at **Abydos** and among the finds was an arm with fine jewellery of the period. His tomb was later identified as the tomb of **Osiris**. See also **Djet.**

DJET (reigned c.3000 BC). Fourth king of **Dynasty 1**. Successor of **Djer**. His tomb has been excavated at **Abydos** and among the finds was a finely carved **stela** with the royal name written as a serpent, now in the **Lou-**

vre. His son and successor **Den** may have been a child on his accession as Djer's wife **Merneith** appears to have acted as regent.

DJOSER (reigned c.2667–2648 BC). Horus name Netjerihet. Probably first king of **Dynasty 3**. He is famed for his tomb, the first step-**pyramid** and the first building constructed in stone, supposedly designed by his **vizier Imhotep**. Nothing is known about his reign. See also **Sanakhte**.

DOOMED PRINCE. A literary tale from the **Ramesside Period** known from one partial manuscript. It describes the adventures of a young prince who is fated to die as a result of an attack by a snake, a dog, or a crocodile. He refuses to bow to his fate and goes abroad where he overcomes other suitors to win the hand of a princess locked in a tower. She saves him from his first fate, and he eludes the attack of a dog only to fall into the clutches of a crocodile. At this point the manuscript breaks off. It is assumed that he overcomes his fate and lives happily ever after.

DUAMUTEF see **SONS OF HORUS**.

DUDIMOSE (reigned c.1674 BC). Throne name Djedneferre. One of the last rulers of **Dynasty 13**. He is generally identified with the ruler Tutimaios, mentioned by the historian Josephus probably following **Manetho**, in whose reign the **Hyksos** seized power in Egypt. However, it has recently been suggested that the passage in Josephus does not contain a royal name and Dudimose should be assigned to **Dynasty 16**. See also **Second Intermediate Period**.

DYNASTIES. The Egyptian writer **Manetho** divided Egyptian rulers into numbered dynasties or families. His original manuscript apparently contained 30 dynasties and later copyists apparently added **Dynasty 31**, the later **Persian** kings, but the Macedonian and Ptolemaic kings and Roman emperors were never part of the numbered sequence. This concept of dynastic tabulation has been followed by modern Egyptologists. The concept appears already in use in the **Ramesside Period** in the **Turin Royal Canon**.

DYNASTY 0 (c.3500–3100 BC). The designation given by Egyptologists to those kings of **Upper Egypt** before the official union of Egypt. They are attested mostly by their tombs at **Abydos**. It is not clear how much of **Lower Egypt** they controlled. The system of **hieroglyphic** writing had not developed sufficiently for their names to be clearly read so they are known by their royal symbols such as King **Scorpion**.

DYNASTY 1 (c.3100–2890 BC). First dynasty of the Archaic or **Early Dynastic Period**. Stated by **Manetho** to comprise eight kings of **Thinis**, the dynasty was founded by the legendary **Menes**, the first king of united Egypt. All can be identified from later **king-lists**. The royal seal of Dynasty 1, recently discovered at **Abydos**, confirms the order of the first five kings from **Narmer** who may be identified with Menes. The kings were buried at **Abydos** and their high officials at **Saqqara**.

DYNASTY 2 (c.2890–2686 BC). Stated by **Manetho** to comprise nine kings of **Thinis**. The names given by Manetho and earlier **king-lists** are difficult to reconcile with those on contemporary inscriptions. The rulers were buried either at **Saqqara** or in the royal cemetery at **Abydos.**

DYNASTY 3 (c.2686–2613 BC). Stated by **Manetho** to comprise nine kings of **Memphis**. Very little is known of this dynasty, the most famous ruler being **Djoser** for whose burial the step-**pyramid** was allegedly designed by **Imhotep**. These rulers were buried at **Saqqara**. This dynasty is usually considered to mark the beginning of the **Old Kingdom**.

DYNASTY 4 (c.2613–2494 BC). Sometimes considered the first dynasty of the **Old Kingdom**. Stated by **Manetho** to consist of eight kings of **Memphis** belonging to a different line. Most of these rulers can be identified from contemporary monuments and later **king-lists** although the number varies. The rulers include **Snefru**, who built two **pyramids** at **Dahshur**, and **Khufu**, **Khafre**, and **Menkaure**, the builders of the three pyramids at **Giza**.

DYNASTY 5 (c.2494–2345 BC). Stated by **Manetho** to consist of eight kings from **Elephantine** although he names nine. All nine are easily identifiable on monuments and later **king-lists**. They were buried in **pyramids** at **Abusir** and **Saqqara**, notably **Unas** whose pyramid was the first to be inscribed.

DYNASTY 6 (c.2345–2181 BC). Stated by **Manetho** to comprise six kings of **Memphis**. The first five, notably **Pepy II**, are all identifiable from contemporary monuments and later **king-lists**. They were buried in

pyramids at **Saqqara**. The last, **Nitocris**, is known from the **Turin Royal Canon** and later legend.

DYNASTY 7 (c.2181 BC). Stated by **Manetho** to consist of 70 kings of **Memphis**, who reigned for 70 days. No rulers have been identified and the whole dynasty may be non-existent.

DYNASTY 8 (c.2181–2125 BC). Stated by **Manetho** to comprise 27 kings of **Memphis**, who reigned for 146 years. This dynasty, or the preceding if it existed, marks the beginning of the **First Intermediate Period**. A number of rulers are known from **king-lists**.

DYNASTY 9 (c.2160–2130 BC). Stated by **Manetho** to consist of 19 kings of **Herakleopolis** who reigned for 146 years. See the following.

DYNASTY 10 (c.2130–2040 BC). Stated by **Manetho** to consist of 19 kings of **Herakleopolis** who reigned for 185 years. The numbers and figures for Dynasties 9 and 10 are dubious. The **Turin Royal Canon** seems to list 18 rulers for both dynasties, but they are ignored on other **king-lists**. Contemporary monuments mention kings with the name of **Khety**, and **Merykare** is known from literature. Dynasty 10 was contemporary in part with **Dynasty 11** and was overthrown by **Mentuhotep II**.

DYNASTY 11 (c.2125–1985 BC). Stated by **Manetho** to consist of 16 kings of **Thebes** who reigned for 43 years. Only seven kings are known although the first **Mentuhotep I** never reigned but was honoured with the royal title by his descendants. The family may have been governors of Thebes originally, but independence was probably declared by **Intef I** who adopted the royal title. **Mentuhotep II** reunited Egypt and inaugurated the **Middle Kingdom**. The later kings were buried at **Deir el-Bahri**.

DYNASTY 12 (c.1985–1795 BC). Stated by **Manetho** to comprise seven kings of **Thebes.** In fact, there were eight as the founder **Amenemhat I** was erroneously mentioned by **Manetho** under Dynasty 11. Much detail on this dynasty is preserved in the **Turin Royal Canon** and on many contemporary monuments. The dynasty moved its capital to Itjtawy, modern **Lisht**, and the kings were buried in **pyramids** in the **Fayum** area and **Dahshur**.

DYNASTY 13 (c.1795–1650 BC). Stated by **Manetho** to consist of 60 kings of **Thebes** who reigned for 453 years. With this dynasty began the **Second Intermediate Period**. Manetho's numbers and total of years are clearly inaccurate, but the **Turin Royal Canon** reveals a long list of kings, many with short reigns. Many can be identified from contemporary monuments.

DYNASTY 14 (c.1750–1650 BC). Stated by **Manetho** to comprise 76 kings of **Xois** who reigned for 184 years. Nothing is known of this dynasty which was probably contemporary with **Dynasty 13** in part. Some of the minor **Hyksos** kings have recently been assigned to this dynasty rather than Dynasty 16. Manetho's figures are again suspect.

DYNASTY 15 (c.1650–1550 BC). The dynasty of the **Hyksos**. Stated by **Manetho** to comprise six kings although the figures for this dynasty vary in different versions from 250 to 284 years. The **Turin Royal Canon** gives a more accurate assessment of 108 years. Few monuments survive, but most kings can be identified from **scarabs** or other references, notably **Khayan** and **Apepi**.

DYNASTY 16 (c.1650–1580 BC). The surviving sources of **Manetho** are completely confused regarding this dynasty. Versions range from 32 **Hyksos** rulers reigning for 518 years to five kings of **Thebes** for 190. Some Egyptologists assign minor Hyksos chieftains, probably contemporary with **Dynasty 15**, to this dynasty, but more recently it has been suggested that some of the Theban rulers, previously listed in **Dynasty 17**, should be listed here.

DYNASTY 17 (c.1580–1550 BC). Again the versions of **Manetho** are confused, sometimes identifying this dynasty with **Dynasty 15** or naming 43 kings of **Thebes**. Egyptologists place here some of the rulers of Thebes before the reunification of Egypt under **Dynasty 18**, many of which are known from the **Turin Royal Canon** or contemporary monuments.

DYNASTY 18 (c.1550–1295 BC). The first dynasty of the **New Kingdom** starting with **Ahmose I** who drove out the **Hyksos** and reunified Egypt. **Manetho** names 14 or 16 kings of **Thebes**, but his names are not all identifiable with evidence from contemporary monuments which yield detailed information on 14 rulers.

DYNASTY 19 (c.1295–1186 BC). The famous Ramesside dynasty founded by **Ramesses I**. The sources for **Manetho** name five kings of **Thebes** reigning for 194 to 209 years, but Ramesses I is usually misplaced in **Dynasty 18**. Contemporary monuments yield eight rulers.

DYNASTY 20 (c.1186–1069 BC). Manetho names 12 kings of **Thebes** reigning for 135 years. Contemporary monuments name 10 kings from the founder **Sethnakhte** to **Ramesses XI**. With the exception of the first all kings bore the dynastic name Ramesses. The rulers were all buried in the **Valley of the Kings** except the last whose tomb was unfinished.

DYNASTY 21 (c.1069–945 BC). Stated by **Manetho** to consist of seven kings of **Tanis** reigning for 130 years. Most can be identified from contemporary sources. The dynasty was founded by **Nesbanebdjed** (Smendes), ruler of Tanis, but apparently only ruled the north of the country while the south was virtually independent under the **high priest of Amun** at **Thebes**. Some royal burials have been discovered at Tanis.

DYNASTY 22 (c.945–715 BC). The Libyan dynasty founded by **Sheshonq I**. Stated by **Manetho** to consist of nine kings of **Bubastis** reigning for 120 years. Nine kings with the names of **Sheshonq, Osorkon**, and **Takelot** can be identified from contemporary monuments, but the situation is confused as **Dynasty 23** was in part contemporary with Dynasty 22 and other local rulers also assumed pharaonic **titularies**. The royal burials have been discovered at **Tanis**.

DYNASTY 23 (c.818–715 BC). Manetho's excerptors name three kings of **Tanis** reigning for 44 years or four kings reigning for 89 years. This dynasty was wholly contemporary with **Dynasty 22** and appears to have consisted of local rulers of Libyan origin, possibly offshoots of the previous dynasty, who became independent. The first ruler **Pedubast I** and the second **Osorkon III** are easily identifiable from contemporary monuments. It is not clear exactly where their capital city was located but they were recognized in **Thebes**.

DYNASTY 24 (c.727–715 BC). Stated by the copyists of **Manetho** to comprise one king of **Sais**, Bocchoris, who reigned for six or 44 years. The former figure is probably more accurate. That king, whose Egyptian name was **Bakenrenef**, is known from contemporary sources but Egyptologists also include his predecessor **Tefnakhte** in this dynasty.

DYNASTY 25 (c.747–656 BC). Manetho names three Nubian rulers, **Shabaqo, Shebitqo,** and **Taharqo,** who reigned for 40 or 44 years. Contemporary monuments confirm these three as well as two previous rulers **Kashta** and **Piye** and a final one **Tantamani** whose rule was recognized in parts of Egypt.

DYNASTY 26 (664–525 BC). Manetho names nine rulers of **Sais** reigning for 150 to 167 years of whom the first three appear to have been only local rulers of Sais. The first authenticated member of the dynasty was **Nekau I** (d. 664 BC) and his son **Psamtik I** was the first to rule a reunited Egypt. The later kings are well attested on contemporary monuments and documents. The dynasty was overthrown by the invasion of King **Cambyses** of Persia in 525 BC.

DYNASTY 27 (525–404 BC). The kings of **Persia** who ruled in Egypt from **Cambyses** to Darius II. **Manetho** lists eight kings reigning for 120 or 124 years four months, but the names vary slightly in his copyists. The kings are known from some monuments in Egypt and Persian and classical sources.

DYNASTY 28 (404–399 BC). Stated by **Manetho** to consist of **Amyrtaeos** of **Sais** who reigned for six years. The king is known from contemporary classical sources. He was evidently deposed by the founder of the succeeding dynasty.

DYNASTY 29 (399–380 BC). Manetho lists four kings of **Mendes** who reigned for 21 years four months, but actually gives five names. Some of the kings such as **Nefaarud** and **Hagor** are known from contemporary documentation.

DYNASTY 30 (380–343 BC). Stated by **Manetho** to consist of three kings from **Sebennytos** who reigned for 20 or 38 years. The names of these rulers—**Nakhtnebef, Djedhor,** and **Nakhthorheb**—appear on contemporary monuments and in classical sources. The last ruler of this dynasty was forced to flee to **Nubia** by the second **Persian** invasion in 343 BC.

DYNASTY 31 (343–332 BC). This dynasty was apparently added to **Manetho** and refers to the kings of **Persia** who ruled Egypt following the conquest by Artaxerxes III until the arrival of **Alexander the Great.**

- E -

EARLY DYNASTIC PERIOD (c.3100–2686 BC). The term used by Egyptologists for the period of **Dynasties 1–2**; some also include **Dynasty 3**. The term Archaic Period is also used for this era. This period witnessed the development of the unitary Egyptian state, the growth of royal power as shown in the tombs at **Abydos,** and most importantly the development of writing in the form of **hieroglyphs**.

ECONOMY. The Egyptian economy was primarily based on **agriculture** as the fertility of the soil engendered by the **Nile** flood allowed a crop surplus to the population's basic needs. The excess could be collected, stored, and recirculated. Egypt's natural resources provided for most of her mineral needs, in particular her control of the gold mines of **Nubia**.

Egypt never developed a monetary economy, but a sophisticated barter system was used. Goods were valued in measures of wheat if of low worth, or weights of copper, silver, or gold for higher valued objects. They would be paid for with goods of a similar value and not usually with the materials used in the valuation.

Major imports were normally received as part of state diplomatic relations. These included wood from Lebanon, tin, lapis lazuli, and other luxury goods accepted as tribute when Egypt was strong or reciprocated with Egyptian products such as gold. There is little evidence for a strong merchant class in Egypt, and foreign trade, not on the diplomatic level, appears to have been carried out by foreigners based in their own quarters in **Memphis** or later in special areas such as **Naukratis**.

EDFU. Modern name for a site on the west bank of the **Nile** in southern **Upper Egypt**, halfway between **Thebes** and **Elephantine** (Aswan), ancient Egyptian *Djeba,* Greek Apollonospolis where a major **temple** is located dedicated to the god **Horus** which was rebuilt in the **Ptolemaic Period**. The inscriptions include a long text which may be the text of a ritual play. Remains of the earlier temple have been uncovered in the foundations. Excavations have taken place under Auguste **Mariette** about 1860 and by a French expedition in 1914–33 and a Franco-Polish team in 1937–39. The temple inscriptions are being published by a French team. The main town site, largely buried under the modern town, has not been excavated.

EGYPT. Modern name derived from the Greek *Aigyptos* for the country comprising the **Nile** Delta and the Nile Valley up to **Elephantine**

(Aswan) and the adjacent deserts. The Greek name may be derived from the name *Hikuptah* which was sometimes used for ancient **Memphis.** The ancient Egyptians called their country *Kemet*, the Black Land, referring to the fertile soil left by the Nile inundation.

EGYPT EXPLORATION FUND (later SOCIETY). This organization was founded in London in 1882 largely through the efforts of the novelist Amelia Edwards to sponsor excavations in Egypt. The name was changed from Fund to Society in 1919. It has been responsible for archaeological work at many sites in Egypt, notably at **Tanis** and **Bubastis** in the Delta, **Abydos, Amarna, Deir el-Bahri, Saqqara,** and **Buhen** and **Qasr Ibrim** in **Nubia.** Among the archaeologists employed by the Society have been Flinders **Petrie** and Howard **Carter.** The Society has also encouraged the copying of tomb and **temple** reliefs and inscriptions and from 1895 to 1907 the work of Bernard Grenfell and Arthur Hunt in collecting Graeco-Roman **papyri**, notably at **Oxyrhynchus**, which are still in the course of publication. The Society received in the past from the Egyptian authorities a division of the antiquities which had been found during its excavations, which were then distributed to various museums throughout the world.

ELEPHANTINE. Greek name for the Egyptian *Abu,* modern Aswan, capital of the first **nome** of **Upper Egypt**. The site located on an island in the **Nile** marked the southern limit of the border of Egypt proper and was the main entrepôt for goods imported from the south, notably ivory from which its name in Egyptian and Greek derives. Remains have been found from the **Early Dynastic** to **Roman Periods**. The principal deity worshipped at the main **temple** was the ram-headed god **Khnum** together with the goddesses **Satis** and **Anukis**. The important shrine of the deified **Heqaib** is also located here. Rock tombs from the **Old Kingdom** to the **New Kingdom** are located on the west bank of the river at Qubbet el-Hawa. The Nilometer records the levels of the flood and dates from the Roman Period. Interesting records of a Jewish colony in the **Persian** Period have been discovered here. The site has been excavated by German archaeologists in 1906–07, by a French team in 1907–09, by Egyptian archaeologists in 1932 and 1946–47, and by a Swiss archaeologist in 1953–54 and has been systematically excavated by a German expedition from 1969. The nearby tombs were examined by a second German expedition in 1960–73. See also **Nubia**.

ELKAB. Arabic name for a site in **Upper Egypt** south of **Thebes**, ancient Egyptian *Nekheb*, Greek Eileithyiapolis, on the east side of the **Nile** in the third **nome** of Upper Egypt of which it became the capital in the **New Kingdom**. The principal deity of the city was the goddess **Nekhbet**, tutelary goddess of Upper Egypt. Remains date from the **Predynastic Period** and include the **temple** of Nekhbet and tombs from **Dynasties 18–19**. Those of **Ahmose** son of Ebana and Ahmose Pennekhbet contain biographical texts concerning the war against the **Hyksos** and the early rulers of Dynasty 18. The site was excavated by British archaeologists in the period 1892–1904 and has been worked by a Belgian expedition from 1937.

ELOQUENT PEASANT. A literary tale from the **Middle Kingdom** which describes the pleadings of the peasant Khunanup for justice at the hands of the Egyptian bureaucracy. His complaints were so eloquently put that his case was prolonged by officials in order to hear his words until its eventual successful conclusion.

ESNA. Modern name for a site in southern **Upper Egypt** on the west bank of the **Nile**, ancient Egyptian *Iunet*, Greek Latopolis. The surviving **temple** dedicated to **Khnum** dates to the **Ptolemaic** and **Roman Periods** and includes a relief of **Septimius Severus** with his family. The site was excavated by the British archaeologist John Garstang in 1905–06 and has since 1951 been excavated and the temple inscriptions copied by a French expedition.

EXECRATION TEXTS. These texts are found in the **Middle Kingdom** inscribed on figures and pots which have then been ritually broken. They contain curses against the enemies of the king both internal and external. The ceremony of breaking their names may have been thought to render these enemies powerless. The texts range from the general to the specific giving names of individuals and foreign princes in Palestine and **Nubia** otherwise unknown.

EXODUS. A book of the Hebrew Bible which describes the captivity of the Israelites in Egypt and their delivery by Moses from the oppression of **Pharaoh**. Much has been written to try to identify the route of the Exodus out of Egypt and the pharaoh concerned. The pharaoh of the oppression has usually been identified as **Ramesses II** or his son **Merenptah**. However, the story as described in Exodus is in some respects legendary. Most Egyptologists would not accept the complete tale as historical fact. Some doubt its entire historicity, while others are willing to subscribe to a minor flight of slaves but not the full dramatic account. It has been recently argued that the Exodus is to some extent a rewriting of the expulsion of the **Hyksos** from a Canaanite or Israelite point of view.

- F -

FARAS. Modern Arabic name for a site in **Nubia**, Greek name Pachoras, south of **Abu Simbel** in the modern Sudan. The earliest remains appear to date to the Meroitic Period as blocks of **Thutmose III** found here are now known to have been reused from **Buhen**. The most extensive period of occupation dates to the **Coptic** Period and includes several churches and a cathedral with frescoes. The site was briefly excavated in 1905 by an expedition from the University of Pennsylvania, in 1910–13 by Francis L. Griffith for the University of Oxford, in 1960–62 by the Sudan Antiquities Service, and in 1961–64 by a Polish expedition which discovered the cathedral and much inscriptional evidence. The area was flooded in 1964 by the waters of the Aswan High Dam. The frescoes have been rescued and divided between the National Museums in Khartoum and Warsaw.

FAYUM. A fertile depression south of **Memphis** where a large lake was located in the pharaonic period. The area was developed during the course of **Dynasty 12** whose capital at **Lisht** was close to the Fayum. Several of the rulers were buried either in the Fayum at **Hawara** or nearby at **Lahun**. The principal god of the region was the crocodile god **Sobek**.

The area was further extensively settled in the **Ptolemaic Period** due to major drainage works carried out to release new land for retired Greek soldiers of the royal army. The area was quite prosperous at this time and in the **Roman Period**, and the remains of many settlements exist from which many objects, notably literary and non-literary **papyri** and **mummy** portraits, have been recovered.

FIRST INTERMEDIATE PERIOD (c.2181–2055 BC). The term used by Egyptologists to denote the period from the end of **Dynasty 6** to the reunification of Egypt under **Dynasty 11**. The era is marked by the collapse of royal power and the growth of the authority of the local rulers or nomarchs of the **nomes**. Local autonomy also led to distinct provincial art styles. Following the disappearance of the ruling line in **Memphis**, the governors of **Herakleopolis (Dynasties 9–10)** and **Thebes** (Dynasty 11) vied for supreme authority and the period came to an end with the victory of **Mentuhotep II** of Thebes who reunited the country under his rule. See also **Middle Kingdom, Old Kingdom**.

- G -

GEB. Egyptian god of the earth. Son of **Shu** and **Tefnut**, husband of the sky goddess **Nut**, and father of **Osiris, Isis, Seth**, and **Nephthys**. According to legend, Geb and Nut were separated in the act of sexual union, and he can be depicted lying flat as the earth with the overvaulting Nut as the sky.

GEBEL EL-SILSILA. Sandstone quarry on the banks of the **Nile** between **Thebes** and **Elephantine** (Aswan) which was used from the **New Kingdom** onwards. There are remains of rock-cut shrines, notably one of **Horemheb**.

GEBEL EL-ZEIT. Modern name for a site in the Eastern Desert on the Red Sea coast north of modern Hurghada where the lead mines exploited by the ancient Egyptians from the **Middle Kingdom** to the **New Kingdom** were located. The site was discovered and excavated in 1982–86 by a French expedition. Apart from the mines, the site included small sanctuaries erected by the miners, notably to the deities **Hathor, Horus**, and **Min**, as well as graffiti. The lead was used for the production of eye make-up known by the Arabic word *kohl*.

GEBELEIN. Modern name for a site in **Upper Egypt** where remains from the **Old Kingdom** to the **Roman Period** have been uncovered, including an important early **papyrus**. The site was excavated by an Italian expedition in 1910–14, 1919–20, and again in 1930, 1935, and 1937.

GERF HUSSEIN. Former location of a sandstone **temple** in **Nubia** built by the **viceroy of Kush** Setau in honour of **Ptah** and the deified **Ramesses II**. The inscriptions of the temple were copied and certain parts cut out before the site was flooded by the lake caused by the Aswan High Dam in the 1960s.

GERMANICUS (15 BC–19 AD). Roman prince. Son of Nero Claudius Drusus and Antonia, daughter of Marcus **Antonius**. He was born probably in Rome on 24 May 15 BC. Original name probably Nero Claudius Germanicus but known as Germanicus Julius Caesar following his adoption by the Emperor Tiberius in 4 AD. He was destined to succeed to imperial power and held several high appointments, including governor of Germany and Syria. In 19 AD he travelled to Egypt despite the ban on senatorial visits and was well received in **Alexandria**. He died in Antioch on his return on 10 October 19 AD.

GILUKHEPA (fl. c.1380 BC). A princess of **Mitanni**, daughter of Shuttarna II who married **Amenhotep III** in his tenth year. Her fate is unknown although she is mentioned when arrangements were made for the marriage of her niece **Tadukhepa** to the king. See also **Tiy**.

GIZA. Modern name for the area near modern Cairo which was the main burial site for the rulers of **Dynasty 4**. The site is dominated by the three **pyramid** complexes of **Khufu**, his son **Khafre**, and his grandson **Menkaure**. The **Sphinx** appears to have been constructed under Khafre but was renovated by the later king **Thutmose IV**. The pyramids are surrounded by the tombs of the wives, children, and officials of the monarchs.

The most important early excavations here were carried out by the Italian Giovanni Battista Caviglia in 1817 and the British John Perring and Howard Vyse in 1837–38. In more modern times, the site has been excavated by several expeditions, the most notable being by Auguste **Mariette** in 1853; Flinders **Petrie** in 1880–81; the **Boston Museum of Fine Arts** under George **Reisner** in 1902–1939, whose discoveries included the tomb of **Hetepheres** in 1924–27; the Italian Ernesto Schiaparelli in 1903; the Austrian Hermann Junker in 1912–29; the American Clarence Fisher for the University of Pennsylvania in 1915; and the Egyptian archaeologists Selim Hassan in 1929–39, Abdel-Moneim Abu Bakr in 1949–50, an Egyptian team who in 1954 excavated one of the boat graves beside the pyramid of Khufu, and more recently in 1978, 1980, and from 1989 the work of Zahi Hawass and Mark Lehner.

GOD'S FATHER. Title used from the **Middle Kingdom** for the father of a ruler who was not himself a king. In late **Dynasty 18** it may have designated a king's father-in-law although the exact reason that it was used by the future king **Ay** is unclear. It is not to be confused with the minor priestly title of god's father used for priests of a certain god.

GOD'S WIFE OF AMUN. Title first attested for queens and some princesses in **Dynasty 18**. The office was eventually bestowed on unmarried princesses who were regarded as brides of the god **Amun** rather than the king. The first known princess to hold the office under these conditions was Isis, daughter of **Ramesses VI** of **Dynasty 20**. The importance of the office gradually eclipsed the status of that of **high priest of Amun** by **Dynasty 25** and the latter office fell into disuse in **Dynasty 26**, the title being absorbed by the God's Wife. The office was used by both Dynasties 25 and 26 to exert control over **Thebes** by having their princesses installed although true power doubtless rested with the steward of the God's Wife. The last attested God's Wife was **Ankhnesneferibre**, daughter of **Psamtik II** who was in office at the time of the **Persian** invasion in 525 BC. Classical sources in the **Ptolemaic Period** imply the office may have continued or been revived on a more modest scale.

GRAECO-ROMAN PERIOD (332 BC–642 AD). A term used by Egyptologists for the entire span of rule by the Greeks and later the Romans in Egypt. It is more usually divided into the **Ptolemaic**, **Roman**, and **Byzantine Periods**.

GUROB. Modern name for a site in the **Fayum** 25 kilometres west of the **Nile**; ancient Egyptian *Merwer*. A palace complex and associated town and cemetery were located here during **Dynasties 18–19**. The area was excavated by Flinders **Petrie** in 1888–90 and again by his team in 1903–04 and in 1920. The finds included imported Mycenaean pottery. It is believed that the famous sycamore head of Queen **Tiy** now in the **Berlin Egyptian Museum** came from this vicinity.

- H -

HADRIAN (76–138 AD). Roman emperor. Original name Publius Aelius Hadrianus. He was born in Baetica in 76, son of Publius Aelius Hadrianus and Domitia Paulina, and was great-nephew of the Emperor Trajan who adopted him on his deathbed in 117. Hadrian was noted for his policy of favouring Greek culture and his constant travels throughout the empire. He visited Egypt in 130 along with his wife Vibia Sabina and his favourite Antinous who was drowned in the Nile. Hadrian founded the city of **Antinoopolis** in his honour. His visit to the Colossi of **Memnon** is recorded on graffiti.

HAKOR (reigned 393–380 BC). The Greek version of his name was Achoris. Throne name Khnummaatre setepenkhnum. Second ruler of **Dynasty 29** and successor of **Nefaarud I.** He allied with Greek states and rebels in Cyprus against **Persian** rule.

HAPY. Fertility god who was a personification of the annual **Nile** flood. He is depicted as a fat effeminate man with large breasts and marsh plants on his head. A different god Hapy with a baboon head was one of the **Sons of Horus**.

HARDJEDEF (fl. c.2570 BC). Son of **Khufu** of **Dynasty 4**. In later times he was regarded as the author of a text of **wisdom literature** and he was named among the princes in the literary tale of the **Westcar Papyrus**. An isolated later text writes his name in a royal **cartouche**. In later legend he was credited with the discovery of the text of the **Book of the Dead**. See also **Djedefre, Kawab, Khafre**.

HARKHUF (fl. c.2280 BC). Egyptian official in the reigns of **Nemtyemsaf I** and **Pepy II** of **Dynasty 6** who held the post of governor of **Upper Egypt** possibly as successor to **Weni**. He was buried at **Elephantine** and his tomb contains a major autobiographical inscription. He undertook four expeditions to **Nubia** during which he acquired exotic goods for the royal court including a pygmy or dwarf for which he was personally congratulated by the king.

HARMACHIS see **HARWENNEFER**.

HARNEDJITEF (reigned c.1770 BC). Ruler at the beginning of **Dynasty 13**. Throne name Hetepibre. Possibly son of a previous ruler **Ameny Qemau** whose name appears in his **cartouche** and has wrongly been interpreted as meaning "the Asiatic". A statue of him has been found in the Delta near **Avaris**. An object with his throne name has recently been found in the Syrian city of Ebla indicating trade and political links with the Levant were still active in this period. See also **Second Intermediate Period**.

HARSAPHES see **HERYSHEF**.

HARSIESE (reigned c.870–860 BC). Throne name Hedjkheperre setepenamun. Son of the **high priest of Amun** Sheshonq, who may have succeeded as **Sheshonq II**, and Nestanebtashru. Grandson of **Osorkon I** of **Dynasty 22** and great-grandson of **Pasebakhaenniut II** of **Dynasty 21**. He succeeded as high priest of Amun and then adopted the royal **titulary** in the reign of his cousin **Osorkon II**. On his death, Osorkon II installed his own son **Nimlot** as high priest to reassert central control of **Thebes**. See also **Karomama, Maatkare**.

HARWENNEFER (reigned c.205–199 BC). Rebel king in the reign of **Ptolemy V**. The Greek version of his name is Haronnophris and was previously wrongly read as Harmachis. His rebellion was centred in the south, and he controlled the area from south of **Thebes** to north of **Abydos**, while the Ptolemaic government remained in control of **Elephantine** and the north. Thebes was retaken in 199 BC when Harwennefer was succeeded in unknown circumstances by **Ankhwennefer**.

HATHOR. Egyptian goddess of sexual love and music. She was originally the mother of the sky-god **Horus** and so mother of the king who was identified with Horus. Later she was regarded as the daughter of **Re** and the wife of Horus. She is depicted as a cow or as a human figure with the ears of a cow or wearing a crown with the horns of a cow. Her principal place of worship was **Dendera**, but she also had connections with desert and foreign areas, such as **Serabit el-Khadim** where she was worshipped as the lady of turquoise. She is also associated as a protective deity with the necropolis area of **Thebes**.

HATNUB. Site in the Eastern Desert used as a quarry for Egyptian alabaster from the **Early Dynastic Period** to the **Roman Period**.

HATSHEPSUT (reigned c.1472–1458 BC). Queen-regnant of Egypt, throne name Makare. She was the daughter of **Thutmose I** and his queen **Ahmose** and married her half-brother **Thutmose II** by whom she had at least one daughter, **Nefrure**. Hatshepsut became regent for her step-son **Thutmose III**, but soon ascended the throne in her own right although the date for this act is disputed. She claimed that she had been designated as heir to the throne by her father. Hatshepsut built her mortuary temple at **Deir el-Bahri** with scenes showing the great events of her reign, an expedition to **Punt**, and the erection of an **obelisk**. The work was supervised by her chief architect **Senenmut** whose relations with the queen have been the subject of much speculation.

Her reign ended after 21 years presumably with her death and her step-son became sole ruler. Hatshepsut appears to have been buried with her father in a joint tomb (no. 20) in the **Valley of the Kings**, but her body has not been identified. Thutmose III later attempted to expunge all mention of his aunt although he appears to have been on relatively good terms with her during her reign. See also **Women**.

HAWARA. Modern name for the area in the **Fayum** where the **pyramid** complex of **Amenemhat III** of **Dynasty 12** was built. The remains of the mortuary **temple** were later identified by the Greeks as the Labyrinth. The area was excavated by Flinders **Petrie** in 1888–89 and 1911 when in a cemetery close to the complex he discovered pits of the **Roman Period** which contained many burials with fine painted portraits. In 1955–56 an Egyptian expedition uncovered the intact burial of Princess **Nefruptah**, daughter of the king.

HEIRESS CONCEPT. Theory invented by Egyptologists whereby the right to the throne passed through a woman and thus necessitated brother-sister marriages by the ruler. The theory was based on the inscriptions of **Hatshepsut** and the number of brother-sister marriages in early **Dynasty 18**. This concept has now been shown to be false as succession passed through the male and many rulers chose not to marry their sisters but preferred commoners.

HEKANAKHTE (fl. c.1950 BC). Landholder and priest at **Thebes** during the reign of **Senusret I**. He is known from his letters which were discovered in 1921–22 at **Deir el-Bahri**. These letters were written to his household while he was away in the north and give details on the practice of Egyptian **agriculture** as well as the personal relations within his family. See also **Hieratic**.

HELIOPOLIS. Greek name for the Egyptian city of *Iunu*, capital of the 13th **Lower Egyptian nome** in the suburbs of present-day Cairo. Its main **temple** was dedicated to the creator-god **Atum** who was identified with the sun-god **Re** elevated to the chief god in Egypt from **Dynasty 5**. Very little remains of the original city and temple apart from an **obelisk** of **Senusret I**. Many of the monuments appear to have been transported to decorate **Alexandria** in the **Ptolemaic** and **Roman Periods**. Excavations were carried out by an Italian expedition in 1903, the University of Cairo in 1976–81, and Egyptian inspectors in 1988.

HELWAN. Modern name for a site 25 kilometres south of Cairo where a major cemetery of the **Early Dynastic Period** was excavated in 1942–54 by the Egyptian archaeologist Zaki Saad. Objects from **Dynasties 1–2**, including pottery, stone vessels, palettes, and jewellery, were recovered.

HEMAKA (fl. c.2950 BC). High official of King **Den** of **Dynasty 1**. His large tomb (no. 3035) excavated at **Saqqara** has been ascribed to the king but is now generally accepted as that of his chancellor. It was discovered by Cecil Firth, a British archaeologist working for the Egyptian Antiquities Service in 1931, and cleared by his successor Walter B. Emery in 1936.

HENTTAWY. The name of several ladies related to the family of the **high priests of Amun** and the royal family during **Dynasty 21**. The most important seems to have been the wife of **Pinudjem** I and daughter of Queen **Tentamun**. Unfortunately, the inscriptions concerning these women are not always precise so their exact relationships are still uncertain.

HEQAIB (fl. c.2240 BC). Military official and probable governor of **Elephantine** at the end of the **Old Kingdom**. His full name was Pepinakht also known as Heqaib and he was buried at Qubbet el-Hawa (tomb no. 35) on the western bank opposite the island of Elephantine. He appears to have played a leading role in Egyptian military activity in **Nubia** and was deified after his death. A shrine was built in his honor by Sarenput I, governor of Elephantine at the beginning of **Dynasty 12**. It was excavated in 1932 and 1946 by Egyptian archaeologists and yielded a large number of statues, **stelae**, and offering-tables of kings and officials of **Dynasties 12–13**. The shrine was abandoned in the **Second Intermediate Period**.

HERACLIUS (c.575–641 AD). Byzantine emperor. Son of Heraclius, the governor of Africa, of Armenian origin, and Epiphania. His father organized a revolt against the usurper Phocas in 610 sending a nephew Nicetas to secure Egypt, while the younger Heraclius sailed to Constantinople where he was crowned emperor on 7 October 610. The new emperor tried without success to reconcile the religious differences within the empire between the orthodox and monophysite beliefs. He had to fight and expel the **Persians** who occupied Egypt between 617 and 629 and other eastern provinces, only to lose them to the Arabs in 641–42. He died in Constantinople on 11 February 641. See also **Benjamin, Cyrus**.

HERAKLEOPOLIS. Greek name, more properly Herakleopolis Magna, for the Egyptian site of *Nen-nesu*, modern Ihnasya el-Medina in **Middle Egypt**. It became the capital of Egypt under **Dynasties 9–10** until the overthrow of the last ruler by the prince of **Thebes**. Its main **temple** was dedicated to the local god **Heryshef** and enlarged by **Ramesses II**. The city was an important military garrison in **Dynasty 22** and a branch of the royal family was established there. Excavations were carried out by British archaeologists in 1890–91 and 1903–04 and more recently by a Spanish expedition in 1966–69, 1976–79, and from 1984 which has uncovered tombs of the royal family of Dynasty 22.

HERIHOR (fl. c.1075 BC). High priest of Amun and military general of unknown but possibly Libyan origin at the end of **Dynasty 20**. It is not certain if he preceded or followed **Piankh** in office. He adopted the style of king at **Thebes**, using his title as high priest as his throne name, and was virtually an independent ruler in the south. His rule may not have ended peacefully as his figure on one **stela** is defaced. He may have been the first of a line of independent Theban high priests.

HERMOPOLIS. Greek name, more properly Hermopolis Magna, for the ancient Egyptian *Khmunu*, modern el-Ashmunein, capital of the 15th **nome** of **Upper Egypt**. The site is much destroyed, but there are remains from the **Middle Kingdom** to the **Roman Period**. It has been excavated by expeditions from Italy in 1903, Germany in 1929–39, the University of Alexandria in the late 1940s, and by various Egyptian inspectors, and more recently by a **British Museum** expedition in 1980–90. Many of the blocks from **Amarna** were reused in construction work here by **Ramesses II**. See also **Akhenaten**.

HERODOTUS (c.484–420 BC). Greek author from Halicarnassus. He visited Egypt in the course of his travels and his *Histories* contains valuable information on Egyptian history and customs. Much of this information would have been supplied by Egyptian priests and is uneven in content.

HERYSHEF. Chief god of **Herakleopolis** whose Greek name was Arsaphes and who was identified with the Greek god Herakles. He is depicted as a ram-headed human figure.

HESIRE (fl. c.2650 BC). A high official of **Dynasty 3**. His tomb at **Saqqara** yielded delicately carved wooden panels depicting the owner and his titles. The tomb was first discovered by Auguste **Mariette** and later recleared in 1911–12.

HESUNEBEF (fl. c.1210–1175 BC). Workman in the **Deir el-Medina** community during **Dynasties 19–20**. He is first attested as a **slave** boy of the foreman Neferhotep who obviously freed him and arranged a post for him as a workman as well as obtaining a bride for him from a community family. He remained in the workforce after his patron's death, but the new foreman **Paneb**, Neferhotep's adopted son, was later accused of adulterous relations with his wife and also sexual misconduct with his daughter who was then passed on to Paneb's son. The truth of this accusation is unclear, but certainly Hesunebef and his wife were divorced. In the reign of **Ramesses III**, he rose to the post of deputy foreman. He remained loyal to the memory of his patron, naming his son after him and erecting a **stela** in honour of Neferhotep.

HETEPHERES. The name of several princesses and queens of **Dynasty 4**. The most important was Hetepheres I, the wife of **Snefru** and mother of **Khufu**. Her intact burial without any body was recovered at **Giza** by George **Reisner** in 1925–27. Hetepheres II was the daughter of Khufu, wife of her brother **Kawab**, and mother of **Meresankh** III.

HIBA, El-. Modern name for the Egyptian *Teudjoi* and Greek Ankyronpolis. This place was an important military garrison in **Dynasties 21–22**. The cemetery of the **Roman Period** was excavated by British explorers in 1903 and **papyri** and **mummy** portraits were found. It was investigated by an American expedition in 1980.

HIERAKONPOLIS. Greek name for the Egyptian city of *Nekhen*, modern Kom el-Ahmar. This city, south of **Thebes**, was a major settlement in the **Predynastic** and **Early Dynastic Periods** and probably the capital of the kings of **Upper Egypt** before the unification of the country. Important remains and objects from this period were discovered here by a British expedition in 1897–99, including the famous **Narmer** palette and the **Scorpion** macehead. The main deity of the city was the falcon-god **Horus**. The site continued to be occupied through the **Roman** and **Coptic Periods**. Further excavation took place by the University of Liverpool in 1905–06, the Brooklyn Museum in 1907–08, a British expedition in 1927, and the New York **Metropolitan Museum of Art** in 1934–35. Work was resumed by an American expedition in 1967–69 and from 1978.

HIERATIC. Modern term derived from the Greek for the abbreviated form of writing the **hieroglyphic** script which developed from the **Early Dynastic Period** and was used primarily on **papyri** or **ostraca** for correspondence and religious and literary texts. The earliest complete texts are the **Abusir Papyri** of **Dynasty 5**. The script fell out of use in the **Saite Period** when it was largely replaced by **demotic**, but persisted in use in religious texts until the **Roman Period**.

HIEROGLYPHIC. Modern term derived from the Greek used to describe the standard form of Egyptian writing to express the Egyptian **language**. The earliest forms appear at the end of the **Predynastic Period** and the early Dynastic Period, but the script does not become fully intelligible until the **Old Kingdom**. The writing consists of two types of signs: phonograms which represent single consonants or consonantal clusters (biliterals or triliterals), and ideograms which indicate the sense of the word, usually written at the end of the word to reinforce the meaning. The basic consonantal alphabet consists of 24 signs; vowels were not written. The hieroglyphic writing was soon replaced by **hieratic** for ordinary usage, and the hieroglyphic script was reserved for monumental work in stone or paint and for religious texts. The script was deciphered in modern times by Jean-François **Champollion**, building on the work of Thomas Young, with the help of bilingual texts such as the **Rosetta Stone**. The subsequent realization that **Coptic** was a later form of the same language immeasurably aided the understanding of ancient Egyptian texts. See also **Demotic**.

HIGH PRIEST OF AMUN. The chief religious office in the **temple** of **Amun** at **Karnak** in **Thebes**. The office grew in importance and wealth with the elevation of Amun to the position of chief god of Egypt in **Dy-**

nasty **18** and the extensive endowments bestowed on the temple by various rulers. The appointment of the high priest appears to have been carefully controlled by the ruler to avoid any conflict of power, and often incumbents were chosen not from the Theban clergy but from priesthoods in other cities or from court officials. The reforms of **Akhenaten** appeared in part designed to limit the influence of the priesthood of Amun.

In **Dynasty 20** the office became more influential and hereditary in one family, resulting in a civil war in Thebes under **Ramesses XI** whose generals **Herihor** and **Piankh** suppressed the high priest Amenhotep but took over his office and power. In **Dynasty 21** the south was virtually independent under the family of high priests descended from Piankh. Under **Dynasty 22** an attempt was made to control Thebes through the appointment of royal princes as high priests, but conflict soon arose, especially over the appointment of the high priest **Osorkon**. In **Dynasty 25** the office was still held by royal descendants of the dynasty, but appears to have been suppressed in **Dynasty 26** when the titles were assumed by the **God's Wife of Amun**. The office is again attested in the **Ptolemaic Period** when it appears to have been primarily religious and shorn of political power.

HIGH PRIEST OF PTAH. Chief religious office in the **temple** of **Ptah** at **Memphis**. The lack of documentation limits knowledge of the influence and power of this office. As administrator of the main temple of the second capital of Egypt, he had great resources under his control, but any political power would have been limited by the proximity of the court which resided in the north in the **New Kingdom**. There is no evidence of conflict as is recorded in the case of the **high priest of Amun**. The officeholders include Prince **Khaemwese**, son of **Ramesses II**, and several princes during **Dynasty 22**, but also local priests allegedly of one family. An inscription listing many of the officeholders and the rulers they served is an important chronological tool in studying Egyptian history. The office took on new importance in the **Ptolemaic Period** when the high priest served as the chief Egyptian religious official at the royal court and many funerary inscriptions of the family survive. The office may have been suppressed by the Roman government as only one high priest is attested after the conquest.

HITTITES. The Hittites were an Indo-European-speaking people who established a kingdom in central Anatolia (modern Turkey) which in the second millennium BC gradually built up an empire that included much of Anatolia and Syria. The Hittites helped to destroy the kingdom of **Mitanni** and sought to inherit their overlordship in Syria, leading them into conflict with Egypt in the reign of **Akhenaten**. The Hittite king Shuppiluliumas I managed to detach the Egyptian vassal kingdom of Amurru from Egyptian control. On the death of **Tutankhamun**, his widow **Ankhesenamun** sought a Hittite husband, but this plan proved abortive.

Sety I and **Ramesses II** sought to restore Egyptian control in Syria, but the Egyptians were driven back at the battle of **Kadesh** in 1274 BC. Eventually a peace treaty was signed between the two powers in 1258 BC whereby the border between the two empires in Syria was recognized with the loss of Amurru to the Hittites. About 1245 BC a marriage was arranged by Ramesses II with the daughter of the Hittite king who was known in Egypt as Maathornefrure, and he later appears to have married a second daughter. Relations between the two powers remained friendly until the destruction of the Hittite kingdom about 1195 BC probably as a result of the movement of the **Sea Peoples** perhaps aided by local tribesmen.

HOR (reigned c.1760 BC). Throne name Awibre. Ruler of **Dynasty 13**. He was buried at **Dahshur** where statues of the king have been recovered from his tomb. See also **Second Intermediate Period.**

HOREMHEB (reigned c.1323–1295 BC). Throne name Djeserkheperure. Of unknown parentage from Henes. Possibly to be identified with Paatonemheb attested in the reign of **Akhenaten**, he was military commander in the reign of **Tutankhamun**. He was married to **Mutnodjmet**, possibly sister of **Nefertiti**. He conducted campaigns in **Nubia** and Palestine to restore Egyptian power and with **Ay** conducted affairs in the minority of Tutankhamun and helped organize the return to orthodoxy after the **Amarna Period**. His tomb at **Saqqara**, built when a commoner, was first seen in the nineteenth century and was rediscovered and excavated by an expedition of the **Egypt Exploration Society** in 1975–80.

He succeeded to the throne on the death of Ay and continued the policy of rebuilding Egypt at home and abroad and suppressed the names of his immediate predecessors since **Amenhotep III**. He died childless and appears to have arranged the succession of his **vizier Ramesses I**, founder of **Dynasty 19**. He was buried in tomb no. 57 in the **Valley of the Kings**, but his **mummy** has not been recovered or identified. See also **Dynasty 18.**

HORUS. Egyptian god. Originally Horus was a sky-god identified with the ruler in the **Early Dynastic Period** who bore a Horus name in a **serekh** as part of the royal **titulary**. In later legend Horus became the son of **Osiris** and **Isis** and the legitimate ruler of Egypt on his father's death. In his former aspect he was worshipped as Haroeris or Horus the elder and in the latter as Harpocrates or Horus the child, often depicted as a youth with a sidelock protected by his mother Isis. Horus was also identified with the sun-god **Re** and worshipped as Re-Harakhty. His sacred animal was the hawk and his particular places of worship were at **Hierakonpolis** and **Edfu.** The *udjat*-eye of Horus was considered a potent amulet.

HOTEPSEKHEMWY (reigned c.2880 BC). First ruler of **Dynasty 2.** The reasons for his accession and the start of a new dynasty are unknown. His tomb appears to have been at **Saqqara.** See also **Raneb.**

HUNI (reigned c.2637–2613 BC). Last ruler of **Dynasty 3.** He is often said to have been buried in the **pyramid** at **Meidum,** but this may well have been built for **Snefru** or completed by him. There is no basis for the contention that Snefru was his son since Snefru's mother does not have a queenly title. No reason is known for the change in dynasty.

HYKSOS. Greek version of the Egyptian *Heka Khasut,* "ruler of foreign lands". This title was used by the Egyptians for the various Asiatic chieftains in Palestine and Syria. The later derivation of "shepherd kings" is erroneous. The Egyptians were always wary of Asiatic encroachment and in **Dynasty 12 Amenemhat I** built a wall to exclude unwanted Asiatics. Nevertheless some immigration was permitted as an Asiatic settlement grew up around **Avaris** and Asiatic travellers are depicted at **Beni Hasan.** During the **Second Intermediate Period** large numbers of Asiatics settled in Egypt and eventually took over most of the country, founding the Hyksos **Dynasty 15** and adopting many of the attributes of Egyptian rulers. **Thebes** apparently became a vassal state but ultimately rebelled and succeeded in capturing the Hyksos capital at Avaris and driving them from Egypt.

- I -

IAH. Moon-god of Egypt. He was popular at the beginning of **Dynasty 18** when royal names such as **Ahmose** and **Ahhotep** were composed from his name. He was later identified with **Khons.**

IANNAS (reigned c.1590 BC). Greek name, given by the Hebrew historian Josephus who derived it from **Manetho**, for one of the **Hyksos** kings of **Dynasty 15**. A **stela** fragment, recently discovered at **Avaris**, bears the **cartouches** of **Khayan** and names his eldest son Ianassi, presumably to be identified with the future king. Nothing is known of his actual reign.

IBI (reigned c.2140 BC). Throne name Kakare. A minor ruler of **Dynasty 8**. Nothing is known of his reign, but he was buried in a **pyramid** at **Saqqara** which was excavated in the 1930s. See also **First Intermediate Period**.

IMHOTEP (fl. c.2660 BC). Vizier of **Djoser** of **Dynasty 3**. He is credited with devising the construction of the step-**pyramid**, the first stone structure in Egypt. He had a reputation for wisdom and was deified after his death and worshipped as a minor deity. He is usually depicted as a seated scribe with an open **papyrus** on his lap. He was identified by the Greeks with Aesculapius, god of medicine.

IMSETY see **SONS OF HORUS**.

INAROS (fl. c.459–454 BC). Greek form of the Egyptian name Irethorru. Son of Psamtik, a local Egyptian dynast. Egyptian rebel against the rule of **Persia**. Allied with forces from Athens, he took **Memphis** and defeated and killed the **satrap Achaemenes** in 459 BC, but his army was later crushed by superior Persian troops. He was captured and taken to Persia where he was executed. His son Amyrtaeos was said to have been reinstated in his father's possessions and may have been an ancestor of the later king **Amyrtaeos**.

INENI (fl. c.1510–1470 BC). A high official at the beginning of **Dynasty 18**, serving in the reigns of **Amenhotep I**, **Thutmose I**, **Thutmose II**, and **Thutmose III** with the title of overseer of the granary of **Amun**. Son of the judge Ineni and the lady Sit-Djehuty. He was in charge of building works at **Karnak** for the first two rulers and also supervised the construction of the royal tomb of Thutmose I in the **Valley of the Kings**. He was buried in a tomb (no. 81) at **Thebes** which contains a detailed biographical inscription.

INTEF I (reigned c.2125–2112 BC). First declared ruler of **Dynasty 11**. **Horus** name Sehertawy. Son of **Mentuhotep I**. As first governor of

Thebes, he appears to have revolted against **Herakleopolis** and adopted the title of king although he did not adopt the full royal **titulary**. He was buried in a rock-cut tomb on the west bank at Thebes.

INTEF II (reigned c.2112–2063 BC). Successor to **Intef I** of **Dynasty 11.** **Horus** name Wahankh. Son of the lady **Nefru** and possibly **Mentuhotep I** so brother of his predecessor. He consolidated Theban control of **Upper Egypt,** capturing **Thinis.** He was buried in a rock-cut tomb on the west bank at **Thebes** where a funerary **stela** mentioning his pet dogs was set up. This stela is mentioned in a tomb robbery **papyrus** of **Dynasty 20** and part of it was recovered by Auguste **Mariette** in excavations in 1860.

INTEF III (reigned c.2063–2055 BC). Successor and presumably son of **Intef II** of **Dynasty 11** and the lady **Nefru. Horus** name Nakhtnebtepnefer. Little is known of his brief reign except that a famine occurred in the region of **Abydos.** He too was buried in a rock-cut tomb at **Thebes.** He married the lady Iah by whom he had his son and successor **Mentuhotep II** who conquered the rest of Egypt and ended the **First Intermediate Period**.

INTEF (fl. c.2150 BC). Governor of **Thebes** in the **First Intermediate Period**. Son of the lady Ikuy. He was worshipped as the ancestor of the later rulers of **Dynasty 11** and so was probably the father or ancestor of **Mentuhotep I**.

INTEFYOKER (fl. c.1945–1950 BC). Vizier of **Amenemhat I** and **Senusret I** of **Dynasty 12**. He is attested in office towards the end of the reign of Amenemhat I and was presumably one of the most powerful officials of the period. He was buried in a tomb near the **pyramid** of Amenemhat I at **Lisht**. However, his family is cursed in the **execration texts** so it may be speculated that they eventually fell from power.

IPUT. The name of two queens of **Dynasty 6.** Iput I would appear to have been the wife of **Teti** and mother of **Pepy I** and was buried in a subsidiary **pyramid** next to that of Teti. Iput II was the wife of **Pepy II** and was buried in a subsidiary pyramid next to her husband's.

IPUWER. The ostensible author of a text of **wisdom literature** composed in the **Middle Kingdom** which describes the country in a state of chaos.

This has been taken as a reference to the **First Intermediate Period**, but it may have simply been a literary device.

ISIS. Greek name of the major female deity of Egypt, Egyptian *Ast*. Daughter of **Geb** and **Nut** and consort of her brother **Osiris,** mythological ruler of Egypt. Following the murder of her husband by their brother **Seth**, she assiduously collected the remains of Osiris and, according to one version, was impregnated by him after death, if not before. She fought tirelessly for the rights of her son **Horus** to succeed to Egypt in opposition to Seth. This contest is reflected in the bawdy tale *The Contendings of Horus and Seth*. The worship of Isis became particularly strong in the **Graeco-Roman Period** when Osiris was displaced as her husband by the composite god **Sarapis.** Her cult spread throughout the Roman Empire, being particularly attractive to women. It was suppressed at the advent of Christianity.

ISIS (fl. c.1485 BC). The name of a junior wife of **Thutmose II** who was the mother of his successor **Thutmose III**. She is only attested in the reign of her son as the king's mother. A Princess Isis is probably her granddaughter. See also **Hatshepsut.**

ISITNOFRET (fl. c.1300–1245 BC). Junior wife and queen of **Ramesses II**. He married her at the same time as **Nefertari** and she bore his eldest daughter **Bintanat** as well as three sons: his second, Ramesses; his fourth, **Khaemwese**; and his thirteenth, **Merenptah**. She appears to have succeeded Nefertari as chief queen but died before her husband and was replaced by her daughter Bintanat. The name was also borne by other later queens and princesses of **Dynasty 19**.

ISTEMKHEB. The name of several princesses and members of the family of the **high priests of Amun** during **Dynasty 21**. The most important appear to have been a wife of the high priest **Pinudjem** I and a daughter of **Pasebakhaenniut I** who married the high priest **Menkheperre**.

IUPUT. The name of two kings and a royal prince of **Dynasties 22–23**. Iuput (fl. c.944–924), son of **Sheshonq I**, was installed as **high priest of Amun** to control **Thebes** on behalf of his father. Iuput I (reigned c.805–783 BC) is attested as ruler in association with **Pedubast I** of **Dynasty 23**, but nothing is known of him. Iuput II (reigned c.731–720 BC) had the throne name Usimaatre setepenamun and the epithet meryamun si-bast. He is attested as ruler of **Leontopolis** in the **stela** of **Piye**.

- J -

JOSEPH. Biblical hero, son of Jacob and Rachel, who was sold into **slavery** in Egypt and rose to the position of king's chief minister or **vizier**. He later welcomed his father and family to settle in Egypt. The story exhibits knowledge of Egyptian customs, but it is debatable whether Joseph represents a historical figure. The background of the story may refer to the period when the **Hyksos** had gained power in Egypt. See also **Exodus**.

JUBILEE. The *heb-sed* festival or jubilee was usually performed in a king's 30th year and presumably consisted of rituals to rejuvenate him to continue his rule. It is possible that in prehistoric times the king may have been killed if he failed the ritual. Subsequent jubilees were performed at frequent intervals after year 30 until the death of the monarch.

- K -

KADESH. An important city-state, now located in Syria; modern Tell Nebi Mend. The city became part of the Egyptian empire in **Dynasty 18**, but later fell under **Hittite** control. About 1274 BC **Ramesses II** sought to regain the lost Egyptian territory, but his forces were ambushed outside Kadesh by the Hittite army. Although his army was severely mauled, the Egyptian king managed to hold the Hittites back from his camp and avoid capture. The battle itself ended in stalemate, but the campaign was lost and the Egyptians were forced to retreat.

On his return to Egypt, Ramesses II had an account of the battle written and inscribed on **temple** walls to glorify his personal bravery despite the unfortunate outcome of the campaign. The Hittites more succinctly recorded an Egyptian defeat, and the northern part of the Egyptian empire in Syria remained in Hittite hands.

KAGEMNI (fl. c.2613 BC). Legendary **vizier** of **Huni** of **Dynasty 3** and **Snefru** of **Dynasty 4**. He was the recipient of a text of **wisdom literature** which has only survived in fragments and was undoubtedly composed at a later date. A historical vizier of this name is known from the reign of **Teti** of **Dynasty 6** and may have served as a model for the literary text. His tomb was discovered in 1893 and more fully excavated in the 1920s.

KAHUN see **LAHUN.**

KALABSHA. Modern name for the site in **Nubia** 50 kilometres south of **Elephantine** (Aswan) on the west bank of the **Nile**; Greek Talmis. There stood a **temple** rebuilt under **Augustus** dedicated to the Nubian god Mandulis. The area was flooded by the lake formed by the Aswan High Dam, but the temple was removed in 1961–63 to a safer location. In the course of this work a Graeco-Roman gateway was discovered which is now in the **Berlin Egyptian Museum.**

KAMOSE (reigned c.1555–1552 BC). Throne name Wadjkheperre. Last ruler of **Dynasty 17** and prince of **Thebes**. He succeeded Seqenenre **Tao**, who may have been his father, and continued the war against the **Hyksos**. He campaigned up to the walls of the Hyksos capital **Avaris** and also in **Nubia**. A **stela** giving details of his campaign was found at **Karnak**. His fate is unknown, but he was followed by **Ahmose I**, possibly his brother, who expelled the Hyksos from Egypt. See also **Ahhotep.**

KARNAK. The main **temple** of the god **Amun** at **Thebes** known in Egyptian as *Iput-sut*. The temple was known in the **Middle Kingdom** and was enlarged and embellished by successive rulers of the **New Kingdom**. Its great wealth led to an increase of political power for the **high priest of Amun** under whom Thebes became virtually independent in the **Third Intermediate Period**. The temple was sacked by the **Assyrians** in 663 BC and although restored in the **Ptolemaic Period** never regained its prominence. The site has been extensively excavated from the last century and currently is being restored by the Centre Franco-Égyptien. More recent expeditions include the work of the Brooklyn Museum at the subsidiary temple of **Mut** from 1976.

KAROMAMA. Variants Karoma, Kamama. The name of several queens and princesses of **Dynasties 22–23**, the first of which was the wife of **Sheshonq I** and mother of his heir **Osorkon I**. A second was the wife of **Osorkon II**. Another Queen Karomama was the daughter of **Osorkon II**'s Prince **Nimlot**, wife of **Takelot II**, and mother of the **high priest of**

Amun Osorkon. The mother of **Osorkon III** was also named Kamama. A bronze statue, inlaid with gold, silver, and electrum, of the God's Wife **Karomama** is now in the **Louvre Museum.**

KASHTA (fl. c.750 BC). Nubian ruler. He appears to have gained control over the **Theban** region at the end of **Dynasty 23** and installed his daughter **Amenirdis** as the adopted daughter and heiress of the **God's Wife of Amun**. See also **Alara.**

KAWAB (fl. c.2580 BC). Son of **Khufu** of **Dynasty 4**. He was apparently Khufu's eldest son and destined successor, but he died before his father and was buried in a **mastaba** near Khufu's **pyramid** at **Giza.** His widow **Hetepheres** II was then married to his brother **Khafre.**

KEFTYU. A foreign people named in Egyptian accounts mostly during **Dynasty 18** and depicted in certain tomb paintings with local produce. These depictions leave little doubt that they are Minoans from Crete, and the existence of Minoans in Egypt is confirmed by the discovery of Minoan pottery at Egyptian sites from the **Middle Kingdom**. Egyptian stone vessels found in Crete indicate a trading relationship from the **Early Dynastic Period**. An inscription from the reign of **Amenhotep III** names several cities of the Keftyu, notably Knossos, but it is unclear whether the reference is contemporary or based on earlier records. Recent discoveries of Minoan frescoes at **Avaris** confirm the presence of Minoan traders or artists in Egypt from the late **Second Intermediate Period** or early Dynasty 18.

KENHERKHEPESHEF (fl. c.1270–1200 BC). Chief scribe of the **Deir el-Medina** community from the middle of the reign of **Ramesses II** until **Sety II**. Son of Panakht and Sentnefer. He appears to have been adopted by the scribe **Ramose** and succeeded him in his office. He is known as a collector of historical and religious manuscripts including an account of the Battle of **Kadesh** written in his own hand and a dream-book giving interpretations of dreams. His interest in previous rulers is attested by a brief **king-list** also in his own hand. His tomb has not been discovered, and he appears to have died childless. He was survived on his death by his widow Naunakhte who must have been several decades younger than him as she remarried the workman Khaemnun and had eight children. She survived until the reign of **Ramesses V** when her will was written. She apparently inherited the papers of her first husband which were passed on to her sons by the second marriage who added to the archive, notably with the literary text *The Contendings of Horus and Seth.* The archive was uncovered in the 1920s and is now preserved in several museums.

KERMA. Site of a major city in **Nubia** near the Third **Cataract** and apparent capital of a Nubian kingdom of Kush, founded by the C-group people from the **Old Kingdom,** which was especially prominent during the **Second Intermediate Period** when an alliance was attempted with the **Hyksos** against the rulers of **Thebes** of **Dynasty 17**. This kingdom of Kush was regarded as a major threat by the Egyptians and was destroyed in a series of campaigns at the beginning of **Dynasty 18** after which the area was incorporated as a province of Egypt. The site is dominated by two large brick constructions known as the Upper and Lower Deffufas of uncertain usage. The area has been excavated by George **Reisner** in 1913–16 for the **Boston Museum of Fine Arts** and more recently by a Swiss expedition under Charles Bonnet.

KHA (fl. c.1390 BC). Foreman in the community of **Deir el-Medina** during **Dynasty 18**, probably in the reign of **Thutmose IV** and **Amenhotep III**. He is known from his undecorated tomb which was discovered with its contents intact by an Italian expedition in 1906. The **mummies** of Kha and his wife Meret together with the coffins and other objects from the tomb are now preserved in the **Turin Egyptian Museum**.

KHABA (reigned c.2640–2637 BC). Horus name of an obscure king of **Dynasty 3**. He apparently was the builder of the unfinished **pyramid** located at **Zawiyet el-Aryan**.

KHABABASH (reigned c. 338–337 BC). Egyptian ruler who is attested on several documents including an inscription on the **sarcophagus** of an **Apis** bull of his second year. He appears to have held office in the later **Persian** period as a rebel against their rule, but his origin and exact date are not known.

KHAEMWESE (fl. c.1285–1230 BC). Fourth son of **Ramesses II** by **Isitnofret**. He was appointed to the priesthood of **Ptah** and eventually reached the position of **high priest of Ptah** at **Memphis** and briefly served as crown prince before predeceasing his father. He may have been buried in the **Serapeum**. Khaemwese undertook restoration works of older monuments including the **pyramids** at **Abusir** and **Saqqara**. In later literature he is portrayed as a learned but not necessarily wise magician. A like-named son of **Ramesses III**, who died young, is known from his tomb (no. 44) in the **Valley of the Queens**.

KHAFRE (reigned c.2558–2532 BC). His name might be read as Rakhaef and was known in Greek as Chephren. Son of **Khufu** of **Dynasty 4**. He succeeded his brother **Djedefre**. For his burial he moved back to the site at **Giza** and erected the second **pyramid** at that site close to that of his father Khufu. His valley temple was excavated in 1860 and yielded much fine sculpture. It is believed that his architects fashioned the **Sphinx** in his likeness from a rocky outcrop near his pyramid.

KHAKHEPERRESENEB. The ostensible author of a text of **wisdom literature** composed in the **Middle Kingdom** which consists of a series of complaints about the state of the country.

KHAMERERNEBTY. The name of two queens, mother and daughter, of **Dynasty 4**. It is generally thought that the elder married **Khafre** and their daughter then was the wife of **Menkaure**, but formal proof is lacking although it seems likely that the elder was the mother of Menkaure. The younger was buried in a tomb at **Giza** in the cemetery near the **pyramid** of Khafre originally designed for her mother.

KHARGA OASIS. An oasis in the Western Desert west of **Luxor**. Prehistoric remains have been discovered there, but evidence from the Pharaonic Period is lacking. The surviving archaeological sites date from the **Graeco-Roman** and **Byzantine Periods**, apart from the **temple** at Hibis which was begun in the **Persian** Period. The area was excavated by Herbert Winlock for the **Metropolitan Museum of Art** in New York in 1909 and by a French expedition from 1976.

KHASEKHEMWY (reigned c.2600 BC). Final ruler of **Dynasty 2**. Probably identical with a King Khasekhem attested on contemporary monuments. He appears to have ended the religious conflict between the supporters of **Horus** and **Seth** by adopting both gods as part of the **serekh** of the royal **titulary**. His statues found at **Hierakonpolis** represent the king as victorious over northern enemies in **Lower Egypt**. He built an elaborate tomb at **Abydos** as well as a massive palace structure which may have served as a mortuary temple.

KHAYAN (reigned c.1600 BC). Throne name Sewoserenre. **Hyksos** ruler of **Dynasty 15**. Monuments of his have been found in Crete and Baghdad, but it is uncertain when these were removed from Egypt. The discovery of Cretan frescoes at his capital of **Avaris** strengthens the idea of direct relations between Crete and Egypt at this time. A **stela** names his eldest son and presumed successor, **Iannas**.

KHENDJER (reigned c.1750 BC). Throne name Userkare. A ruler of **Dynasty 13**. He is known principally for his **pyramid** tomb which was built at **Saqqara** and excavated by Gustave Jécquier in 1929–31. See also **Second Intermediate Period**.

KHENEMET-NEFER-HEDJET. The name of a princess and two queens of **Dynasty 12**. The princess was a daughter of **Amenemhat II**, but her fate is unknown although she might be identical with the following. Queen Khenemet-nefer-hedjet the elder was the chief wife of **Senusret II** and mother of **Senusret III**, while Khenemet-nefer-hedjet the younger was the wife of Senusret III. The parentage of either queen is uncertain. The name was later used as a royal title for the queen.

KHENTKAUES. The name of two queen-mothers of **Dynasty 5**. Khentkaues I was buried at **Giza** where her tomb was excavated in 1932, while the tomb of Khentkaues II was excavated at **Abusir** in 1978–81. The theory that Khentkaues I was a princess of **Dynasty 4** who linked the two dynasties must be abandoned as she nowhere is styled the daughter of a king. She was the mother or wife of **Userkaf** or **Sahure**, while Khentkaues II was the wife of **Neferirkare** and mother of **Raneferef** and **Niuserre**. It seems that both may have been mothers of two kings and played important political roles, possibly as regents for a minor king or during a disputed succession.

KHETY. The name of several kings of **Dynasties 9–10** based in **Herakleopolis**. Their reigns are obscure and little documentation survives from this period.

KHETY (fl. c.1960 BC). Author and sage who lived during **Dynasty 12**. He was the author of *The Satire on Trades*, a popular composition extolling the profession of scribe and denigrating others. He may also have composed *The Instructions of King Amenemhat I* which was assigned to the king.

KHNUM. Ram-headed creator-god of **Elephantine**. He was believed to fashion the souls of the living on his potter's wheel and so was also a patron of potters. He was associated with **Anukis** and **Satis**.

KHUFU (reigned c.2589–2566 BC). Second king of **Dynasty 4**, son of **Snefru** and **Hetepheres** I. The Greek form of his name was Cheops. The Great Pyramid at **Giza** was built in his reign as his tomb surrounded by the **mastaba** tombs of his family and officials. His reign is little known, but he was remembered in later times as a harsh ruler. See also **Djedefre, Hardjedef, Kawab, Khafre**.

KING-LISTS. Lists of kings and their reign lengths seem to have been kept from early dynastic times for religious and chronological use. No complete list has survived, but the **Turin Royal Canon** written in the **Ramesside Period** is the most complete with many exact reign lengths. Other offering-lists to deceased kings appear in tombs and **temples**. One difficulty with these lists lies in the fact that some rulers reigned contemporaneously as **co-regents** or rivals and this is rarely indicated. See also **Chronology**.

KIYA (fl. c.1340 BC). Secondary wife of **Akhenaten**, of unknown origin. There has been much speculation about her background and possible children, but nothing is known about her except her name which is found erased on many monuments.

KOM ABU BILLO. Modern name for a site in the third **nome** of **Lower Egypt** on the western edge of the Delta; Greek Terenuthis, possibly ancient Egyptian *Perhathornebetmefkat*. The principal deity of the town may have been originally Hathor and later the snake-goddess Renenutet. The necropolis dates from the **Old Kingdom** but has yielded many **stelae** of the **Roman Period** which depict the deceased in Greek costume either standing with arms raised or reclining on a couch often associated with Egyptian gods such as **Anubis** or **Horus**, sometimes with texts in Greek. The area was first excavated on behalf of the **Egypt Exploration Fund** in 1887–88 when remains of a Ptolemaic **temple** were discovered. Further excavations were carried out by the University of Michigan in 1935 and the Egyptian Antiquities Service in 1970–71.

KOM OMBO. The modern name for a site on the east bank of the **Nile** in southern **Upper Egypt**, ancient Egyptian *Nebit*, Greek Ombos. The principal surviving monument consists of a **temple** of the **Ptolemaic Period** dedicated to the gods **Sobek** and **Horus** in the form of Haroeris and their respective wives and sons. The temple was cleared by the Egyptian Antiquities Service in 1893 and is being published by a French expedition. The nearby town has not been excavated.

KOPTOS see **COPTOS.**

KUMMA. Modern name for a site in lower **Nubia** in the Second **Cataract** region where a fortress was erected during **Dynasty 12**, probably by **Senusret III**, as part of the Egyptian garrison. Egyptian *Itnw Pedjut*. The area has now been flooded by the lake of the Aswan High Dam. See also **Askut, Buhen, Mirgissa, Semna, Shalfak, Uronarti.**

- L -

LAHUN. Modern name for a site near the **Fayum**, also known as Illahun, where the **pyramid** complex of **Senusret II** of **Dynasty 12** was built. Nearby at a site called Kahun the village for the workmen who constructed the pyramid was laid out and was later used by the community of priests which served the royal cult. The area was excavated in 1889–90 by Flinders **Petrie** who discovered much material of daily life at Kahun, including **papyri**, and in the pyramid he found jewellery belonging to the Princess **Sithathoriunet.**

LANGUAGE. The ancient Egyptian language belongs to the Afro-Asiatic group of languages and has affinities with both North African and Semitic languages and possibly devolved before these two groups separated. The language did not remain unchanged, but went through five linguistic stages. Old Egyptian was used in the **Old Kingdom** and expressed in written form by **hieroglyphic** and **hieratic** writing. The next phase was Middle Egyptian used firstly in the **Middle Kingdom** and later regarded as the classical form of the language by subsequent generations. Late Egyptian was in use from the **New Kingdom**, but was replaced by **demotic** in the **Late Period**, using new grammatical and written forms until it died out as a written language in the **Roman Period**. Finally **Coptic** was introduced in the Christian period. Regional variations only become apparent in the Coptic period but must have existed in earlier times. During its long history the Egyptian language borrowed many loan words from Semitic languages in the New Kingdom and later from Greek.

LATE PERIOD (664–332 BC). A term used by Egyptologists for the period from the beginning of **Dynasty 26** until the conquest of Egypt by **Alexander the Great**. Some scholars also include **Dynasty 25**. At this time the royal court was located in the Delta at **Sais** and other cities. The Egyptian rulers attempted to maintain the independence of the country against outside aggression from **Persia**, but were ultimately unsuccessful.

LEONTOPOLIS. Greek name for the Egyptian *Ta-remu,* modern Tell Moqdam in the Delta. The city is attested as a royal seat in the **Third Intermediate Period**, and the burial of a Queen **Karomama** has been found there. Little remains of the city now. The city has been investigated by an American expedition from 1992–98.

LEPSIUS, (KARL) RICHARD (1810–1884). German Egyptologist. He was born in Naumburg on 23 December 1810. He studied Egyptology in Paris and Germany. In 1842–45 Lepsius was sent to Egypt with a Prussian expedition which collected antiquities for the **Berlin Egyptian Museum** but he and his colleagues also made copious notes and drawings on standing monuments later published in 12 volumes. In 1846 he was appointed professor at Berlin University and in 1855 vice-director of the Berlin Museum, succeeding as director in 1865. Lepsius continued **Champollion**'s research into ancient Egyptian grammar and helped to perfect the understanding of the ancient language. He died in Berlin on 10 July 1884.

LISHT. Modern name for the city of *Itjtawy,* capital of **Dynasty 12** located in the **Fayum**. The town itself is unexcavated but nearby are located the **pyramids** of **Amenemhat I** and his son **Senusret I** as well as their officials. The site has been excavated by the French in 1894–95 and by the New York **Metropolitan Museum of Art** in 1906–34 and in 1984–89. See also **Intefyoker**.

LITERATURE see **WISDOM LITERATURE**.

LOUVRE MUSEUM. Following the French Revolution, the Louvre Palace in Paris was turned into a museum but contained few Egyptian objects. In 1824 the French government acquired the Durand collection of 1,225 small Egyptian antiquities and in 1826 through the efforts of Jean-François **Champollion** the second collection of Henry Salt, the British consul-general in Egypt, comprising 4,000 pieces was purchased. A separate Egyptian section was established in the Louvre in 1826 with Champollion as its curator. The collection was enriched by further purchases and objects acquired by Champollion during his tour to Egypt in 1828–29.

Further antiquities were received from the excavations of Auguste **Mariette** at the **Serapeum** and the work of the Institut français d'archéologie orientale which was founded in 1880 and undertook excavations throughout Egypt. Among its chief pieces are the **stela** of King **Djet** of **Dynasty 1** from **Abydos**, the seated scribe of **Old Kingdom** date, and the bronze statue inlaid with gold, silver, and electrum of Princess **Karomama** of **Dynasty 22**.

LOWER EGYPT. Ancient Egyptian *Tamehu.* The area of Egypt comprising the **Nile** Delta from the Mediterranean Sea up to **Memphis**. It appears to have evolved into a separate kingdom, possibly with its capital at **Buto**, in the **Predynastic Period** and was united, forcibly or not, with **Upper Egypt** to form a single country, described in Egyptian texts as the Two Lands. The symbol of Lower Egypt was the sedge-plant which formed part of the royal title with the bee of Upper Egypt. The tutelary goddess **Wadjet** was represented as a serpent or **uraeus** on the royal brow. The royal crown of Lower Egypt, known as the red crown, consisted of a flat top with a vertical section at the back.

LUXOR. Modern name for the town on the site of ancient **Thebes.** The name is used by Egyptologists to refer to the **temple** in Luxor, known to the Egyptians as *Iput-rsyt*, as distinct from the temple of **Karnak** or *Iput-sut*, now on the outskirts of the town. The Luxor temple was built by **Amenhotep III** and apparently dedicated to the *ka* or soul of the king. Reliefs feature the **divine birth** of the king. The temple was later enlarged by **Tutankhamun** and **Ramesses II.** A processional way of ram-headed **sphinxes** connected the temple to that of Karnak. During the main religious festival the sacred image of the god **Amun** would proceed from Karnak to Luxor on a barque carried by priests. In the fourth century AD part of the temple was converted to a church and later to a mosque. A Muslim religious festival to a local saint incorporates some features of the ancient Egyptian ritual.

- M -

MAADI. Modern name for a suburb 10 kilometres south of Cairo in which excavations by Cairo University in 1930–53 uncovered a settlement and cemeteries dating to the late **Predynastic Period**. The remains included huts and storage pits for grain and pottery, both local and imported from Palestine. The local culture is different from that of **Upper Egypt** of the **Naqada** Period which is believed to be in part contemporary and was thought to represent a separate culture of **Lower Egypt** although excavations at **Minshat Abu Omar** in the Delta reveal Naqada culture there.

MAAT. The Egyptian concept of righteous order, often translated as truth and symbolized by a feather. The king was obliged to maintain *maat* on earth through just rule and the maintenance of the constant religious rituals in the **temples** which placated the gods. Individuals were supposed to follow *maat* in their daily lives to ensure passage to the next life and, according to religious belief, their heart would be weighed against the feather of *maat* to determine their worthiness to enter the **afterlife**, although **Books of the Dead** were used to avoid any possible problems if there was doubt about the worthiness of the individual.

MAATHORNEFERURE (fl. c.1245 BC). Egyptian name of the **Hittite** princess, daughter of Hattusilis III and Padukhepa, who married **Ramesses II** in his year 34, c.1245 BC. The marriage is recorded on several monuments and this queen is known from **scarabs** and other textual evidence.

MAATKARE (fl. c.1030 BC). Daughter of the **High Priest of Amun Pinudjem** I and **Henttawy** II. She was appointed **God's Wife of Amun**. Her body was recovered from the **royal cache** at **Deir el-Bahri** in 1881. Her virgin status was disputed as a small body, believed to be her child, was found in her coffin, but X-ray analysis later revealed this to be her pet monkey. A later Maatkare, daughter of **Pasebakhaenniut II** of **Dynasty 21**, was the wife of **Osorkon I** of **Dynasty 22**.

MALKATA. Modern name for an area on the west bank of the **Nile** opposite **Thebes** known as *Aten Tjehen*. Here the remains of a palace of **Amenhotep III** have been found as well as a pleasure lake nearby at Birket Habu. The site was discovered in 1888 and excavated by an American, R. Tytus, in 1901–03, the **Metropolitan Museum of Art** of New

York in 1910–20, an American expedition from Pennsylvania in 1971–74, and more recently by a Japanese expedition from Waseda University in 1972–80 and 1985–88.

MANETHO (fl. c.270 BC). Egyptian priest and author in the reign of **Ptolemy II**. He came from **Sebennytos** and appears to have held the post of high priest at **Heliopolis**. He wrote a history of Egypt in Greek entitled *Aegyptiaca* based on **temple** records. The complete text is now lost, but part of it is known from garbled excerpts in the works of other authors. His **king-lists** and division of **dynasties** were instrumental in establishing Egyptian **chronology** but must be carefully evaluated. The names and reign lengths are often distorted and must be checked against contemporary sources. He was also involved in the establishment of the cult of **Sarapis** in Egypt. See also **Dynasty 1** through **Dynasty 30**.

MARIETTE, (FRANÇOIS) AUGUSTE FERDINAND (1821–1881). French excavator. He was born in Boulogne on 11 February 1821 and at first became a teacher. His interest in Egypt was aroused by papers of a relative who had visited there, and he taught himself Egyptian and **Coptic**. In 1850 he was sent to Egypt to purchase Coptic manuscripts but used the money to discover and excavate the **Serapeum** at **Saqqara**.

In 1858 he was appointed head of the newly founded Egyptian Antiquities Service and organized archaeological excavations at all major sites in Egypt, notably **Abydos**, **Thebes**, **Dendera, Saqqara, Giza,** and various sites in the Delta region. In 1863 he opened the first **Cairo Egyptian Museum**. Mariette tried to put an end to illicit excavation and restricted foreign excavators. The bulk of his discoveries went to the **Cairo Egyptian Museum** which henceforth had first choice of excavated material in Egypt. He died in Cairo on 18 January 1881 and he was later reburied in front of the new Cairo Museum.

MARINA EL-ALAMEIN. Modern name for an ancient site on the Mediterranean coast near modern el-Alamein where Egyptian and Polish excavations from 1986 have uncovered a town of the **Graeco-Roman Period** with nearby tombs. The tombs consist of burial chambers off a central altar and a room for the funeral and subsequent feasts in honour of the dead. **Mummy** portraits have been recovered with some of the burials indicating that this practice was also carried on in the north of Egypt; this had not been hitherto attested due to the wetter climate here.

MARRIAGE. Although marriage undoubtedly existed in ancient Egypt, there is no evidence for any marriage ceremonies and it may be that a couple merely declared their intention and lived together. It is probable that there was a family celebration of some sort, but no legal or religious notification was necessary. In the **Late Period** marriage contracts have survived which specify the terms of the relationship. Most Egyptian men appear to have had monogamous marriages with one wife at a time, and certainly this state of affairs was the ideal in **wisdom literature**. In view of the high level of mortality, it is likely that some men and women would have had further partners although evidence for remarriage is not always clearly indicated. Divorce was freely available but was limited by economic and social pressures. A divorced wife or widow was entitled to one-third of the matrimonial property unless guilty of adultery in which case her financial claims were diminished.

Polygamy, although permitted, is rarely attested except for the king. Total fidelity on the part of men was not realistically expected, but most men appear to have preferred to consort with prostitutes, concubines, or **slave** girls rather than take a second wife, a procedure which was expensive and might lead to legal disputes. In one known case of a childless couple, the husband fathered children by a slave girl who were then adopted by the wife.

Apart from the royal family, ancient Egyptians did not marry their sisters. Early Egyptologists were confused by the fact that wives are often referred to as a sister as a term of endearment. The king as a god could marry his sister although this was not obligatory and only a few cases of full brother-sister marriage are recorded during the Pharaonic Period: possibly **Mentuhotep II** and his sister **Nefru**, Seqenenre **Tao** and **Ahhotep**, and **Ahmose I** and **Ahmose-Nefertari**. Others married half-sisters or the identity of the mother of the queen is uncertain. The practice was revived by some of the Ptolemaic kings starting with **Ptolemy II**. Only in the **Graeco-Roman Period** are brother-sister marriages attested for commoners, and this development seems to have arisen as a means to control family property.

MASAHARTA (fl. c.1044–1036 BC). High priest of Amun at **Thebes** during **Dynasty 21.** Son of **Pinudjem** I. He succeeded his father as high priest apparently when the latter adopted royal titles but may have predeceased him. He was eventually succeeded by his brother **Menkheperre**. His body was recovered from the **royal cache.**

MASTABA. Arabic term used by Egyptologists to describe free-standing tombs from the late **Predynastic Period** onwards. The superstructure of these tombs is rectangular in shape and composed of mud-brick or stone. Within the core of the superstructure are various storerooms or chapels, sometimes filled in to present a seemingly solid appearance. A shaft within the body of the tomb leads to the underground burial chamber. See also **Pyramid**.

MEDAMUD. Modern name for a site in **Upper Egypt** just northeast of **Luxor**. Ancient Egyptian *Madu*. The main deity of the site was the god **Montu** whose temple is attested from the **Middle Kingdom** although the surviving remains date to the **Graeco-Roman Period**. A cult of a sacred bull similar to the **Mnevis** is known from here. The site was excavated by French archaeologists in 1929–40.

MEDINET HABU. Modern name for the site of the mortuary **temple** of **Ramesses III** on the west bank at **Thebes**. The temple is well preserved and contains a major inscription detailing the king's war against the **Sea Peoples**. The workmen from **Deir el-Medina** sought refuge here at the end of **Dynasty 20**. The site also contains a temple of **Thutmose III** and later the burial chapels of the **God's Wives of Amun**.

MEIDUM. Modern name for ancient Egyptian *Mertem*, where the earliest known true **pyramid** is located although not originally designed as such. It was built as a step-pyramid but the steps were later filled in, although most of the filling has now collapsed. The pyramid has been attributed to **Huni** or his successor **Snefru**. It is surrounded by the tombs of royal officials, including that of Prince Rahotep which contained fine painted statues of himself and his wife Neferet now in the **Cairo Egyptian Museum**. The site was examined by Auguste **Mariette** and later Flinders **Petrie** in 1890–91 and 1909–10 and more recently in 1984 by an Egyptian expedition.

MEIR. Modern name for a site in **Middle Egypt** south of **Amarna**; ancient Egyptian *Qis*, capital of the 14th **nome** of **Upper Egypt**. The most important features of the area are the rock-cut tombs of the nomarchs from **Dynasties 6–12.** The reliefs were copied by an expedition sponsored by the **Egypt Exploration Society** in 1912–14, 1921, and 1949–50.

MEKETATEN (fl. c.1340 BC). Second daughter of **Akhenaten** and **Nefertiti**. She appears on many monuments with her sisters during the early part of her father's reign. The deathbed scene of this princess is vividly depicted in the royal tomb at **Amarna**. This scene might be interpreted to suggest that she died in childbirth, but this is not certain.

MEKETRE (fl. c.2000 BC). Chancellor at the end of **Dynasty 11** and possibly the beginning of **Dynasty 12**. He was buried at **Deir el-Bahri,** and his tomb was excavated by an expedition from the **Metropolitan Museum of Art** in 1921. Among the objects discovered were fine models of activities of daily life which are a feature of tombs of the **Middle Kingdom**.

MEMNON, COLOSSI OF. The two colossal statues of **Amenhotep III** which stood before his mortuary **temple** on the west bank at **Thebes**. The statues were named by the Greeks after the legendary Ethiopian king Memnon who fought in the Trojan War. One was believed to sing, probably the action of wind through cracks, and became a favourite tourist attraction in the **Roman Period**, being visited notably by **Hadrian** and his wife. This statue was repaired by order of **Septimius Severus** and sang no more. The temple behind the statues was heavily plundered by **Merenptah** who used many blocks and statues for the construction of his own mortuary temple.

MEMPHIS. Greek name for the capital of the first **nome** of **Lower Egypt** located at modern Mit Rahina. The city is said to have been founded by **Menes**. It then served as the capital of a united Egypt and was first called *Inebu-hedj,* "White Wall". It was later known by the name *Men-nefer,* derived from the **pyramid** of **Pepy I**, from which the Greek form of its name developed. Memphis remained the first or second capital of Egypt through most of dynastic history. Its principal monument was the **temple** to its local god **Ptah** which is now in ruins but was largely rebuilt by **Ramesses II**. The remains of smaller temples and palaces, mainly from the **Ramesside Period**, have also been uncovered.

The site has not been systematically excavated and so is less well known than the southern capital at **Thebes**. Investigations were carried out by Jospeh Hekekyan in 1852. Excavations were carried out by Auguste **Mariette**; Flinders **Petrie** in 1909–13; the University of Pennsylvania in 1915–19, 1921–23, and 1955–56; by Egyptian archaeologists, notably in 1931 and 1942 when tombs of the Ramesside Period and **Dy-**

nasty 22 were uncovered; and the **Egypt Exploration Society** from 1981. The kings and courtiers who resided here were buried at the nearby desert sites of **Abusir**, **Dahshur**, **Giza**, **Meidum**, and **Saqqara**.

MENDES. Greek name for the Egyptian *Per-Banebdjet*, now Tell el-Ruba, capital of the 16th **nome** of **Lower Egypt**. The principal deity of the site was the sacred ram Banebdjet. Remains include tombs from the **Old Kingdom** and later eras and the cemetery of the sacred rams. Capital of **Dynasty 29**. The site has been excavated by American Egyptologists from 1964. The nearby site of Tell el-Timai, Greek Thmuis, marked the area of residence in the **Graeco-Roman Period.**

MENES. Legendary first king of Egypt who founded **Dynasty 1** and founder of the city of **Memphis**. There are no certain contemporary references to a king of this name, but he appears on Ramesside **king-lists** 2,000 years later. He may be identified with **Narmer**.

MENKAUHOR (reigned c.2421–2414 BC). Ruler of **Dynasty 5**. Successor of **Niuserre**. Very little is known of his reign, and although the name of his **pyramid** has been discovered, the actual structure has yet to be located either at **Saqqara** or **Abusir**. See also **Djedkare**.

MENKAURE (reigned c.2532–2503 BC). Ruler of **Dynasty 4**. Son and successor of **Khafre** and probably Queen **Khamerernebty** I. The Greek form of his name was Mycerinus. He built the third **pyramid** complex at **Giza** next to that of his father and his grandfather **Khufu**. His pyramid was opened in 1837 and his **sarcophagus** was shipped to London, but was lost at sea. The associated **temples** and chapels were excavated by George **Reisner** for the **Boston Museum of Fine Arts** in 1906–10 and 1923 and yielded fine pieces of sculpture depicting the king with various goddesses.

MENKHEPERRE (fl. c.1060–986 BC). High priest of Amun at **Thebes** during **Dynasty 21**. Son of **Pinudjem** I. He eventually succeeded his brother **Masaharta** at Thebes in year 25 of **Nesbanebdjed** (c.1035 BC) after some political dissension resulting in the banishment of his rivals. Menkheperre held office for about 50 years after which he was followed by his sons Nesbanebdjed and **Pinudjem** II. See also **Third Intermediate Period.**

MENTUEMHAT (fl. c.700–650 BC). Fourth prophet of **Amun** and mayor of **Thebes**, son of Nesptah who had similar titles and Istemkheb. He was the virtual ruler of Thebes and **Upper Egypt** at the end of **Dynasty 25** and is named in **Assyrian** accounts as prince of Thebes. Mentuemhat skilfully kept his position during and after the Assyrian conquest but submitted in 656 BC to **Psamtik I** who recognized his position. He was succeeded by his son Nesptah but Psamtik I eventually managed to remove the family from power.

MENTUHERKHEPESHEF. The name of several princes in **Dynasties 19–20**. The name was first used for the fifth son of **Ramesses II** (fl. 1270 BC). A like-named son of **Ramesses IX** was buried in tomb no. 19 in the **Valley of the Kings**, first rediscovered in 1817.

MENTUHOTEP I (fl. c.2125 BC). Ancestor of **Dynasty 11.** He apparently never actually ruled but was probably a governor of **Thebes** and awarded a posthumous royal **Horus** name as the father of **Intef I**. See also **First Intermediate Period**.

MENTUHOTEP II (reigned c.2055–2004 BC). Throne name Nebhepetre. Son of **Intef III** and Iah, ruler of **Thebes** of **Dynasty 11**. He reestablished the unity of Egypt c.2040 BC by defeating the ruler of **Herakleopolis** of **Dynasty 10** and ended the **First Intermediate Period**. He established Thebes for the first time as capital of Egypt. Mentuhotep II appears to have undertaken campaigns in **Nubia**, in Sinai, and against the Libyans to safeguard and possibly expand Egypt's borders. He built his tomb and mortuary **temple** at **Deir el-Bahri**. He married his sister **Nefru** and the lady Tem, mother of his successor **Mentuhotep III**.

MENTUHOTEP III (reigned c.2004–1992 BC). Throne name Sankhkare. Son and successor of **Mentuhotep II** and Tem. He also built a funerary complex at **Deir el-Bahri**, but this has not survived. This site was examined by George Schweinfurth in 1904 and Flinders **Petrie** in 1909 and was excavated by a Hungarian expedition in 1995–96. See also **Mentuhotep IV**.

MENTUHOTEP IV (reigned c.1992–1985 BC). Throne name Nebtawyre. Successor and probable son of **Mentuhotep III** and Imi. He is not listed in any of the surviving **king-lists** but is known from contemporary documents including inscriptions of mining expeditions to the **Wadi el-**

Hudi and the **Wadi Hammamat**. The latter records a visit by his **vizier** Amenemhat who is generally believed to be the future **Amenemhat I** who may well have overthrown his master.

MENTUHOTEP V–VII. Ephemeral kings of **Dynasty 13** and **Dynasty 17**. Meryankhre Mentuhotep V is known from two statues, Sewadjre Mentuhotep VI from a fragmentary inscription, and Sankhenre Mentuhotep VII from some inscriptions and the **Turin Royal Canon**. See also **Second Intermediate Period**.

MERENPTAH (reigned c.1212–1202 BC). Throne name Baenre. Thirteenth son of **Ramesses II** by **Isitnofret**. He apparently survived all his older brothers or those eligible for the throne and became virtual **co-regent** of his father towards the end of the latter's reign. After his succession he faced invasions from the Libyans and the **Sea Peoples** that were successfully repulsed. He was buried in tomb no. 8 in the **Valley of the Kings** and his **mummy** was found in the **royal cache** in the tomb of **Amenhotep II**.

MERENRE see **NEMTYEMSAF**.

MERERUKA (fl. c.2340 BC). Vizier of **Teti** of **Dynasty 6** and successor of **Kagemni**. Son of the lady Nedjetempet. He married a royal princess, Watetkhekher alias **Sesheseshet**. His tomb is located near the **pyramid** of Teti at **Saqqara** and is one of the largest in the cemetery. There are many fine reliefs of daily life and a massive statue of the deceased in the main hall. The tomb was discovered in 1893 but was only fully copied by an expedition from the University of Chicago in 1930–36. His mother's tomb has recently been discovered next to his own.

MERESANKH. The name of several princesses and queens of **Dynasty 4**. Meresankh I was the mother of **Snefru**. Meresankh II was the daughter of **Khufu** and Meresankh III was the daughter of Khufu's son **Kawab**; both were wives of **Khafre** and were buried at **Giza**.

MERETSEGER. Snake-goddess of **Thebes**. She was worshipped primarily by the royal workmen at **Deir el-Medina**, no doubt to avoid the dangers of snake-bite. She was sometimes represented as a woman with a snake's head. Meretseger was identified with el-Qorn, the highest mountain peak on the west bank of the **Nile** opposite Thebes.

MERIMDA BENI SALAMA. Modern name of an archaeological site in the Delta northwest of Cairo where a prehistoric town settlement was located. The later phases include mud-brick houses apparently built in a town plan. The culture is contemporary with that of el-**Badari** and **Naqada** I, but exhibits differences which were originally thought to indicate separate cultural development for **Lower Egypt**. The site was excavated by a German expedition in 1928–39 and 1977–83. Recent discoveries at **Minshat Abu Omar** indicate that Naqada culture was also present in the north.

MERITAMUN (fl. c.1540–1500 BC). Egyptian princess and queen, sister and wife of **Amenhotep I** of **Dynasty 18** and thus probably daughter of **Ahmose I** and **Ahmose-Nefertari**. She appears to have had no issue. She was buried in tomb no. 358 at **Deir el-Bahri** which was discovered in the 1920s. A body identified as hers in the **royal cache** must be a misattribution.

MERITAMUN (fl. c.1450 BC). Egyptian princess of **Dynasty 18**. Probably daughter of **Thutmose III**. She is attested in the chapel at **Deir el-Bahri** and several other monuments and is not to be confused with the above.

MERITAMUN (fl. c.1352–1338 BC). Original name Meritaten. Eldest daughter of **Akhenaten** and **Nefertiti**. She appears as queen towards the end of **Dynasty 18**, and it has been suggested that she was the wife of **Smenkhkare** or possibly Smenkhkare herself. Her ultimate fate is unknown. A Princess Meritaten-tasherit attested on monuments from **Amarna** may be her daughter. See also **Amarna Period**.

MERITAMUN (fl. c.1279-1240 BC). Daughter of **Ramesses II** and **Nefertari**. She became one of her father's queens and a colossal statue of her was discovered at **Akhmim** in 1981. She was buried in tomb no. 68 in the **Valley of the Queens**.

MERITATEN see **MERITAMUN (fl. c.1352–1338 BC).**

MERNEITH (fl. c.2985 BC). Queen of **Dynasty 1**, wife of **Djet** and mother of **Den**, who appears on the royal seal of her son. She apparently acted as regent or co-ruler with her son, the first woman attested in this position. See also **Early Dynastic Period**.

MEROE. Capital of the Kushite kingdom in **Nubia** from the **Late Period** until the **Roman Period.** Following the expulsion of **Dynasty 25** from Egypt, their successors reigned firstly at **Napata** and then further south at Meroe. The rulers were buried in **pyramid** tombs near the city. Hostilities with the Egyptian authorities occasionally occurred, the most notable being in the reign of **Augustus.** Little is known of the internal workings of the kingdom as the Meroitic script has yet to be deciphered. The city site has been excavated by the British John Garstang in 1909–14 and subsequently by a Canadian expedition in 1965–76, while the pyramid site has been explored by the American George **Reisner** in 1920–23 and more recently by a German expedition.

MERYATUM (fl. c.1270–1230 BC). Sixteenth son of **Ramesses II** by **Nefertari**. He was appointed to the post of high priest of **Re** at **Heliopolis** c.1254 BC.

MERYKARE (reigned c.2050 BC). Throne name of a ruler of **Dynasty 9** or **10** who ruled from **Herakleopolis** during the **First Intermediate Period**. He is known as the recipient of advice in a text of **wisdom literature** where the name of the author is missing but was presumably a King **Khety.** The personal name and fate of King Merykare is unknown.

METROPOLITAN MUSEUM OF ART (NEW YORK). One of the major collections of Egyptian antiquities. The Egyptian galleries were first opened in 1911. The collection was put together from purchases such as the antiquities of the Earl of Carnarvon, donations from the **Egypt Exploration Fund**, and most importantly archaeological work in Egypt carried out by the director Herbert Winlock mainly at **Deir el-Bahri**, **Thebes**, and **Lisht**. Major pieces include the staute of **Sahure** of **Dynasty 5**, the jewellery of Princess **Sithathoriunet**, a wooden statue of **Senusret I**, and the jewellery of the minor wives of **Thutmose III**. Following the **Nubian Rescue Campaign**, the Museum was presented with the **temple** of Dandur by the Egyptian Government.

MIDDLE EGYPT. A geographical term used by modern Egyptologists to refer to the area from **Lisht** to **Asyut** in the **Nile** Valley. In ancient times this was considered to be the northern part of **Upper Egypt**.

MIDDLE KINGDOM (c.2040–1795 BC). The term used by Egyptologists for the period from the reunion of Egypt by **Mentuhotep II** of **Dy-**

nasty 11, which terminated the **First Intermediate Period**, until the end of **Dynasty 12** although some would continue until the middle or end of **Dynasty 13**. This period witnessed Egyptian expansion into **Nubia** and increased influence in the Middle East, the establishment of a new capital at **Lisht** under **Dynasty 12** and increased agricultural development in the **Fayum** region, and the development of Egyptian classical literature. Political instability and pressure from Asiatic neighbors brought about its collapse and the beginning of the **Second Intermediate Period.**

MIN. Egyptian god of fertility represented as a standing mummiform man with an erect phallus and feathered plumes. His right arm is usually raised with a flail at hand. Chief god of **Coptos** and **Akhmim**. Min was also regarded as a protector of desert areas and often identified with **Amun** as a creator god.

MINSHAT ABU OMAR. Modern name for a site of a cemetery in the north-eastern Delta which was excavated by a German expedition in 1978–91. The graves date from the late **Predynastic Period** to the **Early Dynastic Period**, and the pottery shows strong affinities with the **Naqada** culture of **Upper Egypt** but also includes imports from Palestine.

MIRGISSA. Modern name for a site in lower **Nubia** near the end of the Second **Cataract**; ancient Egyptian *Iken.* Here was located a **Dynasty 12** fort which served as a major trading centre and entrepôt. The area was excavated by a French expedition before the site was flooded by the waters of the Aswan High Dam.

MITANNI. A major Asiatic kingdom formed in the middle of the second millennium covering northern Iraq, southern Turkey, and eastern Syria. Its rulers exercised sway over many of the local princes of Syria and Palestine. The invading Egyptian armies from **Thutmose I** onwards clashed with Mitanni, known to the Egyptians as Naharin, and restricted its influence. Peace seems to have been arranged between the powers by the reign of **Thutmose IV** who married a Mitannian princess as did his son **Amenhotep III** who had two Mitannian wives, **Tadukhepa** and **Gilukhepa**. The Mitannian kingdom was reduced to vassal status by the **Hittites** and finally destroyed by the **Assyrians** towards the end of the second millennium.

MNEVIS. Greek name for the sacred bull of **Heliopolis**, regarded as the living embodiment of the sun-god **Re**. He ranked next in importance to the **Apis** bull of **Memphis**. Some burials have been discovered at Heliopolis, but information on the succession of Mnevis bulls is less documented than that of the Apis.

MOALLA, El-. A site in **Upper Egypt** near **Thebes** where painted rock-cut tombs of the **First Intermediate Period** have been discovered. The most interesting of these is that of Ankhtifi who described the civil wars at that time.

MONS CLAUDIANUS. Roman name for the site of the Roman granodiorite quarry and associated settlement in the Eastern Desert 500 kilometres south of Cairo in the mountains bordering the Red Sea. The area was in use from the time of Trajan (98–117 AD). The surviving remains include a fortress with administrative buildings, animal lines, and a temple of **Sarapis**. The site was excavated by a joint British-French expedition in 1987–93 which recovered among other objects 9,000 **ostraca**.

MONS PORPHYRITES. Roman name for the site of the Roman porphyry quarry and associated settlement in the mountains of the Eastern Desert 30 kilometres from the Red Sea coast. The site was discovered in 18 AD and worked throughout the **Roman Period.** Archaeological investigations of the area were conducted by a British expedition in 1994–98.

MONTU. Hawk-headed god of war whose major place of worship was at **Thebes** and nearby **Armant** and **Tod**. Prominent in **Dynasty 11**, he was eclipsed by the popularity of **Amun**.

MOSES see **EXODUS.**

MUMMY. Modern word derived from the Arabic *mumiya* to describe the embalmed bodies of the ancient Egyptians. The earliest preserved bodies from the late **Predynastic Period** c.3200 BC are not mummies strictly speaking since they have been preserved by natural means in the dry Egyptian sand without any human intervention. Possibly inspired by these, the Egyptians came to believe that it was necessary to maintain the body of the deceased as home for the soul. Efforts were undertaken from the **Old Kingdom** to do so. The first results were not very successful. The bodies were wrapped in linen, presumably after the removal of the internal organs and then covered with mud to model human features.

Only a few of these have been discovered intact, notably one in the tomb of **Nefer** during **Dynasty 5**.

By the **New Kingdom**, the method of embalming had been perfected and reached its most advanced state in Dynasty 21. The internal organs were removed and placed in **canopic jars** or returned to the body in packages, apart from the heart which was left in the body. The brain was extracted via the nose and discarded. The body was then dried out with dry natron, a natural salt, packed and anointed with resins and aromatics, and then wrapped in bandages beneath and between which various amulets were often placed.

The method of mummification declined in succeeding periods although the outer covering of bandages became more elaborate and in the **Roman Period** included painted mummy portraits. Mummification was abandoned in the **Coptic** Period as a pagan rite. In the medieval period, bodies were ground down to a powder, known in Arabic as *mumiya,* which was considered beneficial to health. This led to a minor industry of excavating and disposing of mummies which incidentally also resulted in some early archaeological discoveries. The present term mummy derives from the Arabic name of the powder. See also **Afterlife**.

MUT. Egyptian goddess, consort of **Amun.** She is usually depicted as a female figure with a vulture headdress surmounted by the double crown of Egypt, but may be depicted with the head of a lioness. Her sacred animal was a lion, and her principal place of worship was her **temple** at **Karnak** linked to the main temple of Amun. The temple was adorned by many statues of the goddess **Sakhmet** who was thus linked to Mut.

MUTEMWIA (fl. c.1350 BC). Queen-mother of **Amenhotep III** and wife of **Thutmose IV**. She is not attested until the reign of her son and must have been a minor wife of his father. There is no evidence to identify her with the **Mitannian** princess who was also wife to Thutmose IV. In the **temple** of **Luxor** she is depicted in the embrace of the god **Amun** who according to tradition was the father of each Egyptian ruler.

MUTNEFRET (fl. c.1500 BC). Wife of **Thutmose I** and mother of **Thutmose II**. Her origin is unknown but she is generally described by Egyptologists as a minor or secondary wife. There is no evidence for this assertion as she may have been the wife of Thutmose I before his accession to the throne at which time he may then have wed his sister and queen **Ahmose**. Mutnefret may have been the mother of the king's other sons

Amenmose and **Wadjmose**. A Princess Mutnefret was probably her granddaughter or great-granddaughter.

MUTNODJMET (fl. c.1310 BC). Queen of **Horemheb**. She appears in the reign of **Akhenaten** apparently as the sister of his queen **Nefertiti**, but her parentage is unknown. It is not clear when she married Horemheb who appears to have had an earlier wife. She apparently died childless before her husband and is possibly buried in his tomb at **Saqqara**. A later Queen Mutnodjmet was the wife of **Pasebakhaenniut I**.

MYCERINUS see **MENKAURE**.

- N -

NAG HAMMADI CODICES. These 13 codices written in **Coptic** in the fourth century AD were discovered by a peasant in 1945 near the modern city of Nag Hammadi in **Upper Egypt**. After being sold separately, they have now all been reunited in the **Coptic Museum** in Cairo and fully published. The texts are religious tractates pertaining to the dualistic Gnostic sect which combined features of Christianity and paganism and was proscribed following the triumph of Christianity.

NAGA EL-DEIR. Modern name for a site in northern **Upper Egypt** which probably served as a cemetery for the city of **Thinis**. The remains date from the **Predynastic Period** to the **Middle Kingdom**. The site was excavated by the American George **Reisner** in 1901–04, 1912, and 1923–24 and yielded much inscribed material in the form of **stelae** and **papyri**. Two tombs of the **Ramesside Period** are located in the nearby site of Nag el-Mashayikh.

NAKHTHORHEB (reigned 360–343 BC). Last ruler of **Dynasty 30**. The Greek version of his name was Nectanebos, usually rendered as Nectanebo II. Throne name Senedjemibre setepenanhur. Epithet meryhathor. Son of Tjaihepimu, who was the brother of King **Djedhor**. Nakhthorheb accompanied his uncle Djedhor on a campaign in Syria and there rebelled with the assistance of his father who had been left as regent in Egypt. Nakhthorheb was joined by the Greek mercenaries in the army and his uncle fled to **Persia**. He continued the policies of his grandfather **Nakhtnebef** in supporting Egyptian **temples**.

Nakhthorheb faced continued attempts by Persia to reconquer Egypt and eventually in 343 BC his armies were defeated and he was forced to flee to the south, disappearing from history. The **sarcophagus** which he prepared for his burial was reused and is now in the **British Museum**. Later legend views him as a wise magician who escaped to Macedon and through an affair with Queen Olympias fathered **Alexander the Great** who was to drive out the Persians from Egypt. The legend is chronologically impossible but reflects the Egyptian tendency to try to give an Egyptian background to their foreign conquerors.

NAKHTNEBEF (reigned 380–363 BC). The Greek version of his name was Nectanebes, usually rendered as Nectanebo I. Throne name Kheperkare. Founder of **Dynasty 30**. Son of Djedhor, a military officer from **Sebennytos**. He overthrew **Nefaarud** II of **Dynasty 29**. He managed to defeat a **Persian** invasion of Egypt in 373 BC and embarked on a major programme of refurbishing Egypt's **temples**. See also **Djedhor, Nakhthorheb**.

NAME. Ancient Egyptian *rn*. Much importance was attached in ancient Egypt to preserving the name of an individual throughout eternity as this imparted immortality to the deceased. Statues and **stelae** were erected especially in tombs and **temples** for this purpose. One of the standard prayers of an ancient Egyptian was that someone "cause his name to live".

NAOS. Greek name for the sacred shrine of a **temple**. The naos usually consisted of a hollowed-out stone or wooden container fitted with wooden doors into which the image of the deity was placed. Such monuments are depicted on statues and survive from some temples. Model naoi are also known in bronze and wood.

NAPATA. First capital of the later kingdom of Kush in **Nubia**. The site is 30 kilometres south of the Second **Cataract** and appears to have been initially occupied in the **New Kingdom**. Following the Egyptian withdrawal, a Nubian kingdom centred on Napata developed and under **Kashta**, **Piye**, and finally **Shabaqo** conquered Egypt as **Dynasty 25** or the Napatan Dynasty. The area includes the royal cemeteries at el-Kurru and Nuri and the holy mountain of Gebel Barkal with its **temple** to **Amun**. The capital of the kingdom was eventually transferred to the site of **Meroe**.

NAQADA. Modern name for ancient *Nubt*, Greek Ombos, a site in **Upper Egypt** north of **Thebes** where important remains from the late **Predynastic Period** were excavated by Flinders **Petrie** in 1895. The name is now used to denote the final phase of predynastic culture, divided into the periods Naqada I and Naqada II, which last is best attested by its painted designs on pottery.

NARMER (reigned c.3100 BC). First king of **Dynasty 1**, as named in the royal seal of the dynasty. He may be identified with the legendary King **Menes**. He is known from a palette and macehead found at **Hierakonpolis** which record his military victories. He was buried at **Abydos,** where his tomb has recently been re-excavated by a German expedition. See also **Aha**.

NAUKRATIS. Greek name for a site in the fifth **nome** of **Lower Egypt** which became a settlement for Greek merchants during **Dynasty 26**, probably founded by **Psamtik I** rather than **Ahmose II** as stated in **Herodotus**, and flourished into the **Roman Period**. It was excavated by Flinders **Petrie** in 1885, other British archaeologists in 1886, 1899, and 1903, and an American expedition in 1977–78 and 1980–83.

NECHO see **NEKAU**.

NECTANEBO I see **NAKHTNEBEF**.

NECTANEBO II see **NAKHTHORHEB**.

NEFAARUD. The Greek version of the name was Nepherites. The name of two kings of **Dynasty 29** from **Mendes**. Nefaarud I, throne name Baenre merynetjeru, reigned 399–93 BC. He overthrew **Amyrtaeos** but little is known of his reign. Nefaarud II, reigned 380 BC, was in turn ousted by **Nakhtnebef** (Nectanebo I), the founder of **Dynasty 30**.

NEFER (fl. c.2400 BC). The owner of a tomb built at **Saqqara** south of the causeway of the **pyramid** of **Unas** which was discovered by Egyptian archaeologists in 1966. Son of the overseer of singers Kahay and Meretites who were also buried here. Nefer inherited his father's rank and built the tomb for the family during **Dynasty 5**. The tomb contains fine painted reliefs and is remarkable for the survival of a male **mummy** in a fine state of preservation.

NEFEREFRE see **RANEFEREF.**

NEFERHOTEP I (reigned c.1740–1730 BC). Throne name Khasekhemre. Son of the **God's Father** Haankhef and the lady Kemi. The circumstances of his accession to power as 22nd ruler during **Dynasty 13** are unclear. He was one of the more important rulers of this period and recorded his family origins on graffiti near **Elephantine.** He was succeeded by his brothers **Sihathor** and **Sobekhotep IV.** See also **Second Intermediate Period.**

NEFERIRKARE (reigned c.2475–2455 BC). Personal name Kakai. Third ruler of **Dynasty 5.** According to the later **Westcar Papyrus,** he was a brother of his predecessors **Userkaf** and **Sahure,** but this is doubtful. He built his **pyramid** complex at **Abusir** which was excavated by the German Ludwig Borchardt in 1900 and 1903–07. He is the first ruler to use two **cartouches** with his prenomen and nomen in the royal **titulary.** See also **Raneferef.**

NEFERTARI (fl. c.1300–1255 BC). Favourite wife of **Ramesses II** of unknown origin. She is represented in his temples at **Abu Simbel** and has her own magnificent tomb (no. 66) in the **Valley of the Queens.** She had six children: sons **Amenherkhepeshef, Preherwenemef,** Meryre, and **Meryatum** and daughters **Meritamun** and Henuttawy. She carried out diplomatic correspondence with the queen of the **Hittites.** See also **Isitnofret.**

NEFERTI. The fictional author of a literary text set in the reign of **Snefru** in which he prophesies civil war and confusion in Egypt which will be ended by the succession of **Amenemhat I** of **Dynasty 12.** The text was doubtless written in the reign of the latter as a justification of his accession to the throne.

NEFERTITI (fl. c.1370–1336 BC). Chief wife of **Akhenaten** of unknown origin. She is represented as an equal of her husband on reliefs and in a style not previously used for queens. She is best known for the famous bust now in Berlin found at **Amarna.** She was apparently the mother of six daughters: Meritaten (later **Meritamun**), **Meketaten, Ankhesenpaaten** (later **Ankhesenamun,** wife of **Tutankhamun**), Nefernefruatentasherit, Nefernefrure, and Setepenre. Her ultimate fate is unknown, but it has been suggested that she briefly acted as ruler or regent on her husband's death. See also **Ay, Tiy**.

NEFERTUM. Egyptian god of vegetation. Son of **Ptah** and **Sakhmet** and part of the **triad** of **Memphis**. He is represented as a human figure with a beard and a floral headdress of a lotus.

NEFRU. The name of several queens in **Dynasties 11** and **12**. The mothers of **Intef II** and **Intef III** of Dynasty 11 were both named Nefru as was the daughter of Intef III who married her brother **Mentuhotep II**. In Dynasty 12 Nefru, daughter of **Amenemhat I**, married her brother **Senusret I** and was the mother of his successor **Amenemhat II**. She is mentioned at the royal court in the story of **Sinuhe**.

NEFRUPTAH (fl. c.1810 BC). The name of at least two royal princesses of **Dynasty 12**. The more notable was the daughter of **Amenemhat III** whose intact tomb was discovered in 1955–56 at **Hawara** near the **pyramid** of her father. Her body had been dissolved by water seepage, but jewellery and funerary material were recovered. A **sarcophagus** inscribed for her was also found in her father's burial chamber in his pyramid, but was either not used or used only temporarily. Her importance is witnessed by the fact that her name is written in a **cartouche**.

NEFRURE (fl. c.1280–1259 BC). Only daughter of **Thutmose II** and **Hatshepsut**. She was given a prominent role at court by her mother and was placed in the care of **Senenmut**. She was possibly destined to marry her half-brother **Thutmose III**. It is not certain if she survived her mother nor if this marriage took place, but she undoubtedly died fairly young and without issue.

NEHESY (reigned c.1700 BC). Throne name Aasehre. Ruler of **Dynasty 14** during the **Second Intermediate Period**. He is known from several monuments discovered in the eastern Delta region, notably from **Tanis**, **Bubastis**, **Leontopolis**, and **Avaris**. His capital was probably at **Xois** or Avaris, and his rule undoubtedly extended over part of the Delta region.

NEITH. Primeval Egyptian goddess worshipped primarily at **Sais**. She is represented as a woman with the red crown of **Lower Egypt**. Her symbol was a shield with crossed arrows representing an ancient connection with war. She was one of the tutelary goddesses protecting **canopic jars**.

NEITH (fl. c.2275 BC). Egyptian princess and queen. Daughter of **Pepy I**. She married her brother **Pepy II** and was buried in a subsidiary **pyramid** next to his at **Saqqara**.

NEKAU I (d. 664 BC). Throne name Menkheperre. The Greek form of his name was Necho. Originally prince of **Sais**, he was installed as puppet ruler of Egypt by the **Assyrians** and was killed by **Tantamani** in his reconquest of Egypt. He was the ancestor of **Dynasty 26**. See also **Psamtik I**.

NEKAU II (reigned 610–595 BC). Throne name Wehemibre. Son of **Psamtik I**. He attempted to stop the growth of Babylonian power by supporting the remnants of the defeated **Assyrian** army. Nekau defeated the army of King Josiah of Israel, killing the king when the Israelites attempted to block his forces, but was himself defeated by the Babylonians at the battle of Carchemish in 609 BC. He was forced to retreat but prevented a Babylonian invasion of Egypt. See also **Psamtik II**.

NEKHBET. Egyptian goddess of *Nekheb*, modern **Elkab**, represented as a vulture. She was the tutelary deity of **Upper Egypt** and as such appears in the *nebty* or two ladies name of the royal **titulary** and on the royal crown with the **uraeus** of **Wadjet**.

NEMTYEMSAF. The name of two kings of **Dynasty 6** who both had brief reigns. The name was wrongly read Antyemsaf by earlier Egyptologists. Nemtyemsaf I (reigned c.2287–78 BC), throne name Merenre, was the elder son of **Pepy I**. He died young and was buried at **Saqqara**. Nemtyemsaf II (reigned c.2184–83 BC) was the son of **Pepy II** and nephew of his namesake. If a later story reported by **Herodotus** is correct, he was assassinated after a brief reign and succeeded by his sister-queen **Nitocris**.

NEPHERITES see **NEFAARUD**.

NEPHTHYS. Egyptian goddess. Daughter of **Geb** and **Nut** and sister of **Isis**, **Osiris**, and **Seth**, whom she married. She was the chief mourner for Osiris along with Isis. Nephthys was one of the tutelary goddesses protecting coffins and **canopic jars**

NESBANEBDJED (reigned c.1069–1043 BC). The Greek version of his name was Smendes. Throne name Hedjkheperre. Founder of **Dynasty**

21. Mayor of **Tanis** at the end of **Dynasty 20**, he succeeded to the throne after **Ramesses XI** in obscure circumstances. His control of southern Egypt appears to have been minimal. He is mentioned in the story of **Wenamun** together with his wife **Tentamun**.

NESKHONS. The wife of **Pinudjem II, high priest of Amun** at **Thebes**. Possibly daughter of the high priest Nesbanebdjed and so niece of her husband. She was buried in the **royal cache** at Thebes. She bore the title of **viceroy of Kush** which must have been purely nominal and was used for the last time by her. See also **Dynasty 21**.

NEW KINGDOM (c.1550–1069 BC). The term used by Egyptologists to describe the period from **Dynasty 18** to **Dynasty 20** when Egypt was at the height of its power and prosperity and ruled an empire covering **Nubia** and Palestine-Syria. The era begins with the expulsion of the **Hyksos** from Egypt and the reunion of the country under **Ahmose I** ending the **Second Intermediate Period**. There followed the expansion into Nubia and the Levant culminating in the campaigns of **Thutmose III**. The increased wealth generated by these conquests led to major building campaigns, notably at **Karnak** and later under **Ramesses II** at **Pi-Ramesse, Abu Simbel**, and other sites. The god of **Thebes, Amun**, was elevated to the head of the divine pantheon. Increasing political and economic instability and the aggressive external threats led to the gradual abandonment of the empire by the end of **Dynasty 20** and the division of the country, heralding the **Third Intermediate Period**.

NILE. Modern word derived from Greek for the main waterway of ancient Egypt known simply then as the *itrw*, river, since there was no other river. It was the main artery for irrigation and transportation in Egypt. The Nile flooded annually from July to September fed by the rains in Ethiopia and brought fertile topsoil down onto Egyptian farmlands as well as washing out harmful salts. As a result Egypt was guaranteed good crop harvests unless the Nile was exceptionally low or high and thus presented the most stable area for settlement in the Middle East. The Nile also served as the main means of communication throughout its valley up to **Elephantine** (Aswan) where a series of **cataracts** or rapids impeded river traffic and so marked the historical border of Egypt. See also **Agriculture, Chronology**.

NIMLOT. The name of several princes of **Dynasty 22**. The earliest was the brother of King **Osorkon** the Elder and father of **Sheshonq I**. Both

Sheshonq I and **Osorkon II** had sons named Nimlot who were placed in control of the town of **Hierakonpolis**. During the invasion of **Piye**, King Nimlot of **Hermopolis** was one of his chief opponents. See also **Karomama**.

NITOCRIS (reigned c.2183–81 BC). Greek form of the name of a legendary queen. She is alleged by **Herodotus** to have succeeded her assassinated brother and husband and to have executed his murderers before committing suicide. If the legend is correct, she might have been the wife of **Nemtyemsaf II**. The Egyptian name Neithikert appears as the last ruler of **Dynasty 6** in the **Turin Royal Canon**, but nothing historical is known of the ruler who may well have been a man. See also **First Intermediate Period**.

NITOCRIS (fl. c.665–586 BC). Daughter of **Psamtik I** and Mehitenweskhet, daughter of the priest Harsiese. She was appointed in 656 BC as eventual heiress to the title of **God's Wife of Amun** and thereby ensured the recognition of her father as **pharaoh** by the authorities in **Thebes** headed by **Mentuemhat**. She later adopted her great-niece **Ankhnesneferibre** in 595 BC and died on 16 December 586 BC. A second Nitocris, daughter of **Ahmose II**, was destined to be the successor of Ankhnesneferibre, but her fate is unknown after the **Persian** conquest of Egypt.

NIUSERRE (reigned c.2445–2421 BC). Personal name Ini. Ruler of **Dynasty 5**. Son of **Neferirkare** and probably **Khentkaues** II. He was the eventual successor of the short-lived **Raneferef**, possibly after some confusion. He built a sun **temple** at Abu Ghurab near **Abusir**, excavated by a German expedition at the end of the nineteenth century and a **pyramid** and mortuary complex at Abusir excavated by Ludwig Borchardt in 1902–04 from which many fine reliefs were recovered. The **Palermo Stone** indicates that he sent expeditions to **Sinai** and to **Punt**.

NOMARCH see **NOME**.

NOME. Greek name for the 42 provincial divisions of Egypt known as *sepat* to the Egyptians. There were traditionally 22 **Upper Egyptian** nomes and 20 **Lower Egyptian** nomes, each with its own standard and symbols. The governors of the nomes, known as nomarchs in Greek, tended to increase their power at times of weakness of the central government, notably during the **First Intermediate Period**, but their powers were curbed during **Dynasty 12** and the offices may well have been suppressed under **Senusret III**.

NUBIA. Modern name for the area of the **Nile** Valley and its adjacent region south of **Elephantine**. It became important to Egypt as a source of minerals and served as an intermediary between Egypt and sub-Saharan Africa for luxury trade goods. Egyptian expeditions penetrated the area from the late **Predynastic Period** on raiding forays and in the **Old Kingdom** copper was mined and smelted at **Buhen** although it is unclear whether the Egyptian presence was permanent.

During the **Middle Kingdom** a determined attempt was made to subjugate the area and extensive fortresses were built along the Nile with the new border fixed at **Semna**. The collapse in the **Second Intermediate Period** led to an Egyptian withdrawal and the growth of a native kingdom based on **Kerma** in the area now known in Egyptian sources as Kush. The **Hyksos** sought an alliance with Kush against the rulers of **Thebes**, but both were to be destroyed by **Dynasty 18** which renewed the Egyptian conquest of the south, conquering Nubia down to **Napata** by the reign of **Thutmose III** and putting the new province under the rule of the **viceroy of Kush**.

Some native chieftains were allowed to remain, under strict control, but their families were sent to the Egyptian court to be Egyptianized. Nubia was exploited principally for its gold reserves which greatly enhanced Egyptian prestige and power. Numerous **temples** were built and Egyptian religion, especially worship of the god **Amun**, took a strong hold on the population. Egyptian administration collapsed in civil war and confusion at the end of **Dynasty 20**.

A new native kingdom was formed based at **Napata** and eventually under **Piye** and **Shabaqo** conquered Egypt itself to found **Dynasty 25**. The Nubians were driven out of Egypt by **Assyria,** but the dynasty persisted in Nubia and later moved its capital to **Meroe.** Tension remained between the Meroitic kingdom and the Ptolemaic and Roman rulers of Egypt over control of the area just south of Elephantine, and Nubian rulers were assiduous in their worship at the temple of **Philae** even after Egypt was Christianized.

The Meroitic kingdom fell apart in the fourth century AD partly under pressure from invading desert tribes such as the Nobatae which gave the area its modern name. Three local kingdoms developed and adopted Christianity in the sixth century but were eventually overwhelmed by Muslim forces and disappeared in the fifteenth century. The successive constructions of dams at Aswan and the subsequent flooding have led to major archaeological campaigns in Lower Nubia in 1898–1902, 1907–12, 1929–34, and 1960–65 so that, although the region is now flooded, its archaeological record is better attested than many areas of Egypt proper.

NUBIAN RESCUE CAMPAIGN. The construction of the new Aswan High Dam which began in 1960 resulted in the creation of a massive lake flooding much of Lower Nubia from the First **Cataract** at Aswan to nearly the Third **Cataract**. Under the auspices of UNESCO, following an appeal by the Egyptian and Sudanese governments in 1959, an intensive archaeological campaign was organized by the international community in 1960–65, involving 27 nations. Nineteen temples or monuments were removed from threatened sites, notably the temples at **Abu Simbel**, **Dendur**, and **Philae** and parts of the temples of **Gerf Hussein** and **Semna**.

NUN. God of the primeval waters of chaos from which emerged a mound on which the god **Atum** appeared.

NUT. Egyptian goddess of the sky and wife of **Geb**, the god of earth. She is represented as a naked woman often in an arched position over her husband and is depicted on the inside of coffins as a protector of the dead. Mother of **Osiris**, **Isis**, **Seth**, and **Nephthys**.

NYMAATHAP (fl. c.2667 BC). Queen of **Dynasty 3**, either mother or wife of **Djoser**. She has been seen as a link between **Dynasty 2** and Dynasty 3, but no firm evidence has yet been found of her exact position in either dynasty.

NYNETJER (reigned c.2860 BC). Third ruler of **Dynasty 2** and successor to **Raneb**. Part of his reign is recorded on the **Palermo Stone** which mentions military campaigns and the **Apis** bull. He appears to have been buried at **Saqqara**. See also **Peribsen**.

- O -

OBELISK. Modern word for an Egyptian monolithic stone monument consisting of a thin shaft whose top is shaped as a **pyramidion**. Ancient

Egyptian *tekhen*. Small obelisks are known, but most are tall and were located in **temples**. The development of the obelisk was linked to the introduction of the cult of the sun-god **Re** whose rising rays would strike the top of the obelisk, often sheeted in gold. The first obelisks seem to have been constructed at **Heliopolis** and the sun-temples of **Dynasty 5**, but their use in temples in the **New Kingdom** and later was widespread. Two obelisks would be placed in front of the main **pylon** of the major temples. Scenes from the temple of **Hatshepsut** at **Deir el-Bahri** depict the transport of an obelisk from the quarries at Aswan to **Thebes**, while a broken one remains in the quarry. Many obelisks were carried off by the Roman conquerors to decorate Rome, while others were removed in modern times to major European and North American cities.

OLD KINGDOM (c.2686–2181 BC). A term used by Egyptologists to refer to the stable period—from either **Dynasty 3** or **Dynasty 4** to the end of **Dynasty 6**—which followed from the **Early Dynastic Period**. It would appear that Egypt at that time had a highly organized autocratic government which could mobilize its resources and manpower in massive construction works such as the **pyramids**. The period ended with the collapse of central authority possibly due to famine or increasingly powerful regional governors, or nomarchs, ushering in the **First Intermediate Period**.

ONURIS see **ANHUR**.

OSIRIS. Greek form for the Egyptian god of the dead *Wsir,* lord of the underworld. Son of **Geb** and **Nut** and husband of **Isis**. According to legend, he was originally a king of Egypt but was murdered and dismembered by his brother **Seth**. His widow Isis recovered and buried his remains. He was also a god of vegetation and renewal. The dead king, and later any deceased individual, was identified with Osiris but the individual also had to be judged by Osiris before entering the next life. Osiris is depicted as a mummiform figure with a feathered crown holding a crook and flail. He was early amalgamated with the god Khentyamnetyu of **Abydos** which became the principal place of his worship and where his tomb was said to be located.

OSORKON (reigned c. 984–978 BC). A king of **Dynasty 21**, now known to Egyptologists as Osorkon the Elder. Throne name Aakheperre setepenre. Son of the Libyan chief Sheshonq and Mehtenweskhet. He briefly

gained the throne from the Tanite king **Amenemope**, but it then passed
to **Siamun** apparently of another family. His nephew **Sheshonq I** re-
established the Libyans on the throne, founding **Dynasty 22**. The true
form of his name was only established after the later kings Osorkon had
been numbered so he does not appear in that sequence.

OSORKON I (reigned c.924–889 BC). Throne name Sekhemkheperre
setepenre. Epithet meryamun. Son of **Sheshonq I** of **Dynasty 22** and
Karomama. He established a major fortress at Per-Sekhemkheperre. He
is attested in close relations with the port of **Byblos** on the eastern Mediterranean coast. He married Maatkare daughter of **Pasebakhaenniut II**,
by whom he was the father of Sheshonq whom he installed as **high
priest of Amun** in succession to his brother **Iuput**. This son wrote his
name in a royal **cartouche** and may be identified with the ephemeral
king **Sheshonq II**. See also **Takelot I**.

OSORKON II (reigned c.874–850 BC). Throne name Usimaatre setepenamun. Epithet meryamun sibast. Son of **Takelot I** of **Dynasty 22** and
Kapes. He continued the dynastic policy of putting sons in key positions,
installing Sheshonq as **high priest of Ptah** in **Memphis** and Nimlot as
high priest of **Heryshef** in **Herakleopolis** and later **high priest of Amun**
in **Karnak**. He erected a festival hall in **Bubastis** to celebrate his **jubilee**. He was buried at **Tanis** and his intact tomb was rediscovered in
1939. See also **Takelot II**.

OSORKON III (reigned c.777–749 BC). Throne name Usimaatre setepenamun with the epithet siese. Ruler of **Dynasty 23**. Son of Queen
Karomama. He is attested mainly by monuments in **Thebes** and **Middle
Egypt**. He installed his son **Takelot III** as **high priest of Amun** in **Karnak** and his daughter **Shepenwepet I** as **God's Wife of Amun**. He was
recognized as ruler in Thebes and Middle Egypt. See also **Rudamun**.

OSORKON IV (reigned c.730–715 BC). Throne name possibly Aakheperre setepenamun. He was probably the last ruler of **Dynasty 22** and
ruled only in the area of **Tanis** and **Bubastis**. He is named on the **stela**
of **Piye** and attested in **Assyrian** sources in 716 BC. He may be the ruler
who appears in the Bible as So, king of Egypt. He was followed by the
Nubian rulers of **Dynasty 25**.

OSORKON (fl. c.850–785 BC). The name of a **high priest of Amun**, son
of **Takelot II** and Queen **Karomama**. He was installed in office by his

father but faced opposition from the Thebans and was involved in a series of campaigns to claim his office. He recorded his biography on a long inscription on the **temple** wall at **Karnak**. It has been suggested that he is to be identified with a later King **Osorkon III** who also had the title of high priest and is known mainly from monuments in **Thebes** and **Middle Egypt**. If so, Osorkon must have lived to a great age.

OSTRACON. Plural ostraca. Greek name used by Egyptologists to designate flakes of limestone or pottery with ink inscriptions in **hieroglyphic**, **hieratic**, **demotic**, and later Greek which are often found at many sites in Egypt. Some texts may be trial pieces or school exercises, but many are complete documents which may contain literary texts or non-literary material such as legal texts, tax documents, or letters. These often provide valuable contributions to the study of Egyptian literature and daily life, notably the thousands of ostraca found at **Deir el-Medina**.

OXYRHYNCHUS. Greek name of a town in **Middle Egypt,** ancient *Permedjed*, capital of the 19th **Upper Egyptian nome** and modern el-Behnasa. Little is known of the site in the Pharaonic Period as it is attested only from the **New Kingdom**. The principal deity worshipped there was **Seth** along with the sacred oxyrhynchus fish. Remains date from the **Graeco-Roman Period**. The site was excavated in 1896–1907 when thousands of **papyri** from that time were recovered. These have included known and lost literary texts and much documentary material.

- P -

PACHOMIUS (292–346 AD). Egyptian Christian monk and saint. He was born in **Upper Egypt** and later served in the Roman army in Egypt. On leaving the army, he settled at the village of Shenest in **Middle Egypt** and converted to Christianity, becoming an ascetic hermit at Tabennese. He was joined by other disciples whom he organized into the first monastic community with a common rule. This gradually expanded in his lifetime to nine monasteries and two convents. He transformed the previously ascetic solitary style of living into that of a monastic existence which idea soon spread throughout the Christian world. See also **Anthony**.

PALERMO STONE. A fragment of diorite on which is inscribed the annals of the kings of Egypt from the **Predynastic Period** to **Dynasty 5**, now in the Palermo Museum. While the early section is necessarily vague, later reigns are listed year by year with mention of the one important event of the year. Other fragments of this stone or similar ones have been located, but all remain too broken to give a detailed account of the period. See also **Chronology**.

PANEB (fl. c.1235–1190 BC). Foreman of the community of **Deir el-Medina** at the end of **Dynasty 19**. Son of the workman Nefersenut and Iuy. He was adopted by the childless foreman Neferhotep. He appears in the workforce at the end of the reign of **Ramesses II** when he is attested with his wife Wab. On the death of Neferhotep, apparently killed in the civil war between **Sety II** and **Amenmesse**, he succeeded to his adopted father's office. At the end of Dynasty 19 or possibly early **Dynasty 20** he was accused by Amennakhte, brother of Neferhotep, of various crimes including bribing the **vizier** to obtain the office of foreman, stealing from the royal tombs, and oppressive behaviour towards his fellow workmen, notably adultery with some of their wives. He disappears abruptly from the records and a later reference implies that he was punished for his misdeeds.

PAPYRUS. Plural papyri. Aquatic plant found in the swamps of ancient Egypt but now extinct in that country. The name derives from the Greek and probably from ancient Egyptian. The pith of the plant, when cut into strips, was joined using its natural adhesive properties to form sheets which were never more than 50 centimetres high. These sheets in turn could be glued together to form rolls or cut down to form smaller writing surfaces. Papyrus became the standard medium of written communication in ancient Egypt and many examples survive of literary, religious, and documentary usage. The earliest uninscribed example dates to **Dynasty 1**. Papyrus was later used outside of Egypt throughout the ancient world before the invention of paper. See also **Wisdom Literature**.

PASEBAKHAENNIUT I (reigned c.1039–991 BC). The Greek form of his name is Psusennes. Throne name Akheperre setepenre. He ruled in the north while **Thebes** was under the control of the **high priests of Amun**. He was buried in **Tanis** and his tomb was discovered intact by a French expedition headed by Pierre Montet in 1939. See also **Third Intermediate Period**.

PASEBAKHAENNIUT II (reigned 959–945 BC). Throne name Titkheperure setepenre with the epithets Hor and meryamun. Last ruler of **Dy-**

nasty 21. He is generally believed to be identical with the like-named **high priest of Amun**, son of **Pinudjem II**. Little is known of his reign. His daughter **Maatkare** married **Osorkon I**, second ruler of **Dynasty 22**. See also **Third Intermediate Period**.

PASER (fl. c.1300–1255 BC). Southern **vizier** of **Sety I** and **Ramesses II**. Son of the **high priest of Amun** Nebnejteru and Meritre. He began his career as chamberlain and later chief chamberlain to Sety I who promoted him to the post of vizier. Paser continued in office under Ramesses until at least year 21 when he was in correspondence with the **Hittite** court at the time of the peace treaty with Egypt. He was in direct charge of the community at **Deir el-Medina** where he appears to have been much respected. Paser is known from a large number of monuments, including his tomb (no. 106) at **Thebes**. He was later rewarded with the post of high priest of Amun.

PASHERMUT (reigned c.393 BC). The Greek version of his name was Psammuthis. Throne name Userre setepenptah. Obscure ruler of **Dynasty 29** and probable successor to **Nefaarud I** and rival to **Hakor**. He is attested in inscriptions from **Thebes** and **Memphis**.

PEDUBAST I (reigned c.818–793 BC). Founder of **Dynasty 23**. Throne name Usermaatre setepenenamun. Epithet meryamun. He appears to have assumed the royal **titulary** during the reign of **Sheshonq III** of **Dynasty 22** and founded a parallel line of rulers recognized in **Thebes**. Little is known of his reign or that of his contemporary **Iuput** I. His effective successor was **Osorkon III**. See also **Third Intermediate Period**.

PEDUBAST II. Throne name Sehetepibre. Minor kinglet who flourished at the end of the **Third Intermediate Period**. He may well be the king of **Tanis** of this name who is mentioned in an **Assyrian** inscription of 671 BC.

PEFTJAUAWYBAST (reigned c.730 BC). Throne name Neferkare. He is attested as ruler of **Herakleopolis** at the end of the **Third Intermediate Period** when the country was divided into various local kinglets with full royal **titularies**. He married a daughter of **Rudamun** of **Dynasty 23**.

PEPY I (reigned c.2321–2287 BC). Throne name Meryre. Son of **Teti** of **Dynasty 6** and Queen **Iput** I. He had a lengthy reign and is attested at various sites, notably at **Hierakonpolis** where a life-size copper statue of the king and a smaller one, possibly of his son **Nemtyemsaf** I, were discovered. There is a mysterious reference in the inscription of **Weni** to a disgraced queen who was replaced by two sisters both renamed **Ankhesenmeryre** otherwise Ankhesenpepy. His other wives included Nubwenet and Inenek-Inti whose tombs next to the **pyramid** of the king were identified in 1990 and 1992. The king was buried in a pyramid at **Saqqara** whose discovery in 1880 revealed the first examples of **pyramid texts.**

PEPY II (reigned c.2278–2184 BC). Throne name Neferkare. Son of **Pepy I** and **Ankhesenmeryre** II. He succeeded his half-brother **Nemtyemsaf** I. As he was still a child, his mother and her brother apparently ruled on his behalf. Very little information has survived about his reign except its length. Both the **Turin Royal Canon** and **Manetho** imply that he reigned over 90 years. The dynasty ended in confusion shortly after his death so his longevity and increasing weakness of rule may have contributed to its downfall. The king was buried in a **pyramid** at **Saqqara** surrounded by three subsidiary pyramids of his queens **Iput** II, **Neith** (who was his sister or half-sister), and Udjebten as well as **Ankhesenpepy** who was buried in the tomb of Iput.

PERIBSEN (reigned c.2700 BC). Ruler of **Dynasty 2** and successor to **Nynetjer.** There appears to have been a religious conflict in his reign between the followers of the gods **Horus** and **Seth.** Peribsen changed the standard inscription of the royal **titulary,** writing his name in a **serekh** not as a Horus name but as one preceded by that of Seth.

PERSIA. Ancient kingdom situated in modern Iran. The Persian king Cyrus the Great overthrew the Babylonian kingdom and annexed most of western Asia creating the largest empire then known. His son **Cambyses** conquered Egypt in 525 BC and added it to the empire. Persian rule in Egypt was unpopular, and the Persians were later accused of neglecting Egyptian religion and withdrawing **temple** privileges. The Persian governor or **satrap** was usually a member of the royal family. The Persians were expelled in 401 BC by **Amyrtaeos.** In 343 BC the Persian king Artaxerxes III reconquered Egypt, driving out the last native ruler, **Nakhthorheb. Alexander the Great** put an end to Persian rule in 332 BC and was welcomed as a liberator by the Egyptians.

PETOSIRIS (fl. c.330 BC). High priest of **Thoth** at **Hermopolis**. Son of the high priest of Thoth Sishu and Ankhefenkhons. He succeeded his elder brother as high priest and probably held office at the end of the **Persian** Period and the beginning of Greek rule. He was the owner of a magnificent tomb at **Tuna el-Gebel** which was discovered in 1919. In the biographical inscriptions he claims to have restored the neglected **temples** of his city. See also **Graeco-Roman Period**.

PETRIE, WILLIAM MATTHEW FLINDERS (1853–1942). British archaeologist. He was born in Charlton on 3 June 1853 and was educated at home, his interest in archaeology being encouraged by his father. Petrie was first sent to Egypt to survey the **pyramid** of **Khufu** in 1880–82. He later excavated for the **Egypt Exploration Fund** in 1884–86 and again from 1896–1905, but disagreements led to his founding of the Egyptian Research Account and later the British School of Archaeology in Egypt to finance his independent excavations by donations from subscribers. Petrie carried out work in many sites in Egypt, notably **Tanis**, **Abydos**, **Hawara**, **Lahun**, **Amarna**, and **Thebes**. He was the first archaeologist to stress the importance of small uninscribed objects such as amulets and pottery which could be used to date the consecutive archaeological levels of a site and strongly criticized those who sought only monumental inscribed antiquities. He believed in prompt publication, but often then omitted much detailed evidence. Petrie's rather austere lifestyle in the field owed much to his desire to expend his resources on the excavations. He was appointed the first professor of Egyptology at University College, London, in 1892, retiring in 1933. In the 1920s he turned his attention to excavation in Palestine. He died in Jerusalem on 28 July 1942. His personal collection of antiquities, notebooks, and papers are preserved in the Petrie Museum of Archaeology, University College, London.

PHARAOH. Modern word derived through Hebrew to designate the ruler of Egypt. The ancient Egyptian term *peraa,* or great house, was used at first to refer to the royal court as a whole and was not originally a synonym for king, ancient Egyptian *nesu,* but was used with this meaning from the **New Kingdom** onwards. Its first known use as a title is in the reign of **Sheshonq I**.

PHILAE. Greek name for an island in the **Nile** south of **Elephantine** where a **temple** to **Isis** and associated buildings were constructed, dating from the **Late Period** to the **Roman Period**. Temples were also erected to deities from **Nubia**, and the site became a place of pilgrimage for Nubians and Egyptians. The last known **hieroglyphic** inscription (394 AD) and the last **demotic** inscription (452 AD) are recorded here. Following the advent of Christianity in Egypt, the temples remained open to accommodate the worshippers from the empire of **Meroe** until the time of Justinian who closed them. In 1972–79 the buildings on the site were dismantled and reconstructed on a neighboring island to preserve them from the new lake caused by the Aswan High Dam.

PHILIP ARRHIDAEUS (reigned 323–317 BC). Son of Philip II of Macedon and Larinna and half-brother of **Alexander the Great**. Although mentally incompetent, he was proclaimed his brother's successor and ruled jointly with his nephew **Alexander** until he was murdered at the order of his step-mother Olympias. He never visited Egypt but his name is recorded on work in the **temples** of **Karnak**, **Hermopolis**, and **Sebennytos**.

PIANKH (fl. c.1094–1064 BC). High priest of Amun and military general at the end of **Dynasty 20**. He led his army against the **Viceroy of Kush** Panehsi whose forces had overrun **Thebes**, advancing into Nubia although it is not clear if he gained an outright victory. Letters by him on campaign have survived. It is not clear if he followed or preceded **Herihor**, but he was the ancestor of the independent high priests such as **Pinudjem** I who flourished under **Dynasty 21**.

PIANKHY see **PIYE**.

PIMAY (reigned c.773–767 BC). Throne name Usimmatre setepenere or setepenamun. Epithet meryamun. An obscure monarch of **Dynasty 22**. Probably son of **Sheshonq III** or **IV**. He was the father of **Sheshonq V**. See also **Third Intermediate Period**.

PINUDJEM. The name of two **high priests of Amun** who flourished in **Dynasty 21**. Pinudjem I (fl. c.1064–26 BC) was the son of **Piankh** and succeeded as high priest and governor of **Upper Egypt** during the reign of **Nesbanebdjed**. He was effective ruler of the south and later took royal titles with the throne name Khaheperre setepenamun. He was succeeded by his two sons **Masaharta** (fl. c.1044–36 BC) and **Menkheperre** (fl. c.1035–986 BC) and his two grandsons Nesbanebdjed (fl.

c.986–85 BC) and Pinudjem II (fl. c.985–69 BC) who maintained Theban independence. The marriage links between the Theban family and the royal family of Dynasty 21 in **Tanis** are not always clear. His great-grandson **Pasebakhaenniut II** eventually became ruler of the whole country.

PI-RAMESSES. The northern capital city of **Ramesses II** built in the Delta at modern Qantir near the site of the **Hyksos** capital **Avaris**. The building seems to have begun under **Sety I**, but Ramesses II enlarged the city and gave it his name. Several poems in praise of the city survive. The city seems to have been abandoned after **Dynasty 20**, and many of its monuments were used to decorate the cities of **Tanis** and **Bubastis**. It is currently being excavated by a German expedition, which has uncovered the royal stables and other palace buildings.

PIYE (reigned c.747–712 BC). Ruler of **Nubia** formerly known as Piankhy. Successor of **Kashta**. Throne names Usimaatre, Sneferre. He is known principally from a **stela** detailing his military campaign against Egypt. He appears to have inherited control over parts of southern Egypt and he temporarily extended Nubian control throughout the country by defeating local princes, notably **Tefnakhte**, prince of **Sais**, although this was largely lost on his return to **Nubia**. He was buried in el-Kurru near **Napata** and was succeeded by his brother **Shabaqo** who conquered Egypt and founded **Dynasty 25**. See also **Shepenwepet**.

PREDYNASTIC PERIOD (c.5000–3100 BC). The period in Egyptian history from the development of permanent settlements until the creation of the united Egyptian state with **Dynasty I**. The period is subdivided into the cultures named from the sites of el-**Badari** and **Naqada**.

PREHERWENEMEF (fl. c.1280–1260 BC). Third son of **Ramesses II** by **Nefertari**. He is listed as the king's fourth son and appears in inscriptions from the beginning of Ramesses II's reign. His fate is not known but he presumably died before his father and was buried in the tomb of the king's sons (no. 5) in the **Valley of the Kings**. A like-named son of **Ramesses III** is known from his tomb (no. 42) in the **Valley of the Queens**.

PSAMMETICHUS see **PSAMTIK**.

PSAMMUTHIS see **PASHERMUT**.

PSAMTIK I (reigned 664–610 BC). Psammetichus in Greek. Throne name Wahibre. Son of **Nekau I** of **Sais**. On his father's death in battle against **Tantamani** in 664 BC, he fled to **Assyria** and was restored as puppet ruler by Assyrian forces in 663 BC, founding **Dynasty 26**. He skilfully reunited Egypt under his rule with the help of Greek mercenaries and by installing his daughter **Nitocris** as **God's Wife of Amun** in **Thebes**. He gradually disentangled himself from Assyrian control and restored Egyptian independence. See also **Mentuemhat**.

PSAMTIK II (reigned 595–589 BC). Throne name Neferibre. Son and successor of **Nekau II**. He sought to restore Egyptian prestige by a campaign into **Nubia** recorded by graffiti of his soldiers at **Abu Simbel** and also intrigued in Palestine. He arranged the adoption of his daughter **Ankhnesneferibre** as **God's Wife of Amun**. He died on 10 February 589 BC. See also **Wahibre**.

PSAMTIK III (reigned 526–525 BC). Throne name Ankhkaenre. Son of **Ahmose II** and Tantheta, daughter of the priest of **Ptah** Padineith. Shortly after his accession, he faced an invasion by **Cambyses**, king of **Persia**, who conquered Egypt and took him prisoner. He and his son were later executed for plotting against the new ruler.

PTAH. Chief god of **Memphis**, depicted as a mummiform man with a cap and beard, holding a sceptre. His principal epithet was Lord of *Maat* or Truth. He was associated with crafts. Ptah was worshipped throughout the country as one of the main deities. The priests of Memphis credited him with the first act of creation. His consort was the goddess **Sakhmet,** and with their son **Nefertum** they formed the Memphite **triad**. The temple of Ptah at Memphis is now in a ruined state with little remaining of its ancient splendour which may have rivalled that of **Karnak**.

PTAH-SOKAR-OSIRIS see **SOKAR**.

PTAHHOTEP (fl. c.2400 BC). Vizier of **Djedkare** Isesi of **Dynasty 5**. He is the alleged author of a text of **wisdom literature** which is known from later copies from the **Middle** and **New Kingdoms**.

PTAHSHEPSES (fl. c.2440 BC). Vizier who held office under **Niuserre** whose daughter Khamerernebty he married. He had a magnificent tomb built at **Abusir** which has been excavated by a Czech expedition from the 1970s.

PTOLEMAIC PERIOD (323–30 BC). The term used by Egyptologists for the period during which Egypt was ruled by the Macedonian general **Ptolemy I** and his descendants. The beginning of the period varies, as Ptolemy was in charge from 323 BC but did not openly assume independent rule until 305 BC. Many **temples** from **Upper Egypt** erected or refurbished by the Ptolemies survive from this time. However, the government was carried on from **Alexandria** by the Greek ruling class and Egyptian culture, although respected, remained secondary to the interests of the rulers.

PTOLEMY I SOTER (c.367–282 BC). Son of Lagus and Arsinoe. Macedonian nobleman and military commander under **Alexander the Great**. In 323 BC, on the death of Alexander, he secured the governorship of Egypt which he ruled virtually as an independent state after disposing of **Cleomenes**. He expanded his control to Cyprus and parts of Syria, Greece, and Asia Minor. He assumed the title of king in 305 BC. Unlike other would-be successors of Alexander, he had no pretensions to try to control the entire empire. Ptolemy I married several wives: the Persian Artacama, daughter of Artabazus, whom he presumably abandoned; the Macedonian Eurydice, daughter of the regent Antipater; and finally **Berenice I**, leading to court intrigues over his succession until he made his son **Ptolemy II**, by his last wife, **co-regent**. He died apparently in the first half of the year 282 BC. See also **Alexander II**.

PTOLEMY II PHILADELPHUS (308–246 BC). Son of **Ptolemy I** and **Berenice I**. He was named **co-regent** with his father in 285 BC and succeeded to sole rule in 282 BC. His reign was prosperous, allowing the king to undertake major building works including the *Pharos* or Lighthouse, Library, and Museum at **Alexandria**. He scandalized Greek public opinion by divorcing his wife **Arsinoe I** and marrying his full sister **Arsinoe II**. He died in January 246 BC and was succeeded by his son **Ptolemy III**.

PTOLEMY III EUERGETES (c.284–222 BC). Son of **Ptolemy II** and his first wife, **Arsinoe I**. He succeeded to the throne in 246 BC and continued to expand Egypt's control in Syria and Asia Minor. He also acquired **Cyrene** through marriage with its heiress **Berenice II**. He died between October and December 222 BC and was succeeded by his son **Ptolemy IV**.

PTOLEMY IV PHILOPATOR (c.244–205 BC). Son of **Ptolemy III** and **Berenice II**. He married his sister **Arsinoe III**. He pursued an aggressive policy in Asia in an attempt to gain control of Palestine-Syria, but faced a major revolt in the south where native rulers **Harwennefer** and **Ankhwennefer** were proclaimed. He appears to have died in late 205 BC, but his death was initially concealed by his court. He was succeeded by his son **Ptolemy V**.

PTOLEMY V EPIPHANES (210–180 BC). Son of **Ptolemy IV** and **Arsinoe III**. He was born on 9 October 210 and was at first under the regency of various courtiers. He faced difficulties throughout his reign with revolts in Egypt which were eventually suppressed and clashes over Ptolemaic possessions in Syria and Palestine which were lost in 200 BC. He married a Seleucid princess, **Cleopatra I**. He died in September/October 180 BC and was succeeded by his son **Ptolemy VI**.

PTOLEMY VI PHILOMETER (c.186–145 BC). Son of **Ptolemy V** and **Cleopatra I**. He succeeded in 180 BC at a young age under the regency of his mother and later courtiers. When Egypt was threatened by **Antiochus IV**, the royal family was united through his marriage to his sister **Cleopatra II** in 176 BC and their joint rule together with his brother **Ptolemy VIII** from 170 BC. He was briefly captured and then released by Antiochus IV during the latter's invasion in 169 BC, and his rule was restored by a Roman ultimatum to the Syrian king to withdraw from Egypt in 168 BC after a second invasion. His reign was undermined by war with his brother, who was expelled to **Cyrene** in 163 BC. He attempted to regain Egyptian possessions in Syria in 145 BC but died of wounds sustained in a battle near Antioch in which his forces were victorious. His elder son **Ptolemy Eupator** died in his lifetime so he was initially succeeded by his younger son **Ptolemy VII**.

PTOLEMY VII NEOS PHILOPATOR (c.162–145 BC). Son of **Ptolemy VI** and **Cleopatra II**. He was made joint ruler with his father but was killed in 145 BC when his uncle **Ptolemy VIII** returned to Egypt and seized the throne.

PTOLEMY VIII EUERGETES II (c.182–116 BC). Nicknamed Physcon, or pot belly. Younger son of **Ptolemy V** and **Cleopatra I**. He was made joint ruler with his brother **Ptolemy VI** in 170 BC and expelled him from the country in 164 but was himself forced to retire to **Cyrene** in 163 BC. On his brother's death in 145 BC, Ptolemy VIII returned to Egypt and seized the throne, murdering his nephew **Ptolemy VII**. He married firstly in 145 BC his sister **Cleopatra II** by whom he had one son **Ptolemy Memphites,** whom he eventually put to death. Later about 140 BC he married his niece, Cleopatra II's daughter **Cleopatra III**, thus precipitating a civil war with his sister in 132 BC. He was initially driven out of Egypt but regained control in 130 BC. The civil war was finally resolved in 124 BC by the recognition of Cleopatra II's position as senior queen. Ptolemy VIII died on 28 June 116 BC leaving Egypt to Cleopatra III and whichever of her two sons, **Ptolemy IX** or **Ptolemy X**, she chose to rule with her.

PTOLEMY IX SOTER II (142–80 BC). Nicknamed Lathyrus or chickpea. Elder son of **Ptolemy VIII** and **Cleopatra III**. He was possibly born on 18 February 142 BC. King of Cyprus under his father, he succeeded him despite the wishes of his mother who preferred his younger brother, the future **Ptolemy X**. He was forced to divorce his sister-wife **Cleopatra IV** in favor of a younger sister, **Cleopatra V Selene**. He was expelled from Egypt in 107 BC by his mother and brother but was able to return in 88 BC and reign until his death in March 80 BC with his daughter **Cleopatra Berenice III**.

PTOLEMY X ALEXANDER I (c. 140–88 BC). Younger son of **Ptolemy VIII** and **Cleopatra III**. He was his mother's choice as ruler in 116 BC but was forced to acknowledge his elder brother **Ptolemy IX**. Later king of Cyprus, he ousted his elder brother in 107 BC and reigned in Egypt with his niece **Cleopatra Berenice III** as consort until expelled by a popular revolt in 89 BC. He returned with Syrian forces but was again expelled to Lycia. He was killed in a sea battle in March 88 BC as he attempted to flee to Cyprus.

PTOLEMY XI ALEXANDER II (c.105–80 BC). Son of **Ptolemy X** and an unknown wife. He was living in exile until chosen as the consort of his cousin **Cleopatra Berenice III** on the death of her father **Ptolemy IX**. He murdered his wife shortly afterwards and was in turn killed by the Alexandrian mob in June 80 BC. He was succeeded by his cousin **Ptolemy XII**.

PTOLEMY XII THEOS PHILOPATOR PHILADELPHUS NEOS DI-ONYSIUS (d. 51 BC). Illegitimate son of **Ptolemy IX** by an unknown mistress. He was chosen as ruler on the murder of **Ptolemy XI** and soon gained the nickname Auletes, or flute-player. He was expelled in 58 BC, being replaced by his daughter **Berenice IV**, but was restored in 55 BC by Roman troops and executed his daughter. His wife was **Cleopatra VI Tryphaena** and may have been his sister, but it is not known if she was the mother of all his children, notably **Cleopatra VII**. See also **Arsinoe, Ptolemy XIII, Ptolemy XIV**.

PTOLEMY XIII (c.61–47 BC). Elder son of **Ptolemy XII** and possibly **Cleopatra VI Tryphaena**. He succeeded jointly with his sister and wife **Cleopatra VII** but soon fell out with her and civil war broke out between the siblings. The situation was changed by the arrival of Julius **Caesar** who soon supported Cleopatra. The king was defeated in battle against the Roman forces and apparently drowned in the **Nile** during the action in January 47 BC.

PTOLEMY XIV PHILOPATOR (c.59–44 BC). Younger son of **Ptolemy XII** and possibly **Cleopatra VI Tryphaena**. He replaced his older brother as consort of **Cleopatra VII**, but his position was purely nominal and he was probably murdered by her.

PTOLEMY XV PHILOPATOR PHILOMETER (47–30 BC). Son of **Cleopatra VII** who named **Julius Caesar** as the father. The boy was nicknamed Caesarion. He was made joint ruler of Egypt with his mother in 44 BC on the death of his uncle **Ptolemy XIV**. He was executed while trying to escape from Roman forces following the conquest of Egypt in 30 BC.

PTOLEMY EUPATOR (c.163–152 BC). Elder son of **Ptolemy VI** and **Cleopatra II**. He was named **co-regent** with his father but died young.

PTOLEMY MEMPHITES (c.144–131 BC). Son of **Ptolemy VIII** and **Cleopatra II**. Heir to the throne, he was executed by his father in 131 BC after his mother had revolted in an attempt to overthrow her husband.

PTOLEMY PHILADELPHUS (b. 36 BC). Younger son of Marcus **Antonius** and **Cleopatra VII**. He was assigned Syria and the eastern part of the Roman Empire by his father in 34 BC. He was taken prisoner by **Augustus** in 30 BC, but his ultimate fate is unknown.

PUNT. A country located along the Red Sea coast, probably in Somalia, to which Egyptian expeditions were periodically sent from the time of the **Old Kingdom** to the **New Kingdom** to obtain exotic products such as incense. An expedition sent by Queen **Hatshepsut** is recorded in detail on reliefs on her funerary **temple** at **Deir el-Bahri.**

PYLON. Greek name for the massive stone gateway in front of Egyptian **temples** and also within several of the larger temples. The pylon was decorated with scenes of the king triumphant over his enemies and had emplacements for massive flagstaffs. **Obelisks** and large royal sculptures were often placed in front of the pylon.

PYRAMID. Greek name for the four-sided triangular-shaped monument which marked the burial of kings from the **Old Kingdom** to the **Middle Kingdom.** Rulers from **Dynasties 1–2** were buried in mud-brick **mastaba** tombs, but in **Dynasty 3** a new architectural form in stone was evolved ascribed according to legend to the **vizier Imhotep** for his master **Djoser.** The stone step-pyramid at **Saqqara** consisted of a series of six mastabas placed on top of each other covering the burial chamber beneath. The tomb complex also included a mortuary **temple** and other ritual buildings.

This type of complex was used in the course of the dynasty, but at the beginning of **Dynasty 4** the true pyramid with its **pyramidion** capstone was created for **Snefru** at **Meidum** and later **Dahshur.** The pyramids of **Khufu, Khafre**, and **Menkaure** at **Giza** represent the high point of pyramid construction. Each of these pyramids had a mortuary temple associated with it as well as a valley temple reached by water and connected to the main pyramid by a dry causeway. The tombs of the queens in small pyramids and favoured courtiers in mastabas surrounded the king's tomb.

Later pyramids were built on a less lavish scale with rubble cores and only one course of stone masonry on the outside, but were highly decorated with reliefs in the temples and causeway walls and **pyramid texts** inscribed inside the burial chamber. Pyramid-building continued into the **Middle Kingdom** although the pyramids of **Dynasty 12** in the **Fayum** area often had a mud-brick core. At the beginning of **Dynasty 18**, pyramids were abandoned by the rulers in favour of secluded tombs in the **Valley of the Kings**, but the royal mortuary temples remained—now located near the **Nile**—and some of considerable size. Small mud-brick pyramids with a stone pyramidion were now used to mark burials of private individuals. The use of small pyramids for royal burials with associated chapels was revived by **Dynasty 25** at cemeteries near **Napata** and **Meroe**.

PYRAMID TEXTS. Religious texts inscribed on the walls of the royal **pyramid** to enable the king to pass safely to the next life. The earliest texts are inscribed in the pyramid of **Unas**, last ruler of **Dynasty 5**, and were discovered in 1881. The texts were first discovered in 1880 in the pyramid of **Pepy I** of **Dynasty 6**. See also **Afterlife**.

PYRAMIDION. The capstone of a **pyramid.** After pyramids were discontinued for royal burials, mud-brick pyramids were placed on top of private tombs, as at **Thebes** surmounted by a stone pyramidion often inscribed with a prayer to and decorated with a figure of the sun-god **Re-**Harakhty.

- Q -

QAA (reigned c.2915 BC). Eighth and final ruler of **Dynasty 1** and successor to **Semerkhet**. Like his predecessors, he was buried in **Abydos** where his tomb has recently been re-excavated by a German expedition. A fine **stela** of the king is now in the **Louvre Museum**. See also **Dynasty 2**.

QADESH see **KADESH**.

QANTIR see **PI-RAMESSES**.

QASR IBRIM. Modern name for a site in **Nubia** situated on the east bank of the **Nile** 116 kilometres north of Wadi Halfa. Greek name Primis. The site consists of a Roman fortress, but includes isolated blocks and **stelae** from the **New Kingdom** and a **temple** from **Dynasty 25** as well as later Meroitic occupation and a Christian cathedral. The town later housed a Turkish garrison. The construction of the Aswan High Dam in the 1960s has led to flooding of part of the site which is now an island. The site and its vicinity have been excavated by the **Egypt Exploration Society** from 1961. Much documentary material from the **Coptic** and Turkish Periods has been discovered, along with interesting material from the **Roman Period** occupation. Nearby were chapels dedicated by the **viceroys of Kush** of **Dynasties 18–19** and a rock-cut stela of **Sety I** which were removed before the area was covered by the new lake.

QEBEHSENUEF see **SONS OF HORUS**.

QEMAU see **AMENY QEMAU**.

QENHERKHEPESHEF see **KENHERKHEPESHEF**.

QUDSHU. Canaanite fertility goddess whose worship became popular in Egypt during **Dynasties 18–19**. She is represented as a full frontal nude woman and depicted often with the Syrian war-god **Reshep**. See also **Anat**.

QUSTUL see **BALLANA**.

- R -

RAMESSES I (reigned c.1295–1294 BC). Throne name Menpehtyre. Son of a military officer named Sety. First ruler of **Dynasty 19**. He was **vizier** to the apparently childless **Horemheb** and succeeded to the throne on the latter's death. His reign was short, but he left a son **Sety I** to re-establish Egyptian prestige at home and abroad. He was buried in tomb no. 16 in the **Valley of the Kings**, but his **mummy** has not been recovered or identified.

RAMESSES II (reigned c.1279–1212 BC). Throne name Usermaatre setepenre. Epithet meryamun. Son of **Sety I** and Tuya, daughter of the lieutenant of the chariotry Raia. As the apparently only son, he was named crown prince at an early age by his father and provided with the accoutrements of kingship, including a royal harem. On his accession Ramesses II sought to restore Egyptian control in Syria but was defeated by the **Hittites** at the battle of **Kadesh** in year 5 (c.1274 BC). In year 21 (c.1258 BC) he signed a formal treaty with the Hittites ending the conflict. In year 34 (c.1245 BC) he married **Maathorneferure**, the daughter of the Hittite king, to cement the alliance and apparently later married a second daughter.

Ramesses II emphasized Egyptian power through many construction projects notably his new capital at **Pi-Ramesses** and many **Nubian temples** such as **Abu Simbel**. His wives included **Nefertari**, for whom he had a splendid tomb built in the **Valley of the Queens** at **Thebes**, and **Isitnofret**. Ramesses II also married three of his daughters, including the eldest Princess **Bintanat**, **Meritamun**, and Nebttawy. He had about 100 children, including his eldest son **Amenherkhepeshef** by Nefertari, and **Khaemwese** and his eventual heir **Merenptah**, both by Isitnofret. Ramesses II reigned for 66 years and two months and was remembered in legend as a great conqueror. His tomb (no. 7) in the **Valley of the Kings** has suffered severe earthquake damage and awaits a proper publication. An extensive tomb which he had built for his many sons has recently been uncovered there. His **mummy** survived in the **royal cache** and was recovered in 1881.

RAMESSES III (reigned c.1184–1153 BC). Throne name Usermaatre meryamun. Epithet heka iunu. Son of **Sethnakhte** and Tiye-merenese of **Dynasty 20**. His reign was distinguished by his successful campaign against the **Sea Peoples** whose invasion of Egypt he crushed. Ramesses III was able to maintain most of Egypt's Asian empire. His principal surviving monuments are his mortuary **temple** at **Medinet Habu** and his tomb (no. 11) in the **Valley of the Kings**. Ramesses III was apparently assassinated in a harem conspiracy against his appointed heir **Ramesses IV** who successfully countered the plot and punished the conspirators. His **mummy** was recovered from the **royal cache** in 1881.

RAMESSES IV (reigned c.1153–1147 BC). Throne name Usermaatre, later Hekamaatre. Son and successor of **Ramesses III**. He may be identical with a Prince Ramesses, son of Ramesses III, whose tomb (no. 53) was prepared in the **Valley of the Queens** but obviously abandoned on his accession. He successfully overcame the conspirators who assassinated his father and had them tried and punished. The Harris **Papyrus** recording the benefactions of his father was drawn up in his reign. Ramesses IV appears to have intended to undertake massive construction works in the Theban area but died when these were barely begun. He doubled the number of the workmen at **Deir el-Medina** so his tomb (no.

2) in the **Valley of the Kings** would be completed. His body was recovered from the **royal cache** in the tomb of **Amenhotep II** in 1898.

RAMESSES V (reigned c.1147–1143 BC). Throne name Usermaatre sekheperenre. Personal name Amenherkhepeshef. Epithet meryamun. Successor and possibly son of **Ramesses IV**. The principal document of his brief reign is the extensive **Wilbour Papyrus** outlining the possessions of the **temple** of **Amun** at **Thebes** throughout Egypt. He prepared tomb no. 9 in the **Valley of the Kings** for his burial but this was taken over by his successor **Ramesses VI** so it is not certain if he was buried here. His body was recovered from the **royal cache** in the tomb of **Amenhotep II** in 1898.

RAMESSES VI (reigned c.1143–1136 BC). Throne name Nebmaatre meryamun. Personal name Amenherkhepeshef. Epithet netjer heka iunu. Successor of **Ramesses V** and possible son of **Ramesses III**. He installed his daughter Princess Isis as **God's Wife of Amun**, apparently the first known virgin princess to hold the post. He was buried in tomb no. 9 in the **Valley of the Kings** which he had taken over from his predecessor. His body was recovered from the **royal cache** in the tomb of **Amenhotep II** in 1898.

RAMESSES VII (reigned c.1136–1129 BC). Throne name Usermaatre meryamun setepenre. Personal name Itamun. Epithet netjer heka iunu. Successor and possibly son of **Ramesses VI**. He was buried in tomb no. 1 in the **Valley of the Kings**, but his **mummy** has not been identified.

RAMESSES VIII (reigned c.1129–1126 BC). Throne name Usermaatre akhenamun. Personal name Sethherkhepeshef. Epithet meryamun. Successor of **Ramesses VII** and possibly son of **Ramesses III**. His reign was brief and no tomb has been identified for him.

RAMESSES IX (reigned c.1126–1108 BC). Throne name Neferkare setepenre. Personal name Khaemwese. Epithet mereramun. A member of the royal family of **Dynasty 20** whose exact origin is uncertain; successor to **Ramesses VIII**. A large amount of documentation survives from this reign concerning the affairs of **Deir el-Medina** and the Theban area, notably the **Tomb Robbery Papyri** which illustrate the gradual breakdown in law and order and the growing independence of the Theban area under its high priest. He was buried in tomb no. 6 in the **Valley of the Kings**, and his body was recovered from the **royal cache** in 1881.

RAMESSES X (reigned c.1108–1099). Throne name Khepermaatre setepenre. Successor and possibly son of **Ramesses IX**. The length of his reign is uncertain. He was buried in tomb no. 18 in the **Valley of the Kings**, but his **mummy** has not been identified.

RAMESSES XI (reigned c.1099–1069 BC). Throne name Menmaatre setepenptah. Personal name Khaemwese. Epithet mereramun netjer heka iunu. Successor and possibly son of **Ramesses X**. His reign marked the end of **Dynasty 20**. Contemporary documents refer to civil war and tomb robberies in **Thebes**, which became increasingly independent under the **high priest of Amun**. The king's tomb (no. 4) in the **Valley of the Kings** was left unfinished. It is presumed that he spent most of his time in the north, but the circumstances of his death and the change of the dynasty are unknown. His body has not been recovered. See also **Herihor**, **Piankh**.

RAMESSEUM. Modern name for the site of the mortuary **temple** of **Ramesses II** on the west bank of **Thebes** near **Deir el-Bahri**. The temple is noted for its fallen colossal statue of the king which inspired the poetic work of Shelley. The inscriptions also detail the royal children and the king's wars.

RAMESSIDE PERIOD (c.1295–1069 BC). A term used to describe the rule of **Dynasties 19–20** when the most common royal name was Ramesses. This period marked the time of Egypt's imperial power with an empire encompassing **Nubia** and Syria-Palestine. It was also a period when Egypt was open to foreign influence especially from Syria in language and religion.

RAMOSE (fl. c.1300–1240 BC). Chief scribe of the **Deir el-Medina** community. Son of Amenemheb and Kakaia. He previously served at the mortuary **temple** of **Thutmose IV** and was appointed to Deir el-Medina in year 5 of **Ramesses II** and was still in office in year 38. He appears to have been one of the wealthiest members of the community and had three tombs (nos. 7, 212, and 250) built for himself and his dependants. He and his wife Mutemwia were childless and adopted **Kenherkhepeshef** who succeeded to Ramose's office.

RANEB (reigned c.2865 BC). Second ruler of **Dynasty 2** and successor to **Hotepsekhemwy**. Little is known of his reign. **Manetho** credits him with the introduction of the animal cults at **Mendes, Heliopolis,** and **Memphis** although the **Apis** bull cult is attested earlier in **Dynasty 1**. His tomb appears to be located at **Saqqara**. See also **Nynetjer**.

RANEFEREF (reigned c.2448–2445 BC). Variant transcription of the name Neferefre. Personal name Isi. Fourth ruler of **Dynasty 5**. Son of **Neferirkare** and probably **Khentkaues** II. His reign was short and his funerary complex at **Abusir** was left unfinished. It was excavated by a Czech expedition in the 1980s and several pieces of sculpture were recovered as well as more **Abusir papyri.** See also **Niuserre, Shepsekare.**

RE. The ancient Egyptian sun-god whose main place of worship was at **Heliopolis**. The sun-god became the principal god of Egypt from **Dynasty 4**, displacing the sky-god **Horus** with whom Re is often combined in the form of the god Re-Harakhty. He was usually combined with other gods who were placed at the head of the pantheon, notably **Sobek** and **Amun**. In late **Dynasty 18** the worship of Re in the form of the sun's disk or **Aten** was promoted by **Akhenaten** but failed to displace Amun. Re is usually depicted as a human figure with a feathered headdress but can be represented with a hawk head.

RE-HARAKHTY see **RE.**

REISNER, GEORGE ANDREW (1867–1942). American excavator. He was born in Indianapolis on 5 November 1867. A Harvard graduate, he then studied Egyptology at Berlin. Reisner became director of archaeological work in Egypt for the University of California, financed by the Hearst family, in 1899–1905 and then directed the Nubian Archaeological Survey for the Egyptian Antiquities Service in 1907–09. He was appointed curator of the Egyptian Department of the **Boston Museum of Fine Arts** in 1910 and until his death conducted excavations at various sites in Egypt at **Naga el-Deir, Zawiyet el-Aryan**, several sites in **Nubia**, and especially **Giza** where he discovered the tomb of Queen **Hetepheres.** Reisner kept meticulous and detailed notes of his work, but this inevitably delayed publication so many of his excavations were published after his death by his assistant Dows Dunham. He died at Giza on 6 June 1942.

REKHMIRE (fl. c.1425 BC). Vizier towards the end of the reign of **Thutmose III** and the beginning of that of **Amenhotep II**. Son of Neferweben and Bata. He came from a prominent official family as his grandfather Ahmose and his uncle Woser had both held the post of vizier. He was buried at **Thebes** (Theban tomb no. 100), and his tomb contains a major inscription which details the duties of the vizier as well as scenes of foreign peoples bringing tribute to the Egyptian court.

RELIGION. For most of Egyptian history no attempt was made to develop a coherent religious theology for the entire country. Egypt consisted of many cities, each of which had a god or goddess to whom the inhabitants were particularly attached, along with the deity's family represented in a local **triad** and often an animal or animals sacred to the local divinity. For example, Meretseger, the snake-goddess of **Thebes** would represent a purely regional deity. However, some gods and goddesses such as **Ptah** of **Memphis**, **Thoth** of **Hermopolis**, or **Osiris**, the god of the dead, were worshipped on a national level throughout the country. The patronage of the king elevated others to the status of supreme deity, such as the sky-god **Horus**, the sun-god **Re** of **Heliopolis**, the formerly obscure god **Amun** of Thebes, the Ptolemaic deity **Sarapis**, and finally the goddess **Isis** in the **Roman Period**. More influential deities might absorb a local god or combine to form a composite god such as Re-Harakhty or Amun-Re. Various local **temples** as at Heliopolis or Hermopolis conceived different myths of creation in which their god naturally played the crucial role. The only attempt to impose a more uniform worship—that of the **Aten** disk—by **Akhenaten** ended in failure.

In most cities the gods were worshipped in major temples which were built or enlarged through the favour of the king and staffed with priests appointed by him. It was their duty to carry out the rituals to maintain *maat* and appease the gods. The bulk of the priests inherited their rank and were trained in their calling by temple schools and their relations, but the king could and did assign the top posts to royal favourites who could have been from priestly families but also from the royal family, bureaucracy, or military. He could also shift priests from one temple to another. Worship was not confined to the temples.

Unlike the state temples from which the local population would have been largely barred, common folk would have access to small local shrines and chapels, sometimes in their own homes as reflected in the religious practice at **Deir el-Medina**. **Stelae** and statues of the deceased with prayers giving his **name** would have been erected in the shrines, tombs, and temples to keep his memory alive.

RESHEP. Canaanite war-god worshipped in Egypt during the **New Kingdom.** He is usually depicted as a bearded man carrying military weapons. He is found associated with the Canaanite fertility-goddess **Qudshu** and the Egyptian fertility-god **Min** at **Deir el-Medina**.

ROMAN PERIOD (30 BC-395 AD). The term used by Egyptologists to designate the period when Egypt was under the direct rule of Roman emperors in Rome whose representative—the prefect of Egypt—was the effective governor of the country. Egypt was regarded as the private property of the Roman ruler and no Roman citizens were allowed to enter the country without imperial permission. Privileges were granted to Greek residents, but these were strictly defined and more limited than during the **Ptolemaic Period**. Construction work on Egyptian **temples** was undertaken, but there was no official recognition of the use of the Egyptian **language**, especially in legal contexts. After the move of the court to Constantinople, Egypt was ruled as part of the Eastern Empire in the **Byzantine Period**.

ROSETTA STONE. A bilingual decree of 196 BC built into the fort at Rosetta discovered by the French during reconstruction work in 1797. The same decree is written in the **hieroglyphic, demotic,** and Greek scripts. The importance of these texts for the decipherment of the Egyptian scripts was immediately realized and copies were sent to Paris where it was intended to ship the stone. Following the surrender of the French forces in 1801, however, the Rosetta Stone was given, with Turkish approval, to the British by the Treaty of Alexandria and was assigned to the **British Museum** in 1802. Decipherment of the hieroglyphic writing proved difficult and centred on the royal names in **cartouches**. The major breakthrough was made by Jean-François **Champollion** in 1822 when he recognized the alphabetic as well as the ideogrammatic nature of the hieroglyphic text. The Rosetta Stone has become the symbol of the key which unlocks mysteries.

ROYAL CACHES. During **Dynasty 21** the royal **mummies** in the **Valley of the Kings** whose tombs had been plundered were gathered together and reburied in two separate locations, one group in a cliff tomb near **Deir el-Bahri** and a second in the tomb of **Amenhotep II**. The first group was discovered by local residents in the 1870s who sold some of the equipment, leading to the discovery of the tomb in 1881. The second group was recovered in 1898. The mummies include most rulers of **Dynasties 18–20** as well as some queens, princes, and princesses of Dynasty 18 and members of the family of the **high priest of Amun** of Dynasty 21. Most are identified by inscriptions, but it is not absolutely clear that all the identifications made by the priests of Dynasty 21 are correct. Modern attempts to distinguish relationships and ages through bone structure or DNA have so far proved inconclusive.

RUDAMUN (reigned c.734–731 BC). Throne name Usimaatre setepenamun. Epithet meryamun. Younger son of **Osorkon III** of **Dynasty 23** and successor of his brother **Takelot III**. He is attested from a few monuments in **Thebes**. His daughter married **Peftjauawybast**, ruler of **Herakleopolis**. See also **Third Intermediate Period**.

- S -

SAHURE (reigned c.2487–2475 BC). Second ruler of **Dynasty 5**. According to the later **Westcar Papyrus**, he was a brother of his predecessor **Userkaf**, but he was more likely his son. He continued the policy of sun worship, constructing his own sun **temple** and his **pyramid** and temple complex at **Abusir**. The reliefs from the temple depict a trading expedition probably to Lebanon. The area was excavated by the German Ludwig Borchardt in 1907–08. See also **Neferirkare**.

SAIS. Greek name for the Egyptian town *Sau*, modern Sa el-Hagar, on the east bank of the Rosetta branch of the **Nile**. Capital of the fifth **nome** of **Lower Egypt**. The chief deity of the town was the goddess **Neith**. The town gained prominence in the **Third Intermediate Period** when it was ruled by local princes, one of whom, **Nekau I**, was installed by the **Assyrians** as ruler of Egypt and founded **Dynasty 26**. The city became the capital of Egypt at this time, but very little remains at the site today. It has never been properly excavated by archaeologists. In 1997 the **Egypt Exploration Society** began a survey of the area.

SAITE PERIOD (664–525 BC). A term used to describe the rule of **Dynasty 26** from **Sais**. It marked the last dynastic period of Egypt's greatness with political reunification of the country, revival in art which had begun in **Dynasty 25** combining styles from the **Old** and **Middle Kingdoms** in deliberate archaisms, and Egyptian intervention in **Nubia** and Palestine.

SAKHMET. Egyptian goddess, daughter of the sun-god **Re** and wife of the god **Ptah** of **Memphis**. She is usually depicted as a lioness-headed human figure. She is regarded as fierce and bloodthirsty and a destroyer of the king's enemies, but also has a healing aspect. In **Thebes** she was identified with the goddess **Mut** and her statues were erected in the temple of Mut there.

SALITIS. Greek name, given by the Hebrew historian Josephus who derived it from **Manetho**, for the first **Hyksos** ruler of **Dynasty 15**. The Austrian expedition at **Avaris** recently discovered a fragmentary inscription with part of a royal **titulary** of King Seker-Hor who may well be identifiable with the first Hyksos ruler.

SANAKHTE (fl. c.2686–2667 BC). Horus name of a king of **Dynasty 3** whose personal name is uncertain, possibly Nebka. He is known from a relief from Sinai but his order in the dynasty is unclear. He is generally stated to be the first king, but he may have been a successor rather than a predecessor of **Djoser**.

SAQQARA. Modern name for the main necropolis of ancient **Memphis** in use from **Dynasty 1** to the **Roman Period**. The area contains the tombs of the high officials of the **Early Dynastic Period**; the step-**pyramids** of **Dynasty 3**, notably the pyramid complex of **Djoser**; the tomb of **Shepseskaf** of **Dynasty 4**; three pyramids of **Dynasty 5**, including that of **Unas** with the first inscribed **pyramid texts**; the pyramids of **Dynasty 6**; many private tombs from all periods; and the **Serapeum**, the burial place of the **Apis** bull. The area has been under continuous excavation from the late nineteenth century, and recent discoveries by Egyptian, British, and French excavators include the late **Dynasty 18** and **Ramesside Period** cemeteries, notably the tombs of **Horemheb** as a commoner and the **vizier Aperel**.

SARAPIS. Egyptian god prominent in the **Graeco-Roman Period**. The name seems to have been derived from **Osiris Apis**, the deceased form of the Apis bull worshipped at **Memphis**. The deity was adopted by **Ptolemy I** and depicted with Greek features as a bearded man similar to the Greek god Zeus but with attributes derived from other Greek gods such as Dionysius and Aesculapius. Sarapis was promoted to the head of the Egyptian pantheon and considered the husband of **Isis**. He was regarded as a god of fertility and healing.

SARCOPHAGUS. The term used by Egyptologists to denote the stone coffins used in the burials of members of the royal family and high officials and which contained the wooden coffin or coffins in which the **mummy** of the deceased rested. These first appeared in the **Old Kingdom** and were rectangular in shape, being plain or decorated on the outside with a palace facade or **serekh** motif. In some cases the name and titles of the deceased were inscribed on the outside or inside. More lengthy inscribed prayers and decoration were in evidence from the **Middle Kingdom**. In the **New Kingdom** anthropoid sarcophagi came into use with texts on the inside and outside. The sky-goddess **Nut** was often depicted on the inside especially in sarcophagi from the **Late** and **Graeco-Roman Periods**.

The term sarcophagus has also been loosely used to refer to wooden or cartonnage coffins, but is now generally restricted to those of stone.

SATIS. Consort of the god **Khnum** of **Elephantine**. She is depicted as a human female figure with a white crown with horns. She was principally worshipped at Elephantine and in **Nubia**.

SATRAP. The **Persian** term for governor of a province. The Persian satraps of Egypt were generally members of the royal family or nobility. The last Persian satrap surrendered to **Alexander the Great**, on whose death the Macedonian general **Ptolemy** became the last satrap as he eventually took the title of king. See also **Achaemenes**, **Arsames**.

SCARAB. Modern name for the dung beetle which was regarded as sacred by the ancient Egyptians as, according to one perception, the sun was pushed through the sky by a celestial beetle. The ancient Egyptian name for the beetle was *kheper*. The scarab was a popular form of amulet usually made of steatite and then glazed and pierced vertically to fit on necklaces or rings. The underside could carry a prayer or a name when used as a seal. The larger heart scarab was unpierced and made of hard stone such as schist. It was placed over the heart of the **mummy** as the underside carried a spell to enable the heart to act favourably towards the deceased in the **weighing of the heart** ceremony. Winged scarabs and smaller scarabs all made of faience were also placed amid the wrappings of the mummy.

SCORPION (reigned c.3200 BC). A major king of **Dynasty 0** whose name is uncertain but was written as a scorpion hieroglyph. He reigned in **Upper Egypt** but is attested from an inscription in **Nubia**. His principal monument is a decorated macehead found at **Hierakonpolis**. He was buried at **Abydos** and his tomb has recently been excavated by a German expedition.

SEA PEOPLES. A term used by the Egyptians for a group of allied foreign peoples who threatened Egypt from the middle of **Dynasty 19** until the beginning of **Dynasty 20**. They first appear as an entity in year 5 of **Merenptah** when, allied with the Libyans, they invaded Egypt but were driven back and defeated. The Sea Peoples are described as Ekwesh, Lukka, Shekelesh, and Sherden, some of whom had been noted separately in Egyptian texts from late **Dynasty 18**.

The Sea Peoples returned in year 8 of **Ramesses III** after, according to the Egyptians, destroying the **Hittite** empire and several Syrian centres, including **Ugarit**. Their coalition was now described as Denen, Peleset, Shekelesh, Sherden, Tjekker, Teresh, and Weshwesh. Ramesses III claimed to have defeated them and pushed them back from Egypt. The intention of the Sea Peoples was to settle in newly occupied lands as they were accompanied by their families and possessions. Ramesses III stated that he agreed to the defeated forces settling along the Levantine coast in what was then the Egyptian empire, although he may have been obliged to do so since they could not be expelled. The Tjekker are later recorded there in late Dynasty 20 and the Pelest, later known as the Philistines, also settled on the coast. The origin of the Sea Peoples is unclear but they possibly originated in Asia Minor or the northern Aegean. Some groups may have migrated elsewhere such as the Sherden to Sardinia, but this is speculative.

SEBENNYTOS. Greek name for the ancient Egyptian town of *Tjebnetjer*, capital of the 12th **nome** of **Lower Egypt**. Modern Samanud on the west bank of the Damietta branch of the **Nile**. The main temple was dedicated to the god Onuris-**Shu**. Although some objects from the **Old** to **New Kingdoms** have been found in the vicinity, no remains on site earlier than **Dynasty 30**, whose royal family are stated to have come from here, have been found, but the area has not yet been thoroughly excavated.

The town remained prominent in the **Graeco-Roman Period**, its most famous citizen being the historian **Manetho**.

SECOND INTERMEDIATE PERIOD (c.1795–1550 BC). The term used by Egyptologists to designate the period between the end of **Dynasty 12** or, according to some, the middle of **Dynasty 13** until the accession of **Dynasty 18**. In this period the kingship was weak and divided, and Egypt was occupied by the **Hyksos** until driven out by the princes of **Thebes**.

SEKER-HOR see **SALITIS**.

SEKHEMKHET (reigned c.2648–2640 BC). Horus name of a king of **Dynasty 3** and probable successor to **Djoser**. His personal name is uncertain, possibly Djoser Teti. His unfinished **pyramid** at **Saqqara** was excavated between 1951 and 1954 by Zakaria Goneim, an Egyptian archaeologist, but Sekhemkhet's closed **sarcophagus** was found empty. His successor is uncertain. See also **Huni**.

SEMERKHET (reigned c.2915 BC). Seventh ruler of **Dynasty 1** and successor of **Anedjib**. He was buried in an elaborate tomb at **Abydos**, but little is known of his reign, which may have been a time of unrest.

SEMNA. Modern name for a site in **Nubia** near the Second **Cataract** where a fortress, temple, and settlement were erected during **Dynasty 12**, on the west bank, probably begun under **Senusret I** and completed under **Senusret III** after whom it was named *Sekhem-Khakaure*. Nearby was a second fort, now known as Semna South; ancient Egyptian *Dair Seti*. Semna marked the limit of Egyptian control in the **Middle Kingdom**. The site was excavated by George **Reisner** of Boston in 1924–28 and again in the 1960s. The area is now flooded by the lake of the Aswan High Dam, but part of the **temple** was removed to safety.

SENAKHTENRE see **TAO**.

SENENMUT (fl. c.1479–1455 BC). High official in the reign of **Hatshepsut**. Son of Ramose and Hatnefer of apparently humble origin. He held the office of chief steward and tutor of the Princess **Neferure**. He was in charge of the queen's building works, notably at **Deir el-Bahri**. Numerous statues of him survive, most badly damaged although it is not certain when this action took place. There has been much speculation about his relationship with the queen. He may have fallen into disgrace before the end of the reign. No family of his is known. His major tomb at **Thebes** was never completed and is defaced.

SENNEDJEM (fl. c.1280 BC). Workman in the community of royal tomb-builders at **Deir el-Medina**. Son of Khabekhnet and Tahenen. He served in the workforce probably in the reign of **Sety I** and the early part of that of **Ramesses II** during **Dynasty 19**. His tomb (no. 1) was discovered intact in 1886, including several **mummies** of his immediate family along with their burial equipment. Most of the material remains in the **Cairo Egyptian Museum**, but some has been dispersed to other museums. The painted plaster scenes in his tomb are well preserved and remarkable for their vividness.

SENUSRET I (reigned c.1965–1920 BC). Throne name Kheperkare. Son of **Amenemhat I**, founder of **Dynasty 12**. He was named **co-regent** with his father c.1965 BC to secure the new dynasty and succeeded to sole rule following his father's assassination about 1955 BC. The circumstances are mentioned in the tale of **Sinuhe**, but the motive for the assassination and the means by which the conspiracy was crushed remain unclear. He maintained the policy of expansion in **Nubia**. His reign appears to have fostered literary composition as evidenced by the production of the story of *Sinuhe, the Prophecy of Neferti*, and *the Instruction of Amenemhat I*. An important example of his construction work at **Karnak** has survived in the form of a kiosk with intricately carved **hieroglyphs**. He also erected a pair of **obelisks** in the **temple** at **Heliopolis** of which one survives. He was buried in a **pyramid** at **Lisht** which has been excavated by the **Metropolitan Museum of Art**. His principal queen was his sister **Nefru** and he was succeeded by his son **Amenemhat II**.

SENUSRET II (reigned c.1880–1874 BC). Throne name Khakheperre. Son of **Amenemhat II**. He continued the expansionist policy of **Dynasty 12** with trade relations recorded with Palestine. He was buried at **Lahun** in the **Fayum**. His principal wife was Queen **Khenemet-nefer-hedjet** and he was succeeded by his son **Senusret III**.

SENUSRET III (reigned c.1874–1855 BC). Throne name Khakaure. Son of **Senusret II** and **Khenemet-nefer-hedjet**. He undertook military expeditions in **Nubia** where he strengthened Egyptian fortresses and in

Palestine attacking the town of Shechem. He is credited with eliminating the provincial **nomarchs** who are last attested in his reign. He was buried in a **pyramid** of **Dahshur**, recently excavated by the **Metropolitan Museum of Art**. His military activities were later confused with those of **Ramesses II** to form the deeds of conquest of a mythical King Sesostris. His principal wife was **Khenemet-nefer-hedjet** the younger.

SEPTIMIUS SEVERUS (145–211 AD). Roman emperor. Full name Lucius Septimius Severus, son of Publius Septimius Geta and Fulvia Pia. He was born in Leptis Magna in Libya about 145. He had a successful military and senatorial career, finally occupying the post of governor of Pannonia. Severus was proclaimed emperor in 193 and eventually defeated his rivals in the eastern and western parts of the empire. He visited Egypt in 200, granting **Alexandria** and other major cities municipal councils and ordering new building work in Alexandria and the restoration of one of the Colossi of **Memnon** which was alleged to sing but did so no more after this work. Septimius Severus died in York on 4 February 211.

SERABIT EL-KHADIM. Site in the Sinai used as a quarry for turquoise from the **Middle Kingdom**, largely replacing **Wadi Maghara** and location of a **temple** dedicated to **Hathor**, lady of turquoise, where many texts dedicated by the leaders of mining expeditions have been found. The site was first excavated by Major Charles Macdonald in the 1860s and later by Flinders **Petrie** in 1904–05 and a French expedition from 1993. See also **Hatnub**, **Wadi el-Hudi**, **Wadi Hammamat**.

SERAPEUM. Greek name for the catacombs of the sacred **Apis** bull at **Saqqara**. The underground vault contained separate chambers for each burial in a massive **sarcophagus** and on the walls were attached **stelae** of the workmen involved in the burials. The Serapeum was discovered by Auguste **Mariette** in 1851, but the continuous sequence of burials has been traced only from the **Third Intermediate Period** to the **Ptolemaic Period** although a few isolated earlier burials have been located. Prince **Khaemwese**, son of **Ramesses II**, may have been buried here. See also **Memphis**.

SERAPIS see **SARAPIS**.

SEREKH. The stylized palace facade used from **Dynasty 0** to enclose the **Horus** name of the king in the royal **titulary**.

SESEBI. Modern name for a settlement in Upper **Nubia** founded at the end of **Dynasty 18**. The **temple** was dedicated to the Theban **triad**. The area was excavated by a British expedition in 1936–38 but has not been properly published.

SESHESESHET. The name of two royal ladies of **Dynasty 6**. The first was the mother of **Teti**, founder of the dynasty, whose husband is unknown. She apparently was alive at her son's accession and given the title of queen mother. Her granddaughter, Sesheseshet, the daughter of Teti, was the wife of the **vizier Mereruka**.

SETH. Egyptian god of thunder and the desert. Son of **Geb** and **Nut**. Brother of **Osiris, Isis**, and **Nephthys**. According to Egyptian legend, he murdered his brother Osiris in order to claim the crown of Egypt but was thwarted by Isis and her son **Horus**. He was therefore regarded as an evil god and abominated in most parts of Egypt although worshipped in areas of the Delta. He was identified with the Syrian god Baal and hence associated with the **Hyksos**. In another myth he appears as a protector of the sun-god **Re**.

SETHHERKHEPESHEF. The name of several royal princes in **Dynasties 19–20**. The first known was a son of **Ramesses II**, but it appears that this name was merely an alternate name of Prince **Amenherkhepeshef**. The tomb (no. 43) of Sethherkhepeshef (fl. c.1185 BC), son of **Ramesses III**, is located in the **Valley of the Kings**, and it appears from his depiction that he died as a child. A second Prince Sethherkhepeshef succeeded as **Ramesses VIII** and may well have been a younger son of Ramesses III of the same name.

SETHNAKHTE (reigned c.1188–1186 BC). Throne name Userkhaure. Founder of **Dynasty 20** of unknown origin. He overthrew the rule of **Tewosret** and **Bay** but died shortly after leaving the throne to his son **Ramesses III**. He was buried in tomb no. 14 in the **Valley of the Kings** which he had taken over from Tewosret. His body may have been found in the **royal cache** in the tomb of **Amenhotep II** in 1898.

SETY I (reigned c.1294–1279 BC). Throne name Menmare. Son of **Ramesses I** and Sitre. Second ruler of **Dynasty 19**. He pursued a vigorous policy of re-establishing Egyptian control in Palestine and Syria. At home he undertook important construction works, notably the **temple** at

Abydos with a detailed **king-list** and his finely painted tomb (no. 17) in the **Valley of the Kings** discovered in 1817. He established his son **Ramesses II** as his **co-regent**. His **mummy** was recovered in the **royal cache** in 1881.

SETY II (reigned c.1202–1196 BC). Throne name Userkheprure. Son of **Merenptah** of **Dynasty 19**. His claim to the throne was challenged by **Amenmesse** and he only established himself after a civil war which weakened the dynasty. After a short reign, Sety II was followed by his son **Siptah** although power remained in the hands of his widow **Tewosret** and **Bay**. He was buried in tomb no. 15 in the **Valley of the Kings**, and his body was recovered from the **royal cache** in the tomb of **Amenhotep II** in 1898.

SHABAQO (reigned c.716–702 BC). Throne name Neferkare. Son of **Kashta** and successor of **Piye**. **Nubian** ruler who conquered Egypt in 715 BC, executing **Bakenrenef** of **Dynasty 24** and establishing **Dynasty 25** in Egypt. He maintained good relations with **Assyria** whose empire had spread to the Egyptian border. He was buried in a **pyramid** tomb at el-Kurru in **Nubia**. He was succeeded by **Shebitqo** whose relationship to him is uncertain. See also **Taharqo**.

SHABTI. The earliest royal burials of **Dynasties 1–2** were surrounded by the graves of royal retainers who had been sacrificed to accompany their master as servants in the next life. This practice was then abandoned, and models of servants appear in tombs in the **Old** and **Middle Kingdoms**. As the deceased was expected to be asked to perform some manual activities in the **afterlife**, so from the late Middle Kingdom to the **Ptolemaic Period** burials included *shabtis* or servant figures with inscriptions naming the deceased and obliging the figure to carry out any work demanded of him or her. Elaborate burials had 365 *shabtis*—one for each day of the year plus overseer *shabtis* for every ten worker figures. The figures would be placed in *shabti* boxes in the tomb.

SHAI. Egyptian god of fate. He is represented as a human figure.

SHALFAK. Modern name for the site of a fortress in the Second **Cataract** region of **Nubia** probably built by **Senusret III**. Ancient Egyptian *Waf Khasut*.

SHEBITQO (reigned c.702–690 BC). Throne name Djedkaure. Successor of **Shabaqo** of **Dynasty 25**. He faced mounting pressure from the expanding **Assyrian** empire and supported a rebellion of the Palestinian states against Assyrian domination. Egyptian forces under the command of **Taharqo** were defeated at Eltekeh in 701 BC, and **Assyria** remained a constant threat. He was buried at el-Kurru in **Nubia**.

SHENOUTE (d. c.466 AD). Coptic abbot of the White Monastery near modern Sohag. He was born in the village of Shenalolet near **Akhmim** and entered the White Monastery in 371, where he served as a monk and later succeeded his uncle Pjol, the founder of the monastery, as head of the community. His rule was quite strict and harsher than that of **Pachomius**, and Shenoute introduced a written profession of obedience. He was a staunch opponent of paganism and encouraged the destruction of pagan monuments. He took part in 431 in the Council of Ephesus with the patriarch **Cyril**. Many of his literary compositions, all on religious subjects, have survived and Shenoute is regarded as the most original author of the Coptic Period.

SHEPENWEPET. The name of two princesses who succeeded as **God's Wife of Amun**. Shepenwepet I, daughter of **Osorkon III** of **Dynasty 23** and Karoatjet, held office until the advent of the **Nubian Dynasty 25** when she was obliged to adopt **Amenirdis** I, daughter of **Kashta**, as her heir. Shepenwepet II, daughter of **Piye**, succeeded Amenirdis I and adopted Amenirdis II, daughter of **Taharqo**, but in 656 BC was obliged to adopt **Nitocris**, daughter of **Psamtik I** of **Dynasty 26** who had ousted her family from power.

SHEPSEKARE (reigned c.2455–2448 BC). Obscure monarch of **Dynasty 5**. He appears to have been either the predecessor or the successor of **Raneferef**, but no details are known of his reign.

SHEPSESKAF (reigned c.2503–2498 BC). Ruler of **Dynasty 4**. Successor and possibly son of **Menkaure**. The waning power of the monarch is demonstrated by his failure to build a **pyramid**; he was buried in a large **mastaba** tomb near **Saqqara**.

SHESHI. Throne name Maaibre. Ruler of the **Second Intermediate Period** attested on many **scarabs**. He is generally considered to be a member of the **Hyksos Dynasty 15** but may well belong to **Dynasty 14**.

SHESHONQ I (reigned c.945–924 BC). Throne name Hedjkheperre sete-penre. Epithet meryamun. Founder of **Dynasty 22**, son of the Libyan chieftain **Nimlot** and his wife Tentsepeh and nephew of King **Osorkon** the Elder. He succeeded to the throne despite opposition in **Thebes** and re-established Egyptian prestige with a campaign in Palestine, being mentioned in the Bible as Shishak. A statue of him has been discovered at **Byblos**. Sheshonq I described his campaign on a victory relief which was carved in the **temple** of **Karnak**. He placed his sons in strategic positions such as that of **high priest of Amun** to strengthen his rule.

SHESHONQ II (reigned c.890 BC). Throne name Heqakheperre setepe-nre. Epithet meryamun. Ephemeral monarch of **Dynasty 22** who is known from his burial at **Tanis** in the tomb of **Pasebakhaenniut I**. He is usually identified with Prince Sheshonq, son of **Osorkon I** and **Maatkare**, the daughter of **Pasebekhaenniut II** of **Dynasty 21**, but appears never to have reigned alone but only as **co-regent** with his father.

SHESHONQ III (reigned c.825–785 BC). Throne name Usermaatre sete-penre or setepenamun. Epithet meryamun si-bast netjer heka iunu. Successor of **Takelot II** of **Dynasty 22**. It would appear that in his reign the unity of Egypt was broken and a rival line of rulers was established as **Dynasty 23**, beginning with **Pedubast I**. Sheshonq III carried out building works at **Tanis** with material brought from **Pi-Ramesses**. His intact tomb at Tanis was discovered in 1939. A King Usimaatre meryamun Sheshonq is known at this time from **Thebes** and may be a variant of his title or a separate king now to be known as Sheshonq VI. Sheshonq III may have been succeeded by **Sheshonq IV**.

SHESHONQ IV (reigned c.785–773 BC). Throne name Hedjkheperre setepenre or setepenamun. Epithet meryamun si-bast netjer heka iunu. An obscure ruler whose existence has only recently been acknowledged. It is likely that he was a successor to **Sheshonq III**.

SHESHONQ V (reigned c.767–730 BC). Throne name Akheperre setepe-nre. Epithet meryamun si-bast netjer heka waset. Son and successor of **Pimay**. His control appears to have been restricted to the Delta area. Sheshonq V celebrated his **jubilee** and carried out building works at **Tanis**, but is otherwise little known. See also **Osorkon IV**.

SHIPWRECKED SAILOR. A literary tale from the **Middle Kingdom** known from one manuscript. It describes the adventures of a sailor shipwrecked on a mysterious island where he meets a magical serpent. See also **Wisdom Literature**.

SHU. Egyptian god of the air and sunlight. According to the creation myth from **Heliopolis**, he was created by **Atum** and by his union with **Tefnut**, goddess of moisture, produced **Geb** and **Nut**. He is depicted in human form as a kneeling man with upraised arms and a sun disk on his head or as a lion.

SIAMUN (reigned c.978–950 BC). Throne name Netjerkheperre. Penultimate king of **Dynasty 21**. Successor of **Osorkon** the Elder but of unknown origin. Little is known of his reign. He may have undertaken a campaign against Gezer in Palestine, but his identification with the unnamed ruler who took this city mentioned in the Bible is speculative.

SIHATHOR (fl. c.1730 BC). A possible minor ruler of **Dynasty 13**, son of the **God's Father** Haankhef and probably the lady Kemi. According to the **Turin Royal Canon**, he succeeded his brother **Neferhotep I**, but his reign was brief and he was followed by his brother **Sobekhotep IV**. However, contemporary monuments only describe him as a royal prince, and he may have predeceased his elder brother and never reigned. The attribution of the throne name Menwadjre is dubious. See also **Second Intermediate Period**.

SINUHE. Hero of a **Middle Kingdom** story set in the reign of **Senusret I**. Sinuhe flees the country on hearing of the assassination of the king's father **Amenemhat I** and the story outlines his adventures in the Palestine region. In old age, he longs to return to Egypt and is pardoned and welcomed back by the king. The story reflects the strong attachment of Egyptians to their homeland. It is already attested at the end of the Middle Kingdom and was extremely popular in the **New Kingdom** from which time many copies survive. See also **Wisdom Literature**.

SIPTAH (reigned c.1196–1190 BC). Throne name Akhenre, probably son of **Sety II** of **Dynasty 19**. He was proclaimed king with the help of **Bay** when still a child but died after a short reign. His **mummy** reveals that he suffered from a club foot. He was succeeded by his probable stepmother **Tewosret**. He was buried in tomb no. 47 in the **Valley of the Kings**, discovered in 1905, and his body was recovered from the **royal cache** in the tomb of **Amenhotep II** in 1898.

SITAMUN (fl. c.1525 BC). Egyptian princess. Probably daughter of **Ahmose I** and **Ahmose-Nefertari**. She is attested in the reign of her father with the title **God's Wife** and appears to have survived into the reign of her brother **Amenhotep I**.

SITAMUN (fl. c.1355 BC). Egyptian princess. Daughter of **Amenhotep III** and **Tiy**. An item of furniture with her name was found in the tomb of **Yuya**, Tiy's father. She was given the title of queen on inscriptions from her father's reign and so probably married him, but her subsequent fate is not known. See also **Baketaten**.

SITHATHORIUNET (fl. c.1875 BC). A princess of **Dynasty 12** and probable daughter of **Senusret II**. Her tomb was discovered near her father's **pyramid** at **Lahun** and contained a large collection of jewellery now on display at the **Cairo Egyptian Museum** and the **Metropolitan Museum of Art** in New York.

SIWA OASIS. An oasis in the northern part of the Western Desert just east of the present Libyan border. There is no direct evidence for Egyptian control until **Dynasty 26** when the famous **temple** to **Amun** was built, although this does not preclude earlier Egyptian influence. The oracle of the temple became well known in the classical world. **Cambyses** was alleged to have tried and failed to conquer the oasis. The oracle was consulted by **Alexander the Great** and was believed to have confirmed his divine origin.

SLAVERY. Slavery played a minor role in ancient Egypt, contrary to modern expectations. There was no large-scale exploitation of slavery. Most slaves were acquired as booty in war or to a lesser extent from the sale of criminals or debtors. Most slaves were used in a domestic context as local servants although they might be employed in certain industrial concerns, such as slave women used for the preparation of textiles. Slaves seem to have been on the whole well treated and absorbed in due course into the community. There is the example of **Hesunebef**, who was freed by his patron and found a position, and references to slaves who inherited the property of their master or mistress. The position of slaves undoubtedly worsened in the **Graeco-Roman Period** when classical views on slavery prevailed.

SMATAWYTEFNAKHT (fl. c.340–330 BC). A chief priest of **Sakhmet** from **Herakleopolis**, son of the priest of **Amun-Re** Djedsmatawyefankh and Ankhet. He left a long biographical **stela**, discovered in 1765 in Pompeii and now in the Naples Museum, in which he mentions his presence in the battle between the **Persians** and the Greeks, presumably referring to the campaign of **Alexander the Great**.

SMENKHKARE (reigned c.1338–1336 BC). Throne name Ankhkheper-ure. Mysterious and ephemeral ruler at the end of **Dynasty 18** who was **co-regent** and successor of **Akhenaten**. It has been suggested that this ruler was in fact Akhenaten's widow **Nefertiti** or daughter **Meritamun** or a man who reigned with one of these, but his existence remains obscure. It has also been suggested that his presumed body found in tomb no. 55 in the **Valley of the Kings** was in fact that of Akhenaten although the age of the skeleton renders this theory dubious. See also **Ay**, **Horemheb**, **Tutankhamun**.

SNEFRU (reigned c.2613–2589 BC). First king of **Dynasty 4** of unknown origin. His mother **Meresankh** I bore the title of queen mother but not queen so his father is unlikely to have been **Huni**, last ruler of the previous dynasty. He built possibly three **pyramids**, two at **Dahshur** and possibly one at **Meidum**. Snefru undertook campaigns in **Nubia** and had trade relations with Lebanon. He was remembered in the later literature as a wise and just monarch. He was succeeded by **Khufu**, his son by his chief queen **Hetepheres**.

SOBEK. Crocodile-god, often depicted as a crocodile-headed human figure. His principal places of worship were the **Fayum** and **Kom Ombo**. He was especially popular in the late **Middle Kingdom** and early **Second Intermediate Period** when he is often equated with **Re** as the god Sobek-Re.

SOBEKEMSAF. The name of two kings of **Dynasty 17**. The more important was Sobekemsaf II, throne name Sekhemre Shedtawy, of whom several monuments survive, including a colossal statue in the **British Museum**. He was buried on the western bank at **Thebes** and his tomb is recorded as being violated in **Dynasty 20**. See also **Second Intermediate Period**.

SOBEKHOTEP. The name of several kings in **Dynasty 13**, the numbering of whom is not absolutely certain. The most successful appears to have been Sobekhotep III.

SOBEKHOTEP III (reigned c.1740 BC). Throne name Sekhemresewadjtawy. Son of the **God's Father** Mentuhotep and the lady Iuhetibu. He is attested on monuments in **Middle** and **Upper Egypt** and on a graffito near the First **Cataract**. A **papyrus** from his reign documents the presence in Egypt of Asiatic servants.

SOBEKHOTEP IV (reigned c.1730–1722 BC). Throne name Khaneferre. He was a younger son of the **God's Father** Haankhef and the lady Kemi and succeeded his brothers **Neferhotep I** and **Sihathor**. He is attested on several graffiti in the region of **Elephantine** and the **Wadi Hammamat** and on monuments in **Karnak** and Palestine.

SOBEKNEFRU (reigned c.1799–1795 BC). Throne name Sobekkare. Last ruler of **Dynasty 12**. Daughter of **Amenemhat III** and possibly wife of her brother **Amenemhat IV**. She succeeded to the throne presumably for lack of male heirs, but her reign was brief and she was followed by the unstable **Dynasty 13** beginning the **Second Intermediate Period**.

SOCIETY. Ancient Egyptian society consisted basically of two classes divided by the ability to read and write. The bulk of the population were illiterate peasants engaged in **agriculture** together with a relatively small number of craftsmen who either lived alongside the rural communities or, like workers in faience, glass, or jewellery, were attached to wealthy private or government establishments. The literate population of not more than 5 percent comprised the royal court and the bureaucracy—civil, priestly, and military. Although it was an Egyptian ideal for a son to follow in his father's office, the major appointments were the prerogative of the king and the **vizier**, or high officials for more minor offices, so posts often did not follow a hereditary line although the sons of a literate official would find other positions. Thus it is inaccurate to speak of an Egyptian nobility. Rather there existed a hereditary bureaucratic class.

It would have been difficult to rise from one class to another. Presumably an enterprising farmer who managed to build up a small estate such as **Hekanakhte**, might become literate or have his children educated so they could join the official class. Similarly the army might prove the vehicle for the acquisition of land and wealth for someone from a peasant background. But such cases would appear to be rare.

SOKAR. Protective god of the necropolis of **Memphis**. He is usually depicted as a hawk-headed human. As a funerary god, he was often identified with **Osiris** but he was also seen as a craftsman and maker of unguents and so identified with **Ptah**. The composite god Ptah-Sokar-Osiris is attested in the **Middle Kingdom** but becomes more prominent in the **Late Period** when statues dedicated to him become a standard part of funerary equipment.

SOLEB. Modern name for a site in Upper **Nubia** where a major **temple** was erected by **Amenhotep III** dedicated to Amen-Re and the deified king himself as Nebmaatre, lord of Nubia. The site also includes the remains of a town and cemeteries. The area was excavated by an Italian-French expedition in 1957–77.

SONS OF HORUS. The four deities who were associated with the protection of the internal organs removed during the embalming procedure and placed in **canopic jars** or in packages. They were originally represented as human figures but by the **New Kingdom** three had acquired animal heads. Imsety in human form protected the liver; Hapy with a baboon head, the lungs; Duamutef with a jackal head, the stomach; and Qebeh-senuef with a hawk head, the intestines. The gods appear as heads on canopic jars and on amulets placed on the **mummy**.

SOTHIC CYCLE see **CHRONOLOGY.**

SOTHIS. Greek name for the Egyptian astral goddess *Sopdet*, the personification of the dog-star Sirius whose time of best visibility marked the beginning of the **Nile** flood. The goddess is represented as a human female figure with a star on her headdress.

SPHINX. Greek name for the human-headed lion which is depicted in Egyptian art and especially large sculpture. The most famous example is the Great Sphinx at **Giza** which was carved from a rocky knoll in the form of King **Khafre**. This sphinx was later identified with a form of the sun-god Harmakhis. It was especially venerated and restored by **Thutmose IV** who attributed his unexpected succession to its divine intercession. Monumental sphinxes were produced during **Dynasty 12** although wrongly assigned to the **Hyksos** by early Egyptologists.

The Great Sphinx was first cleared by Giovanni Battista Caviglia in

1817 and subsequently by Auguste **Mariette** in 1853, Gaston Maspero in 1889, and Eugene Baraize in 1923–36. It has recently been restored.

STELA. Plural stelae. Greek word used by Egyptologists for a free-standing inscribed stone, often but not necessarily round-topped. A stela can vary in size from several centimetres to several metres. Most record prayers with dedications to gods on behalf of an individual, often naming members of his family, and can run to several registers with inscribed scenes as well as texts. Historical stelae record the deeds of kings. Some inscriptions on **temple** walls or cliffs have a surround in imitation of the free-standing stelae.

- T -

TACHOS see **DJEDHOR.**

TADUKHEPA (fl. c.1350 BC). A princess from **Mitanni**, daughter of King Tushratta, who was married to **Amenhotep III** towards the end of his reign and possibly married his successor **Akhenaten**. She has sometimes been identified with the lady **Kiya**, but there is no evidence for this. See also **Gilukhepa**.

TAHARQO (reigned 690–664 BC). Throne name Khunefertemre. Son of **Piye** and Abar. He was summoned from **Nubia** after the accession of his relation **Shebitqo** and commanded his army in Palestine in 701 BC against the **Assyrians**. He succeeded Shebitqo and undertook extensive building works, especially at **Karnak** where he installed his daughter **Amenirdis** II as prospective **God's Wife of Amun.** He defeated an initial Assyrian invasion but was driven out of Egypt by another invasion in 671 BC in which his family was captured. He retired to Nubia where he died in 664 BC and was buried in the royal cemetery at Nuri near **Napata.** See also **Tantamani.**

TAKELOT I (reigned c.889–874 BC). Throne name Hedjkheperre. Son of **Osorkon I** and Tashedkhons. His reign is obscure. He has recently been identified as the king of this name buried in the tomb of his son **Osorkon II** at **Tanis** whose body was uncovered in 1939 by the French excavator Pierre Montet.

TAKELOT II (reigned c.850–825 BC). Throne name Hedjkheperre sete-penre. Epithet meryamun siese. Successor and probable son of **Osorkon II**. His reign is badly attested, but his attempt to install his son **Osorkon** as **high priest of Amun** in **Karnak** led to prolonged civil strife. See also **Karomama**.

TAKELOT III (reigned c.754–734 BC). Throne name Usermaatre sete-penamun. Epithet meryamun siese. Son of **Osorkon III** of **Dynasty 23** and Tentsai. He held the title of **high priest of Amun** before his acces-sion. He is attested on monuments from **Thebes**. See also **Rudamun**.

TANIS. Greek name for ancient Egyptian *Djane,* modern San el-Hagara, a city in the northeast part of the Delta in the 19th Egyptian **nome**. It came into prominence during **Dynasty 21** as the residence of the royal family founded by **Nesbanebdjed**, mayor of Tanis. The town was decorated with monuments moved from other sites such as **Pi-Ramesses**. The town was excavated by Auguste **Mariette** in the 1860s and Flinders **Petrie** in 1884. A French expedition has been working at the site in 1928–56 under Pierre Montet, in 1965–85 under Jean Yoyotte, and from 1985 under Philippe Brissaud. Inside the **temple** complex dedicated to **Amun**, Montet found the tombs of some of the rulers of Dynasty 21 and **Dynasty 22** in 1939.

TANTAMANI (reigned 664–656 BC). Last ruler of **Dynasty 25** in Egypt. Throne name Bakare. He succeeded **Taharqo** and embarked on a recon-quest of Egypt, defeating the ruler **Nekau I** installed by the **Assyrians**. In 663 BC the Assyrian army returned and defeated him, marching as far south as **Thebes** which was sacked and appointing **Psamtik I** as ruler. Tantamani retreated to **Nubia** but was recognized as ruler in southern Egypt until 657 BC. He died in 656 BC and was buried at el-Kurru. See also **Mentuemhat**.

TAO (reigned c.1555 BC). Throne name Seqenenre. Penultimate ruler of **Dynasty 17** and prince of **Thebes**. Son of Queen **Tetisheri** and possibly Senakhtenre. Possibly a vassal of the **Hyksos**, he later led Theban forces against them in the north. A literary tale implies conflict between him and the Hyksos ruler **Apepi**. His **mummy** was recovered in the **royal cache** and shows that he died violently. He is often referred to as Tao II since his predecessor, whose throne name was Senakhtenre, may have had the same personal name although this is not certain. See also **Ahhotep**, **Ahmose**.

TATENEN. Primeval god of the fertility of the soil left by the **Nile** flood. He was later identified with the god **Ptah** of **Memphis**. He is represented as a human figure with plumes and often painted green.

TAWERET. Egyptian goddess, protector of women in childbirth. She is represented as a pregnant hippopotamus with female breasts and a crocodile tail. Her appearance was supposed to frighten off demons who might harm the pregnant woman or her child.

TEFNAKHTE (reigned c.727–721 BC). Throne name Shepsesre. Prince of **Sais**. He is named as the main opponent of the **Nubian** ruler **Piye** during his invasion of Egypt. Despite his submission, it appears that Tefnakhte later assumed royal status and was succeeded by his son **Bakenref** of **Dynasty 24**.

TEFNUT. Egyptian goddess of moisture. Created by **Atum**, she produced **Geb** and **Nut** from a union with **Shu**, the god of air. She can be depicted as a lioness or a lioness-headed human figure.

TELL EL-MASKHUTA. Modern name for a site excavated by the **Egypt Exploration Fund** in 1883 in the eastern Delta just west of Ismailia. Remains from the **Late Period** to the **Roman Period** have been found. The city has been identified with ancient Egyptian *Pr-Itm* or Pithom, capital of the eighth **nome** of **Lower Egypt**. It has been excavated by an expedition from the University of Toronto in 1978–79.

TELL EL-YAHUDIYA. Modern name for a site in the Delta where remains from the **Middle Kingdom** to the **Graeco-Roman Period** have been excavated. The site has given its name to a form of black pottery juglet decorated with incised designs painted in white which are found throughout the Levant, although their exact place of manufacture is still unclear. The site was excavated by the **Egypt Exploration Fund** in 1887 and by Flinders **Petrie** in 1906.

TEMPLE. The site of worship for a deity or a series of deities located in each Egyptian centre. During the **New Kingdom** and later a major temple would consist of a **pylon** in front of an open courtyard followed by a hypostyle or columned hall and then a series of rooms leading to the **naos** or sacred shrine in which the image of the deity was contained. The general public would be admitted only to the first courtyard and only the priests and officials would have access to the rest of the building. It was believed that in order for stability to be maintained the sacred rituals had to be carried out daily. These consisted of waking the deity in his shrine, clothing the image, and offering food regularly. The image might be carried out into the courtyard or out of the temple on festive days on a sacred boat or barque. The temple would also contain royal and private statuary, as the king and officials would hope that their **names** might be read by the priests and thus become immortal. Religious worship was not confined to the main temples but also took place more directly between supplicant and deity at various small local shrines. Mortuary temples for deceased rulers were initially associated with the burial site but in the New Kingdom were located some distance away. See also **Pyramid**, **Religion**.

TENTAMUN (fl. c.1085 BC). Wife of **Nesbanebdjed**, mayor of **Tanis** and later first ruler of **Dynasty 21**. She is mentioned with her husband in the tale of **Wenamun**. There is no reason to doubt her identification with the Queen Tentamun, daughter of the official Nebseny, and thus she did not have a royal pedigree. Her daughter **Henttawy** apparently married the **high priest of Amun Pinudjem** I.

TEOS see **DJEDHOR**.

TETI (reigned c.2345–2321 BC). Founder of **Dynasty 6** and son of Queen Mother **Sesheseshet**. His origin is unknown, and it is not clear how he came to power. He had a long and apparently successful reign. He was buried in a **pyramid** tomb at **Saqqara**. Nearby were the tombs of his queens **Iput** I, Khuit, and Khentet- whose complete name is lost. The area surrounding his pyramid has been excavated by the Egyptian Antiquities Service in 1893, 1897–99 under Victor Loret, 1905–07 under James Quibell, 1920–22 under Cecil Firth, and since 1993 by the Egyptian archaeologist Zahi Hawass. See also **Pepy I**.

TETISHERI (fl. c.1570–1540 BC). Possibly wife of Senakhtenre, the ruler of **Thebes** of **Dynasty 17**, and daughter of Tjenna and Nefru. She was the mother of **Tao** and grandmother of **Ahmose I** and **Ahmose-Nefertari**. She possibly acted as regent for her grandson and played a prominent role in his reign. A funerary **temple** in her honour was founded in **Abydos**.

TEWOSRET (reigned c.1190–1188 BC). Throne name Sitre. Wife of **Sety II** and step-mother of his successor **Siptah**. On the death of the king she took the throne and counted her regnal years from the death of her husband. She was apparently overthrown by **Sethnakhte**. She prepared tomb no. 14 in the **Valley of the Kings** for her burial, but it was taken over by Sethnakhte. Her body has not been recovered. See also **Bay**.

THEBES. Greek name for the Egyptian city of *Waset* in the fourth **nome** of **Upper Egypt**. Also known as Diospolis Magna. The early history of the city is obscure, but during the **First Intermediate Period** its rulers took the royal title. It became the capital of Egypt when **Mentuhotep I** reunited Egypt under **Dynasty 11**. Although southerners, the rulers of **Dynasty 12** moved the capital to **Itjtawy** in the north, Thebes remaining the most important city in the south. It regained its prominent position at the end of the **Second Intermediate Period** when the princes of Thebes led the fight against the **Hyksos** rulers in the north and reunited Egypt under **Dynasty 18**. Its god **Amun** was elevated to the position of chief god of Egypt and his **temple** at **Karnak** was enlarged and richly endowed. A second major temple was built at **Luxor** within the city. The royal tombs from Dynasty 18 to **Dynasty 20** were constructed on the west bank of the **Nile** opposite the city in the **Valley of the Kings**. The queens, princesses, and some princes were buried in the **Valley of the Queens**, while the tombs of the officials were located in the nearby cliffs. Also on the west bank near the edge of cultivation were constructed the mortuary temples of the kings such as the **Ramesseum** and **Medinet Habu**.

During **Dynasty 19** the king began to reside more frequently in the north, but the city remained the main religious capital and southern administrative centre. It was often known simply as *niwt,* the city. From the end of Dynasty 20 Thebes and the southern region became increasingly independent of central rule under the **high priests of Amun**. The city was sacked during the **Assyrian** invasion of 666 BC and never recovered its prominence. It remained a bastion of Egyptian nationalism during the **Ptolemaic Period** and was held by various rebel kings. Following the Roman conquest, it became a tourist centre. After the adoption of Christianity, its temples were converted into churches or desecrated and abandoned and it reverted to a minor provincial town after the Arabic conquest. The temples and tombs have been cleared and excavated in modern times, but few remains of the living quarters of the ancient city have been located.

THINIS. Greek name for a city in northern **Upper Egypt**, possibly in or near modern Girga. Ancient Egyptian *Tjeny*, capital of the eighth Upper Egyptian **nome.** The major god worshipped at the site was **Anhur**, later identified with the god **Shu**. The city is named by **Manetho** as the native town of the kings of **Dynasties 1** and **2**, and the population may have been buried in the nearby cemetery of **Naga el-Deir**. It is mentioned in texts of the **First Intermediate Period** when it was fought over by rival **Dynasties 10** and **11** until its final capture by **Mentuhotep II**. It is also mentioned in Egyptian texts in the **Middle** and **New Kingdoms** and in the **Third Intermediate Period** became the seat of the **vizier** of Upper Egypt. In the **Ptolemaic Period** the capital of the nome was moved elsewhere. The site has never been securely identified.

THIRD INTERMEDIATE PERIOD (c.1069–716 BC). The term used by some Egyptologists for the period between the end of **Dynasty 20** and the beginning of **Dynasty 26** although some end it with the inception of **Dynasty 25**. During this period Egypt was again divided, with the south virtually independent for much of the time. Later local rulers sprang up in various cities and **Dynasties 22–24** vied for recognition. See also **Late Period, New Kingdom.**

THOTH. Greek name for the Egyptian god *Djehuty*. He is depicted in the form of an ibis-headed human with a moon's disk on his head. His principal seat of worship was **Hermopolis** and the ibis and baboon were sacred to him. He was worshipped throughout Egypt as the god of scribal arts who wrote the judgement of **Osiris** at the **weighing of the heart**.

THUTEMHAT (reigned c.720 BC). Minor kinglet at the end of the **Third Intermediate Period.** Throne name Neferkheperre Kha-khau. He is attested as a ruler in **Hermopolis**, but it is not certain whether he was a predecessor or successor of the king **Nimlot** of Hermopolis attested on the **stela** of **Piye.**

THUTMOSE I (reigned c. 1504–1492 BC). Throne name Akheperre. Son of the lady Seniseneb by an unknown father. He succeeded the childless

Amenhotep I and must have been related to the ruling family. Thutmose I continued Egyptian expansion south in **Nubia** and in Asia penetrating as far as the Euphrates and defeating the army of **Mitanni.** He married his sister **Ahmose**, possibly after his accession, and had two daughters, notably **Hatshepsut**, but his successor **Thutmose II** was the son of another wife, **Mutnefret.** At least two other older sons possibly by Mutnefret, **Amenmose** and **Wadjmose**, predeceased their father. Thutmose I appears to have been the first ruler to be buried in the **Valley of the Kings** and is the first attested ruler at the village of **Deir el-Medina** where the tomb builders were located. The construction of his tomb is described in a text by his official **Ineni** and may have been tomb no. 20 although his final burial might have been in tomb no. 38, discovered in 1899, to which he may have been moved later by his grandson **Thutmose III**. His **mummy** has not been recovered.

THUTMOSE II (reigned c.1492–1479 BC). Throne name Aakheperenre. Son of **Thutmose I** and **Mutnefret**. He may have been fairly young on his accession and married his half-sister **Hatshepsut.** The length of his reign is uncertain. His forces put down a revolt in **Nubia** early in the reign. He left one daughter **Nefrure** by Hatshepsut and a son and successor **Thutmose III** by a minor wife or concubine **Isis.** His tomb has not been identified, but his **mummy** was recovered from the **royal cache** in 1881.

THUTMOSE III (reigned c.1479–1425 BC). Throne name Menkheperre. Son of **Thutmose II** and **Isis**. He succeeded his father as a young child under the regency of his step-mother **Hatshepsut** who soon took the royal title. He remained in relative obscurity until year 21 when Hatshepsut presumably died and he appears at the head of his army invading Palestine-Syria. Thutmose III defeated the local princes at the battle of Megiddo and firmly established Egyptian rule in the area with a series of campaigns which led to the defeat of **Mitanni**. Later in his reign he ordered the removal of all inscriptions concerning his step-mother Hatshepsut. He was regarded in later times as one of the most effective of rulers and **scarabs** with his throne name were produced centuries after his death. It is not clear if he married his half-sister **Nefrure**, but he had at least two other principal wives, Satioh and Meryre-Hatshepsut, not of royal birth, who was the mother of his successor **Amenhotep II** as his eldest son **Amenemhat** had predeceased him. Thutmose III was buried in the **Valley of the Kings** (tomb no. 34, which was discovered in 1898), and his body was recovered from the **royal cache** in 1881. He has been erroneously described as being very short, but this is due to damage of the lower part of his **mummy**.

THUTMOSE IV (reigned c.1400–1390 BC). Throne name Menkheperure. Son of **Amenhotep II** and Tiaa. Thutmose IV was apparently a younger son and not destined to rule, but in his Dream **stela**, he recounts that after hunting in the desert, he rested at the foot of the **Sphinx** and in a dream was promised the throne if he would undertake clearance and restoration of the monument, which he did on his accession. Little is known of his reign, but he concluded peace with **Mitanni** and is the first ruler attested with a Mitannian princess—the daughter of Artatama I—as a wife. His principal wives were Nefertari and the Princess Iaret who was either his sister or daughter. Thutmose IV was succeeded by **Amenhotep III**, his son by a minor wife **Mutemwia** whose origin is not known. He was buried in the **Valley of the Kings** (tomb no. 43, discovered in 1903), and his **mummy** was recovered from the **royal cache** in the tomb of **Amenhotep II** in 1898.

THUTMOSE (fl. c.1330 BC). The name of a sculptor at **Amarna** whose house has been excavated and in which important royal sculptures, notably busts of Queen **Nefertiti**, have been found. He is one of the few Egyptian artists whose works can be identified.

TI (fl. c.2450 BC). High official during **Dynasty 5**. He held the post of overseer of the **pyramids** of **Neferirkare** and **Niuserre** and the sun-temples of **Sahure**, Neferirkare, **Reneferef**, and Niuserre. His **mastaba** tomb at **Saqqara** contains some of the finest carved scenes of daily life from this period. It was discovered by Auguste **Mariette** in 1860.

TITULARY, ROYAL. The full style of the royal titulary consisted of five names and is attested in complete form from the **Middle Kingdom**. In **Dynasty 1** only two names were used: the **Horus** name which identified the king with the sky-god **Horus** and the *nebty* name which associated the king with the goddesses **Nekhbet** and **Wadjet**, the "two ladies", mistresses of **Upper** and **Lower Egypt**. The Horus name was generally used on its own as the royal name in **Dynasties 1–3** so it is difficult to match these with personal names from other sources. The personal name or nomen becomes more prominent from **Dynasty 4** when it appears in a **cartouche** from the reign of **Snefru**, but is clearly distinguished from

Dynasty 5 when there also appears the prenomen or throne name adopted at accession and compounded with the name of the sun-god **Re**. The Golden Horus name gradually evolved from a title and was also adopted on accession. The Horus name was written in a **serekh**, a recessed palace facade, while the prenomen and nomen were written in the cartouche ring. From **Dynasty 19** epithets were adopted to be added to the prenomen and nomen.

TITUS (39–81 AD). Roman emperor. Original name Titus Flavius Vespasianus. He was born in Rome on 30 December 39, son of Titus Flavius Vespasianus, the future Emperor **Vespasian**, and Flavia Domitilla. Titus headed one of the legions which his father took on his campaign against the Jewish Revolt in 67. He accompanied his father to **Alexandria** in 69 when his father was proclaimed emperor and then took over command of the expedition against Jerusalem. Titus captured Jerusalem in August 70 and returned to Rome via Egypt where he was present at **Memphis** for the installation of an **Apis** bull. He became his father's staunchest supporter in Rome and succeeded him in 79. He proved an effective and popular emperor but died after a short rule at Aquae Cutilae on 13 September 81.

TIY (fl. c.1400–1340 BC). Chief wife of **Amenhotep III** and daughter of **Yuya** and Tuya. She was already married in year 2 of the reign and is depicted prominently on many monuments. She was the mother of **Akhenaten** and probably his elder brother, the crown prince Thutmose who predeceased his father, as well as several daughters, notably **Sitamun** who married her father, Henuttaneb, Isis, and Nebetah. Tiy survived into the reign of her son and is depicted at **Amarna** with a Princess **Baketaten** who may have been a daughter or granddaughter. Her original burial place is uncertain and some of her funerary equipment was apparently reused in tomb no. 55 in the **Valley of the Kings.** A previously unidentified female **mummy** in the **royal cache** has recently been identified as the queen.

TIY (fl. c.1370–1323 BC). Wife of **Ay**. She first appears in the **Amarna Period** when she is described as the nurse of **Nefertiti.** It has been conjectured that Ay was the father of Nefertiti in which case Tiy would be her step-mother. She is later depicted as Ay's queen after he ascended the throne which makes it unlikely that he married **Ankhesenamun**. See also **Akhenaten**.

TOD. Modern name for ancient Egyptian *Djerty*, a site in **Upper Egypt** just south of **Thebes** where there are remains of the **temple** of **Montu** from the **Middle Kingdom** to the **Roman Period**. The site was excavated by French archaeologists in 1934–36; in the last year the Tod treasure consisting of silver vessels, bars of precious material, and cylinder seals, dating to the reign of **Amenemhat II** and probably of foreign origin, was discovered.

TOMB ROBBERY PAPYRI. A series of **papyri** dating from the reigns of **Ramesses IX** and **Ramesses XI** consisting of the official reports into claims that the royal tombs in the **Valley of the Kings** and elsewhere on the west bank had been violated and robbed. After some dispute the claims were investigated and the culprits were punished severely.

TRIAD. A term used by Egyptologists to refer to the standard divine family of each city which usually consisted of the chief god of the city, his wife, and his son. For example, the triad from **Thebes** consisted of the god **Amun**, his wife **Mut**, and son **Khons**; and that of **Memphis** comprised the god **Ptah**, his wife **Sakhmet**, and his son **Nefertum**. A triad might also consist of a god or goddess and two consorts. See also **Religion**.

TUNA EL-GEBEL. Arabic name for the necropolis of **Hermopolis** in the desert near the city. A boundary **stela** of **Akhenaten** marks it as the edge of his city at **Amarna**. The site is primarily known for its decorated tombs from the **Persian** to the **Roman Period**, notably that of **Petosiris** discovered in 1920 and underground galleries for the burials of ibis **mummies** sacred to the god **Thoth**. The site has been excavated by the Egyptian Antiquities Service in 1919–20 and 1931–52, and by a German expedition from 1983.

TURA. Modern name for the site south of Cairo of the principal limestone quarry used by the ancient Egyptians for fine stone, notably for the outside blocks for the **pyramids** at **Giza**. The quarries there are still in use. See also **Hatnub**.

TURIN EGYPTIAN MUSEUM. The Museo Egizio, or Egyptian Museum, in Turin, Italy, was founded in 1824 with the purchase of the collection of the French consul-general in Egypt, Bernardino Drovetti. The collection included 100 statues, particularly an extremely fine representation of **Ramesses II**, along with other Egyptian objects, many from **Deir el-Medina**, notably **papyri** and especially the important **Turin Royal Canon**. The collection was further enlarged by the director of the Museum from 1894 to 1927, Ernesto Schiaparelli, who conducted excavations in the **Valley of the Queens**, **Deir el-Medina** where he found the intact tomb of **Kha**, **Giza**, **Heliopolis**, Qau el-Kebir, and **Gebelein**. The Museum took part in the **Nubian Rescue Campaign** and was rewarded with the gift of the **temple** of Ellesiya.

TURIN ROYAL CANON. The only **king-list** to survive on **papyrus** although the text is now damaged and incomplete. It was written during the **Ramesside Period**. When complete, it was extremely detailed, listing almost every king with the years of his reign, all divided into dynasties. A similar text was doubtless used by the later historian **Manetho**.

TUTANKHAMUN (reigned c.1336–1327 BC). Throne name Nebkheperre, formerly Tutankhaten. Son of a king, probably **Akhenaten**. Still a child, he succeeded Akhenaten after the ephemeral rule of **Smenkhkare** presumably under the tutelage of **Ay** and **Horemheb**. His reign is marked by the return to orthodoxy and the worship of **Amun** and the move of the capital back to **Thebes**. He married his probable half-sister **Ankhesenpaaten**, who later changed her name to **Ankhesenamun**, but had no surviving children. He was the last ruler of the family of **Dynasty 18** and was succeeded by Ay who buried him in tomb no. 62 in the **Valley of the Kings**. His memory was suppressed under **Dynasty 19**. The discovery of his intact tomb in 1922 has ensured his fame although, as he died young, he took no independent actions in his reign. See also **Carter, Howard**.

- U -

UDJAHORRESNET (fl. 530–520 BC). Egyptian officer from **Sais**, commander of the navy under **Ahmose II** and **Psamtik III**. He became chief physician to **Cambyses** of **Persia** following his conquest of Egypt in 525 BC and claimed to choose the royal **titulary** of Cambyses. He left a long autobiographical inscription on a statue now in the Vatican Museum. He used his influence to benefit Sais and its **temple**. His tomb has recently been discovered at **Abusir**.

UGARIT. A major town and seaport on the eastern Mediterranean coast in modern Syria, modern Ras Shamra. Relations with Egypt are attested from the **Middle Kingdom** and the city became part of the Egyptian empire in the **New Kingdom** until it switched its allegiance to the **Hittites** at the end of **Dynasty 18**. It was destroyed by the **Sea Peoples** about year 8 of **Ramesses III**. Excavations by a French expedition began in 1928 and have yielded much material, including inscribed tablets.

UNAS (reigned c.2375–2345 BC). Final ruler of **Dynasty 5** and successor of **Djedkare**. His name has also been transcribed as **Wenis**. He is principally known for his **pyramid** tomb at **Saqqara**, opened in 1881, which is the earliest pyramid to be inscribed on the inside walls with the religious texts now known as **pyramid texts**. The causeway to his mortuary **temple** was also decorated with fine reliefs.

UPPER EGYPT. Ancient Egyptian *Shemau*. The area of Egypt comprising the **Nile** Valley from **Memphis** up to **Elephantine** in ancient times. The area seems to have evolved into a separate kingdom with its capital at **Hierakonpolis** in the late **Predynastic Period** and was united with **Lower Egypt** by **Narmer**, probably by conquest. It was one of the two lands ruled by the Egyptian monarch. In the royal **titulary,** the symbol of Upper Egypt was a bee and its crown was the tall white crown. The term is sometimes used by modern Egyptologists with a more restrictive meaning covering the area from **Asyut** south, the northern part being termed **Middle Egypt**.

URAEUS. Name for the cobra, representing the goddess **Wadjet,** which appears on the brow of the headdress of the monarch and so signifies royalty and kingship. During **Dynasty 25** the **Nubian** rulers of Egypt wore a double uraeus. See also **Nekhbet**.

URONARTI. Modern name for a site in Lower **Nubia** in the Second **Cataract** region where a fortress was constructed on an island under **Senusret III** as part of the Egyptian garrison. Egyptian *Khesef Iunu*. It was abandoned in the **Second Intermediate Period**. The site has now been flooded by the lake created by the Aswan High Dam.

USERKAF (reigned c.2494–2487 BC). First ruler of **Dynasty 5**. According to a later legend in the **Westcar Papyrus**, he was the eldest of triplet sons of Rededet, a priestess of **Re**. The story is fictitious, but emphasizes the attachment of the new dynasty to the cult of Re. The king built a sun-**temple** at Abu Ghurab near **Abusir** which was excavated by a Swiss expedition in the 1950s, but he was buried in a **pyramid** at **Saqqara.**

USERKARE (reigned c.2321 BC). An obscure king of **Dynasty 6**. He appears to have been the direct successor of **Teti**, possibly his son by Khentet- (whose full name is lost), but he was quickly followed by **Pepy I** who may have been his brother. It is possible that he was eliminated by his more ambitious brother.

USHABTI see **SHABTI.**

- V -

VALLEY OF THE KINGS. Known in Arabic as Biban el-Moluk. A secluded desert area in the cliffs on the western bank of **Thebes** consisting of two valleys chosen as the burial place for the kings of **Dynasties 18–20**. There are 62 tombs there, mainly in the eastern valley. It is probable that the first ruler to be buried here was **Thutmose I** and with the subsequent burials of the later monarchs it became standard practice to inter royalty here. Apart from kings, there are tombs of some princes and favoured courtiers. The tombs were constructed by a crew of royal workmen based at **Deir el-Medina**. The walls of the tombs were decorated with religious texts and contain very little in the way of historical information. The last tomb built was that of **Ramesses XI**, but it appears never to have been completed, and future rulers were buried in the north where they now lived.

Most of the tombs were plundered at the end of Dynasty 20 and beginning of **Dynasty 21**. Some remained open in the **Graeco-Roman Period** and later periods, while others were rediscovered and excavated in the nineteenth and early twentieth centuries—notably the tomb of **Tutankhamun**, the only royal tomb to be recovered intact. Most tombs still await full publication. Recent work has focused on the unexplored tomb of **Ramesses II** and that of his sons. Following the desecration of the royal tombs, the **mummies** of many of the rulers were gathered together in two secret **royal caches** from which they were recovered in the nineteenth century.

VALLEY OF THE QUEENS. An area on the western bank of **Thebes** where the tombs of the queens and some princes of **Dynasties 19–20**

were constructed. The most notable is the tomb of **Nefertari**, wife of **Ramesses II**.

VESPASIAN (9–79 AD). Roman emperor. Full name Titus Flavius Vespasianus. He was born at Falacrina near Rieti on 17 November 9, son of Titus Flavius Sabinus and Vespasia Polla. He pursued a senatorial career taking part in the conquest of Britain in 43 and governing Africa. He was put in command of the army sent to crush the Jewish revolt in 67. On 1 July 69 he was proclaimed emperor by the prefect of Egypt Tiberius Julius **Alexander** and his forces and supported by all the Eastern and Balkan armies. He moved to **Alexandria** to cut wheat exports to Italy and is recorded as visiting the temple of **Sarapis** there. His forces took Rome in December 69, and he reached Italy in 70. Vespasian proved an effective ruler. He died at Aquae Clutiae near Rieti on 23 or 24 June 79.

VICEROY OF KUSH. Governor of Egyptian **Nubia** in the **New Kingdom** whose title was literally King's Son of Kush although no royal princes ever held this office. The title was established in early **Dynasty 18** and continued until the end of **Dynasty 20** when the Viceroy Panehsi became embroiled in the civil war in the Theban region at first by royal command but was eventually driven back to Nubia by **Piankh**. Egyptian control of Nubia seems to have lapsed at his death, but the title was used purely symbolically by descendants of Piankh.

VIZIER. Modern name based on the Arabic *wazir* for the chief administrative official of the Egyptian kingdom; ancient Egyptian *tjaty*. The office appears to be attested from the **Early Dynastic Period**. From the **New Kingdom** the post was divided into two, one vizier for **Lower Egypt** and one for **Upper Egypt**. The post was the most powerful next to that of the ruler and an ambitious vizier might be a threat to the king as in the case of **Amenemhat I**.

- W -

WADI EL-HUDI. Site in the Eastern Desert used as a quarry for amethyst during **Dynasties 11–13**. The site was rediscovered in 1939 and explored by the Egyptian archaeologist Ahmed Fakhry in 1944–49 when he copied surviving inscriptions. It was again surveyed by A. I. Sadek in 1975.

WADI ES-SEBUA. A site in Lower **Nubia** which contained **temples** of **Amenhotep III** and **Ramesses II**. This has now been flooded by the lake of the Aswan High Dam, but the main temple was removed and re-erected elsewhere. See also **Gerf Hussein**.

WADI HAMMAMAT. Site in the Eastern Desert used as a quarry for silt-stone (greywacke) from the **Old Kingdom**. There are many inscriptions recording expeditions, notably those of **Mentuhotep III** and **Mentuhotep IV** of **Dynasty 11**. The valley was the major access route to the Red Sea coast and the land of **Punt**.

WADI MAGHARA. Site in the Sinai used as a quarry for turquoise from **Dynasty 3** until the **Middle Kingdom** and noted for important royal inscriptions of the **Old Kingdom**. See also **Serabit el-Khadim**.

WADJET. Egyptian goddess of **Buto**, usually represented as a cobra. She was the tutelary goddess of **Lower Egypt** and as such appears as part of the *nebty* or "two ladies" name in the royal **titulary** and as the **uraeus** on the royal crown. In the **Late Period** she is often represented as a lioness-headed goddess. See also **Nekhbet**.

WADJMOSE (fl. c.1504–1490 BC). Egyptian prince of **Dynasty 18.** He was the son of **Thutmose I** probably by the lady **Mutnefret**. He is attested in the reign of his father and may have become heir to the throne after the death of his elder brother **Amenmose**. He predeceased his father and a mortuary **temple** was built in his honour near the **Ramesseum** in which he and Mutnefret were commemorated. See also **Thutmose II**.

WAHIBRE (reigned 589–570 BC). The Greek version of his name is Apries. Throne name Haaibre. Son of **Psamtik II** and Takhut. He embarked on a military expedition against **Cyrene** which ended in failure. His troops mutinied and proclaimed **Ahmose II** as ruler. His own forces were defeated, and he apparently perished then or after his capture.

WEGAF (reigned c.1795–1792 BC). Throne name Khutawyre. He is generally regarded as the first ruler of **Dynasty 13**, although his position in the dynasty has recently been questioned. He appears to have been of common origin, but the circumstances of his accession are obscure. His reign was brief. See also **Second Intermediate Period**.

WEIGHING OF THE HEART. The main feature of the judgement of the dead when the heart of the deceased, regarded by Egyptians as the seat of intelligence, was weighed on a balance against the feather of **maat** representing truth and righteousness. A virtuous heart would balance and admit the deceased to the **afterlife**, while a heavy heart would indicate an evildoer whose heart would then be devoured by a monster and hence denied an afterlife. The **Book of the Dead** was designed to fix the balance with magic spells to enable the deceased to enter the afterlife without difficulty. A heart **scarab** was often placed over the heart of the deceased with the same intention.

WENAMUN. Hero of a literary tale set at the end of **Dynasty 20**. The story outlines his adventures on a trip to Lebanon seeking wood for religious constructions at **Thebes**. The tale reflects the loss of Egyptian influence in the Near East and the political divisions in Egypt. It survives in only one incomplete copy. See also **Sinuhe**.

WENI (fl. c.2325–2275 BC). Royal official in the reigns of **Teti**, **Pepy I**, and **Nemtyemsaf** I of **Dynasty 6**, who rose to the position of governor of **Upper Egypt**. He is known from his autobiographical inscription found at **Abydos** and now in the **Cairo Egyptian Museum**. During his career, he was in charge of quarrying expeditions to **Tura** and **Hatnub**, commanded a military expedition against Asiatic raiders, and was part of a royal inquiry into the conduct of a queen of Pepy I.

WEPWAWET. Egyptian god in the form of a canine, originally a jackal but later identified by the Greeks as a wolf. Chief god of **Asyut**. His name "opener of the ways" associated him with royal conquests and as a protector and guide of the deceased through the Underworld.

WESTCAR PAPYRUS. This **papyrus** contains a literary tale set in the reign of **Khufu** of **Dynasty 4** but predicts the eventual triumph of **Dynasty 5**. The beginning and end of the text are missing. The king is entertained by tales of the feats of magicians, each told by one of his sons. The final magician foretells the end of the dynasty with Khufu's grandson and the advent of **Dynasty 5**. The papyrus is named after its earliest known owner and is now in the **Berlin Egyptian Museum**.

WILBOUR PAPYRUS. This **papyrus** is named after the Egyptologist Charles Wilbour who acquired it in Egypt and whose heirs bequeathed it to the Brooklyn Museum. It outlines in great detail the possessions of the **temple** of **Amun** throughout Egypt and the tenants in place and is important in the understanding of Egyptian land tenure and onomastics in the late **New Kingdom**.

WISDOM LITERATURE. A genre of Egyptian literature which consists of precepts by sages or kings to guide the reader in a virtuous life, known as *sebayet*, or lamentations on the failure of mankind to do so. The earliest texts are alleged to have been composed in the **Old Kingdom**. Surviving examples date from most periods of Egyptian history. The other major form of fictional Egyptian literature, apart from love poems in the **New Kingdom**, were tales such as those of **Sinuhe** or **Wenamun**. Royal inscriptions and religious texts could be written in a poetical vein.

WOMEN. Women in Egypt had the most secure position of women anywhere in the ancient world. In the Pharaonic Period women were recognized as having equal legal rights as men, and therefore had the right to own, inherit, and manage property and to appear in court in their own capacity and not with a male guardian. The wife had a valued position in any household and was normally in a monogamous **marriage** although sexual fidelity on the part of the husband was not expected. In actual fact women would find it difficult to exercise their legal rights unless they were backed by male protection so their legal rights were often more theoretical than practical. In the **Graeco-Roman Period** these rights were restricted in accordance with classical practice.

- X -

XOIS. Greek name for the capital of the sixth **nome** of **Lower Egypt**. Ancient Egyptian *Khasuu*, modern Sakha. Little is known of the site which was briefly excavated by Howard **Carter** in 1912. It is alleged by **Manetho** to have been the seat of **Dynasty 14** during the **Second Intermediate Period**.

- Y -

YAQUB-HER (reigned c.1600 BC). Ruler of the **Second Intermediate Period** attested on **scarabs**. Throne name Meruserre. He is probably one of the **Hyksos** chieftains but it is unclear whether he belongs to **Dynasty 15** or is simply a minor ruler of **Dynasty 14.** His name is similar to the Biblical patriarch Jacob whose sojourn in Egypt might derive from an account of this king.

YUYA (fl. 1390–1360 BC). High official, father of **Tiy** and father-in-law of **Amenhotep III.** He and his wife Tuya were given the honour of a tomb in the **Valley of the Kings** which was discovered intact in 1905. Their **mummies** and funerary equipment are now in the **Cairo Egyptian Museum.**

- Z -

ZAWIYET EL-ARYAN. Modern name for a site six kilometres south of **Giza** where two unfinished **pyramids** are located. The older probably belongs to **Khaba** of **Dynasty 3** and the other to **Dynasty 4.** There are also graves of **Early Dynastic Period, New Kingdom,** and **Roman Period** date. The site was excavated by the Egyptian Antiquities Service in 1903 and by the **Boston Museum of Fine Arts** in 1910–11.

ZENON (fl. c.260–240 BC). Son of Agreophon of Kaunos in Caria, Asia Minor. Secretary and later (c. 256–48 BC) manager of the gift-estate of Apollonius, finance minister of **Ptolemy II,** located at Philadelphia in the **Fayum.** He is known from his voluminous correspondence of over 1,000 **papyri** which give a valuable insight into the administration of Egypt in the early **Ptolemaic Period.**

SELECT BIBLIOGRAPHY

This bibliography is not intended to be an exhaustive and complete reference tool to the vast literature on ancient Egypt. Details on many older books can be found in the more complete bibliographies of Ibrahim Hilmy and Pratt cited below. With few exceptions, only monographs have been cited to limit the bibliography to a reasonable size. Modern works, especially on archaeological excavations, have been preferred to older accounts. There has been bias in favour of books published in English but German and French works have been noted where appropriate.

Contents

History of Egyptology and Travellers to Egypt
Travel
Bibliographies
Periodicals

GENERAL WORKS

Aldred, Cyril. *The Egyptians*. 3rd ed. Revised by Aidan Dodson. London: Thames and Hudson, 1998.

Assmann, Jan. *Ägypten: Eine Sinngeschichte*. Munich: Carl Hanser Verlag, 1996.

Baines, John, and Jaromir Malek. *Atlas of Ancient Egypt*. Oxford: Phaidon, 1980.

Davies, Vivian, and Renée Friedman. *Egypt*. London: British Museum Press, 1998.

Donadoni, Sergio, ed. *The Egyptians*. Chicago: The University of Chicago Press, 1997.

Harris, John R., ed. *The Legacy of Egypt*. 2nd ed. Oxford: Clarendon Press, 1971.

Hayes, William C. *The Scepter of Egypt*. Vol. I. New York: Harper and Brothers, 1953. Vol. II. Cambridge, Mass.: Harvard University Press, 1959.

Helck, Wolfgang, and Eberhard Otto. *Lexikon der Ägyptologie*. 7 vols. Wiesbaden: Otto Harrassowitz, 1972–92.

Kees, Hermann. *Ancient Egypt: A Cultural Topography*. London: Faber and Faber, 1961.

Lustig, Judith, ed. *Anthropology and Egyptology: A Developing Dialogue*. Sheffield, Great Britain: Sheffield Academic Press, 1997.

Malek, Jaromir, ed. *Egypt: Ancient Culture, Modern Land*. Cradles of Civilization. Norman: University of Oklahoma Press, 1993.

Posener, Georges. *A Dictionary of Egyptian Civilisation*. London: Methuen, 1962.

Sasson, Jack M., ed. *Civilizations of the Ancient Near East*. 4 vols. New York: Scribner's, 1995.

Spencer, A. Jeffrey, and Stephen Quirke, eds. *The British Museum Book of Ancient Egypt*. London: British Museum Press, 1992.

HISTORY

General

Beckerath, Jürgen von. *Handbuch der Ägyptischen Königsnamen*. Münchner Ägyptologische Studien 20. Munich: Deutscher Kunstverlag, 1984.

The Cambridge Ancient History. 10 vols. 2nd and 3rd eds. Cambridge: Cambridge University Press, 1981–96.

Davies, W. Vivian, and Louise Schofield, eds. *Egypt, the Aegean and the Levant: Interconnections in the Second Millennium BC*. London: British Museum Press, 1995.

Gardiner, Alan H. *Egypt of the Pharaohs*. Oxford: Oxford University Press, 1961.

Grimal, Nicolas. *A History of Ancient Egypt*. Oxford: Blackwell: 1992.

Helck, Wolfgang. *Die altägyptischen Gaue*. Beihefte zum Tübinger Atlas des Vorderen Orients B 5. Wiesbaden: Dr. Ludwig Reichert, 1974.

Hornung, Erik. *Grundzüge der ägyptischen Geschichte*. 3rd ed. Darmstadt: Wissenschaftliche Buchgesellschaft, 1988.

James, T. G. Henry. *A Short History of Ancient Egypt*. Cairo: Librairie du Liban, 1995.

Kemp, Barry J. *Ancient Egypt: Anatomy of a Civilization*. London: Routledge, 1989.

O'Connor, David, and David P. Silverman, eds. *Ancient Egyptian Kingship*. Leiden: E. J. Brill, 1995.

Trigger, Bruce G., et al. *Ancient Egypt: A Social History*. Cambridge: Cambridge University Press, 1983.

Vandersleyen, Claude. *L'Égypte et la vallée du Nil. Tome 2. De la fin de l'Ancien Empire à la fin du Nouvel Empire*. Paris: Presses Universitaires de France, 1995.

Vercoutter, Jean. *L'Égypte et la vallée du Nil. Tome 1. Des origines à la fin de l'Ancien Empire*. Paris: Presses Universitaires de France, 1992.

Prehistoric and Predynastic Period

Adams, Barbara. *Predynastic Egypt*. Aylesbury, Great Britain: Shire Publications, 1988.

Adams, Barbara, and Krzysztof Cialowicz. *Protodynastic Egypt*. Aylesbury, Great Britain: Shire Publications, 1997.

Bard, Kathryn A. *From Farmers to Pharaohs*. Sheffield, Great Britain: Sheffield Academic Press, 1994.

Baumgartel, Elise. *The Cultures of Prehistoric Egypt*. London: Oxford University Press, 1947.

Hayes, William C. *Most Ancient Egypt*. Chicago: University of Chicago Press, 1965.

Hoffman, Michael A. *Egypt before the Pharaohs: The Prehistoric Foundations of Ancient Egypt*. London: Routledge and Kegan Paul, 1980.

Early Dynastic Period and Old Kingdom

Aldred, Cyril. *Egypt to the End of the Old Kingdom*. London: Thames and Hudson, 1965.

Andreu, Guillemette. *Egypt in the Age of the Pyramids*. Translated by David Lorton. Ithaca, N.Y.: Cornell University Press, 1997.

Emery, Walter B. *Archaic Egypt*. London: Penguin Books, 1961.

Hart, George. *Pharaohs and Pyramids*. London: Herbert Press, 1991.

Malek, Jaroslav, and Werner Forman. *In the Shadow of the Pyramids: Egypt during the Old Kingdom*. London: Orbis, 1986.

Spencer, A. Jeffrey. *Aspects of Early Egypt*. London: British Museum Press, 1996.

———. *Early Egypt*. London: British Museum Press, 1993.

Strudwick, Nigel. *The Administration of Egypt in the Old Kingdom*. London: Kegan Paul International, 1985.

First Intermediate Period, Middle Kingdom, and Second Intermediate Period

Bietak, Manfred. *Pharaonen und Fremde: Dynastien im Dunkel*. Vienna: Museen der Stadt Wien, 1994.

Bourriau, Janine. *Pharaohs and Mortals: Egyptian Art in the Middle Kingdom*. Cambridge: Fitzwilliam Museum, 1988.

Fay, Biri. *The Louvre Sphinx and Royal Sculpture from the Reign of Amenemhat II*. Mainz am Rhein, Germany: Philipp von Zabern, 1996.

Gomaà, Farouk. *Die Besiedlung Ägyptens während des Mittleren Reiches*. 2 vols. Beihefte zum Tübinger Atlas des Vorderen Orients B 66. Wiesbaden: Dr. Ludwig Reichert, 1986.

Matzker, Ingo. *Die letzten Könige der 12. Dynastie*. Frankfurt: Peter Lang, 1986.

Obsomer, Claude. *Sesostris Ier: Étude chronologique et historique du règne*. Paris: Connaissance de l'Égypte ancienne, 1995.

Quirke, Stephen. *Middle Kingdom Studies*. New Malden, Great Britain: SIA Publishing, 1991.

Ryholt, Kim. *The Second Intermediate Period in Egypt, c.1800-1550 B.C.* Copenhagen: Carsten Niebuhr Publications, 1997.

Van Seters, John. *The Hyksos: A New Investigation*. New Haven: Yale University Press, 1966.

New Kingdom: Dynasty 18

Bryan, Betsy. *The Reign of Thutmose IV*. Baltimore: Johns Hopkins University Press, 1991.

Cummings, Barbara, and Benedict Davies. *Egyptian Historical Records of the Later Eighteenth Dynasty*. 5 vols. Warminster, Great Britain: Aris and Phillips, 1982–94.

Della Monica, Madeleine. *Thoutmosis III: Le plus grand des Pharaons*. Paris: Le Léopard d'Or, 1991.

Der Manuelian, Peter. *Studies in the Reign of Amenophis II*. Hildesheimer Ägyptologische Beiträge 26. Hildesheim: Gerstenberg, 1987.

Dorman, Peter. *The Monuments of Senenmut*. London: Kegan Paul International, 1988.

Gitton, Michel. *Les divines épouses de la 18e dynastie*. Besançon: Annales Littéraires de l'Université de Besançon, 1984.

———. *L'épouse du dieu Ahmes Néfertary*. Besançon: Annales Littéraires de l'Université de Besançon, 1975.

Kozloff, Arielle P., and Betsy M. Bryan. *Egypt's Dazzling Sun: Amenhotep III and His World*. Cleveland: Cleveland Museum of Art, 1992.

O'Connor, David, and Eric Cline, eds. *Amenhotep III: Perspectives on his Reign*. Ann Arbor: University of Michigan Press, 1998.

Redford, Donald B. *History and Chronology of the Eighteenth Dynasty of Egypt: Seven Studies*. Toronto: University of Toronto Press, 1967.

Scmitz, Franz-Jürgen. *Amenophis I*. Hildesheimer Ägyptologische Beiträge 6. Hildesheim: Gerstenberg, 1978.

Tyldesley, Joyce. *Hatchepsut: The Female Monarch*. London: Viking, 1996.

Vandersleyen, Claude. *Les guerres d'Amosis*. Brussels: Fondation Égyptologique Reine Élisabeth, 1971.

The Amarna Period

Aldred, Cyril. *Akhenaten and Nefertiti*. London: Thames and Hudson, 1973.

―――. *Akhenaten, King of Egypt*. London: Thames and Hudson, 1988.

Krauss, Rolf. *Das Ende der Amarnazeit*. Hildesheimer Ägyptologische Beiträge 7. Hildesheim: Gerstenberg, 1978.

Martin, Geoffrey T. M. *A Bibliography of the Amarna Period and Its Aftermath: The reigns of Akhenaten, Smenkhkare, Tutankhamun and Ay (c.1350–1321 BC)*. London: Kegan Paul International, 1991.

Moran, William L. *The Amarna Letters*. Baltimore: Johns Hopkins University Press, 1992.

Redford, Donald B. *Akhenaten, the Heretic King*. Princeton: Princeton University Press, 1984.

Thomas, Angela. *Akenaten's Egypt*. Aylesbury, Great Britain: Shire Publications, 1988.

Tyldesley, Joyce. *Nefertiti: Egypt's Sun Queen*. London: Viking, 1998.

Tutankhamun

Beinlich, Horst, and Mohamed Saleh. *Corpus der Hieroglyphischen Inschriften aus dem Grab des Tutanchamun*. Oxford: Griffith Institute, 1989.

Carter, Howard, and Arthur C. Mace. *The Tomb of Tutankhamen*. 3 vols. London: Cassell and Company, 1923.

Černý, Jaroslav. *Hieratic Inscriptions from the Tomb of Tut'ankhamun*. Tut'ankhamun Tomb Series 2. Oxford: Griffith Institute, 1965.

Desroches-Noblecourt, Christiane. *Life and Death of a Pharaoh*: *Tutankhamen*. London: The Connoisseur and Michael Joseph, 1963.

Eaton-Krauss, Marianne. *The Sarcophagus in the Tomb of Tutankhamun*. Oxford: Griffith Institute, 1993.

Eaton-Krauss, Marianne, and Erhart Graefe. *The Small Golden Shrine from the Tomb of Tutankhamun*. Oxford: Griffith Institute, 1985.

Edwards, I. Eiddon S. *Treasures of Tutankhamun*. London: Trustees of the British Museum, 1972.

―――. *Tutankhamun: His Tomb and Its Treasures*. London: Victor Gollancz, 1979.

Jones, Dilwyn. *Model Boats from the Tomb of Tut'ankhamun*. Tut'ankhamun's Tomb Series 9. Oxford: Griffith Institute, 1990.

el-Khouli, A., R. Holthoer, C. Hope, and O. Kaper. *Stone Vessels, Pottery and Sealings from the Tomb of Tut'ankhamun*. Oxford: Griffith Institute, 1993.

Leek, F. Filce. *The Human Remains from the Tomb of Tut'ankhamun.* Tut'ankhamun's Tomb Series 5. Oxford: Griffith Institute, 1972.

Littauer, M. A., and J. H. Crouwel. *Chariots and Related Equipment from the Tomb of Tut'ankhamun.* Tut'ankhamun's Tomb Series 8. Oxford: Griffith Institute, 1985.

el-Mallakh, Kamal, and Arnold C. Brackman. *The Gold of Tutankhamen.* New York: Newsweek Books, 1978.

Manniche, Lise. *Musical Instruments from the Tomb of Tut'ankhamun.* Tut'ankhamun's Tomb Series 6. Oxford: Griffith Institute, 1976.

McLeod, Wallace. *Composite Bows from the Tomb of Tut'ankhamun.* Tutankh'amun's Tomb Series 3. Oxford: Griffith Institute, 1970.

———. *Self Bows and Other Archery Tackle from the Tomb of Tut'ankhamun.* Tut'ankhamun's Tomb Series 4. Oxford: Griffith Institute, 1982.

Murray, Helen, and Mary Nuttall. *A Handlist of Howard Carter's Catalogue of Objects in Tut'ankhamun's Tomb.* Tut'ankhamun's Tomb Series 1. Oxford: Griffith Institute, 1963.

Reeves, Nicholas. *The Complete Tutankhamun: The King, the Tomb, the Royal Treasure.* London: Thames and Hudson, 1990.

Tait, W. John. *Game-Boxes and Accessories from the Tomb of Tut'ankhamun.* Tut'ankhamun's Tomb Series 7. Oxford: Griffith Institute, 1986.

Welsh, Frances. *Tutankhamun's Egypt.* Aylesbury, Great Britain: Shire Publications, 1993.

New Kingdom: Dynasties 19–20

Gomaà, Farouk. *Chaemwese, Sohn Ramses' II und Hohenpriester von Memphis.* Wiesbaden, Germany: Otto Harrasowitz, 1973.

Kitchen, Kenneth A. *Pharaoh Triumphant: The Life and Times of Ramesses II, King of Egypt.* Warminster, Great Britain: Aris and Phillips, 1982.

———. *Ramesside Inscriptions.* 8 vols. Oxford: Blackwell, 1968–90.

———. *Ramesside Inscriptions Translated and Annotated: Notes and Comments.* Vol. I. Oxford: Blackwell, 1993.

———. *Ramesside Inscriptions Translated and Annotated: Translations.* Vols I–II. Oxford: Blackwell, 1993–95.

Murnane, William J. *The Road to Kadesh.* 2nd ed. Chicago: The Oriental Institute of the University of Chicago, 1995.

Peden, Alexander. *Egyptian Historical Inscriptions of the Twentieth Dynasty.* Jonsered, Sweden: Paul Aströms, 1994.

———. *The Reign of Ramesses IV.* Warminster, Great Britain: Aris and Phillips, 1994.

Sourouzian, Hourig. *Les monuments du roi Merenptah.* Deutsches Archäologisches Institut. Abteilung Kairo. Sonderscrift 22. Mainz am Rhein, Germany: Philipp von Zabern, 1989.

Vernus, Pascal. *Affaires et scandales sous les Ramsès.* Paris: Pygmalion, 1993.

Third Intermediate and Late Periods

Der Manulian, Peter. *Living in the Past: Studies in Archaism of the Egyptian Twenty-Sixth Dynasty.* London: Kegan Paul International, 1994.

Gomaà, Farouk. *Die libyschen Fürstentümer des Delta vom Tod Osorkons II. bis zur Wiedervereinigung Ägyptens durch Psametik I.* Beihefte zum Tübinger Atlas des Vorderen Orient B6. Wiesbaden, Germany: Dr. Ludwig Reinart, 1974.

Kienitz, Friedrich K. *Die politische Geschichte Ägyptens vom 7. bis zum 4. Jahrhundert vor der Zeitwende.* Berlin: Akademie Verlag, 1953.

Kitchen, Kenneth A. *The Third Intermediate Period in Egypt.* Rev. ed. Warminster, Great Britain: Aris and Phillips, 1995.

Leahy, Anthony. *Libya and Egypt c1300–750 BC.* London: SOAS, Centre of Near and Middle Eastern Studies and the Society for Libyan Studies, 1990.

Posener, Georges. *La première domination Perse en Égypte.* Cairo: Institut français d'archéologie orientale, 1936.

Vittmann, Günther. *Priester und Beamte im Theben der Spätzeit.* Vienna: Institute für Afrikanistik und Ägyptologie der Universität Wien, 1978.

Ptolemaic and Roman Periods

Bagnall, Roger S. *Egypt in Late Antiquity.* Princeton: Princeton University Press, 1993.

———. *Reading Papyri, Writing Ancient History.* London: Routledge, 1995.

Bianchi, Robert, et al. *Cleopatra's Egypt: Age of the Ptolemies.* Brooklyn: The Brooklyn Museum, 1989.

Bowman, Alan K. *Egypt after the Pharaohs 332 BC-AD 642: From Alexander to the Arab Conquest.* London: British Museum Publications, 1986.

Ellis, Simon. *Graeco-Roman Egypt.* Aylesbury, Great Britain: Shire Publications, 1992.

Hölbl, Günther. *Geschichte der Ptolemäerreiches*. Darmstadt, Germany: Wissenschaftliche Buchgesellschaft, 1994.

Hughes, George R., and Richard Jasnow. *Oriental Institute Hawara Papyri*. Chicago: The Oriental Institute of the University of Chicago, 1997.

Thompson, Dorothy J. *Memphis under the Ptolemies*. Princeton: Princeton University Press, 1988.

Whitehorne, John. *Cleopatras*. London: Routledge, 1994.

Coptic Period

Atiya, Aziz A. *The Coptic Encyclopedia*. 8 vols. New York: Macmillan, 1991.

Badawy, Alexander. *Coptic Art and Archaeology: The Art of the Christian Egyptians from the Late Antique to the Middle Ages*. Cambridge, Mass.: MIT Press, 1978.

Frend, William H. C. *The Rise of the Monophysite Movement*. Cambridge: Cambridge University Press, 1972.

Friedman, Florence D. *Beyond the Pharaohs*. Providence: Museum of Art, Rhode Island School of Design, 1989.

Gould, Graham. *The Desert Fathers on Monastic Community*. Oxford: Clarendon Press, 1993.

MacCoull, Leslie. *Dioscorus of Aphrodito*. Berkeley: University of California Press, 1988.

Rousseau, Philip. *Pachomius*. Berkeley: University of California Press, 1985.

Rubenson, Samuel. *The Letters of St. Anthony*. Minneapolis, Minn.: Fortress Press, 1995.

Timm, Stefan. *Ägypten: Das Christentum bis zur Araberzeit (bis zum 7. Jahrhundert)*. Wiesbaden: Dr. Ludwig Reichert Verlag, 1983.

———. *Das christlich-koptische Ägypten in arabischer Zeit*. 6 vols. Wiesbaden: Dr. Ludwig Reichert Verlag, 1984–92.

The Bible and Egypt

Freedman, David Noel, ed. *The Anchor Bible Dictionary*. 6 vols. New York: Doubleday, 1992.

Frerichs, Ernest S., and Leonard H. Lesko, eds. *Exodus: The Egyptian Evidence*. Winona Lake, Ind.: Eisenbrauns, 1998.

Hoffmeier, James. *Israel in Egypt: The Evidence for the Authority of the Exodus Tradition*. Oxford: Oxford University Press, 1997.

Kurth, Amélie. *The Ancient Near East c.3000–330 BC.* 2 vols. London: Routledge, 1995.

Mitchell, Terence C. *The Bible in the British Museum.* London: British Museum Publications, 1988.

Pritchard, James B. *Ancient Near Eastern Texts Relating to the Old Testament.* 2nd ed. Princeton: Princeton University Press, 1955.

———. *The Ancient Near East in Pictures Relating to the Old Testament.* 3rd ed. Princeton: Princeton University Press, 1974.

Rainey, Anson F. *Egypt, Israel, Sinai.* Tel Aviv: Tel Aviv University, 1987.

Redford, Donald B. *Egypt, Canaan, and Israel in Ancient Times.* Princeton: Princeton University Press, 1992.

Tubb, Jonathan, and Rupert L. Chapman. *Archaeology and the Bible.* London: British Museum Publications, 1990.

NUBIA

Adams, William Y. *Nubia, Corridor to Africa.* London: Allen Lane, 1977.

Brooklyn Museum. *Africa in Antiquity: The Arts of Ancient Nubia and the Sudan.* 2 vols. New York: The Brooklyn Museum, 1978.

Säve-Söderbergh, Torgny. *Temples and Tombs of Ancient Nubia: The International Rescue Campaign at Abu Simbel, Philae and Other Sites.* London: Thames and Hudson, 1987.

Taylor, John H. *Egypt and Nubia.* London: British Museum Press, 1991.

Trigger, Bruce C. *Nubia under the Pharaohs.* London: Thames and Hudson, 1976.

Welsby, Derek. *The Kingdom of Kush: The Napatan and Meroitic Empires.* London: British Museum Press, 1996.

ARCHAEOLOGY: GENERAL

Assman, Jan, et al., eds. *Problems and Priorities in Egyptian Archaeology.* London: Kegan Paul International, 1987.

Brink, Edwin C. M. van den. *The Archaeology of the Nile Delta: Problems and Priorities.* Amsterdam: Netherlands Foundation for Archaeological Research in Egypt, 1988.

Butzer, Karl W. *Early Hydraulic Civilization in Egypt: A Study in Cultural Ecology.* Chicago: University of Chicago Press, 1976.

James, T. G. Henry, ed. *Excavating in Egypt: The Egypt Exploration Society 1882–1982.* London: British Museum Publications, 1982.

Nims, Charles F. *Thebes of the Pharaohs.* London: Elek Books, 1965.

Vandier, Jacques. *Manuel d'archéologie égyptienne.* 6 vols. Paris: Éditions A. et J. Picard, 1952–78.

ARCHAEOLOGY: EXCAVATIONS AND SURVEYS

Abu Roash

Bisson de la Roque, Fernand. *Rapport sur les fouilles d'Abu-Roasch.* 3 vols. Cairo: Institut français d'archéologie orientale, 1924-25.

Swelim, Nabil. *The Brick Pyramid at Abu Rawash Number 'I' by Lepsius.* Alexandria: The Archaeological Society of Alexandria, 1987.

Abu Simbel

el-Achirie, Hassan, and Jean Jacquet. *Le Grand Temple d'Abou Simbel. Vol. I.1. Architecture.* Cairo: Centre de Documentation, 1984.

Černý, Jaroslav, and A. A. Youssef. *Abou-Simbel: Chapelle de Rê-Herakhty.* Cairo: Centre de Documentation Égyptologique, [1963].

Desroches-Noblecourt, Christiane, Sergio Donadoni, et al. *Le Grand Temple d'Abou Simbel. Vol. II. La Bataille de Qadesh.* Cairo: Centre de Documentation, 1971.

Desroches-Noblecourt, Christiane, and Charles Kuentz. *Le petit temple d'Abou Simbel.* Cairo: 1968.

Donadoni, Sergio, and Hassan el-Achirie. *Le grand temple d'Abou Simbel.* Vol. III. Cairo: Centre de Documentation, 1975.

MacQuitty, William. *Abu Simbel.* London: 1965.

Abusir

Borchardt, Ludwig. *Das Grabdenkmal des Königs Nefer-ir-ka3-re.* Leipzig: J. C. Hinrichs, 1909.

———. *Das Grabdenkmal des Königs Ne-user-re.* Leipzig: J. C. Hinrichs, 1907.

———. *Das Grabdenkmal des Königs Sa3-hu-re'.* Leipzig: J. C. Hinrichs, 1910–13.

Charvát, Peter. *The Mastaba of Ptahshepses: The Pottery.* Prague: Charles University, 1981.

Posener-Kriéger, Paule. *Les archives du Temple funéraire de Néferirkare-Kakai (Les papyrus d'Abousir)*. Cairo: Institut français d'archéologie orientale, 1976.

Strouhal, Eugen, and Ladislav Bareš. *Secondary Cemetery in the Mastaba of Ptahshepses at Abusir*. Prague: Charles University, 1993.

Verner, Miroslav. *Abusir I: The Mastaba of Ptahshepses Reliefs*. I. Prague: Charles University, 1977.

———. *Abusir II: Baugraffiti der Ptahschepses Mastaba*. Prague: Charles University, 1992.

———. *Abusir III: The Pyramid Complex of Khentkaus*. Prague: Charles University, 1995.

———. *Forgotten Pharaohs, Lost Pyramids*. Prague: Academia, Academy of Sciences of the Czech Republic, 1994.

Abydos

Abdalla, Aly. *Graeco-Roman Funerary Stelae from Upper Egypt*. Liverpool: Liverpool University Press, 1992.

Amelineau, Émile. *Les nouvelles fouilles d'Abydos*. 4 vols. Paris: Ernest Leroux, 1899–1905.

———. *Le tombeau d'Osiris*. Paris: Ernest Leroux, 1899.

Ayrton, Edward R., et al. *Abydos*. III. London: Egypt Exploration Fund, 1904.

Calverley, Amice M. *The Temple of King Sethos I at Abydos*. 4 vols. London and Chicago: The Egypt Exploration Society and the University of Chicago Press, 1933–58.

Frankfort, Henri. *The Cenotaph of Seti I at Abydos*. London: Egypt Exploration Society, 1930.

Mariette, Auguste. *Abydos: Description des fouilles exécutées sur l'emplacement de cette ville*. 2 vols. Paris: A. Franck, 1869-80.

———. *Catalogue général des monuments d'Abydos découverts pendant les fouilles de cette ville*. Paris: Imprimerie nationale, 1880.

Murray, Margaret. *The Osireion at Abydos*. London: Egyptian Research Account, A. Franck, 1904.

Naville, Édouard, and Thomas E. Peet. *The Cemeteries of Abydos*. 3 vols. London: Egypt Exploration Fund, 1913–14.

Petrie, W. M. Flinders. *Abydos*. 2 vols. London: Egypt Exploration Fund, 1902–03.

———. *The Royal Tombs of the Earliest Dynasties*. 2 vols. London: Egypt Exploration Fund, 1900–01.

Simpson, William Kelly. *Inscribed Material from the Pennsylvania-Yale Excavations at Abydos*. New Haven and Philadelphia: The Peabody Museum of Natural History of Yale University and The University of Pennsylvania Museum of Archaeology and Anthropology, 1995.

———. *The Terrace of the Great God at Abydos: The Offering Chapels of Dynasties 12 and 13*. New Haven and Philadelphia: The Peabody Museum of Natural History of Yale University and the University of Pennsylvania Museum of Archaeology and Anthropology, 1974.

Akhmim

Kanawati, Naguib. *A Mountain Speaks: The First Australian Excavation in Egypt*. Sydney: Macquarie University, 1988.

———. *The Rock Tombs of el-Hawawish: The Cemetery of Akhmim*. 10 vols. Sydney: Macquarie University, 1980–92.

Kuhlman, Klaus. *Materialien zur Archäologie und Geschichte des Raumes von Achmim*. Mainz am Rhein, Germany: Philipp von Zabern, 1983.

McNally, Sheila, and Ivancica D. Schrunk. *Excavations in Akhmim, Egypt: Continuity and Change in City Life from Late Antiquity to the Present*. BAR International Series 590. Oxford: BAR, 1993.

Alexandria

Borkowski, Zbigniew. *Alexandrie II: Inscriptions des factions à Alexandrie*. Warsaw: PWN-Éditions scientifiques de Pologne, 1981.

Empereur, Jean-Yves. *Alexandria Rediscovered*. London: British Museum Press, 1998.

Grimm, Günter. *Alexandria: Die eiste Königsstadt der hellenistischen Welt*. Mainz am Rhein, Germany: Philipp von Zabern, 1998.

Kiss, Zsolt. *Alexandrie V: Les ampoules de Saint Ménas découvertes à Kôm el-Dikka (1961–1981)*. Warsaw: PWN-Éditions scientifiques de Pologne, 1988.

———. *Alexandrie IV: Sculptures des fouilles polonaises à Kôm el-Dikka (1960–1982)*. Warsaw: PWN-Éditions scientifiques de Pologne, 1988.

Kolataj, Wojciech. *Alexandrie VI: Imperial Baths at Kom-el-Dikka*. Warsaw: Zaklad Archeologii Srodziemnomorskiej Polskiej Akademii Nauk, 1992.

La Riche, William. *Alexandria: The Sunken City*. London: Weidenfeld and Nicolson, 1996.

Rodziewicz, Mieczyslaw. *Alexandrie I: La céramique romaine tardive d'Alexandrie.* Warsaw: PWN-Éditions scientifiques de Pologne, 1976.

————. *Alexandrie III: Les habitations romaines tardives d'Alexandrie à la lumière des fouilles polonaises à Kôm el-Dikka.* Warsaw: PWN-Editions scientifiques de Pologne, 1984.

Steen, Gareth L., ed. *Alexandria: the Site and the History.* New York: New York University Press, 1993.

Tkaczow, Barbara. *Topography of Ancient Alexandria (An Archaeological Map).* Travaux du Centre d'Archéologie Méditerranéenne de l'Académie Polonaise des Sciences No. 32. Warsaw: Zaklad Archeologii Srodziemnomorskiej Polskiej Akademii Nauk, 1993.

Amada

el-Achiery, Hassan, Barguet, Paul, Dewachter, Michel, et al. *Le Temple d'Amada.* 5 vols. Cairo: Centre de Documentation et d'Études sur l'Égypte ancienne, 1967.

Amara West

Spencer, Patricia A. *Amara West I: The architectural report.* London: Egypt Exploration Society, 1997.

Amarna

Borchardt, Ludwig, and Herbert Ricke. *Die Wohnhäuser in Tell el-Amarna.* Berlin: Gebr. Mann, 1980.

Davies, Norman de G. *The Rock Tombs of El Amarna.* 6 vols. London: Egypt Exploration Society, 1903–08.

Kemp, Barry J., ed. *Amarna Reports.* 6 vols. London: Egypt Exploration Society, 1984–95.

Kemp, Barry J., and Salvatore Garfi. *A Survey of the Ancient City of el-Amarna.* London: Egypt Exploration Society, 1993.

el-Khouly, Aly, and Geoffrey T. Martin. *Excavations in the Royal Necropolis at El-'Amarna.* Supplément aux Annales du Service des Antiquités de l'Égypte No. 33. Cairo: Service des Antiquités de l'Égypte, 1987.

Martin, Geoffrey T. *The Royal Tomb at el-Amarna.* 2 vols. London: Egypt Exploration Society, 1974–89.

Murnane, William J., and Charles C. Van Siclen. *The Boundary Stelae of Akhenaten.* London: Kegan Paul International, 1993.

Peet, Thomas E., et al. *The City of Akhenaten*. 3 vols. London: Egypt Exploration Society, 1923–51.
Petrie, W. M. Flinders. *Tell el-Amarna*. London: Methuen and Co., 1894.

Aniba

Heykal, F., and A. Abou-Bakr. *Tombeau de Pennout à Aniba*. Cairo: Centre de Documentation Égyptologique, [1963].
Steindorff, Georg. *Aniba*. 2 vols. Glückstadt, Germany: 1935–37.

Armant

Mond, Robert, and Oliver H. Myers. *The Bucheum*. 3 vols. London: Egypt Exploration Society, 1934.
———. *Cemeteries of Armant I*. London: Egypt Exploration Society, 1937.
———. *Temples of Armant: A Preliminary Survey*. London: Egypt Exploration Society, 1940.

Askut

Smith, Stuart T. *Askut in Nubia*. London: Kegan Paul International, 1995.

Athribis

Petrie, W. M. Flinders. *Athribis*. London: British School of Archaeology in Egypt, 1908.
Vernus, Pascal. *Athribis*. Cairo: Institut français d'archéologie orientale, 1978.

Avaris

Bietak, Manfred. *Avaris, Capital of the Hyksos: Recent Excavations*. London: British Museum Press, 1996.
———. *Avaris and Piramesse*. 2nd ed. Oxford: 1986.
———. *Tell el-Dab'a II: Der Fundort im Rahmen einer archäologisch-geographischen Untersuchung über das ägyptische Ostdelta*. Vienna: Österreichische Akademie der Wissenschaften, 1975.
Bietak, Manfred, et al. *Tell el-Dab'a V: Ein Friedhofsbezirk der Mittleren*

Bronzezeit mit Totentempel und Siedlungsschichten. Vienna: Österei-chische Akademie der Wissenschaften, 1991.

Boessneck, Joachim. *Tell el-Dab'a III: Die Tierknochenfunde 1966-1969.* Vienna: Österreichische Akademie der Wissenschaften, 1976.

Boessneck, Joachim, and Angela von den Driesch. *Tell el-Dab'a VII: Tiere und historische Umwelt im Norost-Delta im 2. Jahrtausend anhand der Knochenfunde der Ausgrabungen 1975–1986.* Vienna: Österreichische Akademie der Wissenschaften, 1991.

Winkler, Eike-Meinrad, and Harald Wilfling. *Tell el-Dab'a VI: Anthropologische Untersuchungen an der Skelettresten der Kampagnen 1966–69, 1975–80, 1985.* Vienna: Östereichische Akademie der Wissenschaften, 1991.

Badari, el-

Brunton, Guy, et al. *Qau and Badari.* 3 vols. London: British School of Archeology in Egypt, 1927–30.

Brunton, Guy, and Caton-Thompson, Gertrude. *The Badarian Civilisation and Prehistoric Remains near Badari.* London: British School of Archeology in Egypt, 1928.

Bahriya Oasis

Fakhry, Ahmed. *Bahria Oasis.* 2 vols. Cairo: Government Press, 1942–50.

———. *The Oases of Egypt II: Bahriyah and Farafra Oases.* Cairo: The American University in Cairo Press, 1974.

Giddy, Lisa. *Egyptian Oases.* Warminster, Great Britain: Aris and Phillips, 1987.

Balamun, Tell el-

Spencer, A. Jeffrey. *Excavations at Tell el-Balamun 1991–1994.* London: British Museum, 1996.

Ballana and Qustul

Emery, Walter B., and Laurence P. Kirwan. *The Royal Tombs of Ballana and Qustul.* Cairo: Service des Antiquités de l'Égypte, 1938.

Farid, Shafik. *Excavations at Ballana 1958–1959.* Cairo: Antiquities Department of Egypt, 1963.

Williams, Bruce B. *Excavations between Abu Simbel and the Sudan Frontier.* Oriental Institute Nubia Expedition. 9 vols. Chicago: The Oriental Institute of the University of Chicago, 1986–91.

Beni Hasan

Newberry, Percy E., et al. *Beni Hasan.* 4 vols. London: Trench, Trubner & Co. Ltd., 1893-1900.

Shedid, Abdel Ghaffar. *Die Felsgräber von Beni Hassan in Mittelägypten.* Zaberns Bildbände zur Archäologie 16. Mainz am Rhein, Germany: Philipp von Zabern, 1994.

Bubastis

Bakr, Mohamed I. *Tell Basta I: Tombs and Burial Customs at Bubastis. The Area of the So-Called Western Cemetery.* Cairo: Egyptian Antiquities Organization, 1992.

Habachi, Labib. *Tell Basta.* Supplément aux Annales du Service des Antiquités de l'Égypte No. 22. Cairo: Service des Antiquités de l'Égypte, 1957.

Naville, Édouard. *Bubastis (1887–1889).* London: Egypt Exploration Fund, 1891.

el-Sawi, Ahmad. *Excavations at Tell Basta.* Prague: Charles University, 1979.

Buhen

Caminos, Ricardo. *The New-Kingdom Temples of Buhen.* 2 vols. London: Egypt Exploration Society, 1974.

Emery, Walter B., et al. *The Fortress of Buhen.* 2 vols. London: Egypt Exploration Society, 1976–79.

Buto

Köhler, E. Christiana. *Tell el-Faraîn: Buto III. Die Keramik von der späten Naqada-Kultur bis zum frülen Alten Reich.* Deutsches Archäologisches Institut. Abteilung Kairo. Archäologische Veröffentlichungen 94. Mainz am Rhein, Germany: Philipp von Zabern, 1998.

Von der Way, Thomas. *Tell el-Faraîn: Buto I. Ergebnisse zum fruhen Kontext Kampagnen der Jahre 1983–1989.* Deutsches Archäologisches Institut. Abteilung Kairo. Archäologische Veröffentlichungen 83. Mainz am Rhein, Germany: Philipp von Zabern, 1997.

Coptos

Petrie, W. M. Flinders. *Koptos.* London: Bernard Quaritch, 1896.
Reinach, Adolphe J. *Rapport sur les fouilles de Koptos.* Paris: Ernest Leroux, 1910.

Dahshur

Arnold, Dieter. *Der Pyramidenbezirk des Königs Amenemhet III in Dahschur.* Deutsches Archäologisches Institut. Abteilung Kairo. Archäologische Veröffentlichungen 53. Mainz am Rhein, Germany: Philipp von Zabern, 1987.
Fakhry, Ahmed. *The Monuments of Sneferu at Dahshur.* 2 vols. Cairo: 1959–61.
Morgan, Jacques de. *Fouilles à Dahchour.* 2 vols. Paris: 1895–1903.

Dakhla Oasis

Fakhry, Ahmed. *Denkmäler der Oase Dachla.* Deutsches Archäologisches Institut. Abteilung Kairo. Archäologische Veröffentlichungen 28. Mainz am Rhein, Germany: Philipp von Zabern, 1982.
Giddy, Lisa. *The Egyptian Oases.* Warminster, Great Britain: Aris and Phillips, 1987.
Minault-Gout, Anne. *Balat II: Le mastaba d'Ima-pépi.* Cairo: Institut français d'archéologie orientale, 1992.
Vallogia, Michel. *Balat I: Le mastaba de Medou-Nefer.* Cairo: Institut français d'archéologie orientale, 1986.
———. *Le monument funéraire d'Ima-Pepy/Ima-Meryrê: Balat IV.* 2 vols. Cairo: Institut français d'archéologie orientale, 1998.
Winlock, Herbert E., ed. *Dakhleh Oasis.* New York: The Metropolitan Museum of Art, 1936.

Deir el-Bahri

Arnold, Dieter. *Der Tempel des Königs Mentuhotep von Deir el-Bahari I: Architectur und Deuting.* Deutsches Archäologisches Institut. Abteilung

Kairo. Archäologische Veröffentlichungen 8. Mainz am Rhein, Germany: Philipp von Zabern, 1974.

———. *Der Tempel des Königs Mentuhotep von Deir el-Bahari II: Die Wandreliefs des Sanktuares.* Deutsches Archäologisches Institut. Abteilung Kairo. Archäologische Veröffentlichungen 11. Mainz am Rhein, Germany: Philipp von Zabern, 1974.

———. *Der Tempel des Königs Mentuhotep von Deir el-Bahari III: Die Königlichen Beigaben.* Deutsches Archäologisches Institut. Abteilung Kairo. Archäologische Veröffentlichungen 23. Mainz am Rhein, Germany: Philipp von Zabern, 1981.

———. *The Temple of Mentuhotep at Deir el-Bahari.* Publications of the Metropolitan Museum of Art Egyptian Expedition 21. New York: The Metropolitan Museum of Art, 1979.

Godlewski, Wlodzomierz. *Deir el-Bahari V: Le monastère de St. Phoibammon.* Warsaw: PWN-Éditions scientifiques de Pologne, 1986.

Laskowska-Kusztal, Ewa. *Deir el-Bahari III: Le sanctuaire ptolémaique de Deir el-Bahari.* Warsaw: PWN-Éditions scientifiques de Pologne, 1984.

Lipinska, Jadwiga. *Deir el-Bahari II: The Temple of Tuthmosis III. Architecture.* Warsaw: PWN-Éditions scientifiques de Pologne, 1977.

———. *Deir el-Bahari IV: The Temple of Tuthmosis IV. Statuary and Votive Monuments.* Warsaw: PWN-Éditions scientifiques de Pologne, 1984.

Marciniak, Marek. *Deir el-Bahari I: Les inscriptions hiératiques du temple de Thoutmosis III.* Warsaw: PWN-Éditions scientifiques de Pologne, 1974.

Maspero, Gaston. *La trouvaille de Deir-el-bahari.* Cairo: F. Mourés and Cie, 1881.

Naville, Édouard. *The Temple of Deir el-Bahari.* 7 vols. London: Egypt Exploration Fund, 1894–1908.

Winlock, Herbert E. *Excavations at Deir el-Bahari, 1911–31.* New York: Macmillan, 1942.

———. *Models of Daily Life in Ancient Egypt from the Tomb of Meket-re' at Thebes.* Cambridge, Mass.: The Metropolitan Museum of Art, 1955.

———. *The Slain Soldiers of Neb-hepet-re' Mentu-hotpe.* New York: The Metropolitan Museum of Art, 1945.

Deir el-Ballas

Lacovara, Peter. *Deir el-Ballas: Preliminary Report on the Deir el-Ballas Expedition, 1980–1986.* Winona Lake, Ind.: Eisenbrauns, 1990.

———. *The New Kingdom Royal City.* London: Kegan Paul, 1997.

Deir el-Bersha

Brovarski, Edward, et al. *Bersheh Reports I*. Boston: Museum of Fine Arts, 1992.

Newberry, Percy E., and Francis L. Griffiths. *El-Bersheh*. 2 vols. London: Egypt Exploration Fund, 1892.

Deir el-Medina

Bruyère, Bernard. *Mert Seger à Deir el-Médineh*. 2 vols. Cairo: Institut français d'archéologie orientale, 1929–30.

———. *Rapport sur les fouilles de Deir el Médineh*. 17 vols. Cairo: Institut français d'archéologie orientale, 1924–53.

———. *La tombe no 1 de Sen-nedjem à Deir el-Médineh*. Cairo: Institut français d'archéologie orientale, 1959.

———. *Tombes à décors monochromes*. Cairo: Institut français d'archéologie orientale, 1952.

Bruyère, Bernard, and Charles Kuentz. *Tombes thébaines: La nécropole de Deir el-Médineh. La Tombe de Nakht-Min et la tombe d'Ari-Nefer*. Cairo: Institut français d'archéologie orientale, 1926.

Černý, Jaroslav. *Catalogue des ostraca hiératiques non littéraires de Deir el-Médineh*. 6 vols. Cairo: Institut français d'archéologie orientale, 1935–70.

———. *Graffiti hiéroglyphiques et hiératiques de la nécropole thébaine (nos 1060–1405)*. Cairo: Institut français d'archéologie orientale, 1956.

———. *Papyrus hiératiques de Deir el-Médineh*. 2 vols. Cairo: Institut français d'archéologie orientale, 1978–86.

Gasse, Annie. *Catalogue des ostraca figurés de Deir el-Médineh*. Cairo: Institut français d'archéologie orientale, 1986.

———. *Catalogue des ostraca hiératiques littéraires de Deir el-Médina*. Cairo: Institut français d'archéologie orientale, 1990.

Koenig, Yvan. *Catalogue des étiquettes de jarres hiératiques de Deir el-Médineh*. 2 vols. Cairo: Institut français d'archéologie orientale, 1979–80.

Maystre, Charles. *Tombes de Deir el-Médineh: La tombe de Nebenmât (no. 219)*. Cairo: Institut français d'archéologie orientale, 1936.

Posener, Georges. *Catalogue des ostraca hiératiques littéraires de Deir el-Médineh*. 3 vols. Cairo: Institut français d'archéologie orientale, 1934–80.

Schiaparelli, Ernesto. *Relazione sui lavori della missione archaeologica italiana in Egitto II: La tomba intatta dell'architetto Kha*. Turin: 1927.

Shedid, Abdel Ghaffar. *Das Grab des Sennedjem*. Mainz am Rhein, Germany: Philipp von Zabern, 1994.

Valbelle, Dominique. *La tombe de Hay à Deir el-Medineh*. Cairo: Institut français d'archéologie orientale, 1975.

Vandier, Jacques. *Tombes de Deir el-Médineh: La tombe de Nefer-abou*. Cairo: Institut français d'archéologie orientale, 1935.

Vandier, Jacques, and G. Jourdain. *Deux tombes de Deir el-Médineh*. Cairo: Institut français d'archéologie orientale, 1939.

Vandier d'Abbadie, Jeanne. *Catalogue des ostraca figurés de Deir el-Médineh*. 4 fasc. Cairo: Institut français d'archéologie orientale, 1936–59.

Wild, Henri. *La tombe de Néfer.hotep (I) et Neb.néfer à Deir el-Medina [No 6] et autres documents les concernant. II*. Cairo: Institut français d'archéologie orientale, 1979.

Zivie, Alain. *La tombe de Pached à Deir el-Médineh (no 3)*. Cairo: Institut français d'archéologie orientale, 1979.

Dendera

Castel, Georges, François Daumas, and Jean-Claude Golvin. *Les fontaines de la porte nord*. Cairo: Institut français d'archéologie orientale, 1984.

Cauville, Sylvie. *Dendera I: Traduction*. Louvain: Peeters, 1998.

———. *Dendera: les chapelles osiriennes*. 3 vols. Cairo: Institut français d'archéologie orientale, 1997.

———. *Le temple de Dendera*. Cairo: Institut français d'archéologie orientale, 1990.

Chassinat, Émile. *Le mystère d'Osiris au mois de Khoiak*. Cairo: Institut français d'archéologie orientale, 1966–68.

Chassinat, Émile, François Daumas, and Sylvie Cauville. *Le temple de Dendera*. 10 vols. Cairo: Institut français d'archéologie orientale, 1934–97.

Daumas, François. *Dendera et le temple d'Hathor, notice sommaire*. Cairo: Institut français d'archéologie orientale, 1969.

———. *Les Mammisis de Dendera*. Cairo: Institut français d'archéologie orientale, 1959.

Mariette, Auguste. *Denderah*. 4 vols. Paris: F. Vieweg, 1870–80.

Petrie, W. M. F. *Dendereh*. London: Egypt Exploration Fund, 1900.

Waitkus, Wolfgang. *Der Texte in den Unteren Krypten des Hathortempels von Dendera*. Mainz am Rhein, Germany: Philipp von Zabern, 1997.

Edfu

Cauville, Sylvie. *Edfou.* Cairo: Institut français d'archéologie orientale, 1984.

———. *Essai sur la théologie du temple d'Horus à Edfou.* 2 vols. Cairo: Institut français d'archéologie orientale, 1987.

———. *La théologie d'Osiris à Edfou.* Cairo: Institut français d'archéologie orientale, 1983.

Michalowski, Kazimierz, et al. *Tell Edfou.* 4 vols. Cairo: 1937–50.

Rochemonteix, F. J. Maxence de Chalvet, Marquis de, Émile Chassinat, and Sylvie Cauville. *Le temple d'Edfou.* 15 vols. plus 2 rev. vols. Paris: E. Leroux, 1897; Cairo: Institut francais d'archéologie orientale, 1918–90.

Elephantine

Bresciani, Edda, et al. *Assuan.* Pisa: Giardini, 1978.

Dreyer, Günter. *Elephantine VIII: Der Tempel der Satet. Die Funde der Frühzeit und der Alten Reiches.* Deutsches Archäologisches Institut. Abteilung Kairo. Archäologische Veröffentlichungen 39. Mainz am Rhein, Germany: Philipp von Zabern, 1986.

Edel, Elmar. *Die Felsengräber der Qubbet el-Hawa bei Assuan.* Wiesbaden, Germany: 1967–80.

Gempeler, Robert D. *Elephantine X: Die Keramik römischer bis früharabischer Zeit.* Deutsches Archäologisches Institut. Abteilung Kairo. Archäologische Veröffentlichungen 43. Mainz am Rhein, Germany: Philipp von Zabern, 1993.

Grossmann, Peter. *Elephantine II: Kirche und spätantike Hausanlagen im Chnumtempelhof.* Deutsches Archäologisches Institut. Abteilung Kairo. Archäologische Veröffentlichungen 25. Mainz am Rhein, Germany: Philipp von Zabern, 1980.

Habachi, Labib. *Elephantine IV: The Sanctuary of Heqaib.* Deutsches Archäologisches Institut. Abteilung Kairo. Archäologische Veröffentlichungen 33. Mainz am Rhein, Germany: Philipp von Zabern, 1985.

Jaritz, Horst. *Elephantine III: Die Terrassen vor den Tempeln des chnum und des Satet.* Deutsches Archäologisches Institut. Abteilung Kairo. Archäologische Veröffentlichungen 32. Mainz am Rhein, Germany: Philipp von Zabern, 1980.

Jenni, Hanna. *Elephantine XVII: Die Dekoration des Chnumtempels auf Elephantine durch Nektanebos II.* Deutsches Archäologisches Institut. Abteilung Kairo. Archäologische Veröffentlichungen 90. Mainz am Rhein, Germany: Philipp von Zabern, 1998.

Junge, Friedrich. *Elephantine XI: Funde und Bauteile.* Deutsches Archäologisches Institut. Abteilung Kairo. Archäologische Veröffentlichungen 49. Mainz am Rhein, Germany: Philipp von Zabern, 1987.

Laskowska-Kusztal, Ewa. *Elephantine XV: Die Dekorfragmente der ptolemäisch-römischen Tempel von Elephantine.* Deutsches Archäologisches Institut. Abteilung Kairo. Archäologische Veröffentlichungen 73. Mainz am Rhein, Germany: Philipp von Zabern, 1995.

Pilgrim, Cornelius von. *Elephantine XVIII: Untersuchungen zur Stadt Elephantine im mittleren Reich unter der Zweiten Zwischenzei*t. Deutsches Archäologisches Institut. Abteilung Kairo. Archäologische Veröffentlichungen 91. Mainz am Rhein, Germany: Philipp von Zabern, 1995.

Zierman, Martin. *Elephantine XVI: Befestigungsanlagen und Stadtentwicklung in der Frühzeit und im frühen Alten Reich.* Deutsches Archäologisches Institut Abteilung Kairo. Archäologische Veröffentlichungen 87. Mainz am Rhein, Germany: Philipp von Zabern, 1993.

Elkab

Bingen, Jean, and Willy Clarysse. *Elkab III: Les ostraca grecs.* Brussels: Fondation Égyptologique Reine Élisabeth, 1989.

Derchain, Philippe. *Elkab I: Les monuments religieux à l'entrée de l'Ouady Hellal.* Brussels: Fondation Égyptologique Reine Élisabeth, 1971.

Fondation Égyptologique Reine Élisabeth. *Elkab IV: Topographie.* Brussels: Fondation Égyptologique Reine Élisabeth, 1991.

―――. *Fouilles de El Kab Documents.* Brussels: Fondation Égyptologique Reine Élisabeth, 1940.

Hendrickx, Stan. *Elkab V: The Naqada III Cemetery.* Brussels: Fondation Égyptologique Reine Élisabeth, 1994.

Quibell, James E. *El-Kab.* London: Egyptian Research Account, 1898.

Tylor, Joseph J. *Wall Drawings and Monuments of El Kab: The Tomb of Paheri.* London: Egypt Exploration Fund, 1895.

―――. *Wall Drawings and Monuments of El Kab: The Tomb of Renni.* London: B. Quaritch, 1900.

―――. *Wall Drawings and Monuments of El Kab: The Tomb of Sobeknakht.* London: B. Quaritch, 1896.

Vermeersch, Pierre. *Elkab II: L'Elkabien, Épipalaeolithique de la Vallée du Nil Égyptien.* Brussels: Fondation Égyptologique Reine Élisabeth, 1978.

Esna

Downes, Dorothy. *The Excavations at Esna 1905–1906.* Warminster, Great Britain: Aris and Phillips, 1974.

Sauneron, Serge. *Esna.* 7 vols. Cairo: Institut français d'archéologie orientale, 1959–82.

Sauneron, Serge, and Jean Jacquet. *Les ermitages chrétiens du désert d'Esna.* 4 vols. Cairo: Institut français d'archéologie orientale, 1972.

Faras

Dzierzykray-Rogalski, Tadeusz. *Faras VIII: The Bishops of Faras. An Anthropological-Medical Study.* Warsaw: PWN-Éditions scientifiques de Pologne, 1985.

Godlewski, Wlodzimierz. *Faras VI: Les baptistères nubiens.* Warsaw: PWN-Éditions scientifiques de Pologne, 1979.

Jakobielski, Stefan. *Faras III: A History of the Bishopric of Pachoras.* Warsaw: PWN-Éditions scientifiques de Pologne, 1972.

Karkowski, Janusz. *Faras V: The Pharaonic Inscriptions from Faras.* Warsaw: PWN-Éditions scientifiques de Pologne, 1981.

Kubinska, Jadwiga. *Faras IV: Inscriptions grecques et chrétiennes.* Warsaw: PWN-Éditions scientifiques de Pologne, 1974.

Martens-Czarnecka, Malgorzata. *Les éléments décoratifs sur les peintures de Faras.* Warsaw: PWN-Éditions scientifiques de Pologne, 1982.

Michalowski, Kazimierz. *Faras I: Fouilles polonaises 1961.* Warsaw: PWN-Éditions scientifiques de Pologne, 1962.

———. *Faras II: Fouilles polonaises 1961–62.* Warsaw: PWN-Éditions scientifiques de Pologne, 1965.

———. *Faras: Wall Paintings in the Collection of the National Museum in Warsaw.* Warsaw: Wydawnictwo Artystyczno-Graficzne, 1974.

Vantini, John. *The Excavations at Faras.* Bologna: Editrice Nigrizia, 1970.

Fayum

Caton-Thompson, Gertrude, and Ernest W. Gardner. *The Desert Fayum.* London: The Royal Anthropological Institute of Great Britain and Ireland, 1934.

Griggs, C. Wilfred, et al. *Excavations at Seila, Egypt.* Provo, Utah: Brigham Young University, 1988.

Husselman, Elinor M. *Karanis: Excavations of the University of Michigan in Egypt 1928–1935.* Ann Arbor: The University of Michigan Press, 1979.

Gebel el-Silsila

Caminos, Ricardo A., and T. G. H. James. *Gebel es-Silsilah I.* London: Egypt Exploration Society, 1963.

Gebel el-Zeit

Castel, Georges, and Georges Soukiassian. *Gebel el-Zeit I.* Cairo: Institut français d'archéologie orientale, 1989.

Gerf Hussein

Jacquet, Jean, and Hassan el-Achirie. *Gerf Hussein I.* Cairo: Centre de Documentation et d'Études sur l'ancienne Égypte, 1978.

el-Tanbouli, M., et al. *Gerf Hussein II-IV.* Cairo: Centre de Documentation et d'Études sur l'ancienne Égypte, 1974–78.

Giza

Abu-Bakr, Abdel-Moneim. *Excavations at Giza 1949–1950.* Cairo: Government Press, 1953.

Badawy, Alexander. *The Tomb of Nyhetep-Ptah at Giza and the Tomb of 'Ankhm'ahor at Saqqara.* Berkeley: University of California Press, 1978.

———. *The Tombs of Iteti, Sekhem'ankh-Ptah, and Kaemnofret at Giza.* Berkeley: University of California Press, 1976.

Brunner-Traut, Emma. *Die altägyptische Grabkammer Seschemnofers III. aus Gîsa.* Mainz am Rhein, Germany: Philipp von Zabern, 1977.

Curto, Silvio. *Gli scavi italiani a El-Ghiza (1903).* Rome: Centro per le Antichità e la Storia dell'Arte del Vicino Oriente, 1963.

Dunham, Dows, and William Kelly Simpson. *Giza Mastabas 1: The Mastaba of Queen Mersyankh III, G 7530–7540.* Boston: Museum of Fine Arts, 1974.

Fisher, Clarence. *The Minor Cemetery at Giza.* Philadelphia: University Museum, 1924.

Hölscher, Uvo. *Das Grabdenkmal des Königs Chephren.* Leipzig: J. Hinrich, 1912.

Jenkins, Nancy. *The Boat beneath the Pyramid.* London: Thames and Hudson, 1980.

Junker, Hermann. *Giza.* 12 vols. Vienna: Österreichische Akademie der Wissenschaften, 1929–55.

Kromer, Karl. *Nezlet Batran: Eine Mastaba aus dem Alten Reich bei Giseh (Ägypten)*. Vienna: Österrreichischen Akademie der Wissenschaften, 1991.

———. *Siedlungsfunde aus dem frühen Alten Reich in Giseh*. Vienna: Österreichische Akademie der Wissenschaften, 1978.

Lehner, Mark. *The Pyramid Tomb of Hetep-heres and the Satellite Pyramid of Khufu*. SDAIK 19. Mainz am Rhein, Germany: Philipp von Zabern, 1985.

Nour, Muhammad Zaki, et al. *The Cheops Boats*. Part I. Cairo: Antiquities Department of Egypt, 1960.

Petrie, W. M. Flinders. *Gizeh and Rifeh*. London: Egyptian Research Account, 1907.

———. *The Pyramids and Temples of Gizeh*. London: Field and Tuer, 1883. Reprint with update by Zahi Hawass, London: Histories and Mysteries of Man, 1990.

Reisner, George A. *A History of the Giza Necropolis I*. Cambridge, Mass.: Harvard University Press, 1942.

———. *A History of the Giza Necropolis II. The Tomb of Hetepheres the mother of Kheops*. Cambridge, Mass.: Harvard University Press, 1955.

———. *Mycerinus: The Temples of the Third Pyramid at Giza*. Cambridge, Mass.: Harvard University Press, 1931.

Roth, Anne M. *Giza Mastabas 6: A Cemetery of Palace Attendants*. Boston: Museum of Fine Arts, 1995.

el-Sadek, Wafaa. *Twenty-Sixth Dynasty Necropolis at Gizeh*. Beiträge zur Ägyptologie 5. Vienna: Institut für Africanistik und Ägyptologie Universität Wien, 1984.

Simpson, William Kelly. *Giza Mastabas 2: The Mastabas of Qar and Idu, G 7101–7102*. Boston: Museum of Fine Arts, 1976.

———. *Giza Mastabas 3: The Mastabas of Kawab, Khafkhufu I and II, G 7110–20, 7130–40, and 750 and Subsidiary Mastabas of Street 7100*. Boston: Museum of Fine Arts, 1978.

———. *Giza Mastabas 4: Mastabas of the Western Cemetery, Part I*. Boston: Museum of Fine Arts, 1980.

Weeks, Kent R. *Giza Mastabas 5: Mastabas of Cemetery G6000*. Boston: Museum of Fine Arts, 1994.

Zivie, Christiane. *Giza au Deuxième Millénaire*. Cairo: Institut français d'archéologie orientale, 1976.

———. *Giza au Premier Millénaire*. Boston: Museum of Fine Arts, 1991.

Gurob

Brunton, Guy, and Reginald Engelbach. *Gurob*. London: British School of Archaeology in Egypt, 1927.

Loat, Leonard. *Gurob*. London: British School of Archaeology in Egypt, 1905.

Petrie, W. M. Flinders. *Illahun, Kahun and Gurob*. London: D. Nutt, 1891.

————. *Kahun, Gurob and Hawara*. London: Kegan Paul, Trench, Trübner and Co., 1890.

Thomas, Angela. *Gurob: A New Kingdom Town*. Warminster, Great Britain: Aris and Phillips, 1981.

Hawara

Farag, Naguib, and Zaki Iskander. *The Discovery of Neferwptah*. Cairo: Antiquities Department of Egypt, 1971.

Petrie, W. M. Flinders. *Hawara, Biahmu and Arsinoe*. London: Field and Tuer, 1889.

————. *The Hawara Portfolio*. London: British School of Archaeology in Egypt, 1913.

————. *Kahun, Gurob and Hawara*. London: Kegan Paul, Trench, Trübner and Co., 1890.

Petrie, W. M. Flinders, Gerald A. Wainwright, and Ernest Mackay. *The Labyrinth, Gerzeh and Mazguneh*. London: British School of Archaeology in Egypt, 1912.

Heliopolis

Debono, Fernand, and Bodil Mortensen. *The Predynastic Cemetery at Heliopolis*. Deutsches Archäologisches Institut. Abteilung Kairo. Archäologische Veröffentlichungen 63. Mainz am Rhein, Germany: Philipp von Zabern, 1988.

Petrie, W. M. Flinders, and Ernest Mackay. *Heliopolis, Kafr Ammar and Shurafa*. London: British School of Archaeology in Egypt, 1915.

Saleh, Abdel-Aziz. *Excavations at Heliopolis*. 2 vols. Cairo: Cairo University, 1981–83.

el-Sawi, Ahmad, and Farouk Gomaa. *Das Grab des Panehsi, Gottesvaters von Heliopolis in Matariya*. Wiesbaden: Harrassowitz, 1993.

Helwan

Saad Zaki. *The Excavations at Helwan.* Norman: University of Oklahoma Press, 1969.

————. *Royal Excavations at Saqqara and Helwan 1941–1945.* Cairo: Service des Antiquités de l'Egypte, 1947.

Herakleopolis

Lopez Grande, Maria José, Fernando Quesada Sanz, and Miguel Angel Molinero. *Excavaciones en Ehnasya el Medina (Heracleopolis Magna).* Vol. 2. Madrid: Ministerio de Cultura, 1995.

Mukhtar, Mohamed Gamal el-din. *Ihnâsya el-Medina (Herakleopolis Magna): Its Importance and Its Role in Pharaonic History.* Cairo: Institut français d'archéologie orientale, 1983.

Naville, Édouard. *Ahnas al Medineh (Heracleopolis Magna).* London: Egypt Exploration Fund, 1894.

Perez-Die, Maria del Carmen, and Pascal Vernus. *Excavaciones en Ehnasya el Medina (Heracleopolis Magna).* Vol. 1. Madrid: Ministerio de Cultura, 1992.

Petrie, W. M. Flinders. *Ehnasya 1904.* London: Egypt Exploration Fund, 1905.

————. *Roman Ehnasya (Herakleopolis Magna) 1904.* London: Egypt Exploration Fund, 1905.

Hermopolis

Hanke, Rainer. *Amarna-reliefs aus Hermopolis.* Hildesheimer Ägyptologische Beiträge 2. Hildesheim: Gerstenberg, 1978.

Roeder, Günther. *Amarna-Reliefs aus Hermopolis.* Hildesheim: Gebrüder Gerstenberg, 1969.

————. *Hermopolis 1929–1939.* Hildesheim: Gebrüder Gerstenberg, 1959.

Snape, Steven. *A Temple of Domitian at El-Ashmunein.* British Museum Occasional Paper 68. London: British Museum, 1989.

Snape, Steven, and Donald M. Bailey. *The Great Portico at Hermopolis Magna: Present State and Past Prospects.* British Museum Occasional Paper 63. London: British Museum, 1988.

Spencer, A. Jeffrey, and Donald M. Bailey. *Excavations at El-Ashmunein.* 5 vols. London: British Museum Press, 1983–98.

Hiba, el-

Wenke, Robert J. *Archaeological Investigations at el-Hibeh 1980: Preliminary Report.* Malibu, Calif.: Undena Publications, 1984.

Hierakonpolis

Adams, Barbara. *Ancient Hierakonpolis.* 2 vols. Warminster, Great Britain: Aris and Phillips, 1974.
———. *Ancient Nekhen.* New Malden, Great Britain: SIA Publishing, 1995.
———. *The Fort Cemetery at Hierakonpolis (excavated by John Garstang).* London: Kegan Paul International, 1988.
Hoffman, Michael. *The Predynastic of Hierakonpolis.* Cairo: Cairo University Herbarium, 1982.
Quibell, James E., and Frederick W. Green. *Hierakonpolis.* 2 vols. London: Egyptian Research Account, 1900–02.

Kalabsha

Daumas, François. *Le ouabet de Kalabscha.* Cairo: Centre de Documentation et d'Études sur l'ancienne Égypte, 1970.
De Meulenare, Herman. *La chapelle ptolémaïque de Kalabcha.* Cairo: Centre de Documentation et d'Études sur l'ancienne Égypte, 1964–70.
Siegler, Karl Georg. *Kalabsha: Architektur und Baugeschichte des Tempels.* Deutsches Archäologisches Institut. Abteilung Kairo. Archäologische Veröffentlichungen 1. Berlin: Gebr. Mann, 1970.
Strouhal, Eugen. *Wadi Qitna and Kalabsha South.* Vol. 1. *Archaeology.* Prague: Charles University, 1984.
Wright, G. R. H. *Kalabsha: The Preserving of the Temple.* Deutsches Archäologisches Institut. Abteilung Kairo. Archäologische Veröffentlichungen 2. Berlin: Gebr. Mann, 1972.
———. *Kalabsha III. The Ptolemaic Sanctuary of Kalabsha.* Deutsches Archäologisches Institut. Abteilung Kairo. Archäologische Veröffentlichungen 3,1. Mainz am Rhein, Germany: Philipp von Zabern, 1987.

Karnak

Azim, Michel, et al. *Karnak et sa Topographie: Vol. 1. Les relèves modernes du temple d'Amon-Rê.* Paris: Éditions CNRS, 1998.

Benson, Margaret, and Janet Gourlay. *The Temple of Mut in Asher*. London: John Murray, 1899.

Centre Franco-Égyptien d'Étude des Temples de Karnak. *Cahiers de Karnak V-X*. 5 vols. 1975–95. Previous reports in the journal *Kemi*.

Chevrier, Henri. *Le temple reposoir de Séti II à Karnak*. Cairo: Service des Antiquités Egyptiennes, 1940.

Epigraphic Survey. *Reliefs and Inscriptions at Karnak*. 4 vols. Chicago: The Oriental Institute of the University of Chicago, 1936–86.

————. *The Temple of Khonsu*. 2 vols. Chicago: The Oriental Institute of the University of Chicago, 1979–81.

Gohary, Jocelyn. *Akhenaten's Sed-Festival at Karnak*. London: Kegan Paul International, 1992.

Lacau, Pierre, and Henri Chevrier. *Une chapelle d'Hatshepsout à Karnak*. 2 vols. Cairo: Service des Antiquités de l'Égypte, 1977–79.

————. *Une chapelle de Sésostris Ier à Karnak*. 2 vols. Cairo: Service des Antiquités de l'Égypte, 1956–69.

Lauffray, Jean, Claude Traunecker, F. Le Saout, and Olivier Masson. *La chapelle d'Achôris à Karnak*. Paris: Éditions ADPF, 1981-95.

Le Fur, Daniel. *La Conservation des peintures murales des temples de Karnak*. Paris: Éditions Recherche sur les Civilisations ADPF, 1994.

Legrain, Georges. *Les Temples du Karnak*. Brussels: 1929.

Nelson, Harold H. *The Great Hypostyle Hall at Karnak I, Part 1. The Wall Reliefs*. Chicago: The Oriental Institute of the University of Chicago, 1981.

Parker, Richard, Jean Leclant, and Jean-Claude Goyon. *The Edifice of Taharqa by the Sacred Lake of Karnak*. Providence: Brown University Press, 1979.

Redford, Donald B. *The Akhenaten Temple Project 3: The Excavations of Kom el-Ahmar and Environs*. Toronto: University of Toronto, 1994.

Rondot, Vincent. *La grand salle hypostyle de Karnak: Les architraves*. 2 vols. Paris: Éditions Recherche sur les Civilisations, 1998.

Sauneron, Serge. *La porte ptolémaïque de l'enceinte de Mout à Karnak*. Cairo: Institut français d'archéologie orientale, 1983.

Smith, Ray W., and Donald B. Redford. *The Akhenaten Temple Project I*. Warminster, Great Britain: Aris and Phillips, 1977.

Van Siclen, Charles. *The Alabaster Shrine of King Amenhotep II*. San Antonio: Van Siclen Books, 1986.

Kerma

Bonnet, Charles. *Kerma: Territoire et métropole*. Cairo: Institut français d'archéologie orientale, 1986.

Dunham, Dows. *Excavations at Kerma*. Part VI. Boston: Museum of Fine Arts, 1982.

Reisner, George A. *Excavations at Kerma I-V.* 2 vols. Cambridge, Mass.: 1923.

Kharga Oasis

Barakat, Hala N., and Nathalie Baum. *La végétation antique de Douch (Oasis de Kharga)*. Cairo: Institut français d'archéologie orientale, 1992.

Bousquet, Bernard. *Tell-Douch et sa région*. Cairo: Institut français d'archéologie orientale, 1996.

Caton-Thompson, Gertrude. *Kharga Oasis in Prehistory*. London: The Athlone Press, 1952.

Cruz-Uribe, Eugene. *Hibis Temple Project I*. San Antonio, Tx.: Van Siclen Books, 1988.

Cuvigny, H., and G. Wagner. *Les ostraca grecs de Douch*. 3 fascs. Cairo: Institut français d'archéologie orientale, 1986–92.

Dunand, Fernand, et al. *La nécropole de Douch (Oasis de Kharga)*. Cairo: Institut français d'archéologie orientale, 1992.

Reddé, Michel. *Le trésor de Douch (Oasis de Kharga)*. Cairo: Institut français d'archéologie orientale, 1992.

Winlock, Herbert. *The Temple of Hibis in the el-Khargheh Oasis*. 2 vols. New York: The Metropolitan Museum of Art, 1938–41.

Kom Abu Billo

Abd el-Al, Abdel-Hafeez, Jean-Claude Grenier, and Guy Wagner. *Stèles funéraires de Kom Abu Bellou*. Paris: Éditions Recherche sur les Civilisations, 1985.

Hooper, Finley A. *Funerary Stelae from Kom Abou Billou*. Ann Arbor, Mich.: Kelsey Museum of Archaeology, 1961.

Kom Ombo

Gutbub, Adolphe. *Kom Ombo I*. Cairo: Institut français d'archéologie orientale, 1995.

Morgan, Jacques de, et al. *Kom Ombos*. 2 vols. Vienna: A. Holzhausen, 1895–1909.

Kumma

(see **Semna**)

Lahun

Luft, Ulrich. *Das Archiv von Illahun Briefe 1.* Hieratische Papyri aus den Staatlichen Museen zu Berlin I. Berlin: Akademie Verlag, 1992.

Petrie, W. M. Flinders. *Illahun, Kahun and Gurob.* London: D. Nutt, 1891.

———. *Kahun, Gurob and Hawara.* London: Kegan Paul, Trench, Trübner and Co., 1890.

Petrie, W. M. F., G. Brunton, and M. A. Murray. *Lahun II.* London: 1923.

Lisht

Arnold, Dieter. *The South Cemeteries of Lisht I: The Pyramid of Senwosret I.* New York: Metropolitan Museum of Art, 1988.

———. *The South Cemeteries of Lisht III: The Pyramid Complex of Senwosret I.* New York: Metropolitan Museum of Art, 1992.

Arnold, Felix. *The South Cemeteries of Lisht II: The control notes and team marks.* New York: Metropolitan Museum of Art, 1990.

Goedicke, Hans. *Re-used Blocks from the Pyramid of Amenemhet I at Lisht.* New York: The Metropolitan Museum of Art, 1971.

Mace, Arthur C., and Herbert Winlock. *The Tomb of Senebtisi at Lisht.* New York: The Metropolitan Museum of Art, 1916.

Luxor

Abdel-Raziq, Mahmud. *Die Darstellugen und Texte des Sanktuars Alexander des Grossen im Tempel von Luxor.* Deutsches Archäologisches Institut. Abteilung Kairo. Archäologische Veröffentlichungen 16. Mainz am Rhein, Germany: Philipp von Zabern, 1984.

———. *Das Sanktuar Amenophis, III im Luxor Tempel.* Studies in Egyptian Culture 3. Tokyo: Waseda University, 1986.

Brunner, Hellmut. *Die südlichen Räume des Tempels von Luxor.* Deutsches Archäologisches Institut. Abteilung Kairo. Archäologische Veröffentlichungen 18. Mainz am Rhein, Germany: Philipp von Zabern, 1977.

Epigraphic survey. *Reliefs and Inscriptions at Luxor Termple I: The Festival Procession of Opet in the Colonnade Hall.* Chicago: The Oriental Institute of the University of Chicago, 1994.

Gayet. Albert. *Le temple de Louxor*. Paris: Ernest Leroux, 1894.

Kuentz, Charles. *La faces sud du massif est du pylone de Ramsès II à Louxor*. Cairo: Centre de Documentation et d'Études sur l'ancienne Égypte, 1971.

el-Saghir, Mohammed. *Das Statuenversteck im Luxortempel*. Mainz am Rhein, Germany: Philipp von Zabern, 1992.

el-Saghir, Mohammed, Jean-Claude Golvin, et al. *Le camp romain de Louqsor*. Cairo: Institut français d'archéologie orientale, 1986.

Maadi

Menghin, Oswald, and Mustafa Amer. *The Excavations of the Egyptian University in the Neolithic Site at Maadi*. 2 vols. Cairo: Government Press, 1932–36.

Rizkana, Ibrahim, and Jürgen Seeher. *Maadi*. 4 vols. Deutsches Archäologisches Institut. Abteilung Kairo. Archäologische Veröffentlichungen 64–5, 80–1. Mainz am Rhein, Germany: Philipp von Zabern, 1986–90.

Malkata

Hope, Colin. *Excavations at Malkata and Birket Habu 1971–1974 V*. Warminster, Great Britain: Aris and Phillips, 1978.

Leahy, M. Anthony. *Excavations at Malkata and Birket Habu 1971-1974 IV*. Warminster, Great Britain: Aris and Phillips, 1978.

Tytus, Robb de P. *A Preliminary Report on the Pre-excavation of the Palace of Amenhotep III*. New York: 1903.

Waseda University, Architectural Research Mission for the Study of Ancient Egyptian Architecture. *Studies on the Palace of Malqata 1985–1988* (in Japanese with English summary). Tokyo: Waseda University, 1992.

Waseda University Egypt Archaeological Mission. *The Excavations at Malkata-South 1972–1980*. Studies in Egyptian Culture 1. Tokyo: Waseda University, 1985.

————. *Malkata-South* (in Japanese with English summary). 4 vols. Tokyo: Waseda University, 1983–92.

Watanabe, Yasutada, and Kazuaki Seki. *The Architecture of Kom el Samak at Malkata South: A Study of Architectural Restoration*. Studies in Egyptian Culture 5. Tokyo: Waseda University, 1986.

Medamud

Robichon, Clément, and Alexandre Varille. *Description sommaire du temple primitif de Médamoud.* Cairo: Institut français d'archéologie orientale, 1940.

Medinet Habu

Chicago Epigraphic Survey. *Medinet Habu.* 8 vols. Chicago: 1930-70.
Hölscher, Uvo. *The Excavation of Medinet Habu.* 5 vols. Chicago: 1934–54.

Meidum

el-Khouli, Ali. *Meidum.* Sydney: Macquarie University, 1991.
Petrie, W. M. Flinders. *Meydum.* London: Egypt Exploration Society, 1892.
Petrie, W. M. Flinders, Ernest Mackay, and Gerald Wainwright. *Maydum and Memphis III.* London: British School of Archaeology in Egypt, 1910.

Meir

Blackman, Aylward M. *The Rock Tombs of Meir.* 6 vols. London: Egypt Exploration Society, 1914–53.

Memphis

Abdulla, Said M. A. *A New Temple for Hathor at Memphis.* Warminster, Great Britain: Aris and Phillips, 1978.
Anthes, Rudolf. *Mit Rahineh 1955.* Philadelphia: The University Museum, 1959.
———. *Mit Rahineh 1956.* Philadelphia: The University Museum, 1965.
Engelbach, Reginald. *Riqqeh and Memphis VI.* London: British School of Archaeology in Egypt, 1915.
Jeffreys, David G. *The Survey of Memphis.* London: Egypt Exploration Society, 1985.
Petrie, W. M. Flinders. *Memphis I.* London: British School of Archaeology in Egypt, 1909.
———. *Palace of Apries (Memphis II).* London: British School of Archaeology in Egypt, 1909.

————. *Roman Portraits and Memphis (IV)*. London: British School of Archaeology in Egypt, 1911.

Petrie, W. M. Flinders, Ernest Mackay, and Gerald Wainwright. *Meydum and Memphis (III)*. London: British School of Archaeology in Egypt, 1910.

Petrie, W. M. Flinders, Gerald Wainwright, and Alan H. Gardiner. *Tarkhan and Memphis V.* London: British School of Archaeology in Egypt, 1913.

Mendes

De Meulenaere, Herman, and Pierre Mackay. *Mendes II.* Warminster, Great Britain: Aris and Phillips, 1976.

Hall, Emma S., and Bernard V. Bothmer. *Mendes I.* Warminster, Great Britain: Aris and Phillips, 1977.

Wilson, Karen. *Cities of the Delta, Part II. Mendes: Preliminary Report on the 1979 and 1980 Seasons.* Malibu, Calif.: Undena Publications, 1982.

Merimda Beni Salama

Eiwanger, Josef. *Merimde-Benisalâme.* 3 vols. Deutsches Archäologisches Institut. Abteilung Kairo. Archäologische Veröffentlichungen 47, 51, 59. Mainz am Rhein, Germany: Philipp von Zabern, 1984–93.

Junker, Hermann. *Vorläufer Bericht über die Grabung der Akademie der Wissenschaften in Wien auf der neolitischen Siedlung von Merimde-Beni Salâme.* 6 vols. Vienna: 1929–40.

Meroe

Dunham, Dows, and S. Chapman. *The Royal Cemeteries of Kush III-V.* Boston: Museum of Fine Arts, 1952–63.

Shinnie, Peter L., and Rebecca J. Bradley. *The Capital of Kush I. Meroe Excavations 1965–1972. Meroitica 4.* Berlin: Akademie Verlag, 1980.

Török, László. *Meroe City: An Ancient African Capital. John Garstang's Excavations in the Sudan.* London: The Egypt Exploration Society, 1997.

Minshat Abu Omar

Kroeper, Karla, and Dietrich Wildung. *Minshat Abu Omar: Münchner Ostdelta-Expedition Vorbericht 1978–1984.* Munich: Staatliche Sammlung Ägyptischer Kunst, 1985.

————. *Minshat Abu Omar: Ein vor- und frühgeschichlicher Friedhof im Nildelta I.* Mainz am Rhein, Germany: Philipp von Zabern, 1994.

Mirgissa

Dunham, Dows. *Second Cataract Forts. Vol. II. Uronarti Shalfak Mirgissa.* Boston: Museum of Fine Arts, 1967.
Vercoutter, Jean. *Mirgissa.* 3 vols. Paris: 1970–76.

Moalla, el-

Vandier, Jacques. *Mo'alla, la tombe d'Anktifi et la tombe de Sébekhotep.* Cairo: Institut français d'archéologie orientale, 1950.

Mons Claudianus

Bingen, Jean, et al. *Mons Claudianus: Ostraca Graeca et Latina. I-II.* Cairo: Institut français d'archéologie orientale, 1992–97.
Peacock, Donald, and Valerie Maxfield. *Mons Claudianus: Topography and Quarries.* Cairo: Institut français d'archéologie orientale, 1997.

Mons Porphyrites

Johns, Catherine, and Donald Bailey. "Mons Porphyrites. The source of Imperial Porphyry". *Minerva* 5 No. 5 (1994), 18–20.
Van Rengen, Wilfried. "A New Paneion at Mons Porphyrites". *Chronique d'Égypte* 70 (1995), 240–45.

Naga el-Deir

Dunham, Dows. *Naga-ed-Dêr Stelae of the First Intermediate Period.* Oxford: Oxford University Press, 1937.
Lythgoe, Albert M., and Dows Dunham. *The Predynastic Cemetery N7000. Nag-ed-Dêr IV.* Berkeley: University of California Press, 1965.
Ockinga, Boyo G., and Yahya al-Masri. *Two Ramesside Tombs at El Mashayikh.* Sydney: The Ancient History Documentary Research Centre, Macquarie University, 1988–90.
Podzorski, Patricia V. *Their Bones Shall Not Perish.* New Malden, Great Britain: SIA Publications, 1990.

Reisner, George A. *A Provincial Cemetery of the Pyramid Age: Naga-ed-Dêr.* Oxford: Oxford University Press, 1932.

Reisner, George A., and Arthur Mace. *The Early Dynastic Cemeteries of Naga-ed-Dêr.* Leipzig: J. C. Hinrichs, 1908–09.

Simpson, William Kelly. *Papyrus Reisner I-IV.* Boston: Museum of Fine Arts, 1963–86.

Napata

Dunham, Dows. *The Barkal Temples.* Boston: Museum of Fine Arts, 1970.

———. *The Royal Cemeteries of Kush.* 5 vols. Cambridge, Mass.: Harvard University Press, 1950; Boston: Museum of Fine Arts, 1955–63.

Kendall, Timothy. *Gebel Barkal Epigraphic Survey 1986: Preliminary Report to the Visiting Committee of the Department of Egyptian Art.* Boston: Museum of Fine Arts, 1986.

Naqada

Baumgartel, Elise J. *Petrie's Naqada Excavation: A Supplement.* London: 1970.

Petrie, W. M. Flinders, and James E. Quibell. *Naqada and Ballas.* London: 1896.

Naukratis

Coulson, William D. E. *Ancient Naukratis II, Part I: The Survey at Naukratis.* Oxford: Oxbow Books, 1996.

Coulson, William D. E., and Albert Leonard. *Cities of the Delta I: Naukratis: Preliminary Report on the 1977–78 and 1980 Seasons.* Malibu, Calif.: Undena Publications, 1981.

Gardner, Ernest A. *Naukratis II.* London: Egypt Exploration Fund, 1888.

Petrie, W. M. Flinders, and Ernest A. Gardner. *Naukratis I.* London: Egypt Exploration Fund, 1886.

Qasr Ibrim

Adams, William Y. *Qasr Ibrim: The Late Medieval Period.* London: Egypt Exploration Society, 1996.

Caminos, Ricardo A. *The Shrines and Rock Inscriptions of Ibrim.* London: Egypt Exploration Society, 1968.

Hinds, Martin, and Victor Ménage. *Qasr Ibrim in the Ottoman Period: Turkish and Further Arabic Documents*. London: Egypt Exploration Society, 1991.

Hinds, Martin, and Hamdi Sakkout. *Arabic Documents from the Ottoman Period from Qasr Ibrim*. London: Egypt Exploration Society, 1986.

Mills, Anthony J. *The Cemeteries of Qasr Ibrim*. London: Egypt Exploration Society, 1982.

Plumley, J. Martin. *The Scrolls of Bishop Timotheos*. London: Egypt Exploration Society, 1975.

Plumley, J. Martin, and Gerald M. Browne. *Old Nubian Texts from Qasr Ibrim*. 3 vols. London: Egypt Exploration Society, 1988–91.

Rose, Pamela. *Qasr Ibrim: The Hinterland Survey*. London: Egypt Exploration Society, 1996.

Ramesseum

Goyon, Jean-Claude, et al. *Le Ramesseum X*. 2 vols. Cairo: Centre d'Études et de Documentation sur l'ancienne Égypte, 1976.

Goyon, Jean-Claude, and Hassan el-Achirie. *Le Ramesseum I: Hypostle N*. Cairo: Centre de Documentation et d'Études sur l'ancienne Égypte, 1973.

———. *Le Ramesseum VI: La Salle des Litanies (R)*. Cairo: Centre de Documentation et d'Études sur l'ancienne Égypte, 1974.

Leblanc, Christian, et al. *Le Ramesseum IX 1–2: Les piliers "Osiriaques"*. 2 vols. Cairo: Organisation Égyptienne des Antiquités, 1980–88.

Maher-Taha, M., and A. Loyrette. *Le Ramesseum XI: Les fêtes du dieu Min*. Cairo: Organisation Égyptienne des Antiquités, 1979.

Quibell, James E., et al. *The Ramesseum*. London: Bernard Quaritch, 1898.

Youssef, A. A. H., C. Leblanc, and M. Maher. *Le Ramesseum IV: Les batailles de Tounip et de Dapur*. Cairo: Centre d'Études et de Documentation sur l'ancienne Égypte, 1977.

Sais

el-Sayed, Ramadan. *Documents relatifs à Saïs et ses divinités*. Cairo: Institut français d'archéologie orientale, 1975.

Saqqara

(see also **Serapeum**)

Betro, Maria Carmela. *Saqqara III: I Testi Solari del Portale di Pascerientaisu (BN2)*. Pisa: Giardini, 1989.

Bresciani, Edda., et al. *Saqqara I: Tomba di Boccori. La Galleria di Padineit.* Pisa: Giardini, 1980.

———. *La Tomba di Ciennehebu, Capo della Flotta del Re.* Pisa: Giardini, 1977.

Capart, Jean. *Une rue de tombeaux à Saqqarah.* Brussels: Vromant et Co., 1947.

Davies, W. Vivian, Aly El-Khouli, Alan Lloyd, and A. Jeffrey Spencer. *Saqqara Tombs.* 2 vols. London: Egypt Exploration Society, 1984–90.

Emery, Walter B. *Excavations at Saqqara: Great Tombs of the First Dynasty I.* Cairo: Service des Antiquités de l'Égypte, 1949.

———. *Excavations at Saqqara: The Tomb of Hemaka.* Cairo: Service des Antiquités de l'Égypte, 1938.

———. *Excavations at Saqqara 1937–1938: The Tomb of Hor-Aha.* Cairo: Service des Antiquités de l'Égypte, 1939.

———. *Great Tombs of the First Dynasty II-III.* London: Egypt Exploration Fund, 1954–58.

Épron, Lucienne, François Daumas, and Henri Wild. *Le Tombeau de Ti.* Cairo: Institut français d'archéologie orientale, 1939-66.

el-Fikey, Said A. *The Tomb of the Vizier Re'wer at Saqqara.* Warminster, Great Britain: Aris and Phillips, 1980.

Firth, Cecil, and Battiscombe Gunn. *Excavations at Saqqara: Teti Pyramid Cemeteries.* Cairo: Service des Antiquités de l'Égypte, 1926.

Firth, Cecil, and James E. Quibell. *Excavations at Saqqara: The Step Pyramid.* Cairo: Service des Antiquités de l'Égypte, 1935.

Gaballa, Gabulla A. *The Memphite Tomb Chapel of Mose.* Warminster, Great Britain: Aris and Phillips, 1978.

Giddy, Lisa. *The Anubieion at Saqqara II: The Cemeteries.* London: Egypt Exploration Society, 1992.

Green, Christine I. *The Temple Furniture from the Sacred Animal Necropolis at North Saqqâra 1964–1976.* London: Egypt Exploration Society, 1987.

Hassan, Selim. *Excavations at Saqqara 1937–38.* 3 vols. Cairo: Government Printing Offices, 1975.

James, T. G. Henry. *The Mastaba of Khentika Called Ikheki.* London: Egypt Exploration Society, 1953.

Jécquier, Gustave. *Fouilles à Saqqarah.* 6 vols. Cairo: Service des Antiquités de l'Égypte, 1928–38.

Jeffreys, David, and Henry S. Smith. *The Anubieion at Saqqara I: The Settlement and the Temple Precinct.* London: Egypt Exploration Society, 1988.

Kanawati, Naguib, and Ali Hassan, Ali. *The Teti Cemetery at Saqqara I.* Sydney: Macquarie University, 1996.

Kanawati, Naguib, et al. *Excavations at Saqqara North-west of Teti's Pyramid.* 2 vols. Sydney: Macquarie University, 1984–88.

Labrousse, Audran. *L'Architecture des Pyramides à Texts.* 2 vols. Cairo: Institut français d'archéologie orientale, 1996.

Labrousse, Audran, Jean-Philippe Lauer, and Jean Leclant. *Le temple haut du complexe funéraire du roi Ounas.* Cairo: Institut français d'archéologie orientale, 1977.

Labrousse, Audran, and Ahmed Moussa. *Le temple d'accueil du complexe funéraire du roi Ounas.* Cairo: Institut français d'archéologie orientale, 1996.

Lauer, Jean-Philippe. *Les Pyramides de Saqqarah.* 6th ed. Cairo: Institut français d'archéologie orientale, 1991.

———. *Saqqara: The Royal Cemetery of Memphis: Excavations and Discoveries since 1850.* London: Thames and Hudson, 1976.

Lauer, Jean-Philippe, and Pierre Lacau. *Fouilles à Sakkarah: La Pyramide à degrés I-V.* Cairo: Service des Antiquités de l'Égypte, 1936–65.

Lauer, Jean-Philippe, and Jean Leclant. *Le temple haut du complexe funéraire du roi Téti.* Cairo: Institut français d'archéologie orientale, 1972.

Macramallah, Rizkallah. *Fouilles à Saqqarah: Un cimitière archaïque de la classe moyenne du peuple à Saqqarah.* Cairo: Service des Antiquités de l'Égypte, 1940.

Mariette, Auguste. *Les Mastabas de l'Ancien Empire.* Paris: F. Vieweg, 1889.

Martin, Geoffrey T. *Corpus of Reliefs of the New Kingdom from the Memphite Necropolis and Lower Egypt I.* London: Kegan Paul International, 1987.

———. *The Hidden Tombs of Memphis: New Discoveries from the Time of Tutankhamun and Ramesses the Great.* London: Thames and Hudson, 1991.

———. *The Memphite Tomb of Horemheb, Commander-in-Chief of Tut'ankahmun I: The Reliefs, Inscriptions, and Commentary.* London: Egypt Exploration Society, 1989.

———. *The Sacred Animal Necropolis at North Saqqara.* London: Egypt Exploration Society, 1981.

———. *The Tomb Chapels of Paser and Ra'ia at Saqqara.* London: Egypt Exploration Society, 1985.

———. *The Tomb of Hetepka.* London: Egypt Exploration Society, 1979.

———. *The Tomb of Tia and Tia.* London: Egypt Exploration Society, 1997.

Moussa, Ahmed M., and Hartwig Altenmuller. *Saqqara: Das Grab des Ni-anchchnum und Chnumhotep*. Deutsches Archäologisches Institut. Abteilung Kairo. Archäologische Veröffentlichungen 21. Mainz am Rhein, Germany: Philipp von Zabern, 1977.

———. *The Tomb of Nefer and Ka-Hay*. Deutsches Archäologisches Institut. Abteilung Kairo. Archäologische Veröffentlichungen 5. Mainz am Rhein, Germany: Philipp von Zabern, 1971.

Moussa, Ahmed, and Friedrich Junge. *Two Tombs of Craftsmen*. Deutsches Archäologisches Institut. Abteilung Kairo. Archäologische Veröffentlichungen 9. Mainz am Rhein, Germany: Philipp von Zabern, 1975.

Munro, Peter. *Der Unas-Friedhof Nordwest I*. Mainz am Rhein, Germany: Philipp von Zabern, 1993.

Quibell, James E. *Excavations at Saqqara (1905–6)*. Cairo: Service des Antiquités de l'Égypte, 1907.

———. *Excavations at Saqqara (1906–1907)*. Cairo: Service des Antiquités de l'Égypte, 1908.

———. *Excavations at Saqqara (1907–1908)*. Cairo: Service des Antiquités de l'Égypte, 1909.

———. *Excavations at Saqqara (1908–9, 1909–10): The Monastery of Apa Jeremias*. Cairo: Service des Antiquités de l'Égypte, 1912.

———. *Excavations at Saqqara (1911–12): The Tomb of Hesy*. Cairo: Service des Antiquités de l'Égypte, 1913.

———. *Excavations at Saqqara (1912–14): Archaic Mastabas*. Cairo: Service des Antiquités de l'Égypte, 1923.

Quibell, James E., and Angelo Hayter. *Excavations at Saqqara: Teti Pyramid North Side*. Cairo: Service des Antiquités de l'Égypte, 1927.

Raven, Maarten J. *The Tomb of Irudef*. London: Egypt Exploration Society, 1991.

Ricke, Herbert. *Das Sonnenheiligtum des Königs Userkaf*. Beiträge für Ägyptischen Bauforschung und Altertumskunde 7–8. Cairo: Schweizerisches Institut fur Ägyptische, 1965–69.

Zivie, Alain. *Découverte à Saqqarah: Le vizier oublié*. Paris: Seuil, 1990.

Semna

Caminos, Ricardo. *Semna-Kumma*. 2 vols. London: Egypt Exploration Society, 1998.

Dunham, Dows, and Jozef M. A. Janssen. *Second Cataract Forts. Vol. 1. Semna Kumma*. Boston: Museum of Fine Arts, 1960.

Serabit el-Khadim

Petrie, W. M. Flinders, and Charles T. Curelly. *Researches in Sinai.* London: Murray, 1906.
Valbelle, Dominique, and Charles Bonnet. *Le sanctuaire d'Hathor maîtresse de la turquoise.* Paris: Picard, 1996.

Serapeum

Lauer, Jean-Philippe, and Charles Picard. *Les statues ptolémaïques du Sérapiéion de Memphis.* Paris: Presses Universitaires de France, 1955.
Malinine, Michel, Georges Posener, and Jean Vercoutter. *Catalogue des stèles du Sérapeum de Memphis I.* Paris: Musées Nationaux, 1968.
Mariette, Auguste. *Le Sérapéum de Memphis.* Edited by Gaston Maspero. Paris: F. Vieweg, 1882.

Shalfak

(see **Uronarti**)

Siwa Oasis

Fakhry, Ahmed. *The Oases of Egypt I: Siwa Oasis.* Cairo: The American University in Cairo Press, 1973.
———. *Siwa Oasis.* Cairo: Government Press, 1944.
Giddy, Lisa. *Egyptian Oases.* Warminster, Great Britain: Aris and Phillips, 1987.

Soleb

Giorgini, Michela Schiff. *Soleb.* 2 vols. Florence: Firenze, Sansoni, 1965–71.

Tanis

Brissaud, Philippe. *Cahiers de Tanis I.* Paris: Éditions Recherche sur les Civilisations, 1987.
Montet, Pierre. *Le lac sacré de Tanis.* Paris: C. Klincksieck, 1966.
———. *La nécropole royale de Tanis.* 3 vols. Paris: 1947–60.
———. *Les nouvelles fouilles de Tanis.* Paris: Les Belles lettres, 1933.

Petrie, W. M. Flinders. *Tanis*. 2 vols. London: Egypt Exploration Fund, 1885–87.

Yoyotte, Jean, et al. *Tanis: L'or des pharaons*. Paris: Ministère des Affaires Étrangères, 1987.

Tell el-Maskhuta

Holladay, John S. *Cities of the Delta III: Tell el-Maskhuta*. Malibu, Calif.: Undena Publications, 1982.

Naville, Édouard. *The Store-City of Pithom and the Route of the Exodus*. London: Egypt Exploration Fund, 1885.

Tell el-Yahudiya

Naville, Édouard. *The Mound of the Jew and the City of Onias*. London: Egypt Exploration Fund, 1890.

Petrie, W. M. Flinders. *Hyksos and Israelite Cities*. London: British School of Archaeology in Egypt, 1906.

Thebes: Private Tombs

Arnold, Dieter. *Gräber des Alten und Mittleren Reiches in El-Tarif*. Deutsches Archäologisches Institut. Abteilung Kairo. Archäologische Veröffentlichungen 17. Mainz am Rhein, Germany: Philipp von Zabern, 1976.

———. *Grabung im Asasif 1963–1970 I. Das Grab des Jnj-jtj.f: Die Architectur*. Deutsches Archäologisches Institut. Abteilung Kairo. Archäologische Veröffentlichungen 4. Mainz am Rhein, Germany: Philipp von Zabern, 1971.

Assmann, Jan. *Das Grab des Amenemope (TT41): Theben III*. Mainz am Rhein, Germany: Philipp von Zabern, 1991.

———. *Sonnenhymnen in Thebanischen Gräber: Theben I*. Mainz am Rhein, Germany: Philipp von Zabern, 1983.

———. *Grabung im Asasif 1963–1970 II. Das Grab des Basa (Nr. 389) in der thebanischen Nekropole*. Deutsches Archäologisches Institut. Abteilung Kairo. Archäologische Veröffentlichungen 6. Mainz am Rhein, Germany: Philipp von Zabern, 1973.

———. *Grabung im Asasif 1963–1970 VI. Das Grab des Mutirdis*. Deutsches Archäologisches Institut. Abteilung Kairo. Archäologische Veröffentlichungen 13. Mainz am Rhein, Germany: Philipp von Zabern, 1977.

Bietak, Manfred, and Elfriede Reiser-Haslauer. *Das Grab des 'Anch-hor,-*

Obersthofmeister der Gottesgemahlin Nitokris. 2 vols. Untersuchungen der Zweigstelle Kairo des Österreichischen Archäologischen Institut IV-V. Vienna: Österreichischen Akademie der Wissenschaften, 1978–82.

Brack, Annelies, and Artur Brack. *Das Grab des Haremheb: Theben Nr. 78.* Deutsches Archäologisches Institut. Abteilung Kairo. Archäologische Veröffentlichungen 35. Mainz am Rhein, Germany: Philipp von Zabern, 1980.

—————. *Das Grab des Tjanuni: Theban Nr. 74.* Deutsches Archäologisches Institut. Abteilung Kairo. Archäologische Veröffentlichungen 19. Mainz am Rhein, Germany: Philipp von Zabern, 1977.

Burkard, Günter. *Grabung im Asasif 1963–1970 III. Die Papyrusfunde.* Deutsches Archäologisches Institut. Abteilung Kairo. Archäologische Veröffentlichungen 22. Mainz am Rhein, Germany: Philipp von Zabern, 1986.

Davies, Norman de G. *The Tomb of Ken-amun at Thebes.* New York: The Metropolitan Museum of Art, 1930.

—————. *The Tomb of Nakht at Thebes.* New York: The Metropolitam Museum of Art, 1917.

—————. *The Tomb of Nefer-hotep at Thebes.* New York: The Metropolitan Museum of Art, 1933.

—————. *The Tomb of Rekh-mi-re at Thebes.* New York: The Metropolitan Museum of Art, 1943.

—————. *The Tomb of Two Sculptors at Thebes.* New York: The Metropolitan Museum of Art, 1925.

Dorman, Peter. *The Tombs of Senenemut.* New York: The Metropolitan Museum of Art, 1991.

Dziobek, Eberhard. *Das Grab des Ineni: Theben Nr. 81.* Deutsches Archäologisches Institut. Abteilung Kairo. Archäologisches Veröffentlichungen 68. Mainz am Rhein, Germany: Philipp von Zabern, 1991.

—————. *Die Gräber des Vezirs User-Amun: Theben Nr. 61 und 131.* Deutsches Archäologisches Institut. Abteilung Kairo. Archäologische Veröffentlichungen 84. Mainz am Rhein, Germany: Philipp von Zabern, 1994.

Dziobek, Eberhard, and Mahmud Abdel Raziq. *Das Grab des Sobekhotep: Theben Nr. 63.* Deutsches Archäologisches Institut. Abteilung Kairo. Archäologische Veröffentlichungen 71. Mainz am Rhein, Germany: Philipp von Zabern, 1990.

Eigner, Dieter. *Die Monumentalen Grabbauten der Spätzeit in der Thebanischen Nekrople.* Denkschriften der Gesamtakademie VIII. Vienna: Österreichische Akademie der Wisenschaften, 1984.

Epigraphic Survey. *The Tomb of Kheruef: Theban Tomb 192.* Chicago: The Oriental Institute of the University of Chicago, 1980.

Feucht, Erika. *Das Grab des Nefersecheru (TT 296): Theben II.* Mainz am Rhein, Germany: Philipp von Zabern, 1985.

Graefe, Erhart. *Das Grab des Ibi.* Brussels: Fondation Égyptologique Reine Élisabeth, 1990.

Guksch, Heike. *Das Grab des Benja gennant Paheqamen: Theben Nr. 343.* Deutsches Archäologisches Institut. Abteilung Kairo. Archäologische Veröffentlichungen 7. Mainz am Rhein, Germany: Philipp von Zabern, 1978.

————. *Die Gräber des Nacht-Min und des Men-cheper-Ra-Seneb: Theben Nr. 87 und 79.* Deutsches Archäologisches Institut. Abteilung Kairo. Archäologische Veröffentlichungen 34. Mainz am Rhein, Germany: Philipp von Zabern, 1995.

Habachi, Labib, and Pierre Anus. *Le tombeau de Nay à Gournet Mar'ei.* Cairo: Institut français d'archéologie orientale, 1977.

Hari, Robert. *La tombe thébaine du père divin Neferhotep (TT 50).* Geneva: Éditions de Belles-Lettres, 1985.

Hegazy, El Sayed A., and Mario Tosi. *A Theban Private Tomb no. 295.* Deutsches Archäologisches Institut. Abteilung Kairo. Archäologische Veröffentlichungen 45. Mainz am Rhein, Germany: Philipp von Zabern, 1978.

Hofmann, Eva. *Das Grab des Neferrenpet gen. Kenro (TT 178): Theben IX.* Mainz am Rhein, Germany: Philipp von Zabern, 1995.

Jaroš-Deckert, Brigitte. *Grabung im Asasif 1963–1970 V. Das Grab des Jnj-jtj.f: Die Wandmalereien der XI. Dynastie.* Deutsches Archäologisches Institut. Abteilung Kairo. Archäologische Veröffentlichungen 12. Mainz am Rhein, Germany: Philipp von Zabern, 1984.

Kampp, Friederike. *Die thebanische Nekropole: Theben XIII.* Mainz am Rhein, Germany: Philipp von Zabern, 1993.

Kuhlmann, Klaus, and Wolfgang Schenkel. *Das Grab des Ibi, Obergutsverwalters der Gottesgemahlin des Amun (Thebanischen Garb Nr. 36) I.* Deutsches Archäologisches Institut. Abteilung Kairo. Archäologische Veröffentlichungen 15. Mainz am Rhein, Germany: Philipp von Zabern, 1983.

Manniche, Lise. *Lost Tombs.* London: Kegan Paul International, 1988.

————. *The Wall Decoration of Three Theban Tombs (TT 77, 175, and 249).* The Carsten Niebuhr Institute of Ancient Near Eastern Studies Publications 4. Copenhagen: Museum Tusculanum Press, 1988.

Mostafa, Maher F. *Das Grab des Neferhotep und des Meh: Theben VIII.* Mainz am Rhein, Germany: Philipp von Zabern, 1995.

Negm, Maged. *The Tomb of Simut: Theban Tomb 409 at Qurnah.* Warminster, Great Britain: Aris and Phillips, 1997.

Polz, Daniel. *Das Grab des Hui und des Kel: Theben Nr. 54.* Deutsches Archäologisches Institut. Abteilung Kairo. Archäologische Veröffentlichungen 74. Mainz am Rhein, Germany: Philipp von Zabern, 1996.

Redford, Susan, and Donald Redford. *The Akhenaten Temple Project 4: The Tomb of Re'a.* Toronto: University of Toronto, 1994.

Saleh, Mohammed. *Three Old-Kingdom Tombs at Thebes.* Deutsches Archäologisches Institut. Abteilung Kairo. Archäologische Veröffentlichungen 14. Mainz am Rhein, Germany: Philipp von Zabern, 1977.

Säve-Söderbergh, Torgny, et al. *Private Tombs at Thebes.* 4 vols. Oxford: Griffith Institute, 1957–63.

Seele, Keith. *The Tomb of Tjanefer at Thebes.* Chicago: The Oriental Institute of the University of Chicago, 1959.

Seidel, Matthias, and Abdel Ghaffar Shedid. *Das Grab des Nacht.* Mainz am Rhein, Germany: Philipp von Zabern, 1992.

Seyfried, Karl-Joachim. *Das Grab des Amonmose (TT 373): Theben IV.* Mainz am Rhein, Germany: Philipp von Zabern, 1990.

———. *Das Grab des Djehutiemhab (TT 194): Theben VII.* Mainz am Rhein, Germany: Philipp von Zabern, 1995.

———. *Das Grab des Paenkhemenu (TT 68) und die Anlage TT 227: Theben VI.* Mainz am Rhein, Germany: Philipp von Zabern, 1991.

Strudwick, Nigel. *The Tombs of Amenhotep, Khnummose, and Amenmose at Thebes (Nos. 294, 253, and 254).* Oxford: Griffith Institute, 1996.

Vandier d'Abbadie, Jeanne. *Deux tombes ramessides à Gournet-Mouraï.* Cairo: Institut français d'archéologie orientale, 1954.

Thebes: West Bank Temples

(see also **Medinet Habu** and **Ramesseum**)

Bickel, Susanne. *Untersuchungen im Totentempel des Merenptah in Theben III: Tore und andere Wiederverwendete Bauteile Amenophis' III.* Beiträge zur Ägyptischen Bauforschung und Altertumskunde 16. Stuttgart: Franz Steiner, 1997.

Haeny, Gerhard. *Untersuchungen im Totentempel Amenophis' III.* Beiträge zur Ägyptischen Bauforschung und Altertumskunde 11. Wiesbaden: Franz Steiner Verlag, 1981.

Osing, Jürgen. *Der Tempel Sethos' I in Gurna: Die Reliefs und Inschriften I.* Deutsches Archäologisches Institut. Abteilung Kairo. Archäologische Veröffentlichungen 20. Mainz am Rhein, Germany: Philipp von Zabern, 1977.

Petrie, W. M. Flinders. *Six Temples at Thebes 1896*. London: Bernard Quaritch, 1897.

Thebes: Valley of the Kings

(apart from Tutankhamun for whom see **History: Tutankhamun**)
Hornung, Erik. *Das Grab des Haremhab im Tal der Könige*. Bern: Francke Verlag, 1971.
————. *The Tomb of Pharaoh Seti I*. Zurich: Artemis Verlag, 1991.
————. *The Valley of the Kings: Horizon of Eternity*. Translated by David Warburton. New York: Timken Publishers, 1990.
————. *Zwei ramessidische Königsgräber: Ramses IV. und Ramses VII. Theben XI*. Mainz am Rhein, Germany: Philipp von Zabern, 1990.
Reeves, C. Nicholas. *After Tut'ankhamun*. London: Kegan Paul International, 1992.
————. *Valley of the Kings: The Decline of a Royal Necropolis*. London: Kegan Paul International, 1990.
Reeves, Nicholas, and Richard H. Wilkinson. *The Complete Valley of the Kings*. London: Thames and Hudson, 1996.

Thebes: Valley of the Queens

Hassanein, F., and M. Nelson. *La tombe du Prince Amon-(her)-khepchef*. Cairo: Centre d'Études et de Documentation sur l'ancienne Égypte, 1976.
Leblanc, Christian. *Ta Set Nefrou: Une nécropole de Thèbes-Ouest et son histoire*. Cairo: Nubar Printing House, 1989.
Schiaparelli, Ernesto. *Esplorazione della 'Valle delle Regine'*. Turin: 1923.
Schmidt, Heike C., and Joachim Willeitner. *Nefertari-Gemahlin Ramses' II*. Mainz am Rhein, Germany: Philipp von Zabern, 1994.
Thausing, Gertrud, and Hans Goedicke. *Nofretari*. Graz, Austria: Akademische Druck- u. Verlagsanstalt, 1971.

Tod

Bisson de la Roque, F., G. Conteneau, and F. Chapouthier. *Le trésor de Tôd*. Cairo: Institut français d'archéologie orientale, 1953.

Tuna el-Gebel

Boessneck, Joachim, Angela von der Dreisch, and Dieter Kessler. *Tuna el-Gebel I: Die Tiergalerien.* Hildesheimer Ägyptologische Beiträge 24. Hildesheim: Gerstenberg, 1987.
Gabra, Sami, Étienne Drioton, Paul Perdrizet, and William G. Waddell. *Rapport sur les fouilles d'Hermopolis Ouest.* Cairo: 1941.
Lefebvre, Gustave. *Le Tombeau de Petosiris.* Cairo: Service des Antiquités de l'Égypte, 1923.

Uronarti

Dunham, Dows. *Second Cataract Forts. Vol. II. Uronarti Shalfak Mirgissa.* Boston: Museum of Fine Arts, 1967.

Wadi el-Hudi

Fakhry, Ahmed. *The Inscriptions of the Amethyst Quarries at Wadi el Hudi.* Cairo: Service des Antiquités de l'Egypte, 1952.
Sadek, Ashraf I. *The Amethyst Mining Inscriptions of Wadi el-Hudi.* 2 vols. Warminster, Great Britain: Aris and Phillips, 1980–85.

Zawiyet el-Aryan

Dunham, Dows. *Zawiyet el-Aryan.* Boston: Museum of Fine Arts, 1978.

ART AND ARCHITECTURE

Aldred, Cyril. *Egyptian Art: In the Days of the Pharaohs, 3100–320 BC.* London: Thames and Hudson, 1980.
Arnold, Dieter. *Building in Egypt: Pharaonic Stone Masonry.* Oxford: Oxford University Press, 1991.
———. *Lexikon der ägyptischen Baukunst.* Zurich: Artemis, 1994.
Aufrère, Sydney, and Jean-Claude Golvin. *L'Égypte restituée.* 3 vols. Éditions Errance, 1991–97.
Badawy, Alexander. *A History of Egyptian Architecture.* 3 vols. Berkeley: University of California Press, 1966–68.
Bothmer, Bernard V. *Egyptian Sculpture of the Late Period 700 BC to AD 100.* New York: Arno Press, 1969 (corrected reprint).

Davies, Nina M., and Alan H. Gardiner. *Ancient Egyptian Painting.* 3 vols. Chicago: University of Chicago Press, 1936.

Dodson, Aidan. *Egyptian Rock-cut Tombs.* Aylesbury, Great Britain: Shire Publications, 1991.

Doxiadis, Euphrosyne. *The Mysterious Fayum Portraits: Faces from Ancient Egypt.* London: Thames and Hudson, 1996.

James, T. G. Henry. *Egyptian Painting and Drawing in the British Museum.* London: British Museum Publications, 1985.

James, T. G. Henry, and W. Vivian Davies. *Egyptian Sculpture.* London: British Museum Publications, 1983.

Josephson, Jack A. *Egyptian Royal Sculpture of the Late Period 400–246 B.C.* Mainz am Rhein, Germany: Philipp von Zabern, 1997.

Kischkewitz, Hannelore, and Werner Forman. *Egyptian Art: Drawings and Paintings.* London: Hamlyn, 1989.

Lange, Kurt, and Max Hirmer. *Egypt: Architecture, Sculpture, Painting in Three Thousand Years.* London and New York: Phaidon, 1956.

Mekhitarian, Arpag. *Egyptian Painting.* Geneva: Skira, 1954.

Michalowski, Kazimierz. *The Art of Ancient Egypt.* London: Thames and Hudson, 1969 (2nd ed. Jean-Pierre Corteggiani and Alessandro Roccati. *L'Art de l'Égypte.* Paris: Citadelles et Mazenod, 1994).

Peck, William H., and John G. Ross. *Drawings from Ancient Egypt.* London: Thames and Hudson, 1978.

Robins, Gay. *The Art of Ancient Egypt.* London: British Museum Press, 1997.

———. *Egyptian Painting and Relief.* Aylesbury, Great Britain: Shire Publications, 1986.

———. *Proportion and Style in Ancient Egyptian Art.* London: Thames and Hudson, 1994.

Russmann, Edna R. *Egyptian Sculpture: Cairo and Luxor.* Austin: University of Texas Press, 1989.

Schäfer, Heinrich. *Principles of Egyptian Art.* Edited by Emma Brunner-Traut; translated and edited by John Baines. Oxford: Clarendon Press, 1974.

Shore, A. F. *Portrait Painting from Roman Egypt.* London: British Museum Publications, 1972.

Smith, W. Stevenson. *The Art and Architecture of Ancient Egypt.* Rev. ed. by W. K. Simpson. London: Penguin Books, 1981.

Spencer, A. Jeffrey. *Brick Architecture in Ancient Egypt.* Warminster, Great Britain: Aris and Phillips, 1979.

Walker, Susan, and Morris Bierbrier. *Ancient Faces.* London: British Museum Press, 1997.

PYRAMIDS AND OBELISKS

Edwards, I. Eiddon S. *The Pyramids of Egypt*. London: Penguin, 1993.

Fakhry, Ahmed. *The Pyramids*. 2nd ed. Chicago: University of Chicago Press, 1969.

Jenkins, Nancy. *The Boat beneath the Pyramid: King Cheops' Royal Ship*. London: Thames and Hudson, 1980.

Habachi, Labib. *The Obelisks of Egypt: Skyscrapers of the Past*. New York: Charles Scribner, 1977.

Iversen, Erik. *Obelisks in Exile*. 2 vols. Copenhagen: G. E. C. Gad, 1968–72.

Lehner, Mark. *The Complete Pyramids*. London: Thames and Hudson, 1997.

Stadelmann, Rainer. *Die ägyptischen Pyramiden: Vom Ziegelbau zum Weltwunder*. Mainz am Rhein, Germany: Philipp von Zabern, 1985.

Watson, Philip. *Egyptian Pyramids and Mastaba Tombs*. Aylesbury, Great Britain: Shire Publications, 1987.

RELIGION

(See also **Mummification and Funerary Practices**)

Allen, James P. *Genesis in Egypt: The Philosophy of Ancient Egyptian Creation Accounts*. Yale Egyptological Studies 2. New Haven: Yale Egyptological Seminar, 1974.

Assmann, Jan. *Ägypten: Theologie und Frömmigkeit einer frühen Hochkultur*. Stuttgart: W. Kohlhammer, 1984.

———. *Ma'at: Gerechtigkeit und Unsterblichkeit im Alten Ägypten*. Munich: C. H. Beck, 1990.

———. *Egyptian Solar Religion in the New Kingdom: Re, Amun and the Crises of Polytheismus*. Translated by A. Alcock. London: KPI, 1995.

Frankfurter, David. *Religion in Roman Egypt*. Princeton: Princeton University Press, 1998.

Hart, George. *A Dictionary of Egyptian Gods and Goddesses*. London: British Museum Press, 1986.

———. *Egyptian Myths*. London: British Museum Press, 1990.

Hornung, Erik. *Conceptions of God in Ancient Egypt: The One and the Many*. Translated by John R. Baines. London: Routledge and Kegan Paul, 1983.

Meeks, Dimitri, and Christine Meeks-Favard. *Daily Life of the Egyptian*

Gods. Translated by G. M. Goshgarian. Ithaca, N.Y.: Cornell University Press, 1996.

Morenz, Siegfried. *Egyptian Religion.* Translated by Ann E. Keep. London: Methuen and Co., 1973.

Otto, Eberhard. *Egyptian Art and the Cults of Osiris and Amon.* London: Thames and Hudson, 1968.

Pinch, Geraldine. *Magic in Ancient Egypt.* London: British Museum Press, 1994.

Quirke, Stephen. *Ancient Egyptian Religion.* London: British Museum Press, 1992.

———. *The Temple in Ancient Egypt.* London: British Museum Press, 1997.

Sauneron, Serge. *The Priests of Ancient Egypt.* Translated by Ann Morrissett. London: Evergreen Books, 1960.

Shafer, Byron E., ed. *Religion in Ancient Egypt: Gods, Myths and Personal Practice.* Ithaca, N.Y.: Cornell University Press, 1991.

———. *Temples of Ancient Egypt.* London: I. B. Tauris, 1998.

Snape, Steven. *Egyptian Temples.* Aylesbury, Great Britain: Shire Publications, 1996.

Thomas, Angela. *Gods and Myths.* Aylesbury, Great Britain: Shire Publications, 1986.

MUMMIFICATION AND FUNERARY PRACTICES

Adams, Barbara. *Egyptian Mummies.* Aylesbury, Great Britain: Shire Publications, 1984.

Andrews, Carol. *Egyptian Mummies.* London: British Museum Publications, 1984.

Aubert, Jacques-F., and Liliane Aubert. *Statuettes égyptiennes: Chaouabtis, ouchebtis.* Paris: Adrien Maisonneuve, 1974.

Balout, Lionel, and C. Roubet. *La Momie de Ramsès II.* Paris: Éditions Recherche sur les Civilisations, 1985.

Budge, E. A. T. Wallis. *The Mummy: A Handbook of Egyptian Funerary Archaeology.* 2nd ed. Cambridge: Cambridge University Press, 1925.

Cockburn, Aidan, and Eve Cockburn, eds. *Mummies, Disease and Ancient Cultures.* Cambridge: Cambridge University Press, 1980.

Davies, W. Vivian, and Roxie Walker, eds. *Biological Anthropology and the Study of Ancient Egypt.* London: British Museum Press, 1993.

Dodson, Aidan. *The Canopic Equipment of the Kings of Egypt.* London: Kegan Paul International, 1994.

Faulkner, Raymond O. *The Ancient Egyptian Book of the Dead.* Rev. ed. by C. A. R. Andrews. London: British Museum Publications, 1985.

————. *The Ancient Egyptian Coffin Texts.* 3 vols. Warminster, Great Britain: Aris and Phillips, 1973–78.

————. *The Ancient Egyptian Pyramid Texts.* Oxford: Clarendon Press, 1969.

Faulkner, Raymond O., and Ogden Goelet. *The Egyptian Book of the Dead: The Papyrus of Ani.* San Francisco: Chronicle Books, 1994.

Forman, Werner, and Stephen Quirke. *Hieroglyphs and the Afterlife in Ancient Egypt.* London: British Museum Press, 1996.

Harris, James E., and Kent R. Weeks. *X-Raying the Pharaohs.* London: Macdonald and Co., 1973.

Harris, James E., and Edward F. Wente. *An X-Ray Atlas of the Royal Mummies.* London: University of Chicago Press, 1980.

Ikram, Salima, and Aidan Dodson. *The Mummy in Ancient Egypt.* London: Thames and Hudson, 1998.

————. *Royal Mummies in the Egyptian Museum.* Cairo: American University in Cairo Press, 1997.

Petrie, W. M. Flinders. *Shabtis.* Reprint of 1935 London ed. Warminster, Great Britain: Aris and Phillips, 1974.

Schneider, Hans D. *Shabtis.* 3 vols. Leiden: Rijkmuseum van Oudheden, 1977.

Smith, G. Elliott, and Warren R. Dawson. *Egyptian Mummies.* Reprint of 1924 ed. London: Kegan Paul International, 1991.

Spencer, A. Jeffrey. *Death in Ancient Egypt.* Harmondsworth, Great Britain: Penguin Books, 1982.

Stewart, Harry M. *Egyptian Shabtis.* Aylesbury, Great Britain: Shire Publications, 1995.

Taylor, John H. *Egyptian Coffins.* Aylesbury, Great Britain: Shire Publications, 1989.

————. *Unwrapping a Mummy.* Egyptian Bookshelf. London: British Museum Press, 1995.

SCARABS AND AMULETS

Andrews, Carol. *Amulets of Ancient Egypt.* London: British Museum Press, 1994.

Hornung, Erik, and Elisabeth Staehelin, eds. *Skarabäen und andere Siege-lamulette aus Basler Sammlungen.* Mainz am Rhein, Germany: Philipp Von Zabern, 1976.

Müller-Winkler, Claudia. *Die ägyptischen Objekt-Amulette.* Freiburg, Switzerland: Éditions Universitaires, and Göttingen, Germany: Vanden-hoeck and Ruprecht, 1987.

Petrie, W. M. Flinders. *Buttons and Design Scarabs.* Reprint of 1925 ed. Warminster, Great Britain: Aris and Phillips, 1974.

————. *Scarabs and Cylinders with Names.* Reprint of 1925 ed. Warmins-ter, Great Britain: Aris and Phillips, 1974.

Tufnell, Olga, and William A. Ward. *Studies on Scarab Seals.* 2 vols. War-minster, Great Britain: Aris and Phillips, 1978–84.

DAILY LIFE

Bierbrier, Morris. *The Tomb-Builders of the Pharaohs.* London: British Museum Publications, 1982. New ed. Cairo: The American University in Cairo Press, 1989.

Brovarski, Edward., et al., eds. *Egypt's Golden Age: The Art of Living in the New Kingdom 1558–1085 BC.* Boston: Museum of Fine Arts, 1982.

Darby, William, Paul Ghalioungui, and Louis Grivetti. *Food: The Gift of Osiris.* 2 vols. London: Academic Press, 1977.

Decker, Wolfgang. *Sports and Games of Ancient Egypt.* Translated by Allen Guttmann. New Haven: Yale University Press, 1992.

Erman, Adolf. *Life in Ancient Egypt.* Reprint of 1894 ed. New York: Dover, 1971.

Filer, Joyce. *Disease.* Egyptian Bookshelf. London: British Museum Press, 1995.

Hall, Rosalind. *Egyptian Textiles.* Aylesbury, Great Britain: Shire Publica-tions, 1986.

Hepper, F. Nigel. *Pharaoh's Flowers: The Botanical Treasures of Tutank-hamun.* London: HMSO, 1990.

Hope, Colin. *Egyptian Pottery.* Aylesbury, Great Britain: Shire Publica-tions, 1991.

James, T. G. Henry. *Pharaoh's People: Scenes from Life in Imperial Egypt.* London: The Bodley Head, 1984.

Janssen, Jac. J. *Commodity Prices from the Ramesside Period.* Leiden: E. J. Brill, 1975.

Janssen, Rosalind M. and Jac. J. *Egyptian Household Animals*. Aylesbury, Great Britain: Shire Publications, 1989.

————. *Growing Old in Ancient Egypt*. London: The Rubicon Press, 1996.

————. *Growing Up in Ancient Egypt*. London: The Rubicon Press, 1990.

Lewis, Naphtali. *Life in Egypt under Roman Rule*. Oxford: Clarendon Press, 1984.

Malek, Jaromir. *The Cat in Ancient Egypt*. London: British Museum Press, 1993.

Manniche, Lise. *An Ancient Egyptian Herbal*. London: British Museum Publications, 1989.

————. *Ancient Egyptian Musical Instruments*. Münchner Ägyptologische Studien 34. Munich: Deutscher Kunstverlag, 1975.

————. *Music and Musicians in Ancient Egypt*. London: British Museum Press, 1991.

————. *Sexual Life in Ancient Egypt*. London: KPI, 1987.

Nunn, John F. *Ancient Egyptian Medicine*. London: British Museum Press, 1996.

Petrie, W. M. Flinders. *Objects of Daily Use*. Reprint of 1927 ed. Warminster, Great Britain: Aris and Phillips, 1974.

Reeves, Carole. *Egyptian Medicine*. Aylesbury, Great Britain: Shire Publications, 1992.

Robins, Gay. *Women in Ancient Egypt*. London: British Museum Press, 1993.

Scheel, Bernd. *Egyptian Metalworking and Tools*. Aylesbury, Great Britain: Shire Publications, 1995.

Shaw, Ian. *Egyptian Warfare and Weapons*. Aylesbury, Great Britain: Shire Publications, 1991.

Strouhal, Eugen. *Life in Ancient Egypt*. Cambridge: Cambridge University Press, 1992.

Tooley, Angela. *Egyptian Models and Scenes*. Aylesbury, Great Britain: Shire Publications, 1995.

Vogelsang-Eastwood, Gillian. *Pharaonic Egyptian Clothing*. Leiden: E. J. Brill, 1993.

Wilkinson, Alix. *The Garden in Ancient Egypt*. London: The Rubicon Press, 1998.

Wilson, Hilary. *Egyptian Food and Drink*. Aylesbury, Great Britain: Shire Publications, 1988.

APPLIED ARTS

Aldred, Cyril. *Jewels of the Pharaohs: Egyptian Jewellery of the Dynastic Period*. London: Thames and Hudson, 1971.

Andrews, Carol A. R. *Ancient Egyptian Jewellery*. London: British Museum Publications, 1996.

Baker, Hollis S. *Furniture in the Ancient World: Origins and Evolution. 3100–475 B.C.* London: The Connoisseur, 1966.

Friedman, Florence D., ed. *Gifts of the Nile: Ancient Egyptian Faience*. London: Thames and Hudson, 1998.

Grose, David Fred. *The Toledo Museum of Art: Early Ancient Glass*. New York: Hudson Hills Press, 1989.

Killen, Geoffrey. *Ancient Egyptian Furniture*. 2 vols. Warminster, Great Britain: Aris and Phillips, 1980, 1994.

———. *Egyptian Woodworking and Furniture*. Aylesbury, Great Britain: Shire Publications, 1994.

Nicholson, Paul T. *Egyptian Faience and Glass*. Aylesbury, Great Britain: Shire Publications, 1993.

Ogden, Jack. *Jewellery of the Ancient World*. London: Trefoil Books, 1982.

Tait, Hugh, ed. *Five Thousand Years of Glass*. London: British Museum Press, 1991.

———. *Seven Thousand Years of Jewellery* . London: British Museum Publications, 1986.

Wilkinson, Alix. *Ancient Egyptian Jewellery*. London: Methuen and Co., 1971.

LANGUAGE AND LITERATURE

Andrews, Carol A. R. *The Rosetta Stone*. London: British Museum Publications, 1982.

Andrews, Carol A. R., and Stephen Quirke. *The Rosetta Stone: Facsimile Drawing*. London: British Museum Publications, 1988.

Černý, Jaroslav. *Paper and Books in Ancient Egypt*. Reprint of 1952 ed. Chicago: Ares Publishers, 1977.

Davies, W. Vivian. *Egyptian Hieroglyphs*. London: British Museum Publications, 1987.

Englund, Gertie. *Middle Egyptian: An Introduction*. Uppsala, Sweden: Uppsala University Press, 1988.

Faulkner, Raymond O. *A Concise Dictionary of Middle Egyptian*. Oxford: Griffith Institute, 1962.

Fischer, Henry George. *Ancient Egyptian Calligraphy: A Beginner's Guide to Writing Hieroglyphics*. 2nd ed. New York: Metropolitan Museum, New York, 1983.

Gardiner, Alan. H. *Egyptian Grammar: Being an Introduction to the Study of Hieroglyphics.* 3rd ed. Oxford: Oxford University Press, 1957.

Lewis, Naphtali. *Papyrus in Classical Antiquity.* Oxford: Clarendon Press, 1974.

Lichtheim, Miriam. *Ancient Egyptian Autobiographies Chiefly of the Middle Kingdom: A Study and an Anthology* . Orbis Biblicus et Orientalis 84. Fribourg, Switzerland: Universitätsverlag, 1988.

———. *Ancient Egyptian Literature: A Book of Readings.* 3 vols. Berkeley: University of California Press, 1973–80.

Loprieno, Antonio. *Ancient Egyptian: A Linguistic Introduction.* Cambridge: Cambridge University Press, 1995.

Loprieno, Antonio, ed. *Ancient Egyptian Literature: History and Forms.* Leiden: E. J. Brill, 1996.

Malek, Jaromir. *A B C of Egyptian Hieroglyphs.* Oxford: Ashmolean Museum, 1994.

Parkinson, Richard. *Tale of Sinuhe.* Oxford: Oxford University Press, 1997.

———. *Voices from Ancient Egypt: An Anthology of Middle Kingdom Writings.* London: British Museum Press, 1991.

Parkinson, Richard, and Stephen Quirke. *Papyrus.* Egyptian Bookshelf. London: British Museum Press, 1995.

Simpson, William Kelly, et al. *The Literature of Ancient Egypt: An Anthology of Stories, Instructions, and Poetry.* 2nd ed. New Haven: Yale University Press, 1973.

Turner, Eric. *Greek Papyri: An Introduction.* Oxford: Clarendon Press, 1968.

Wente, Edward F. *Letters from Ancient Egypt.* Atlanta: Scholars Press, 1990.

Zauzich, Karl-Theodor. *Discovering Egyptian Hieroglyphs: A Practical Guide.* London: Thames and Hudson, 1992.

MATHEMATICS AND ASTRONOMY

Chace, Arnold Buffum. *The Rhind Mathematical Papyrus.* Reprint of 1927–29 ed. Reston, Va.: National Council of Teachers of Mathematics, 1979.

Gillings, Richard J. *Mathematics in the Time of the Pharaohs.* Cambridge, Mass.: MIT Press, 1972.

Neugebauer, Otto E. *The Exact Sciences in Antiquity.* Reprint of 2nd ed. New York: Harper and Brothers, 1962.

Neugebauer, Otto E., and Richard A. Parker. *Egyptian Astronomical Texts.* 3 vols. London: Brown University Press, 1960–69.

Parker, Richard A. *The Calendars of Ancient Egypt.* Studies in Ancient Oriental Civilization 26. Chicago: University of Chicago Press, 1950.

Robins, Gay, and Charles Shute. *The Rhind Mathematical Papyrus: An Ancient Egyptian Text.* London: British Museum Publications, 1987.

SCIENCE AND TECHNOLOGY

Bowman, Sheridan. *Radiocarbon Dating.* London: British Museum Publications, 1990.

David, Rosalie A., ed. *Science in Egyptology.* Manchester, Great Britain: Manchester University Press, 1986.

Hope, Colin. *Egyptian Pottery.* Aylesbury, Great Britain: Shire Publications, 1993.

Lucas, Arthur. *Ancient Egyptian Materials and Industries.* 4th ed., revised by J. R. Harris. London: Edward Arnold, 1962.

Singer, Charles, et al. *A History of Technology.* Vol. I. Oxford: Clarendon Press, 1954.

NATURAL ENVIRONMENT

Brewer, Douglas, and Renée Friedman. *Fish and Fishing in Ancient Egypt.* Warminster, Great Britain: Aris and Phillips, 1989.

Brewer, Douglas, Donald Redford, and Susan Redford. *Domestic Plants and Animals.* Warminster, Great Britain: Aris and Phillips, 1994.

Germer, Renate. *Flora des pharaonischen Ägypten.* Mainz am Rhein, Germany: Philipp von Zaber, 1985.

Houlihan, Patrick. *The Animal World of the Pharaohs.* Cairo: The American University in Cairo Press, 1996.

———. *The Birds of Ancient Egypt.* Warminster, Great Britain: Aris and Phillips, 1986.

Klemm, Rosemarie, and Dietrich Klemm. *Steine und Steinebrüche im Alten Ägypten.* Berlin: Springer Verlag, 1993.

Malek, Jaromir. *The Cat in Ancient Egypt.* London: British Museum Press, 1993.

Osburn, Dale. *Mammals of Ancient Egypt.* Warminster, Great Britain: Aris and Phillips, 1998.

Vartavan, Christian de, and Victoria Asensi Amorós. *Codex of Ancient Egyptian Plant Remains*. London: Triade Exploration, 1997.

NAVIGATION

Glanville, Stephen R., and Raymond O. Faulkner. *Catalogue of Egyptian Antiquities in the British Museum II: Wooden Model Boats*. London: Trustees of the British Museum, 1972.

Jones, Dilwyn. *Boats*. Egyptian Bookshelf. London: British Museum Press, 1995.

Landström, Björn. *Ships of the Pharaohs: 4000 Years of Egyptian Shipbuilding*. London: Allen and Unwin, 1970.

Vinson, Steve. *Egyptian Boats and Ships*. Aylesbury, Great Britain: Shire Publications, 1994.

MUSEUM COLLECTIONS

Australia

Cambitoglou, A. *Egyptian Collection, Nicholson Museum*. 4th ed. Sydney: University of Sydney, 1978.

Lawler, C. *Treasures from the Nicholson Museum*. Sydney: 1979.

Austria

Vienna

Egner, Roswitha, and Elfriede Haslauer. *Kunsthistorisches Museum Wien: Ägyptisch-Orientalische Sammlung. Lieferung 10: Särge der dritten Zwischenzeit, Teil 1*. Corpus Antiquitatum Aegyptiacarum. Mainz am Rhein, Germany: Philipp von Zabern: 1994.

Hein, Irmgard, and Helmut Satzinger. *Kunsthistorisches Museum Wien: Ägyptisch-Orientalische Sammlung. Lieferung 4: Stelen des mittleren Reiches, einschliesslich der I und II Zwischenzeit, Teil 1*. Corpus Antiquitatum Aegyptiacarum. Mainz am Rhein, Germany: Philipp von Zabern, 1989.

———. *Kunsthistorisches Museum Wien: Ägyptisch-Orientalische Sammlung. Lieferung 7: Stelen des mittleren Reiches, einschliesslich der I und II Zwischenzeit, Teil 2.* Corpus Antiquitatum Aegyptiacarum. Mainz am Rhein, Germany: Philipp von Zabern, 1993.

Jaroš-Deckert, Brigitte. *Kunsthistorisches Museum Wien: Ägyptisch-Orientalische Sammlung. Lieferung 1: Statuen des mittleren Reichs und der 18 Dynastie.* Corpus Antiquitatum Aegyptiacarum. Mainz am Rhein, Germany: Philipp von Zabern, 1987.

Jaroš-Deckert, Brigitte, and Eva Rogge. *Kunsthistorisches Museum Wien: Ägyptisch-Orientalische Sammlung. Lieferung 15: Statuen des alten Reiches.* Corpus Antiquitatum Aegyptiacarum. Mainz am Rhein, Germany: Philipp von Zabern, 1993.

Reiser-Haslauer, Elfriede. *Kunsthistorisches Museum Wien: Ägyptisch-Orientalische Sammlung. Lieferung 2: Die Kanopen, Teil 1.* Corpus Antiquitatum Aegyptiacarum. Mainz am Rhein, Germany: Philipp von Zabern, 1989.

———. *Kunsthistorisches Museum Wien: Ägyptisch-Orientalische Sammlung. Lieferung 3: Die Kanopen, Teil 2.* Corpus Antiquitatum Aegyptiacarum. Mainz am Rhein, Germany: Philipp von Zabern, 1989.

———. *Kunsthistorisches Museum Wien: Ägyptisch-Orientalische Sammlung. Lieferung 5: Uschebti, Teil 1.* Corpus Antiquitatum Aegyptiacarum. Mainz am Rhein, Germany: Philipp von Zabern, 1990.

———. *Kunsthistorisches Museum Wien: Ägyptisch-Orientalische Sammlung. Lieferung 8: Uschebti, Teil 2.* Corpus Antiquitatum Aegyptiacarum. Mainz am Rhein, Germany: Philipp von Zabern, 1992.

Rogge, Eva. *Kunsthistorisches Museum Wien: Ägyptisch-Orientalische Sammlung. Lieferung 6: Statuetten des neuen Reiches und der dritten Zwischenzeit.* Corpus Antiquitatum Aegyptiacarum. Mainz am Rhein, Germany: Philipp von Zabern, 1990.

———. *Kunsthistorisches Museum Wien: Ägyptisch-Orientalische Sammlung. Lieferung 9: Statuen der Spätzeit.* Corpus Antiquitatum Aegyptiacarum. Mainz am Rhein, Germany: Philipp von Zabern, 1992.

Satzinger, Helmut. *Das Kunsthistorische Museum in Wien: Die Ägyptisch-Orientalische Sammlung.* Mainz am Rhein, Germany: Philipp von Zabern, 1994.

Belgium

Antwerp

Museum Vleeshuis. *Egypte Onomwonden: Egyptische oudheden van het museum Vleeshuis.* Antwerp: Pandora, 1995.

Brussels

Limme, Luc. *Stèles égyptiennes: Musée de Bruxelles.* Brussels, 1979.
Van de Walle, Baudoin, et al. *La collection égyptienne: Les étapes marquantes de son développement.* Brussels: Musées Royaux d'Art et d'Histoire, 1980.

Mariemont

Musée royal de Mariémont, *Choix d'oeuvres, Égypte 1.* Mariémont, 1990.

Namur

Bruwier, Marie-Cécile. *Présence de l'Égypte dans les collections de la Bibliothèque Universitaire Moretus Plantin.* Namur: Namur University Press, 1994.

Brazil

Kitchen, Kenneth A. *Catalogue of the Egyptian Collection in the National Museum, Rio de Janeiro.* Rio de Janeiro: Museum Nacional, and Warminster, Great Britain: Aris and Phillips, 1990.

Croatia

Monnet Saleh, Janine. *Les Antiquités Égyptiennes de Zagreb.* Paris: Mouton, 1970.

Cuba

Lipinska, Jadwiga. *Monuments de l'Égypte ancienne au Palacio de Bellas Artes à la Havane et du Museo Bacardí à Santiago de Cuba.* Corpus Antiquitatum Aegyptiacarum. Mainz am Rhein, Germany: Philipp von Zabern, 1982.

Czech republic

Pavlasová, Sylva. *The Land of Pyramids and Pharaohs: Ancient Egypt in the Náprstek Museum Collection* (in Czech and English). Prague: Národní Museum, 1997.
Verner, Miroslav. *Altägyptische Särge in den Museen und Sammlungen der*

Tschechoslowakei. Lieferung 1:1. Corpus Antiquitatum Aegyptiacarum. Prague: Charles University, 1982.

————. *Altägyptische Särge in den Museen und Sammlungen der Tschechoslowakei Lieferung 1:2.* Corpus Antiquitatum Aegyptiacarum. Prague: Univerzita Karlova, 1982.

————. *Altägyptische Särge in den Museen und Sammlungen der Tschechoslowakei Lieferung 1:3.* Corpus Antiquitatum Aegyptiacarum. Prague: Univerzita Karlova, 1982.

Denmark

Copenhagen: National Museum

Buhl, Marie-Louise. *A Hundred Masterpieces from the Ancient Near East.* Copenhagen: The National Museum of Denmark, 1974.

Mogensen, Maria. *Inscriptions hiéroglyphiques du Musée National de Copenhague.* Copenhagen: A. F. Hörst et fils, 1918.

Copenhagen: Ny Carlsberg

Frandsen, Paul. J. *The Carlsberg Papyri I: Demotic Texts from the Collection.* Copenhagen: Museum Tusculanum Press, 1991.

Jorgensen, Mogens. *Egypt I (3000–1550 BC): Ny Carlsberg Glyptotek.* Copenhagen: Ny Carlsberg Glyptotek, 1996.

Koefod-Petersen, Otto. *Catalogue des bas-reliefs et peintures égyptiens.* Copenhagen: Ny Carlsberg Glyptotek, 1956.

————. *Catalogue des sarcophages et cercueils égyptiens.* Copenhagen: Ny Carlsberg Glyptotek, 1951.

————. *Catalogue des statues et statuettes égyptiennnes.* Copenhagen: Ny Carlsberg Glyptotek, 1950.

————. *Egyptian Sculpture in the Ny Carlsberg Glyptotek.* Copenhagen: Bianco Lunos Bogtrykkeri, 1951.

————. *Recueil des inscriptions hiéroglyphiques de la Glyptothèque Ny Carlsberg.* Brussels: Fondation Égyptologique Reine Élisabeth, 1936.

————. *Les stèles égyptiennes.* Copenhagen: Ny Carlsberg Glyptotek, 1948.

Egypt

Alexandria

Breccia, Evaristo. *Le Musée gréco-romain d'Alexandrie, 1925–1931.* Rome: "L'Erma" di Bretschneider, 1970.

————. *La necropoli di Sciatbi (Musée d'Alexandrie)*. Cairo: Service des Antiquités de l'Égypte, 1912.

Empereur, Jean-Yves. *A Short Guide to the Graeco-Roman Museum Alexandria*. Alexandria: Sarapis Publications, 1995.

Aswan

Gaballa, Gaballa Ali. *Nubia Museum*. Aswan: Ministry of Culture, n.d.

Cairo: Coptic Museum

Gabra, Gawdat. *Cairo: The Coptic Museum and Old Churches*. Cairo: The Egyptian International Publishing Co., 1993.

Robinson, James M., ed. *The Nag Hammadi Library in English*. 4th rev. ed. Leiden: E. J. Brill, 1996.

Cairo: Egyptian Museum

Abou-Ghazi, Dia, and Alexandre Moret. *Denkmäler des Alten Reiches*. Vol. III, Fascs. 1–2. Cairo: Service des Antiquités de l'Égypte, 1980.

Bénédite, Georges. *Miroirs*. Cairo: Service des Antiquités de l'Égypte, 1907.

————. *Objets de toilettes: Vol. I. Peignes, etc.* Cairo: Service des Antiquités de l'Égypte, 1911.

Bissing, Friedrich W. von. *Fayencegefässe*. Vienna: Adolf Holzhausen, 1902.

————. *Metalgefässe*. Vienna: Adolf Holzhausen, 1901.

————. *Steingefässe*. 2 vols. Vienna: Adolf Holzhausen, 1904–07.

————. *Tongefässe: Teil I*. Vienna: Adolf Holzhausen, 1913.

Borchardt, Ludwig. *Denkmäler des Alten Reiches (ausser den Statuen)*. Vol. I. Berlin: Reichsdruckerei, 1937. Vol. II. Cairo: Service des Antiquités de l'Égypte, 1964.

————. *Statuen und Statuetten von Königen und Privatleuten*. 5 vols. Berlin: Reichsdruckerei, 1911–36.

Carter, Henri, and Percy E. Newberry. *The Tomb of Thoutmosis IV*. London: Archibald Constable and Co., 1904.

Černý, Jaroslav. *Ostraca hiératiques*. 2 vols. Cairo: Service des Antiquités de l'Égypte, 1930–37.

Chassinat, Émile. *La seconde Trouvaille de Deir-el-Bahari (Sarcophages)*. I, i. Cairo: Service des Antiquités de l'Égypte, 1909.

Crum, Walter E. *Coptic Monuments.* Cairo: Service des Antiquités de l'Égypte, 1902.

Curelly, Charles T. *Stone Implements.* Cairo: Service des Antiquités de l'Égypte, 1913.

Daressy, Georges. *Cerceuils et cachettes royales.* Cairo: Service des Antiquités de l'Égypte, 1909.

———. *Fouilles de la Vallée des Rois 1898–9.* Cairo: Service des Antiquités de l'Égypte, 1902.

———. *Ostraca.* Cairo: Service des Antiquités de l'Égypte, 1901.

———. *Statues de divinités.* Cairo: Service des Antiquités de l'Égypte, 1906.

———. *Textes et dessins magiques.* Cairo: Service des Antiquités de l'Égypte, 1903.

Edgar, Campbell C. *Graeco-Egyptian Coffins, Masks and Portraits.* Cairo: Service des Antiquités de l'Égypte, 1905.

———. *Graeco-Egyptian Glass.* Cairo: Service des Antiquités de l'Égypte, 1905.

———. *Greek Bronzes.* Cairo: Service des Antiquités de l'Égypte, 1903.

———. *Greek Moulds.* Cairo: Service des Antiquités de l'Égypte, 1903.

———. *Greek Sculpture.* Cairo: Service des Antiquités de l'Égypte, 1903.

———. *Greek Vases.* Cairo: Service des Antiquités de l'Égypte, 1911.

———. *Sculptors' Studies and Unfinished Works.* Cairo: Service des Antiquités de l'Égypte, 1906.

Gaillard, Claude, and Georges Daressy. *La faune momifiée de l'antique Égypte.* Cairo: Service des Antiquités de l'Égypte, 1905.

Gauthier, Henri. *Cercueils anthropoides des prêtres de Montou.* Cairo: Service des Antiquités de l'Égypte, 1913.

Golenischeff, Vladimir S. *Papyrus hiératiques.* Fasc. I. Cairo: Service des Antiquités de l'Égypte, 1927.

Grenfell, Bernard P., and Arthur S. Hunt. *Greek Papyri.* Oxford: Oxford University Press, 1903.

Kamal, Ahmad. *Stèles ptolemaïques et romaines.* 2 vols. Cairo: Service des Antiquités de l'Égypte, 1904–05.

———. *Tables d'Offrandes.* Cairo: Service des Antiquités de l'Égypte, 1906–09.

Kuentz, Charles. *Obélisques.* Cairo: Service des Antiquités de l'Égypte, 1932.

Lacau, Pierre. *Sarcophages antérieurs au Nouvel Empire.* 2 vols. Cairo: Service des Antiquités de l'Égypte, 1904–06.

———. *Stèles du Nouvel Empire.* 2 fascs. Cairo: Service des Antiquités de l'Égypte, 1909–26.

Lange, Hans O., and Heinrich Schaefer. *Grab- und Denksteine des Mittel Reichs.* 4 vols. Berlin: Reichsdruckerei, 1902–25.

Lefebvre, Gustave. *Papyrus du Ménandre.* Cairo: Service des Antiquités de l'Égypte, 1911.

Legrain, Georges. *Statues et statuettes des rois et des particuliers.* 3 vols. Cairo: Service des Antiquités de l'Égypte, 1906–14.

Maspero, Gaston. *Sarcophages des époque persane et ptolemaïque.* 2 vols. Cairo: Service des Antiquités de l'Égypte, 1908–14.

Maspero, Jean. *Papyrus grecs d'époque byzantine.* 3 vols. Cairo: Service des Antiquités de l'Égypte, 1911–16.

Milne, Joseph G. *Greek Inscriptions.* Oxford: Oxford University Press, 1905.

Moret, Alexandre. *Sarcophages de l'époque bubastite à l'époque saïte.* Cairo: Service des Antiquités de l'Égypte, 1913.

Munier, Henri. *Manuscrits coptes.* Cairo: Service des Antiquités de l'Égypte, 1916.

Munro, Irmtraut. *Die Totenbuch-Handschriften der 18. Dynastie im Ägyptischen Museum Cairo.* 2 vols. Wiesbaden: Harrassowitz, 1994.

Newberry, Percy E. *Funerary Statuettes and Model Sarcophagi.* Fascs. 1–2. Cairo: Service des Antiquités de l'Égypte, 1930–37.

———. *Scarab-shaped Seals.* London: Archibald Constable and Co., 1907.

Quibell, James E. *Archaic Objects.* 2 vols. Cairo: Service des Antiquités de l'Égypte, 1905.

———. *The Tomb of Yuaa and Thuiu.* Cairo: Service des Antiquités de l'Égypte, 1908.

Reisner, George A. *Amulets.* Cairo: Service des Antiquités de l'Égypte, 1907.

———. *Canopics.* Cairo: Service des Antiquités de l'Égypte, 1967.

———. *Models of Ships and Boats.* Cairo: Service des Antiquités de l'Égypte, 1913.

Roeder, Günther. *Naos.* Leipzig: Breitkopf und Härtel, 1914.

Saleh, Mohamed, and Hourig Sourouzian. *The Egyptian Museum, Cairo.* Mainz am Rhein, Germany: Philipp von Zabern, 1987.

Smith, Grafton Elliot. *The Royal Mummies.* Cairo: Service des Antiquités de l'Égypte, 1913.

Spiegelberg, Wilhelm. *Demotische Denkmäler I: Inschriften.* Leipzig: W. Drugulin, 1904.

———. *Demotische Denkmäler. II: Papyrus.* 2 vols. Strassburg: Elsässiche Druckerei and Dumont, Schauberg, 1906–08.

————. *Demotische Denkmäler. III. Demotische Inschriften Papyrus.* Berlin: Reichsdruckerei, 1932.

Strzygowski, Josef. *Koptische Kunst.* Vienna: Adolf Holzhausen, 1904.

Vernier, Émile. *Bijoux et Orfèvreries: Text and Plates.* Cairo: Service des Antiquités de l'Égypte, 1927.

Weigall, Arthur E. P. *Weights and Balances.* Cairo: Service des Antiquités de l'Égypte, 1908.

Luxor

Romano, James F. *The Luxor Museum of Ancient Art Catalogue.* Cairo: American Research Center in Egypt, 1979.

Supreme Council of Antiquities. *Mummification Museum.* Luxor: S. C. A. Press, 1997.

France

Aix-en-Provence

Barbotin, Christophe. *Musée Granet. Collection égyptienne.* Aix-en-Provence: Musée Granet, 1995.

Aix-les-Bains

(see *Annecy*)

Amiens

Perdu, Olivier, and Elsa, Rickal. *La collection égyptienne du Musée de Picardie.* Amiens: Musée de Picardie, 1994.

Angers

Affholder-Gérard, Brigitte, and Marie-Jeanne Cornic. *Angers, Musée Pincé: La collection égyptienne.* Paris: Réunion des Musées Nationaux, 1990.

Annecy

Ratié, Suzanne. *Annecy, musée-château; Chambéry, musées d'art et d'histoire; Aix-les-Bains, musée archéologique: Collections égyptiennes.* Paris: Éditions de la Réunion des Musées Nationaux, 1984.

Autun

Pinette, Mathieu. *Les collections égyptiennes dans les musées de Saône et Loire.* Autun: Ville d'Autun, 1988.

Avignon

Foissy-Aufrère, Marie-Pierre. *Égypte & Provence.* Avignon: Fondation du Muséum Calvet, 1985.

Besançon

Gasse, Annie. *Loin du sable.* Besançon: Ville de Besançon, 1990.

Bordeaux

Orgogozo, Chantal, et al. *Égypte et Mediterranée: Objets antiques du Musée d'Aquitaine.* Bordeaux: Ville de Bordeaux, 1992.

Cannes

Margaine, Anne-Marie. *L'Égypte ancienne: Petits guides des Musées de Cannes 1.* Cannes: Musée de la Castre, 1984.

Chalon-sur-Saône

(see *Autun*)

Chambéry

(see *Annecy*)

Figeac

Dewachter, Michel. *La collection égyptienne du Musée Champollion.* Figeac: Musée Champollion, 1986.

Grenoble

Kueny, Gabrielle, and Jean Yoyotte. *Grenoble, Musée des Beaux Arts: Collection égyptienne.* Paris: Éditions de la Réunion des Musées Nationaux, 1979.

Marseilles

Cahier du Musée d'Archéologie Méditerranéenne: La collection égyptienne. Guide du visiteur. Marseilles: 1995.

Paris: Bibliothèque Nationale

Ledrain, Eugène. *Les monuments égyptiens de la Bibliothèque Nationale (Cabinet des médailles et antiques).* Paris: F. Vieweg, 1879.

Lucchesi, Elisabeth. *Répertoire des manuscrits coptes (sahidiques) de la Bibliothèque Nationale, Cahiers d'orientalisme I.* Geneva: Patrick Cramer, 1981.

Paris: Cluny Museum

Lorquin, Alexandra. *Les tissus coptes au Musée National du Moyen Age.* Paris: Réunion des Musées Nationaux, 1992.

Paris: Louvre

Andreu, Guillemette. *La statuette d'Ahmès Nefertari.* Paris: Réunion des Musées Nationaux, 1997.

Andreu, Guillemette, Marie-Hélène Rutschowscaya, and Christiane Ziegler. *L'Égypte ancienne au Louvre.* Paris: Réunion des Musées Nationaux, 1997.

Bénazeth, Dominique. *L'Art du metal au début de l'ère chrétienne.* Paris: Réunion des Musées Nationaux, 1992.

Delange, Elisabeth. *Catalogue des statues égyptiennes du Moyen-Empire.* Paris: Réunion des Musées Nationaux, 1987.

———. *Rites et beauté: Objets de toilette égyptiens.* Paris: Réunion des Musées Nationaux, 1993.

———. *Le scribe Nebmeroutef.* Paris: Louvre Service Culturel, 1997.

Du Bouguet, Pierre. *Catalogue des étoffes coptes.* Paris: 1964.

Dunand, Françoise. *Terres cuites gréco-romaines d'Égypte.* Paris: Réunion des Musées Nationaux, 1990.

Malinine, Michel, Georges Posener, and Jean Vercoutter. *Catalogue des stèles du Serapeum de Memphis.* Paris: Éditions des Musées Nationaux, 1968.

Musée du Louvre. *Guide des antiquités égyptiennes.* Paris: Réunion des Musées Nationaux, 1997.

———. *Guide des antiquités égyptiennes romaines.* Paris: Réunion des Musées Nationaux, 1997.

Pierret, Paul. *Recueil d'inscriptions inédites du Musée égyptien du Louvre.* Paris: A. Franck, 1874–78.

Rutschowscaya, Marie-Hélène. *Catalogue des bois de l'Égypte copte.* Paris: Réunion des Musées Nationaux, 1986.

———. *La peinture copte.* Paris: Réunion des Musées Nationaux, 1992.

Vandier d'Abbadie, Jeanne. *Catalogue des objets de toilette égyptiens.* Paris: Éditions des Musées Nationaux, 1972.

Ziegler, Chistiane. *Catalogue des instruments de musique égyptiens.* Paris: Réunion des Musées Nationaux, 1979.

———. *Egyptian Antiquities.* London: Scala Publications, 1990.

———. *Le mastaba d'Akhethetep: Une chapelle funéraire de l'Ancien Empire.* Paris: Réunion des Musées Nationaux, 1993.

———. *Catalogue des stèles, peintures et reliefs égyptiens de l'Ancien Empire et de la Première Période Intermédiaire.* Paris: Réunion des Musées Nationaux, 1990.

———. *Statues de l'Ancien Empire au Louvre.* Paris: Réunion des Musées Nationaux, 1997.

Roanne

Moinet, Eric. *Catalogue des antiquités égyptiennes du Musée Joseph Déchelette.* Roanne: Musée J. Déchelette, 1990.

Rouen

Aufrère, Sydney. *Collections égyptiennes.* Rouen: Musées départementaux de Seine Maritime, 1987.

Sèvres

Bulté, Jeanne. *Catalogue des collections égyptiennes du Musée National de Céramique à Sèvres.* Paris: Centre National de la Recherche Scientifique, 1981.

Toulouse

Ramond, Pierre. *Les stèles égyptiennes du Musée G. Labit à Toulouse.* Cairo: Institut français d'archéologie orientale, 1977.

Varzy

Matoïan, Valérie, and Henri Loffet. *Les antiquités égyptiennes et assyriennes de Musée Auguste Grasset de Varzy.* Musées de la Nièvre. Études et Documents 1. Nevers: Conseil Général de la Nièvre, 1997.

Germany

Berlin

Priese, Karl-Heinz. *Ägyptisches Museum: Museuminsel Berlin.* Mainz am Rhein, Germany: Philipp von Zabern, 1991.

Settgast, Jürgen. *Ägyptisches Museum Berlin.* 1st ed. Mainz am Rhein, Germany: Philipp von Zabern, 1983. English translation *Egyptian Museum Berlin.* 3rd ed., 1986.

Bremen

Martin, Karl. *Übersee-Museum Bremen. Lieferung I: Die Altägyptischen Denkmäler. Teil 1.* Corpus Antiquitatum Aegyptiacarum. Mainz am Rhein, Germany: Philipp von Zabern, 1991.

Frankfurt-am-Main

Bayer-Niemeier, Eva, et al. *Liebieghaus-Museum Alter Plastik: Ägyptische Bildwerke. Band III. Skulptur, Malerei, Papyri und Särge.* Melsungen, Germany: Gutenberg, 1993.

von Droste zu Hülshoff, Vera, et al. *Liebieghaus-Museum Alter Plastik: Ägyptische Bildwerke. Band II. Statuetten, Gefässe und Geräte.* Melsungen, Germany: Gutenberg, 1991.

Gessler-Löhr, Beatrix, et al. *Ägyptische Kunst im Liebieghaus.* Frankfurt-am-Main: Museum Alter Plastik, 1981.

Schlick-Nolte, Birgit, and Vera von Droste zu Hülshoff. *Liebieghaus-Museum Alter Plastik: Ägyptische Bildwerke. Band I. Skarabäen, Amulette und Schmuck.* Melsungen, Germany: Gutenberg, 1990.

Hannover

Beste, Irmtraut. *Kestner-Museum Hannover. Lieferung 1: Skarabäen, Teil 1.* Corpus Antiquitatum Aegyptiacarum. Mainz am Rhein, Germany: Philipp von Zabern, 1978.

——. *Kestner-Museum Hannover. Lieferung 2: Skarabäen, Teil 2.* Corpus Antiquitatum Aegyptiacarum. Mainz am Rhein, Germany: Philipp von Zabern, 1979.

——. *Kestner-Museum Hannover. Lieferung 3: Skarabäen, Teil 3.* Corpus Antiquitatum Aegyptiacarum. Mainz am Rhein, Germany: Philipp von Zabern, 1979.

Drenkhahn, Rosemarie. *Ägyptische Reliefs im Kestner-Museum Hannover.* Hannover: Kestner-Museum, 1989.

Woldering, Irma. *Aegyptische Kunst. Bildkataloge des Kestner-Museums Hannover I: Ausgewählte Werke der Aegyptischen Sammlung.* Hannover: Kestner-Museum, 1955.

Heidelberg

Feucht, Erika. *Vom Nil zum Neckar.* Berlin: Springer, 1986.

Hildesheim

Eggebrecht, Arne, ed. *Pelizaeus-Museum Hildesheim: The Egyptian Collection.* Mainz am Rhein, Germany: Philipp von Zabern, 1996.

Eggebrecht, Eva. *Pelizaeus-Museum Hildesheim. Lieferung 2: Spätantike und Koptische Textilien, Teil 1.* Corpus Antiquitatum Aegyptiacarum. Mainz am Rhein, Germany: Philipp von Zabern, 1978.

Martin, Karl. *Pelizaeus-Museum, Hildesheim. Lieferung 3: Reliefs des Alten Reiches, Teil 1.* Corpus Antiquitatum Aegyptiacarum. Mainz am Rhein, Germany: Philipp von Zabern, 1978.

———. *Pelizaeus-Museum, Hildesheim. Lieferung 7: Reliefs des Alten Reiches, Teil 2.* Corpus Antiquitatum Aegyptiacarum. Mainz am Rhein, Germany: Philipp von Zabern, 1979.

———. *Pelizaeus-Museum, Hildesheim. Lieferung 8: Reliefs des Alten Reiches, Teil 3.* Corpus Antiquitatum Aegyptiacarum. Mainz am Rhein, Germany: Philipp von Zabern, 1980.

Martin-Pardey, Eva. *Pelizaeus-Museum, Hildesheim. Lieferung 1: Plastik des Alten Reiches, Teil 1.* Corpus Antiquitatum Aegyptiacarum. Mainz am Rhein, Germany: Philipp von Zabern, 1977.

———. *Pelizaeus-Museum, Hildesheim. Lieferung 4: Plastik des Alten Reiches, Teil 2.* Corpus Antiquitatum Aegyptiacarum. Mainz am Rhein, Germany: Philipp von Zabern, 1978.

———. *Pelizaeus-Museum, Hildesheim. Lieferung 5: Eingeweidegefässe.* Corpus Antiquitatum Aegyptiacarum. Mainz am Rhein, Germany: Philipp von Zabern, 1980.

———. *Pelizaeus-Museum, Hildesheim. Lieferung 6: Grabbeigaben, Nachträge und Ergänzungen.* Corpus Antiquitatum Aegyptiacarum. Mainz am Rhein, Germany: Philipp von Zabern, 1991.

Leipzig

Krauspe, Renate. *Das Ägyptische Museum der Universität Leipzig.* Mainz am Rhein, Germany: Philipp von Zabern, 1997.

Munich

Schoske, Sylvia, et al. *Staatliche Sammlung Ägyptischer Kunst München.* Mainz am Rhein, Germany: Philipp von Zabern, 1995.

Rhine Region

von Droste zu Hülshoff, Vera, and Birgit Schlick-Nolte. *Museen der Rhein-Main-Region. Lieferung 1: Aegyptiaca Diversa, Teil 1.* Corpus Antiquitatum Aegyptiacarum. Mainz am Rhein, Germany: Philipp von Zabern, 1984.

Tübingen

Brunner-Traut, Emma, and Hellmut Brunner. *Die Ägyptische Sammlung der Universität Tübingen.* Mainz am Rhein, Germany: Philipp von Zabern, 1981.

Hungary

Varga, Edith, and Vilmos Wessetzky. *Szépmüvészeti Múzeum. Egyiptomi Kiállítás.* Budapest: Múzeumi Ismeretterjesztö Központ, 1964.
Török, Làszló. *Coptic Antiquities.* 2 vols. Rome: L'Erma di Bretschneider, 1993.

Italy

Asti

Leospo, Enrichetta. *Museo Archeologico di Asti: La collezione egizia.* Turin: Comune di Asti, 1986.

Bergamo

Guidotti, M. Christina. *Civiltà egizia nel Civico Museo Archeologico di Bergamo.* Bergamo: Comune di Bergamo, 1987.

Bologna

Besciani, Edda. *Le stele egiziane del Museo Civico Archeologico di Bologna.* Bologna: Grafis Edizioni, 1985.
Pernigotti, Sergio. *La collezione egiziana: Museo Civico Archeologico di Bologna.* Bologna: Leonardo Arte, 1994.

————. *La statuaria egiziana nel Museo Civico Archeologico di Bologna.* Bologna: Instituto per la Storia di Bologna, 1980.

Como

Guidotti, M. Christina, and Enrichetta Leospo. *La collezione egizia del civico Museo Archeologico di Como.* Como: Comune di Como, 1994.

Cortona

Botti, Giuseppe. *Le antichità egiziane del Museo dell'Accademia di Cortona: Ordinate e descritte.* Florence: Leo S. Olschki, 1955.

Florence

Bosticco, Sergio. *Le stele egiziane.* 3 vols. Rome: Instituto Poligrafico dello Stato, 1959–72.

Milan

Lise, Giorgio. *Museo Archeologico: Raccolta egizia.* Milan: Electa Editrice, 1979.

Naples

Hölbl, Günther. *Le stele funerarie della collezione egizia.* Rome: Instituto Poligrafico e Zecca dello Stato, 1985.

Parma

Botti, Giuseppe. *I cimeli egizi del Museo di Antichità de Parma.* Florence: Leo S. Olschki, 1964.

Pisa

Bresciani, Edda, and F. Silvano. *La collezione Schiff Giorgini: Catalogo delle collezione egittologiche, Università di Pisa—Musei di Ateneo, 1.* Pisa: Giardini, 1992.

Rome

Careddu, Giorgio. *Museo Barracco de Scultura Antica: La collezione egizia.* Rome: Istituto Poligrafico e Zecca dello Stato, 1985.

Vittozzi, Serena E. *Musei Capitolini: La collezione egizia*. Rome: Silvana Editoriale, 1990.

Turin

Botti, Giuseppe. *L'archivio demotico da Deir el Medineh, tomo I (Testo) e II (Tavole), n. 55501–55547*. Serie I—Monumenti e Testi, Vol. I. Florence: Le Monnier, 1967.

Curto, Silvio. *L'antico Egitto nel Museo Egizio di Torino*. Turin: Tipografia Torinese Editrice, 1984.

————. *Storia del Museo Egizio di Torino*. Turin: Centro Studi Piemontesi, 1976.

Delorenzi, Enzo, and Renato Grilletto. *Le mummie del Museo Egizio di Torino, n. 13001–13026*. Serie II—Collezioni, Vol. VI. Milan: Cisalpino-La Goliardica, 1989.

Dolzani, Claudia. *Vasi Canopi, n. 19001–19153*. Serie II—Collezioni, Vol. IV. Milan: Cisalpino-La Goliardica, 1982.

Donadoni Roveri, Anna Maria. *Egyptian Civilization*. 3 vols. Milan: Electa, 1988–89.

————. *Museo Egizio*. Turin: Barisone Editore, 1996.

Habachi, Labib. *Tavole d'offerta, are e bacili da libagione, n. 22001–22067*. Serie II—Collezioni, Vol. II. Turin: Edizioni d'Arte Fratelli Pozzo, 1977.

Leospo, Enrichetta. *La mensa Isiaca di Torino*. Serie I—Monumenti e Testi, Vol. IV. Leiden: E. J. Brill, 1978.

López, Jesus. *Ostraca ieratici*. Serie II—Collezioni, Vol. III, 1–4. Milan: Cisalpino-La Goliardica, 1978–84.

Omlin, Joseph A. *Der Papyrus 55001 und Satirisch-erotische Zeichnungen und Inschriften*. Serie I—Monumenti e Testi, Vol. III. Turin: Edizione d'Arte Fratelli Pozzo, 1970.

Pestman, Pieter W. *L'archivio di Amenothes, figlio di Horos*. Serie I—Monumenti e Testi, Vol. V. Milan, Cisalpino-La Goliardica, 1981.

————. *Il processo di Hermias e altri documenti dell'archivio dei Choachiti*. Serie I—Monumenti e Testi, Vol. VI. Turin: Ministry of Culture, 1992.

Roccati, Alessandro. *Papiro ieratico n. 54003. Estratti magici e rituali del primo Medio Regno*. Serie I—Monumenti e Testi, Vol. II. Turin: Edizioni d'Arte Fratelli Pozzo, 1970.

Ronsecco, Paolo. *Due libri dei morti del principio del Nuovo Regno il lenzuolo funerario della principessa Ahmosi et le tele del Sa-nesu Ahmosi.*

Serie I-Monumenti e Testi Vol. VII. Turin: Ministero per i Beni Culturali e Ambientali, 1996.

Tosi, Mario, and Alessandro Roccati. *Stele e altre epigrafi di Deir el Medina, n. 50001–50262.* Serie II—Collezioni, Vol. I. Turin: Edizione d'Arte Fratelli Pozzo, 1972.

Netherlands

Amsterdam

Van Haarlem, Willem. *Allard Pierson Museum, Fasc. I: Selection from the Collection. Vol. I.* Corpus Antiquitatum Aegyptiacarum. Mainz am Rhein, Germany: Philipp von Zabern, 1986.

———. *Allard Pierson Museum, Fasc. II, vols. 1–2: Shabtis.* Amsterdam: Allard Pearson Museum, 1990.

———. *Allard Pierson Museum, Fasc. III: Stelae and Reliefs.* Corpus Antiquitatum Aegyptiacarum. Amsterdam: Allard Pearson Museum, 1995.

Van Haarlem, Willem, and Scheurleer, R. A. L. *Gids voor de Afdeling Egypte.* Amsterdam: Allard Pierson Museum, 1986.

Leiden

Schneider, Hans D. *Egyptisch Kunsthandwerk.* Amsterdam: De Bataafsche Leeuw, 1995.

———. *De Egyptische Outheid.* Gravenhage: Staatsuitgeverij, 1981.

The Hague

Spiegelberg, Wilhelm, *Die Aegyptische Sammlung des Museum-Meermanno-Westreenianum im Haag.* Strassburg: Karl J. Trübner, 1896.

Norway

Naguib, Saphinaz Amal. *Etnografisk Museum Oslo, Fasc. I: Funerary Statuettes.* Corpus Antiquitatum Aegyptiacarum. Mainz, Germany: Philipp von Zabern, 1985.

———. *Etnografisk Museum Oslo, Fasc. 2: Predynastic Pottery.* Corpus Antiquitatum Aegyptiacarum. Oslo: Novus Forlag, 1987.

Russia

Berlev, Oleg, and Svetlana Hodjash. *Catalogue of the Monuments of ancient Egypt from the Museums of the Russian Federation, Ukraine, Bie-*

lorussia, Caucasus, Middle Asia and the Baltic States. Fribourg: UP, 1998.

Moscow

Hodjash, Svetlana, and Oleg Berlev. *The Egyptian Reliefs and Stelae in the Pushkin Museum, Moscow.* Leningrad: Aurora Art Publishers, 1982.

St Petersburg

Piotrovsky, Boris, ed. *Egyptian Antiquities in the Hermitage.* Leningrad: Aurora Art Publishers, 1974.

Switzerland

Chappaz, Jean-Luc, and Sandra Poggia. *Collections égyptiennes publiques de Suisse.* Cahiers de la Société d'Égyptologie, vol. 3. Geneva: Société d'Egyptologie Genève, 1996.

Geneva

Castioni, Christiane, et al. *Égypte.* Geneva: Musée d'Art et d'Histoire, 1977.

Chappaz, Jean-Luc. *Les figurines funéraires du Musée d'Art et d'histoire de Genève.* Geneva: Musée d'Art et d'Histoire Genève, 1984.

Vodoz, Irene. *Les scarabées gravés du Musée d'Art et d'Histoire de Genève.* Geneva: Musée d'Art et d'Histoire, 1978.

United Kingdom

Cambridge

Vassilika, Eleni. *Egyptian Art: Fitzwilliam Museum Handbooks.* Cambridge: Cambridge University Press, 1995.

Glasgow

McDowell, Andrea G. *Hieratic Ostraca in the Hunterian Museum, Glasgow.* Oxford: 1993.

Ipswich

Plunkett, Steven. *From the Mummy's Tomb. Ancient Egyptian Treasures in Ipswich Museum.* Ipswich: Ipswich Borough Council, 1993.

Liverpool

Bienkowski, Piotr, and Edmund Southworth. *Egyptian Antiquities in the Liverpool Museum. Vol. I: A list of the provenanced objects.* Warminster, Great Britain: Aris and Phillips, 1986.

Bienkowski, Piotr, and Angela M. J. Tooley. *Gifts of the Nile. Ancient Egyptian Arts and Crafts in the Liverpool Museum.* London: HMSO, 1995.

London: British Museum

Anderson, Robert D. *Catalogue of Egyptian Antiquities in the British Museum, Vol. III: Musical Instruments.* London: British Museum Publications, 1976.

Andrews, Carol A. R. *Catalogue of Egyptian Antiquities in the British Museum, Vol. VI: Jewellery from the Earliest Times to the 17th Dynasty.* London: British Museum Publications, 1981.

———. *Catalogue of Demotic Papyri in the British Museum. Vol. IV: Ptolemaic Legal Texts from the Theban Area.* London: British Museum Publications, 1990.

Bierbrier, Morris L. *Hieroglyphic Texts from Egyptian Stelae in the British Museum. Part 10.* London: British Museum Publications 1982.

———. *Hieroglyphic Texts from Egyptian Stelae in the British Museum. Part 11.* London: British Museum Publications, 1987.

———. *Hieroglyphic Texts from Egyptian Stelae in the British Museum. Part 12.* London: British Museum Press, 1993.

Birch, Samuel. *Select Papyri in the Hieratic Character from the Collections of the British Museum.* Parts 1–2. London: British Museum, 1844–60.

British Museum. *Hieroglyphic Texts from Egyptian Stelae, etc. in the British Museum.* Parts 1–12. London: British Museum: 1911–1993. (Parts 7–12 also under authors' names.)

Budge, E. A. Wallis. *Facsimiles of Egyptian Hieratic Papyri in the British Museum.* London: British Museum, 1910.

———. *Facsimiles of Egyptian Hieratic Papyri in the British Museum, 2nd Series.* London: British Museum, 1923.

Cooney, John D. *Catalogue of Egyptian Antiquities in the British Museum, Vol. IV: Glass.* London: British Museum Publications, 1976.

Davies, W. Vivian. *Catalogue of Egyptian Antiquities in the British Museum, Vol. VII: Tools and Weapons.* London: British Museum Publications, 1987.

Dawson, Warren R., and Peter H. K. Gray. *Catalogue of Egyptian Antiquities in the British Museum, Vol. I: Mummies and Human Remains.* London: British Museum, 1968.

Edwards, I. Eiddon S. *Hieratic Papyri in the British Museum, 4th Series: Oracular Amuletic Decrees of the Late New Kingdom.* London: British Museum, 1960.

———. *Hieroglyphic Texts from Egyptian Stelae, etc. Part 8.* London: British Museum, 1939.

Gardiner, Alan H. *Hieratic Papyri in the British Museum, 3rd Series: Chester Beatty Gift.* London: British Museum, 1935.

Glanville, Stephen R. K. *Catalogue of Demotic Papyri in the British Museum, Vol. I: A Theban Archive of the Reign of Ptolemy I, Soter.* London: British Museum, 1939.

———. *Catalogue of Demotic Papyri in the British Museum, Vol. II: The Instructions of 'Onchsheshonqy (P. BM 10508).* London: British Museum: 1955.

———. *Catalogue of Egyptian Antiquities in the British Museum, Vol. II: Wooden and Model Boats.* London: British Museum, 1972.

Hall, Henry R. *Hieroglyphic Texts from Egyptian Stelae, etc. in the British Museum. Part 7.* London: British Museum, 1925.

James, T. G. Henry. *Hieroglyphic Texts from Egyptian Stelae in the British Museum. Part 9.* London: British Museum, 1970.

Janssen, Jack J. *Hieratic Papyri in the British Museum VI. Late Ramesside Letters and Communications.* London: British Museum Publications, 1991.

Lapp, Günter. *Catalogue of the Books of the Dead in the British Museum, Vol. I: The Papyrus of Nu (BM EA 10477).* London: British Museum Press, 1997.

Posener-Kriéger, Paule, and Jean L. de Cenival. *Hieratic Papyri in the British Museum, 5th Series: Abu Sir Papyri.* London: British Museum, 1968.

Robins, Gay, and Charles Shute. *The Rhind Mathematical Papyrus.* London: British Museum Publications, 1987.

Smith, Mark. *Catalogue of Demotic Papyri in the British Museum, Vol. III: The Mortuary Texts of P. BM 10507.* London: British Museum Publications, 1987.

Spencer, A. Jeffrey. *Catalogue of Egyptian Antiquities in the British Museum, Vol. V: Early Dynastic Objects.* London: British Museum Publications, 1980.

Thompson, Herbert. *A Family Archive from Siut from Papyri in the British Museum.* Oxford: Clarendon Press, 1934.

London: Petrie Museum

Adams, Barbara. *Sculptured Pottery from Koptos.* Warminster, Great Britain: Aris and Phillips, 1986.

Page, Anthea. *Ancient Egyptian Figured Ostraca from the Petrie Collection.* Warminster, Great Britain: Aris and Phillips, 1983.

Raisman, Vivian, and Geoffrey T. Martin. *Canopic Equipment in the Petrie Museum.* Warminster, Great Britain: Aris and Phillips, 1984.

Samson, Julia. *Amarna, City of Akhenaten and Nefertiti: Key Pieces from the Petrie Collection.* Warminster, Great Britain: Aris and Phillips, 1979.

Stewart, Harry M. *Egyptian Stelae, Reliefs and Paintings from the Petrie Collection.* 3 vols. Warminster, Great Britain: Aris and Phillips, 1976–83.

———. *Mummy Cases and Inscribed Funerary Cones in the Petrie Collection.* Warminster, Great Britain: Aris and Phillips, 1985.

London: Victoria and Albert Museum (now in British Museum)

Adams, Barbara. *Egyptian Objects in the Victoria and Albert Museum.* Warminster, Great Britain: Aris and Phillips, 1979.

Macclesfield

David, A. Rosalie. *The Macclesfield Collection of Egyptian Antiquities.* Warminster, Great Britain: Aris and Phillips, 1980.

Oxford

Moorey, P. Roger S. *Ancient Egypt: University of Oxford. Ashmolean Museum.* Oxford: Ashmolean Museum, 1970.

Payne, Joan Crowfoot. *Catalogue of the Predynastic Egyptian Collection in the Ashmolean Museum, Oxford.* Oxford: Clarendon Press, 1993.

United States

Baltimore

Steindorff, Georg. *Catalogue of the Egyptian Sculpture in the Walters Art Gallery.* Baltimore: Walters Art Gallery, 1946.

Boston

Brovarski, Edward. *Museum of Fine Arts, Boston. Fasc. I: Canopic Jars.* Corpus Antiquitatum Aegyptiacarum. Mainz am Rhein, Germany: Philipp von Zabern, 1978.

Dunham, Dows. *The Egyptian Department and Its Excavations*. Boston: Museum of Fine Arts, 1958.

Leprohon, Ronald J. *Museum of Fine Arts, Boston. Fasc. II: Stelae 1, The Early Dynastic Period to the Late Middle Kingdom*. Corpus Antiquitatum Aegyptiacarum. Mainz am Rhein, Germany: Philipp von Zabern, 1985.

————. *Museum of Fine Arts, Boston. Fasc. III: Stelae 2, The New Kingdom to the Coptic Period*. Corpus Antiquitatum Aegyptiacarum. Mainz am Rhein, Germany: Philipp von Zabern, 1991.

New Haven

Scott, Gerry D., III. *Ancient Egyptian Art at Yale*. Yale: University Art Gallery, 1986.

New York: Brooklyn Museum

Fazzini, Richard A., et al. *Ancient Egyptian Art in The Brooklyn Museum*. Brooklyn: The Brooklyn Museum and Thames and Hudson, 1989.

Hayes, William C. *A Papyrus of the Late Middle Kingdom in The Brooklyn Museum*. Brooklyn: The Brooklyn Museum, reprint 1972.

James, T. G. Henry. *Corpus of Hieroglyphic Inscriptions in The Brooklyn Museum I*. Brooklyn: The Brooklyn Museum, 1974.

Jasnow, Richard. *A Late Period Hieratic Wisdom Text (P. Brooklyn 47.218.135)*. Chicago: The Oriental Institute of the University of Chicago, 1992.

Riefstahl, Elisabeth. *Ancient Egyptian Glass and Glazes in The Brooklyn Museum*. Brooklyn: The Brooklyn Museum, 1968.

Sauneron, Serge. *Le papyrus magique illustré de Brooklyn*. Brooklyn: The Brooklyn Museum: 1970.

Thompson, Deborah. *Coptic Textiles in The Brooklyn Museum*. Brooklyn: The Brooklyn Museum, 1971.

New York: Metropolitan Museum of Art

Wilkinson, Charles, and Marsha Hill. *The Metropolitan Museum of Art's Collection of Facsimiles*. New York: The Metropolitan Museum of Art, 1983.

Metropolitan Museum of Art. *Guide to the Metropolitan Museum of Art*. New York: Metropolitan Museum of Art, 1972.

Pittsburgh

Patch, Diana C. *Reflections of Greatness: Ancient Egypt at The Carnegie Museum of Natural History.* Pittsburgh: The Carnegie Museum of Natural History, 1990.

Vatican City

Botti, Giuseppe, and Pietro Romanelli. *Le sculture del Museo Gregoriano Egizio.* Vatican City: Poliglotta Vaticana, 1951.

Gasse, Annie. *Les papyrus hiératiques et hiéroglyphiques du Museo Gregoriano Egizio.* Vatican City: Monumenti, Musei e Gallerie Pontificie 1993.

————. *Les sarcophages de la troisième periode intermèdiaire du Museo Gregoriano Egizio.* Vatican City: Monumenti, Musei e Gallerie Pontificie, 1996.

Grenier, Jean-Claude. *Museo Gregoriano Egizio: Guide cataloghi musei Vaticani.* Rome: L'Erma di Bretschneider, 1993.

————. *Les statuettes funéraires du Museo Gregoriano Egizio.* Vatican City: Monumenti, Musei e Gallerie Pontificie, 1996.

CLASSICAL SOURCES

Burton, Anne. *Diodorus Siculus. Book I: A Commentary.* Leiden: E. J. Brill, 1972.

Diodorus Siculus. *The Library of History, Book I.* Translated by C. H. Oldfather. Loeb Classical Library. London: William Heinemann, 1933.

Griffiths, J. Gwyn. *Apuleius of Madauros: The Isis Book, Metamorphoses Book XI.* Leiden: E. J. Brill, 1975.

————. *Plutarch's De Iside et Osiride.* Cambridge: University of Wales Press, 1970.

Herodotus. *Histories, Book II.* Translated by A. D. Godley. Loeb Classical Library. London: William Heinemann, 1921.

Horapollo. *The Hieroglyphics.* Translated by George Boas. Bollinger Series XXIII. New York: Pantheon Books, 1950. Edition with new foreword, Princeton: Princeton University Press, 1993.

Lloyd, Alan B. *Herodotus Book II: Introduction and Commentary.* 3 vols. Leiden: E. J. Brill, 1975–88.

Manetho. *Aegyptiaca.* Translated by W. G. Wadell. Loeb Classical Library. London: William Heinemann, 1940.

Strabo. *The Geography of Strabo VIII, Book 17.* Translated by H. L. Jones. Loeb Classical Library. London: William Heinemann, 1982.

HISTORY OF EGYPTOLOGY AND TRAVELLERS TO EGYPT

Champollion, Jean-François. *Monuments de l'Égypte et de la Nubie.* 2 vols. Reprint of 1835 ed. Geneva: Éditions de Belles-Lettres, 1972.

Clayton, Peter A. *The Rediscovery of Ancient Egypt.* London: Thames and Hudson, 1984.

Curl, James Stevens. *The Egyptian Revival.* London: George Allen and Unwin, 1982.

Dawson, Warren R., and Eric P. Uphill. *Who Was Who in Egyptology.* 3rd ed., revised by M. L. Bierbrier. London: Egypt Exploration Society, 1995.

Dewachter, Michel, and Charles C. Gillispie. *Monuments of Egypt: The Napoleonic Expedition.* Princeton, N.J.: Princeton Architectural Press, 1987.

Donadoni, Sergio, et al. *Egypt from Myth to Egyptology.* Milan: Fabbri Editori, 1990.

Drower, Margaret S. *Flinders Petrie: A Life in Archaeology.* London: Victor Gollancz, 1985.

Greener, Leslie. *The Discovery of Egypt.* London: Cassell, 1966.

James, T. G. Henry. *Howard Carter: The Path to Tutankhamun.* London: Kegan Paul International, 1992.

Lepsius, Carl Richard. *Denkmaeler aus Aegypten und Aethiopien.* 3 vols. Reprint of 1849–59 ed. Geneva: Éditions de Belles-Lettres, 1975.

Mayes, Stanley. *The Great Belzoni.* London: Putnam, 1959.

Sim, Katherine. *Desert Traveller: The Life of Jean Louis Burckhardt.* London: Victor Gollancz, 1969.

Thompson, Jason. *Sir Gardner Wilkinson and His Circle.* Austin: University of Texas Press, 1992.

Tillett, Selwyn. *Egypt Itself: The Career of Robert Hay, Esquire of Linplum amd Nunraw, 1799–1863.* London: SD Books, 1984.

Wilson, John. *Signs and Wonders upon Pharaoh.* Chicago: University of Chicago Press, 1964.

TRAVEL

Brunner-Traut, Emma. *Ägypten.* 6th ed., revised. Stuttgart: W. Kohlhammer, 1988.

Kamil, Jill. *Luxor: A Guide to Ancient Thebes.* 2nd ed. London: Longman, 1977.

———. *Sakkara: A Guide to the Necropolis of Sakkara and the Site of Memphis.* London: Longman, 1978.

———. *Upper Egypt: Historical Outline and Descriptive Guide to the Ancient Sites.* London: Longman, 1983.

Murnane, William J. *The Penguin Guide to Ancient Egypt.* Harmondsworth, Great Britain: Penguin Books, 1983.

Seton-Williams, Veronica, and Peter Stocks. *Blue Guide to Egypt.* London: A. and C. Black, 1984.

BIBLIOGRAPHIES

Beinlich-Seeber, Christine. *Bibliographie Altägypten 1822–1946.* 3 vols. Wiesbaden: Harrasowitz, 1998.

Henrickx, Stan. *Analytical Bibliography of the Prehistory and Early Dynastic Period of Egypt and Northern Sudan.* Leuven, Belgium: Leuven University Press, 1995.

Hilmy, Ibrahim. *The Literature of Egypt and the Soudan from the Earliest Times to the Year 1885 Inclusive.* 2 vols. London: Trübner and Co., 1886.

Janssen, Jozef M. A., Louis, Zonhoven, et al. *Annual Egyptological Bibliography.* Leiden: E. J. Brill, 1947–76; Warminster, Great Britain: Aris and Phillips, 1977–81; Leiden: International Association of Egyptologists, 1982– .

Kalfatovic, Martin R. *Nile Notes of a Howadji: A Bibliography of Travelers' Tales from Egypt from the Earliest Times to 1918.* Metuchen, N.J.: The Scarecrow Press, 1992.

Kammerer, Wilfred. *Coptic Bibliography.* Ann Arbor: University of Michigan Press, 1950.

Porter, Bertha, and Rosalind L. B. Moss. *Topographical Bibliography of Ancient Egyptian Hieroglyphic Texts, Reliefs and Paintings.* 7 vols. Oxford: Clarendon Press, 1927–60. New edition in progress, vols. 1–3, 1960–81; from 1974 edited by Jaromir Málek.

Pratt, Ida A. *Ancient Egypt.* Sources for Information in the New York Public Library. 2 vols. New York: The New York Public Library, 1925–42.

Weeks, Kent R. *An Historical Bibliography of Egyptian Prehistory.* American Research Center in Egypt. Catalogs, No. 6. Winona Lake, Ind.: Eisenbrauns, 1985.

PERIODICALS

Bibliotheca Orientalis. Leiden, 1947– . Annually.

Bulletin Copte. Cairo, 1935– . Annually.

Bulletin de la Société d'Égyptologie Genève. Geneva, 1979– . Annually.

Bulletin de la Société française d'Égyptologie. Paris, 1949– . Three times per year.

Bulletin de l'Institut français d'Archéologie orientale. Cairo, 1901– . Annually.

Bulletin of the Egyptological Seminar. New York, 1979– . Annually.

Cahier de recherches de l'Institut de Papyrologie et d'Égyptologie de Lille. Lille, 1973– . Annually.

Chronique d'Égypte. Brussels, 1925– . Annually.

Discussions in Egyptology. Oxford, 1985– . Biannually.

Egyptian Archaeology. London, 1991–93. Annually. 1994– . Biannually.

Enchoria. Wiesbaden, 1971– . Annually.

Göttinger Miszellen. Göttingen, 1972– .

Journal of Egyptian Archaeology. London, 1914– . Annually.

Journal of Near Eastern Studies. Chicago, 1942– . Annually.

Journal of the American Research Center in Egypt. New York, 1962– . Annually.

Journal of the Society for the Study of Egyptian Antiquities. Toronto, 1970– .

KMT. San Francisco, 1990– . Quarterly.

Lingua Aegyptia. Göttingen, 1991– . Annually.

Mitteilungen des Deutschen Archäologischen Instituts Abteilung Kairo. Mainz am Rhein, Germany, 1930– . Annually.

Orientalia. Rome, 1920– . Annually.

Studien zur Altägyptischen Kultur. Hamburg, 1974– . Annually.

Zeitschrift für ägyptische Sprache und Altertumskunde. Berlin, 1863– . Annually.

APPENDIX 1

DYNASTIC LIST

All dates before 690 BC are approximate. Some dynasties or kings were contemporary with each other.

PREHISTORIC PERIOD to c.5000 BC

PREDYNASTIC PERIOD c.5000–3100 BC

EARLY DYNASTIC PERIOD c.3100–2686 BC

FIRST DYNASTY c.3100–2890 BC
Narmer c.3100 BC
Aha c.3080 BC
Djer c.3050 BC
Djet c.3000 BC
Den c.2985 BC
Anedjib c.2935 BC
Semerkhet c.2925 BC
Qaa c.2915 BC

SECOND DYNASTY c.2890–2686 BC
Hotepsekhkemwy c.2890 BC
Raneb c.2865 BC
Nynetjer c.2860 BC
Peribsen c.2700 BC
Khasekhem (Khasekhemwy) c.2600 BC

OLD KINGDOM c.2686–2181 BC

THIRD DYNASTY c.2686–2613 BC
Sanakhte 2686–2667 BC

Netjerkhet Djoser 2667–2648 BC
Sekhemkhet 2648–2640 BC
Huni 2637–2613 BC

FOURTH DYNASTY c.2613–2494 BC
Snefru 2613–2589 BC
Khufu (Cheops) 2589–2566 BC
Radjedef 2566–2558 BC
Khafre (Chephren) 2558–2532 BC
Menkaure (Mycerinus) 2532–2503 BC
Shepseskaf 2503–2498 BC

FIFTH DYNASTY c. 2494–2345 BC
Userkaf 2494–2487 BC
Sahure 2487–2475 BC
Neferirkare Kakai 2475–2455 BC
Shepseskare 2455–2448 BC
Raneferef Isi 2448–2445 BC
Niuserre 2445–2421 BC
Menkauhor 2421–2414 BC
Djedkare Isesi 2414–2375 BC
Unas 2375–2345 BC

SIXTH DYNASTY c.2345–2181 BC
Teti 2345–2323 BC
Userkare 2323–2321 BC
Meryre Pepy I 2321–2287 BC
Merenre Nemtyemsaf I 2287–2278 BC
Neferkare Pepy II 2278–2184 BC
Merenre Nemtyemsaf II 2184–2183 BC
Nitocris 2183–2181 BC

FIRST INTERMEDIATE PERIOD c.2181–2000 BC

SEVENTH/EIGHTH DYNASTIES c.2181–2125 BC

NINTH/TENTH DYNASTIES c.2160–2130 BC, c.2130–2040 BC
Meryibre Khety
Wahkare Khety
Merykare c.2050 BC

ELEVENTH DYNASTY c.2125–1985 BC

RULERS OF THEBES
Mentuhotep I c.2125 BC

Sehertawy Intef I 2125–2112 BC
Wahankh Intef 2112–2063 BC
Nakhtnebtepnefer Intef 2063–2055 BC

MIDDLE KINGDOM c.2040–1795 BC

KINGS OF EGYPT
Nebhepetre Mentuhotep II 2055–2004 BC
Sankhkare Mentuhotep III 2004–1992 BC
Nebtawyre Mentuhotep IV 1992–1985 BC

TWELFTH DYNASTY c.1985–1795 BC
Sehetepibre Amenemhat 1985–1955 BC
Kheperkare Senusret I 1965–1920 BC
Nubkaure Amenemhat II 1922–1878 BC
Khakheperre Senusret II 1880–1874
Khakaure Senusret III 1874–1855 BC
Nymaatre Amenemhat III 1855–1808 BC
Maakherure Amenemhat IV 1808–1799 BC
Sobekkare Sobeknefru 1799–1795 BC

SECOND INTERMEDIATE PERIOD c.1795–1550 BC

THIRTEENTH DYNASTY c.1795–1650 BC
Khutawyre Wegaf
Sekhmkare Amenemhat V Senebef
Sehetepibre
Iufni
Seankhibre Amenemhat VI
Semenkare Nebnun
Hetepibre Harnedjitef
Sewadjkare
Nedejemibre
Khaankhre Sobekhotep I
Renseneb
Awibre Hor
Sedjefakare Amenemhat VII
Sekhemre-khutawy Sobekhotep II
Userkare Khendjer
Semenkhkare Imiermesha
Sehetepkare Intef IV

Seth
Sekhemre-sewadjtawy Sobekhotep III
Khasekhemre Neferhotep I
Sihathor
Khaneferre Sobekhotep IV
Khahetepre Sobekhotep V
Wahibre Iaib
Merneferre Ay
Merhetepre Sobekhotep VI
Seankhenre-sewadjtu
Mersekhemre Ined
Sewadjkare Hori
Merkare Sobekhotep VII
Djednefere Dudimose

FOURTEENTH DYNASTY c.1750–1650 BC
Aasehre Nehesy

FIFTEENTH DYNASTY (Hyksos) c.1650–1550 BC
Salitis (= ?Seker-her)
Meruserre Yaqub-her
Seuserenre Khayan
Iannas
Aauserre Apepi
Khamudy

SIXTEENTH DYNASTY c.1650–1580 BC

RULERS OF THEBES
Sekhemresementawy Djehuty
Sekhemrewosertawy Sobekhotep VIII
Seakhemre-seankhtawy Neferhotep III Iykhernefret
Seankhenre Mentuhotep
Sewadjenre Nebirirau I
Seuserenre Bebiankh

SEVENTEENTH DYNASTY c.1580–1550 BC

RULERS OF THEBES
Sekhemre-wahkaw Rahotep
Sekhemre-shedtawy Sobekemsaf I
Sekhemre-wepmaat Intef V
Nubkheperre Intef VI

Sekhemre-herhermaat Intef VII
Sekhemre-wadjkhaw Sobekemsaf II
Senakhtenre
Seqenenre Taa
Wadjkheperre Kamose

NEW KINGDOM c.1550–1069 BC

EIGHTEENTH DYNASTY c.1550–1295 BC
Nebpehtyre Ahmose I 1550–1525 BC
Djeserkare Amenhotep I 1525–1504 BC
Aakheperkare Thutmose I 1504–1492 BC
Aakheperenre Thutmose II 1492–1479 BC
Maatkare Hatshepsut 1472–1458 BC
MenkheperreThutmose III 1479–1425 BC
Aakheperure Amenhotep II 1427–1400 BC
Menkheperure Thutmose IV 1400–1390 BC
Nebmaatre Amenhotep III 1390–1352 BC
Neferkheperure waenre Amenhotep IV (Akhenaten) 1352–1336 BC
Neferneferuaten Smenkhkare 1338–1336 BC
Nebkheperure Tutankhamun 1336–1327 BC
Kheperkheperure Ay 1327–1323 BC
Djeserkheperure Horemheb 1323–1295 BC

NINETEENTH DYNASTY c.1295–1186 BC
Menpehtyre Ramesses I 1295–1294 BC
Menmaatre Sety I merenptah 1294–1279 BC
Usermaatre setepenre Ramesses II meryamun 1279–1213 BC
Baenre meryamun Merenptah hotephermaat 1213–1203 BC
Menmire setepenre Amenmesse heka waset 1203–1200 BC
Userkheperure setepenre/meryamun Sety II merenptah 1200–1194 BC
Sekhaenre meryamun Ramesses Siptah, later Akhenre setepenre Siptah
    merenptah 1194–1188 BC
Sitre meritamun Tewosret setepenmut 1188–1186

TWENTIETH DYNASTY c.1186–1069 BC
Userkhaure setepenre meryamun Sethnakhte mereramun 1186–1184 BC
Usermaatre meryamun Ramesses III heka iunu 1184–1153 BC
Usermaatre setepenamun, later Hekamaatre setepenamun Ramesses IV
    heka maat meryamun 1153–1147 BC
Usermaatre sekheperenre Ramesses V Amenherkhepeshef meryamun
    1147–1143 BC

Nebmaatre meryamun Ramesses VI Amenherkhepeshef nejter heka iunu
1143–1136 BC

Usermaatre setepenre meryamun Ramesses VII Itamun netjer heka iunu
1136–1129 BC

Usermaatre akhenamun Ramesses VIII Sethherkhepeshef meryamun
1129–1126 BC

Neferkare setepenre Ramesses IX Khaemwaset meryamun 1126–1108 BC

Khepermaatre setepenre Ramesses X Amenherkhepeshef meryamun
1108–1099 BC

Menmaatre setepenptah Ramesses XI Khaemwaset mereramun netjer heka
iunu 1099–1069 BC

THIRD INTERMEDIATE PERIOD c.1069–656 BC

TWENTY-FIRST DYNASTY c.1069–945 BC

Hedjkheperre setepenre Nesbanebded (Smendes) meryamun 1069–1043
BC

Neferkare heka waset Amenemnisu meryamun 1043–1039 BC

Aakheperre setepenamun Pasebakhaenniut (Psusennes) I meryamun
1039–991 BC

Usermaatre setepenamun Amenemope meryamun 993–984 BC

Aakheperre setepenre Osorkon 984–978 BC

Netjerkheperre setepenamun Siamun meryamun 978–959 BC

Titkheperure setepenre Hor-Pasebakhaenniut (Psusennes) II meryamun
959–945 BC

TWENTY-SECOND DYNASTY c.945–715 BC

Hedjkheperre setepenre Sheshonq I meryamun 945–924 BC

Sekhemkheperre setepenre Osorkon I meryamun 924–889 BC

Hekakhepere setepenre Sheshonq II meryamun 890 BC

Hedjkheperre setepenre Takelot I meryamun 889–874 BC

Usermaatre setepenamun Osorkon II sibast meryamun 874–850 BC

Hedjkheprre setepenamun Harsiese meryamun

Hedjkheperre setepenre Takelot II siese meryamun 850–825 BC

Usermaatre setepenre/setepenamun Sheshonq III si-bast meryamun netjer
heka iunu 825–785 BC

Hedjkeheperre setepenre Sheshonq IV si-bast meryamun netjer heka iunu
785–773 BC

Usermaatre setepenamun Pimay meryamun 773–767 BC

Aakheperre setepenre Sheshonq V meryamun si-bast netjer heka waset
767–730 BC

Aakhepere setepenamun Osorkon IV meryamun 730–715 BC

TWENTY-THIRD DYNASTY c.818–715 BC
Usermaatre setepenamun Pedibast I si-bast meryamun 818–793 BC
Iuput I meryamun 805–783 BC
Usermaatre setepenamun Osorkon III si-ese meryamun 777–749 BC
Usermaatre setepenamun Takelot III si-ese meryamun 754–734 BC
Usermaatre setepenamun Rudamun meryamun 734–731 BC
Usermaatre setepenamun Iuput II si-bast meryamun 731–720 BC

TWENTY-FOURTH DYNASTY c.727–715 BC
Shepsesre Tefnakht
Wahkare Bakenrenef (Bocchoris)

TWENTY-FIFTH DYNASTY (Nubian or Kushite) c.747–656 BC
Menkheperre/Usermaatre/Seneferre Piye (Piankhi) 747–716 BC
Neferkare Shabaqo 716–702 BC
Djedkaure Shebitqu 702–690 BC
Khunefertemre Taharqa 690–664 BC
Bakare Tanutamani 664–656 BC

RULER OF SAIS
Menkheperre Nekau I 672–664 BC

LATE PERIOD 664–332 BC

TWENTY-SIXTH DYNASTY (Saite) 664–525 BC
Wahibre Psamtek I 664–610 BC
Wehemibre Nekau II 610–595 BC
Neferibre Psamtek II 595–589 BC
Haaibre Wahibre (Apries) 589–570 BC
Khnemibre Ahmose II (Amasis) si-neith 570–526 BC
Ankhkaenre Psamtek III 526–525 BC

TWENTY-SEVENTH DYNASTY (Persian Kings) 525–404 BC
Mesutire Cambyses 525–522 BC
Stutre Darius I 522–486 BC
Xerxes 486–465 BC
Artaxerxes I 465–424 BC
Darius II 424–405 BC
Artaxerxes II 405–359 BC

TWENTY-EIGHTH DYNASTY 404–399 BC
Amyrtaeos (Amenirdis) 404–399 BC

TWENTY-NINTH DYNASTY 399–380 BC
Baenre merynetjeru Nefaarud (Nepherites) I 399–393 BC
Userre setepeenptah Pasherenmut (Psamuthis) 393 BC
Khnemmaatre setepenkhnum/setepenanhur Hakor (Achoris) 393–380 BC
Nefaarud II 380 BC

THIRTIETH DYNASTY 380–343 BC
Kheperkare Nakhtnebef (Nectanebo I) 380–362 BC
Irmaatenre Djedhor (Teos) setepenanhur 362–360 BC
Snedjemibre setepenanhur/setepenhathor Nakhthorheb (Nectanebo II)
   meryanhur sibastt/sihathor 360–343 BC

PERSIAN KINGS 343–332 BC
Artaxerxes III Ochus 343–338 BC
Arses (Artaxerxes IV) 338–336 BC
Darius III 336–332 BC

MACEDONIAN KINGS 332–305 BC

Alexander the Great 332–323 BC
Philip Arrhidaeus 323–317 BC
Alexander IV 317–305 BC

THE PTOLEMIES 305–30 BC

Ptolemy I Soter I 305–282 BC
Ptolemy II Philadelphus 285–246 BC
Ptolemy III Euergetes I 246–222 BC
Ptolemy IV Philopator 222–205 BC
Ptolemy V Epiphanes 205–180 BC
Ptolemy VI Philometer 180–145 BC
Ptolemy VII Neos Philopator 145 BC
Ptolemy VIII Euergetes II 170–163, 145–116 BC
Ptolemy IX Soter II (Lathyros) 116–107 BC
Ptolemy X Alexander I 107–88 BC
Ptolemy IX Soter II (restored) 88–80 BC
Ptolemy XI Alexander II 80 BC
Ptolemy XII Neos Dionysos (Auletes) 80–58, 55–51 BC
Berenice Cleopatra III 58–55 BC
Ptolemy XIII 51–47 BC
Cleopatra VII Philopator 51–30 BC
Ptolemy XIV 47–44 BC

Ptolemy XV (Caesarion) 44–30 BC

ROMAN EMPERORS 30 BC–395 AD

Augustus 30 BC–14 AD
Tiberius 14–37 AD
Gaius (Caligula) 37–41 AD
Claudius 41–54 AD
Nero 54–68 AD
Galba 68–69 AD
Otho 69 AD
Vespasian 69–79 AD
Titus 79–81 AD
Domitian 81–96 AD
Nerva 96–98 AD
Trajan 98–117 AD
Hadrian 117–138 AD
Antoninus Pius 138–161 AD
Marcus Aurelius 161–180 AD
Lucius Verus 161–169 AD
Commodus 180–192 AD
Septimius Severus 193–211 AD
Caracalla 198–217 AD
Geta 209–212 AD
Macrinus 217–218 AD
Diadumenianus 218 AD
Severus Alexander 222–235 AD
Gordian III 238–244 AD
Philip 244–249 AD
Decius 249–251 AD
Gallus and Volusianus 251–253 AD
Valerian 253–260 AD
Gallienus 253–268 AD
Macrianus and Quietus 260–261 AD
Aurelian 270–275 AD
Probus 276–282 AD
Diocletian 286–305 BC
Galerius 293–311 AD
Constantine I 306–337 AD
Constantius 337–361 AD

Julian 361–363 AD
Jovian 363–364 AD
Valens 364–378 AD
Theodosius I the Great 379–395 AD

BYZANTINE EMPERORS 395–642 AD

Arcadius 395–408 AD
Theodosius II 408–450 AD
Marcian 450–457 AD
Leo I 457–474 AD
Zeno 474–491 AD
Anastasius I 491–518 AD
Justin I 518–527
Justinian I 527–565 AD
Justin II 565–578 AD
Tiberius 578–582 AD
Maurice 582–602 AD
Phocas 602–610 AD
Heraclius 610–642 AD

ARABIC CONQUEST 642 AD

APPENDIX 2

MUSEUMS WITH EGYPTIAN COLLECTIONS

An asterisk indicates large or important collections.

ARGENTINA

Buenos Aires
Programa de Estudios de Egiptologia
Florida, 165
Entrada San Martin, Piso 5°, Of. 542
1333 Buenos Aires

AUSTRALIA

Melbourne
Museum of Victoria
328 Swanson Street
Melbourne, Victoria 3000

Sydney
Australian Museum
6–8 College Street
Sydney, NSW 2000

Nicholson Museum of Antiquities*
University of Sydney
Sydney, NSW 2006

AUSTRIA

Vienna
Kunsthistorisches Museum*
Ägyptisch-Orientalische Sammlung

Burgring 5
A-1010 Wien

BELGIUM

Antwerp
Museum Vleeshuis
Vleeshouwersstraat, 38
2000 Antwerp

Brussels
Musées Royaux d'Art et d'Histoire*
Collection Égyptienne
Parc du Cinquantenaire, 10
B-1000 Bruxelles

Liège
Musée Curtius
13 quai de Maastricht
4000 Liège

Mariemont
Musée Royal de Mariemont
Section Égypte et Proche-Orient
100 Chaussée de Mariemont
B-7140 Morlanwelz-Mariemont

Namur
Bibliothèque Universitaire Moretus Plantin
Rue Grandgagnage 19
B-5000 Namur

BRAZIL

Rio de Janeiro
Museu Nacional
Quinta da Boa Vista
20942 Rio de Janeiro

CANADA

Montreal
Montreal Museum of Fine Arts
1379 Sherbrooke Street West
Montreal, Quebec H3G 1K3

Redpath Museum
McGill University
859 Sherbrooke Street West
Montreal, Quebec H3A 2K6

Toronto
Royal Ontario Museum*
Department of Near Eastern and Asian Civilizations
100 Queen's Park
Toronto, Ontario M5S 2C6

CROATIA

Zagreb
Arheoloski Muzej
41000 Zagreb
Zrinjski trg 19

CUBA

Havana
Museo Nacional de Bellas Artes
Animas entre Zulueta y Monserrate
CP 10200 Havana

CZECH REPUBLIC

Prague
Náprstkovo Muzeum
Betlémské námestí 1
CZ-11000 Praha 1

Univerzita Karlova
Cesky egyptologicky ústav
Celetná 20
CZ-11000 Praha 1

DENMARK

Copenhagen
The National Museum of Denmark*
Department of Classical and Near Eastern Antiquities
Ny Vestergade, 10
DK-1220 Copenhagen

Ny Carlsberg Glyptotek*
Egyptian Collection
Dantes Plads
DK-1556 Copenhagen

Thorvaldsens Museum
Porthusgade, 2
1213 Copenhagen

EGYPT

Alexandria
Greco-Roman Museum
Al Mathaf Street
Alexandria

Aswan
Aswan Museum
Elephantine Island
Aswan

Nubia Museum
Aswan

Cairo
Coptic Museum*
Masr Ateeka
Old Cairo
Cairo

The Egyptian Museum*
Midan el-Tahrir
Cairo

Luxor
Luxor Museum*

Mummification Museum

Mallawi
Mallawi Museum
Mallawi

FRANCE

Aix-en-Provence
Musée Granet
Place Saint-Jean-de-Malte
13100 Aix-en-Provence

Aix-les-Bains
Musée Archéologique
Place Maurice-Mollard
73100 Aix-les-Bains

Amiens
Musée de Picardie
48 rue de la République
80000 Amiens

Angers
Musée Pincé
32 bis rue Lenepveu
49100 Angers

Annecy
Musée-Château
Place du Château
74000 Annecy

Autun
Musée Rolin
5 rue des Bancs
71400 Autun

Avignon
Musée Calvet
Fine Arts Section
65 rue Joseph Vernet
84000 Avignon

Bordeaux
Musée d'Aquitaine
20 cours Pasteur
33000 Bordeaux

Cannes
Musée-château de la Castre
Le Suquet
06400 Cannes

Chalon-sur-Saône
Musée Vivant Denon
Place de l'Hôtel de Ville
7100 Chalon-sur-Saône

Chambéry
Musées d'Art et d'Histoire
Chambéry

Figeac
Musée Champollion
4 rue Champollion
46100 Figeac

Grenoble
Musée de Beaux-Arts
Place de Verdun
38000 Grenoble

Lille
Institut de Papyrologie et d'Égyptologie
URA 1275 CNRS
Université Charles-de-Gaulle—Lille III
59653 Villeneuve d'Ascq Cedex

Limoges
Musée Municipal
Place de la Cathédrale
87000 Limoges

Lyon
Musée des Beaux-Arts
20 place des Terreaux
69001 Lyon

Marseilles
Musée d'Archéologie Mediterranéenne*
Collection Égyptienne
2 Rue de la Charité
13002 Marseille

Meudon
Musée Rodin
Meudon

Nantes
Musée Dobrée
18 rue Voltaire
Nantes

Orléans
Musée Historique et Archéologique de l'Orléanais
Hôtel Cabu
Square Abbé Desnoyers
45000 Orléans

Paris
Bibliothèque Nationale
Département des Monnaies, Médailles et Antiques
58 rue Richelieu
75002 Paris Cedex 02

Musée de Cluny
6 Place Paul Painlevé
75005 Paris

Musée du Louvre*
Département des Antiquités égyptiennes
Palais du Louvre
75058 Paris Cedex 01

Musée Jacquemart André
158 Blvd Haussmann
75008 Paris

Roanne
Musée Joseph Déchelette
22 rue Anatole France
42300 Roanne

Rouen
Musée des Antiquités de la Seine-Maritime
198 rue Beauvoisine
76000 Rouen

St-Germain-en-Laye
Chateau de St-Germain
St-Germain-en-Laye

Sèvres
Musée National de Céramique
Place de la Manufacture
92310 Sèvres

Strasbourg
Université de Strasbourg
Institut d'Égyptologie
Palais Universitaire
67000 Strasbourg

Toulouse
Musée Georges-Labit
43 rue des Martyrs de la Libération
31000 Toulouse

Varzy
Musée Auguste Grasset
Varzy

GERMANY

Berlin
Ägyptisches Museum und Papyrussammlung*
Staatliche Museen zu Berlin—Preussischer Kulturbesitz
Bodestrasse, 1–3
D-10178 Berlin

Charlottenburg Division
Schlossstrasse, 70
D-14059 Berlin (Charlottenburg)

Bremen
Übersee-Museum Bremen
Bahnhofsplatz, 13
D-28195 Bremen

Darmstadt
Hessisches Landesmuseum Darmstadt
Friedensplatz, 1
D-64283 Darmstadt

Dresden
Staatliche Kunstsammlungen Dresden
Georg-Treu-Platz, 1
Albertinum
O-8012 Dresden

Essen
Museum Folkwang
Goethestrasse, 41
D-4300 Essen 1

Frankfurt-am-Main
Städtische Galerie Liebieghaus
Museum Alter Plastik
Schaumainkal, 71
D-60596 Frankfurt-am-Main

Gotha
Schlossmuseum
Schloss Friedenstein
Ägyptische Sammlung
D-99867 Gotha

Hamburg
Hamburgisches Museum für Völkerkunde
Binderstrasse, 14
D-2000 Hamburg 13

Museum für Kunst und Gewerbe Hamburg
Steintorplatz, 1
D-2000 Hamburg 1

Hannover
Kestner-Museum
Trammplatz, 3
D-30159 Hannover

Heidelberg
Sammlung des Ägyptologischen Instituts der Universität Heidelberg
Marstallhof, 4
D-69117 Heidelberg

Hildesheim
Pelizaeus-Museum*
Am Steine, 1–2
D-31134 Hildesheim

Karlsruhe
Badisches Landesmuseum
Schlossplatz, 1
D-7500 Karlsruhe

Leipzig
Ägyptisches Museum der Universität Leipzig
Schillerstrasse, 6
D-04109 Leipzig

Munich
Staatliche Sammlung Ägyptischer Kunst*
Hofgartenstrasse
D-80333 München

Tübingen
Ägyptologisches Institut der Universität Tübingen
Schloss Hohentübingen
D-72070 Tübingen

Würzburg
Martin von Wagner Museum der Universität
Bayerisches-Julius-Maximilians-Universität
Sanderring, 2
D-97070 Würzburg

GREECE

Athens
National Archaeological Museum
1 Tositsa Street
82 Athens 147

HUNGARY

Budapest
Szépmüvészeti Múzeum
Egyiptomi Osztály
Dózsa György út 41
H-1396 Budapest 62

IRELAND

Dublin
National Museum of Ireland
Kildare Street
Dublin 2

ISRAEL

Haifa
The Reuben and Edith Hecht Museum
University of Haifa
Mount Carmel
Haifa 31905

Jerusalem
Bible Lands Museum
Granot, 25
Jerusalem 93706

Israel Museum
Department of Egyptian Art
Hakiriya
Jerusalem 91710

ITALY

Asti
Museo Archeologico e Paleontologico
Corso Alfieri, 2
14100 Asti

Bergamo
Civico Museo Archeologico
Piazza Cittadella, 9
24100 Bergamo

Bologna
Museo Civico Archeologico*
Via dell'Archiginnasio, 2
I-40124 Bologna

Como
Museo Civico Archeologico 'P Giovio'
Piazza Medaglie d'Oro, 1
22100 Como

Cortona
Museo dell'Accademia Etrusca
Piazza Signorelli
52044 Cortona

Florence
Museo Archeologico*
Via della Colonna, 38
I-50121 Florence

Mantua
Museo di Palazzo Ducale
Piazza Sordello
46100 Mantua

Milan
Civiche Raccolte Archeologiche e Numismatiche
Castella Sforzesco
20121 Milano

Naples
Museo Archeologico Nazionale
Via Museo, 18
80135 Naples

Palermo
Museo Regionale Archeologico
Piazza Olivella
90133 Palermo

Parma
Museo Archeologico Nazionale
Via della Pilctta, 4
43100 Parma

Pisa
Collezioni Egittologiche di Ateneo
Via S. Frediano, 12
I-56126 Pisa

Rome
Museo Barracco
Corso Vittorio Emanuele, 168
00186 Rome

Museo Capitolino
Piazza del Campidoglio, 1471
00186 Rome

Museo Nazionale Romano
Piazza dei Cinquecento, 79
00185 Rome

Rovigo
Museo dell'Accademia dei Concordi
Piazza V. Emanuele II, 14
45100 Rovigo

Trieste
Civico Museo di Storia ed Arte
Via Cattedrale, 15
34121 Trieste

Turin
Museo Egizio
Via Accademia delle Scienze, 6
I-10123 Torino

Venice
Museo Archeologico Nazionale
Piazzetta San Marco, 17
30124 Venice

JAPAN

Tokyo
Ancient Orient Museum
1–4 Higashi Ukebukuro 3 chome
Toshima-ku
Tokyo 170

Tokyo National Museum
13–9 Ueno Park
Taitoku
Tokyo 110

Kyoto
Heian Museum of Ancient History
3rd Archaeological Section
8–1 Takeda Nanasegawa Fushimu-ku
Kyoto 612

LITHUANIA

Kaunas
M. K. Ciurlionis National Museum of Art
Vlado Putvinskio 55
LT-3000 Kaunas

MEXICO

Mexico City
Museo Nacional de Antropología
Paseo de la Reforma y Gandhi
México 5

NETHERLANDS

Amsterdam
Allard Pierson Museum
Oude Turfmarkt, 127
1012 GC Amsterdam

The Hague
Museum Meermanno-Westreenianum
Prinsessegracht, 30
2514 AP The Hague

Leiden
Rijksmuseum van Oudheden*
Egyptische afdeling
Rapenburg, 28
2301 EC Leiden

Otterlo
Rijksmuseum Kröller-Müller
Nationale Park de Hoge Veluwe
Houtkampweg, 6
6731 AW Otterlo

NORWAY

Oslo
Etnografisk Museum
Frederiksgate, 2
N-0164 Oslo

POLAND

Kraków
Archaeological Museum
Department of Mediterranean Archaeology and the Ancient Cultures of
America
3 Senacka Str.
31–002 Kraków

Czartoryski Museum (Foundation) at The National Museum Kraków
ul. Pijarska 8 (The Town Arsenal)
31–015 Kraków

Jagellonian University
Department of Mediterranean Archaeology
ul. Golebia 11
31–007 Kraków

Poznan
Museum Archeologiczne
Palac Górków
Dzial Archeologii Powszechnej
(Department of Extra-European Archaeology)
ul. Wodna 27
61–781 Poznan

Warsaw
Muzeum Narodowe*
Gallery of Ancient Art
Al. Jerozolimskie, 3
00–495 Warszawa

PORTUGAL

Lisbon
Fundação Calouste Gulbenkian
Av. Berna 45
1093 Lisboa

Museu Nacional de Arqueologia
Colecção de Antiguidades Egípcias
Praça do Império
P-1400 Lisboa

RUSSIA

Moscow
State Pushkin Museum of Fine Arts*
Oriental Department
Volchonka, 12
121019 Moscow

St Petersburg
Hermitage Museum*
Oriental Department
Dvortsovaya Naberezhnaya, 34
191186 St Petersburg

SPAIN

Barcelona
Museu Egipci de Barcelona
Fundació Arquelògica Clos
Rambla de Catalunya, 57–59
E-08007 Barcelona

Madrid
Museo Arqueológico Nacional
Departamento de Antigüedafes Egipcias y del Próximo Oriente
Serrano, 13
E-28001 Madrid

SUDAN

Khartoum
National Museum*
El Neel Avenue
P. O. Box 178
Khartoum

SWEDEN

Stockholm
Medelhavsmuseet*
Egyptiska Samlingen
Fredsgatan, 2
S-11484 Stockholm

Uppsala
Institute of Egyptology
Victoriamuseet för egyptiska fornsaker
Gustavianum
S-75220 Uppsala

SWITZERLAND

Basel
Ägyptologisches Seminar der Universität
Schönbeinstrasse, 20
4056 Basel

Antikenmuseum Basel und Sammlung Ludwig
St Albangraben, 5
CH-4051 Basel

Museum für Völkerkunde
POB 1048
Augustinergasse, 2
4051 Basel

Bern
Bernisches Historisches Museum
Helvetiaplatz, 5
3005 Bern

Burgdorf
Museum für Völkerkunde
Kirchbühl, 11
3400 Burgdorf

Fribourg
Institut Biblique de l'Université
Miséricorde
1700 Fribourg

Geneva
Bibliotheca Bodmeriana
Fondation Martin Bodmer
Route de Guignard, 19–21
1223 Cology

Musée d'Art et d'Histoire*
Rue Charles-Galland, 2
CH-1211 Geneva 3

Lausanne
Musée Cantonal d'Archéologie et d'Histoire
Palais de Rumine
Place de la Riponne, 6
1005 Lausanne

Lenzburg
Historisches Museum Aargau
Kantonale Sammlungen
Schloss Lenzburg
5600 Lenzburg

Neuchâtel
Musée d'Ethnographie
Rue Saint-Nicholas, 4
2006 Neuchâtel

Riggisberg
Abegg-Stiftung
Werner Abeggstrasse, 67
3132 Riggisberg

St Gallen
Sammlung für Völkerkunde
Museumstrasse, 50
9000 St Gallen

Yverdon-les-Bains
Musée du Château
Le Château
1400 Yverdon

Zurich
Archäologische Sammlung der Universität Zürich
Rämistrasse, 73
8006 Zürich

UKRAINE

Odessa
Odessa Archaeological Museum
Vul. Lastochkina, 4
Odessa

UNITED KINGDOM

Aberdeen
Aberdeen University Anthropological Museum*
Marischal College
Aberdeen AB9 1AS

Aylesbury
Buckinghamshire County Museum
Church Street
Aylesbury HP20 2QP

Banbury
Banbury Museum
8 Horsefair
Banbury
Oxon

Batley
Bagshaw Museum
Wilton Park Batley
W Yorkshire WF17 0AS

Bedford
Bedford Museum
Castle Lane
Bedford MK40 3XD

Belfast
Ulster Museum
Botanic Gardens
Belfast
N Ireland BT9 5AB

Bexley
Bexley Museum
Hall Place
Bourne Road
Bexley
Kent DA5 1PQ

Birkenhead
Williamson Art Gallery and Museum
Slatey Road
Birkenhead
Wirral L43 4UE

Birmingham
Birmingham City Museums and Art Gallery
Department of Antiquities
Chamberlain Square
Birmingham B3 3DH

Blackburn
Blackburn Museum and Art Gallery
Museum Street
Blackburn
Lancs BB1 7AJ

Bolton
Bolton Museum and Art Gallery*
Le Mans Crescent
Bolton
Lancs BL1 1SE

Bournemouth
Bournemouth Natural Science Society
39 Christchurch Road
Bournemouth
Dorset BH1 3NS

Russell-Cotes Art Gallery and Museum
Russell-Cotes Road
East Cliff
Bournemouth
Dorset BH1 3AA

Brighton
The Royal Pavilion
Art Gallery and Museum
Brighton BN1 1UE

Bristol
City of Bristol Museum and Art Gallery*
Queen's Road
Bristol BS8 1RL

Bromley
Bromley Museum
The Priory
Church Hill
Bromley
Orpington
Kent BR6 0H4

Burnley
Towneley Hall
Art Gallery and Museums
Burnley BB11 3RQ

Cambridge
Fitzwilliam Museum*
Department of Antiquities
Trumpington Street
Cambridge CB2 1RB

University Museum of Archaeology and Anthropology
Downing Street
Cambridge CB2 3DZ

Canterbury
Royal Museum and Art Gallery
High Street
Canterbury CT1 2JE

Carlisle
Carlisle Museums and Art Gallery
Tullie House
Castle Street
Carlisle CA3 8TP

Carmarthen
Carmarthen Museum
Carmarthen
Dyfed

Chelmsford
Chelmsford Museums Service
Civic Centre
Chelmsford
Essex CM1 1JE

Cheltenham

Cheltenham Art Gallery and Museum
Clarence Street
Cheltenham
Glos GL50 3JT

Chiddingstone

Denys Eyre Bower Collection*
Chiddingstone Castle
Chiddingstone
nr Edenbridge
Kent TN8 7AD

Colchester

Colchester and Essex Museums
The Museum Resource Centre
14 Ryegate Road
Colchester
Essex CO1 1YG

Darlington

Borough of Darlington Museum
Tubwell Road
Darlington
Co Durham DL1 1PD

Derby

Derby Museum and Art Gallery
The Strand
Derby DE1 1BS

Dundee

Dundee Art Galleries and Museums
Albert Square
Dundee DD1 1DA

Durham

Oriental Museum*
University of Durham
Elvet Hill
Durham DH1 3TH

Edinburgh
National Museums of Scotland*
Department of History and Applied Art
Royal Museum of Scotland
Chambers Street
Edinburgh EH1 1JF

Exeter
Royal Albert Memorial Museum
Queen Street
Exeter EX4 3RX

Glasgow
Art Gallery and Museum
Kelvingrove
Glasgow G3 8AG

Burrell Collection
2060 Pollockshaws Road
Glasgow G43 1AT

Hunterian Museum and Art Gallery
Egyptian Department
University of Glasgow
University Avenue
Glasgow G12 8QQ

Godalming
The Museum
Charterhouse
Godalming
Surrey GU7 2DX

Grantham
Grantham Museum
St Peter's Hill
Grantham
Lincolnshire NG31 6PY

Greenock
McLean Museum and Art Gallery
9 Union Street
Greenock PA16 8JH

Halifax
Bankfield Museum
Boothtown Road
Halifax
W Yorkshire HX3 6HG

Harrogate
Harrogate Museum and Art Gallery Service
Royal Pump Room Museum
Crown Place
Harrogate HG2 0LZ

Harrow
Old Speech Room Gallery
Harrow School
5 High Street
Harrow on the Hill
Middlesex HA1 3HP

Hartlepool
Gray Art Gallery and Museum
Hartlepool Museum Service
Clarence Road
Hartlepool
Cleveland TS24

Haslemere
Haslemere Educational Museum
78 High Street
Haslemere
Surrey GU27 2LA

Hawick
Roxburgh District Museums Collection
Hawick Museum
Wilton Lodge Park
Hawick
Roxburghshire TD9 7JL

Hereford
Hereford City Museums
Broad Street
Hereford HR4 9AU

Highclere
Highclere Castle
Highclere
nr Newbury
Berkshire RG15 9RN

Ipswich
Ipswich Museum
High Street
Ipswich
Suffolk IP1 3QH

Kendal
Kendal Museum
Station Road
Kendal
Cumbria LA9 6BT

King's Lynn
King's Lynn Museums
Market Street
King's Lynn
Norfolk PE30 1NL

Kingston Lacy
Kingston Lacy House*
Wimborne
Dorset BH21 4EA

Leicester
Leicester Museums and Record Service
96 New Walk
Leicester LE1 6TD

Letchworth
Letchworth Museum and Art Gallery
Broadway
Letchworth
Hertfordshire SG6 3PF

Lincoln
City and County Museum
Greyfriars
Broadgate
Lincoln

Liverpool
Liverpool Museum*
William Brown Street
Liverpool L3 8EN

School of Archaeology, Classics and Oriental Studies
University of Liverpool
P.O. Box 147
Liverpool L69 3BX

London
British Museum*
Department of Egyptian Antiquities
Great Russell Street
London WC1B 3DG

Cuming Museum
155/157 Walworth Road
London SE17 1RS

Freud Museum
Maresfield Gardens
London NW3 5SX

Horniman Museum
London Road
Forest Hill
London SE23 3PQ

Museum of London
London Wall
London EC2Y 5HN

Petrie Museum of Egyptian Archaeology*
University College London
Gower Street
London WC1E 6BT

Soane Museum
Lincoln's Inn Fields
London WC2A 3BP

Victoria and Albert Museum
South Kensington
London SW7 2RL

Macclesfield
West Park Museum
Prestbury Road
Macclesfield
correspondence to:
Macclesfield Museums
The Heritage Centre
Roe Street
Macclesfield
Cheshire SK11 6UT

Maidstone
Maidstone Museum and Art Gallery
St Faith's Street
Maidstone
Kent ME14 1LH

Manchester
Manchester Museum*
University of Manchester
Oxford Road
Manchester M13 9PL

Newbury
Newbury District Museum
The Wharf
Newbury
Berkshire RG14 5AS

Newcastle upon Tyne
Hancock Museum
University of Newcastle upon Tyne
Barras Bridge
Newcastle upon Tyne NE2 4PT

Northampton
Central Museum and Art Gallery
Guildhall Road
Northampton NN1 1DP

Norwich
Castle Museum
Archaeology Department
Norfolk Museums Service
Norwich NR1 3JU

Sainsbury Centre for Visual Arts
University of East Anglia
University Plain
Norwich NR4 7TJ

Nottingham
Castle Museum
Brewhouse Yard Museum
Castle Boulevard
Nottingham NG7 1FB

Oxford
Ashmolean Museum*
Department of Antiquities
University of Oxford
Beaumont Street
Oxford OX1 2PH

Pitt Rivers Museum
South Parks Road
Oxford OX1 3PP

Plymouth
City Museum and Art Gallery
Drake Circus
Plymouth PL4 8AJ

Reading
Ure Museum of Greek Archaeology
Department of Classics
Faculty of Letters
The University
Whiteknights
Reading RG6 2AA

Rochester
Guildhall Museum
High Street
Rochester
Kent ME1 1PY

Saffron Walden
Saffron Walden Museum
Museum Street
Saffron Walden
Essex CB10 1JL

St Albans
Verulamium Museum
St Michaels
St Albans
Herts AL3 4SW

St Helens
St Helens Museum and Art Gallery
College Street
St Helens
Merseyside WA10 1TW

Salford
Salford Museums and Art Galleries
Peel Park
The Crescent
Salford M5 4WU

Scarborough
Rotunda Museum
Vernon Road
Scarborough
N Yorkshire YO11 2PW

Sheffield
Sheffield City Museum
Weston Park
Sheffield S10 2TP

Southend on Sea
Southend Museum Service
Central Museum
Victoria Avenue
Southend on Sea
Essex SS2 6EW

Southport
Botanic Gardens Museum
Goodison Egyptology Collection
Churchtown
Southport PR9 7NB

Stoke on Trent
City Museum and Art Gallery
Hanley
Stoke on Trent ST1 3DW

Swansea
The Wellcome Museum of Egyptian and Graeco-Roman Antiquities
University of Wales Swansea
Singleton Park
Swansea SA2 8PP

Swindon
Thamesdown Museums Service
Bath Road
Swindon
Wiltshire SN5 8AQ

Torquay
Torquay Museum
529 Babbacombe Road
Torquay
S Devon TO1 1HG

Tunbridge Wells
Tunbridge Wells Museum and Art Gallery
Civic Centre
Mount Pleasant
Royal Tunbridge Wells
Kent TN1 1NS

Walsall
Walsall Museum and Art Gallery
Garman Ryan Collection
Lichfield Street
Walsall
W Midlands WS1 1TR

Warrington
Warrington Museum and Art Gallery
Bold Street
Warrington WA1 1JG

Warwick
Warwickshire Museum
Market Hall
Market Place
Warwick CV34 4SA

Welshpool
Powysland Museum
Salop Road
Welshpool
Powys SY21 7EG

West Malling
Kent County Museum Service
Kent County Council
West Malling Air Station
West Malling
Kent ME19 6QE

Windsor
Myers Museum
Eton College
Windsor
Berks SL4 6DB

Wisbech
Wisbech and Fenland Museum
Museum Square
Wisbech
Cambridgeshire PE13 1ES

UNITED STATES OF AMERICA

Ann Arbor (MI)
Kelsey Museum of Ancient and Medieval Archaeology
University of Michigan
434 South State Street
Ann Arbor, MI 48104

Baltimore (MD)
The Johns Hopkins University
Department of Near Eastern Studies
Charles and 34th Street
Baltimore, MD 21218

Walters Art Gallery*
600 North Charles Street
Baltimore, MD 21201–5185

Berkeley (CA)
The Phoebe Apperson Hearst Museum of Anthropology and Archaeology
103 Kroeber Hall
University of California
Berkeley, CA 94720–3712

Boston (MA)
Museum of Fine Arts*
Department of Ancient Egyptian, Nubian and Near Eastern Art
465 Huntington Avenue
Boston, MA 02115

Cambridge (MA)
Fogg Art Museum
Harvard University
Cambridge, MA 02138

Semitic Museum
Harvard University
Cambridge, MA 02138

Chicago (IL)
Field Museum of Natural History
Roosevelt Road at Lake Shore Drive
Chicago, IL 60605

The Oriental Institute Museum*
University of Chicago
1155 East 58th Street
Chicago, IL 60637–1569

Cincinnati (OH)
Art Museum
Eden Park
Cincinnati, OH 45202

Cleveland (OH)
Museum of Art*
Department of Ancient Art
11150 East Boulevard
Cleveland, OH 44106–1797

Dallas (TX)
Dallas Museum of Art
1717 N. Harwood
Dallas, TX 75201

Denver (CO)
Art Museum
100 West 14th Avenue
Parkway
Denver, CO 80204

Detroit (MI)
Detroit Institute of Arts*
Department of Ancient Art
5200 Woodward Avenue
Detroit, MI 48202–4008

Kansas City (MO)
The Nelson-Atkins Museum of Art
4525 Oak Street
Kansas City, MO 64111

Los Angeles (CA)
County Museum of Art
Ancient and Islamic Art
5905 Wilshire Boulevard
Los Angeles, CA 90036

Memphis (TN)
Memphis State University
Institute of Egyptian Art and Archaeology
3750 Norriswood
Memphis, TN 38152

Minneapolis (MN)
Institute of Arts Museum
2400 Third Avenue South
Minneapolis, MN 55404

New Haven (CT)
Peabody Museum
Yale University
New Haven, CT 06520

New York (NY)
Brooklyn Museum*
Department of Egyptian, Classical and Ancient Middle Eastern Art
200 Eastern Parkway
Brooklyn, NY 11238–6052

Metropolitan Museum of Art*
Department of Egyptian Art
1000 Fifth Avenue
New York, NY 10028–0198

Newark (NJ)
Newark Museum
The Classical Collection
49 Washington Street
Newark, NJ 07101–0540

Philadelphia (PA)
University of Pennsylvania Museum of Archaeology and Anthropology*
Egyptian Section
33rd and Spruce Streets
Philadelphia, PA 19104

Pittsburgh (PA)
The Carnegie Museum of Natural History
4400 Forbes Avenue
Pittsburgh, PA 15213

Princeton (NJ)
University Art Museum
Princeton, NJ 08544

Providence (RI)
Museum of Art
Rhode Island School of Design
Department of Antiquities
224 Benefit Street
Providence, RI 02903

Raleigh (NC)
North Carolina Museum of Art
2110 Blue Ridge Boulevard
Raleigh, NC 27607

Richmond (VA)
Virginia Museum of Fine Arts
Department of Ancient Art
2800 Grove Avenue
Richmond, VA 23221

St. Louis (MO)
Art Museum
Forest Park
St. Louis, MO 63110

San Antonio (TX)
San Antonio Museum of Art
200 West Jones
San Antonio, TX 78215

San Jose (CA)
Rosicrucian Egyptian Museum
Rosicrucian Park
1342 Naglee Avenue
San Jose, CA 95191

Seattle (WA)
Seattle Art Museum
Volunteer Park
1400 E. Prospect
Seattle, WA 98112

Toledo (OH)
Toledo Museum of Art
2445 Monroe Street at Scottswood Avenue
Toledo, OH 43697

Washington (DC)
Freer Gallery of Art
Jefferson Drive at 12th Street, SW
Washington, DC 20560

National Museum of Natural History
Smithsonian Institution
Washington, DC 20560

Worcester (MA)
Art Museum
55 Salisbury Street
Worcester, MA 01609

URUGUAY

Montevideo
Museo de Historia del Arte
Ejido, 1326
11100 Montevideo

Museo Egipcio de la Sociedad Uruguaya de Egiptología
4 de Julio, 3068
11600 Montevideo

Museo Nacional de Historia Natural
Buenos Aires, 652
11000 Montevideo

VATICAN CITY

Museo Gregoriano Egizio*
Vatican Museums and Galleries
00120 Vatican City

ABOUT THE AUTHOR

Morris Leonard Bierbrier (B.A., McGill College, Montreal; M.A., University of Toronto; Ph.D., University of Liverpool) is Assistant Keeper in the Department of Egyptian Antiquities, British Museum, London. He is a Fellow of the Society of Antiquaries. Dr. Bierbrier is the author of *The Late New Kingdom in Egypt* and *The Tomb-Builders of the Pharaohs* which has been translated into French, Arabic, and Japanese. He has written numerous articles and reviews in professional journals and is currently editor of *Who Was Who in Egyptology*.